Global Brands

Brands help explain why, in a world focused on science and new technology, several of the world's largest multinational corporations have little to do with either. Rather they are old firms with little critical investment in patents or copyrights.

For these firms, the critical intellectual property is trademarks. *Global Brands* explains how the world's largest multinationals in alcoholic beverages achieved global leadership; the predominant corporate governance structures for firms' marketing-based industries; and why these firms form alliances with direct competitors. Brands also determine the waves of mergers and acquisitions in the beverage industry. Not only do they have personalities of their own, but brands also have the capacity to have independent and eternal lives.

Global Brands contrasts with existing studies by providing a new dimension to the literature on the growth of multinationals through the focus on brands, using an institutional and evolutionary approach based on original and published sources about the industry and the firms.

Teresa da Silva Lopes is a Reader in the School of Business and Management at Queen Mary, University of London. She has previously taught at the University of Oxford and Universidade Católica Portuguesa. She is the author of numerous publications on international business and business history and other topics in journals such as *Business History, Business History Review*, and *Enterprise and Society*. She is currently co-director of the Centre for Globalization Research at Queen Mary, University of London; reviews editor for the journal *Business History*; council member of the Association of Business Historians; and trustee of the American Business History Conference. Lopes has held visiting research fellowships at the University of California, Berkeley, and École Polytechnique in Paris. Currently she is a Fellow of Dynamics of Institutions and Markets in Europe Network, a Research Fellow at Universidade Católica Portuguesa, and a Research Associate of the Centre for International Business History and the Centre for Institutional Performance, both at the University of Reading.

CAMBRIDGE STUDIES IN THE EMERGENCE
OF GLOBAL ENTERPRISE

Editors

Louis Galambos, *The Johns Hopkins University*

Geoffrey Jones, *Harvard Business School*

Other books in the series

National Cultures and International Competition: The Experience of Schering AG, 1851–1950, by Christopher Kobrak, ESCP-EAP, European School of Management

Knowledge and Competitive Advantage: The Coevolution of Firms, Technology, and National Institutions, by Johann Peter Murmann, Australian Graduate School of Management

The World's Newest Profession: Management Consulting in the Twentieth Century, by Christopher D. McKenna, Saïd Business School and Brasenose College, University of Oxford

Global Brands

The Evolution of Multinationals in Alcoholic Beverages

———————

TERESA DA SILVA LOPES

Queen Mary, University of London

CAMBRIDGE UNIVERSITY PRESS
Cambridge, New York, Melbourne, Madrid, Cape Town, Singapore, São Paulo, Delhi

Cambridge University Press
32 Avenue of the Americas, New York, NY 10013-2473, USA

www.cambridge.org
Information on this title: www.cambridge.org/9780521833974

First published 2007

Printed in the United States of America

A catalog record for this publication is available from the British Library.

Library of Congress Cataloging in Publication Data
Lopes, Teresa da Silva, 1968–
Global brands : the evolution of multinationals in alcoholic beverages /
Teresa da Silva Lopes.
p.   cm. – (Cambridge studies in the emergence of global enterprise)
Includes bibliographical references and index.
ISBN 978-0-521-83397-4 (hardback)
1. Alcoholic beverage industry.   2. International business enterprises.
3. Brand name products.   I. Title.
HD9350.5.L66   2007
338.8'87631 – dc22   2006101720

ISBN   978-0-521-83397-4 hardback

To My Father, José da Silva Lopes

Contents

List of Illustrations

Illustrations follow page 170.

List of Figures

List of Tables

Series Editors' Preface

During recent decades brands have rapidly increased their significance at the center of the competitive advantage of global firms. Brands once recognizable only within one country have been taken global. The pursuit of desirable brands has become a prime driver of cross-border mergers and acquisitions. Single brands can now be valued at billions of dollars. Yet the basis of their worth has an elusive quality. Many brands have disappeared over time, while some have gone from strength to strength. As a result, the understanding of the role of brands in the dynamics of global business has proved enormously challenging for researchers in international business and business history.

Teresa da Silva Lopes' *Global Brands: The Evolution of Multinationals in Alcoholic Beverages* represents a radical breakthrough in the literature on brands and the evolution of global business. In the alcoholic beverages industry, whose global market is currently in excess of $800 billion, this study shows that brands and marketing have been key factors in corporate success and failure over recent decades. This book traces their role over half a century in creating today's global giants. It is based on unique access to corporate archives located on three continents and interviews with leading practitioners. The author provides readers with a rich and nuanced international and comparative account of how the world's leading global businesses in alcoholic beverages grew from the 1960s. In the process she delivers compelling insights on the continuing importance of family ownership in many firms, and powerful testimony to the legacy of the past on corporate strategies. This is a book that both academic researchers and industry executives need to read.

Geoffrey Jones
Harvard Business School

Louis Galambos
The Johns Hopkins University

Preface

My interest in global business history and the alcoholic beverages industry antedates my time in the United Kingdom. Growing up in Portugal, where wine was for so long a major field of economic activity and a principal source of foreign trade, I found myself wanting to know why Portugal never created major leading multinationals of alcoholic beverages. For my MPhil (Mestre) degree at Universidade Católica Portuguesa, I studied the evolution of the wine industry, giving particular attention to the most internationalized sector, port wine. In so doing, I found that from the 1960s great changes had taken place in the industry that had led to the fast development of leading multinationals (though none, unfortunately, were Portuguese). These came to dominate the global alcoholic beverages industry by the early twenty-first century. It was from this research that the ideas for this book, based on my PhD dissertation emerged.

Writing this book was a pleasure for multiple reasons. Apart from unique wine, spirits, and beer tasting experiences and lots of traveling, I met a diverse array of generous and helpful people and made many very good friendships, which I am sure will be long lasting.

The two people who most profoundly shaped both my intellectual development and this book are Mark Casson and Geoffrey Jones. They certainly influenced my search for patterns and meaning in the immense amount of empirical data that I had collected. My knowledge of the fields of international business, entrepreneurship, and global business history relies heavily on their work, in more ways than even my copious references in the bibliography can show.

I always had the privilege of having the constant support and guidance of Paul Duguid, an outstanding scholar with interests in the history of brands and alcoholic beverages, as well as an expert in information and knowledge. Having been an important influence on my previous research on port wine, and on the history of the alcoholic beverages industry, Paul extended his support to this book in multiple ways. He read the "thousands" of drafts of chapters and papers I wrote, always providing insightful comments and suggestions, and also encouragement. For all this I am and will always be greatly indebted to Paul.

David Merrett, a distinguished scholar who combines exceptional historical scholarship with a deep understanding of theory, read the penultimate version of this manuscript from beginning to end, providing numerous insightful as well as supportive comments.

Many other academics were important in the collection of information and in the understanding of the industry. I received very useful comments from Alfredo Coelho, Álvaro Aguiar, Roy Church, Anthony Courakis, Joost Dankers, John Dunning, Walter Friedman, Per Hansen, Steve Jones, Bill Lazonick, Bill Mass, Colin Mayer, Christopher McKenna, Avner Offer, Bob Pearce, Gaspar Martins Pereira, Paloma Fernandez Perez, Mary Rose, Mari Sako, Judy Slinn, Keetie Sluyterman, Steen Thomsen, Steven Tolliday, Ronald Weir, Mira Wilkins, and John Wilson.

Early rendering of this research has been presented at conferences and seminars between May 1999 and May 2006 in Aarhus, Athens, Barcelona, Berkeley, Bordeaux, Budapest, Cambridge, Chapel Hill, Copenhagen, Glasgow, Hagley, Helsinki, Kobe, London, Lowell, Maastricht, Macau, Miami, Nottingham, Oslo, Oxford, Porto, Palo Alto, Portsmouth, Reading, Tokyo, and Wilmington. I am particularly grateful for the invitations from Kurt Petersen, Jesper Strandskov, and Peter Sorensen to give a keynote speech at a conference in international business history at Aarhus Business School while I was still a PhD student. I should also thank Paul Duguid and Shawn Parkhurst for inviting me as a visiting scholar to Berkeley in the spring of 2001, where also I gave a seminar, and Martin Iversen for inviting me to give a keynote speech at the annual European Business History Association in Copenhagen, whose location at the Carlsberg Brewery allowed a long-standing dream of giving a presentation with inescapable empirical evidence to come true. The comments, criticisms, and patience of participants at these events were greatly appreciated.

Financial support for this research came from the Portuguese Fundação para a Ciência e a Tecnologia. This made possible the PhD at the University of Reading and my postdoctoral position at Saïd Business School and Brasenose College at the University of Oxford, and also the travel to archives and interviews of managers in different countries. The manuscript was completed after I joined Queen Mary, University of London. I owe a great debt of gratitude to these three very different academic institutions and also Universidade Católica Portuguesa, where I started my academic career.

Many professionals in alcoholic beverages and academics helped me in my research. Interviews provided a particularly important source of information. Jack Keenan from Diageo and Michael Jackaman from Allied Domecq spent hours teaching me about the evolution of the industry in general and the strategies they pursued as CEOs of the firms. They also introduced me to almost everybody I met in the alcoholic beverages industry and greatly helped my access to the archives and libraries of firms. James Espey from

International Distillers and Vintners, Chris Nadin from Diageo, Charles Adriassen from Inbev, Tony Frogatt from Scottish & Newcastle, Jan Beijerink from Heineken, George Sandeman from Seagram, Salvador Guedes from Sogrape, and Kunimasa Himeno and Yoshi Kunimoto both from Suntory, were especially important not only for the interviews they gave but also for putting me in touch with so many other people within their own firms.

The access to archives, private libraries, databases, and information departments of firms was another important source of information. Christine Jones from Diageo was particularly helpful and understanding at different stages of my research, providing crucial primary information even when I was away in London, distant from the archives. I also am indebted to the Hagley Museum and Library, and in particular Roger Horowitz, Michael Nash, and Ellen Morfei, for giving me a grant and support to access the Seagram collection in Wilmington, Delaware. Kasia Odgers and Anthony Duggan from Diageo, Lyne Ouget of Seagram, Gillian Bouzy from Moët & Chandon, Ulla Nymann of Carlsberg, Mary Hall from *International Drinks Bulletin*, Pat Brazier of Canadean, and Laura Linlard and Barbara Esty from Baker Library at the Harvard Business School also helped me find hundreds of reports and historical annual reports of firms from around the world.

Lou Galambos, as editor of this book series "Cambridge Studies in the Emergence of the Global Enterprise," provided invaluable insights and comments in his thorough reading of the whole manuscript, constantly highlighting that I should "toot my horn a bit louder." Frank Smith was the most understanding and supportive of editors at Cambridge University Press, as deadlines came and went. Jill Friedman, Navdeep Singh, and Kate Queram played an indispensable role in editing the manuscript and getting it ready for publication, making the long publication process a pleasant experience.

Finally, Thomas (born while the manuscript was being revised) and Matthew have by now had enough of this manuscript, but it certainly would not have been finished without their support in countless ways. My father's influence on my life – both professionally and personally – make the dedication of this book just a brief gesture of the enormous gratitude and admiration I have for him.

London   Teresa da Silva Lopes

List of Abbreviations

AU	Austria
AUS	Australia
BEL	Belgium
BER	Bermuda
BRA	Brazil
CAN	Canada
CB	Cuba
CEO	Chief Executive Officer
CHI	China
COL	Colombia
CZR	Czech Republic
DCL	Distillers Company Ltd
DC-SL	Distillers Corporation – Seagram Ltd.
DEN	Denmark
EEC	European Economic Community
FDI	Foreign Direct Investment
FR	France
GER	Germany
GRE	Greece
IDV	International Distillers and Vintners
IMF	International Monetary Fund
IND	India
IRE	Ireland
IT	Italy
JAM	Jamaica
JPN	Japan
LVMH	Louis Vuitton Moët-Hennessy
M&A	Mergers and Acquisitions
MEX	Mexico
MNE	Multinational Enterprise
NL	The Netherlands
NOR	Norway
NZ	New Zealand
PER	Peru

PHIL	Philippines
POL	Poland
POR	Portugal
PTO RICO	Puerto Rico
R&D	Research and Development
ROE	Return on Equity
RUS	Russia
SA	South Africa
SAB	South African Breweries
SIC	Standard Industrial Classification
SKOR	South Korea
SPN	Spain
SWE	Sweden
UDV	United Distillers and Vintners
UK	United Kingdom
US	United States of America

1

Brands and the Evolution of Multinationals

Issues

This book is concerned with the growth of multinational firms in the global alcoholic beverages industry since 1960.[1] This is a period when the industry underwent several major changes, the most significant of which was a profound concentration as leading local and regional firms made multiple international mergers and acquisitions, becoming large multinationals. This concentration accompanied rapid internationalization, diversification, and ultimately globalization. Until the 1960s, production and consumption were essentially country and culture specific. Each country consumed predominantly one type of alcoholic beverage, usually domestically produced, and this pattern determined the kind of firms that developed faster.[2]

This story of multinational growth within the alcoholic beverages industry highlights the role of brands in the dynamic evolution of firms and industries. The focus in this book is on developing the understanding of the role of brands in the growth strategies of internationally competing firms.[3] Brands can affect the life of firms in many subtle ways: they can enhance total turnover, bulk up the financial statements, and cause changes in organizational structures. Brands allow firms to take advantage of premium prices, obtain efficiencies in distribution, and accumulate marketing knowledge. These income-enhancing attributes led in the 1980s to important changes in accounting practices by firms that started to include brands in their balance

---

[1] Multinationals are enterprises that have crossed borders, engage in foreign direct investment, and own or control value-adding activities in different regions of the world, even if most of the sales are concentrated in a small number of markets. They operate in distinct institutional environments, not being entirely within the jurisdiction of any single government. Multinationals tend to dominate major international industries, such as alcoholic beverages. John H. Dunning, "The Globalization of Firms and the Competitiveness of Countries," in John H. Dunning, Bruce Kogut, and Magnus Blomström (eds.), *Globalization of Firms and the Competitiveness of Nations* (Lund: Institute of Economic Research, 1990): 9–57; Alan Rugman and Alan Verbeke, "Towards a Theory of Regional Multinationals: A Transactions Cost Economics Approach," *Management International Review*, Vol. 44, No. 4 (2004): 3–15.

[2] See Appendix 1, "Value-Added Chain in Alcoholic Beverages."

[3] See Appendix 2, "Brands Owned by the Leading Multinationals in 2005."

sheets.[4] Since financial analysts tend to favor companies with strong brands, firms find their competitive positions strengthened.

Apart from looking at the role of brands in the growth of firms, I also invert conventional wisdom and examine the role of firms in the life of brands. In particular, I focus on the capacity of some brands to outlive firms and develop independent and eternal lives. This means I look not only at brands traded together with the firms that own them, but also at brands traded independently of firms, more or less as pieces of intellectual property.

Brands have recently become the subject of a vast body of research. However, most of the research is in the management literature and tends to focus on the relationship between brands and consumption, on problems such as adaptation *versus* standardization in different cultures, the social aspects of brands, and brand identity. Indeed, these represent the most pressing issues initially facing the growing number of firms learning how to compete internationally. There is less research using a business historical perspective. Mira Wilkins in 1992 highlighted that problem.[5]

I also explore the importance of other critical determinants, including the role of marketing knowledge, alliances in distribution, and, in particular, different forms of corporate governance in the growth of firms. These factors tend to be neglected by management literature, which focuses essentially on explaining the behavior of large capital-intensive and technology-driven firms. This study of the role of brands in the growth of multinationals in the alcoholic beverages industry is timely for several reasons. First, because it shows the power of brands in determining such growth, and in shaping the structure of industries. Second, because my subject is an industry that, over time, created more homogenous consumption patterns among a large number of consumers from different parts of the world. And third, because I can analyze the process by which industries can move from being national and locally focused to being dominated by a small number of large firms active globally.[6] In addition, the industry offers useful illustrations about

---

[4] C. Napier, "Brand Accounting in the United Kingdom," in Geoffrey Jones and Nicholas Morgan (eds.), *Adding Value: Brands and Marketing in Food and Drink* (London: Routledge, 1994): 76–100; John M. Murphy, "Assessing the Value of Brands," in John M. Murphy (ed.), *Branding a Key Marketing Tool* (London: Macmillan, 1992): 194–97; Peter Doyle, "Building Successful Brands: The Strategic Options," *Journal of Marketing Management*, Vol. 5, No. 11 (1989): 77–95; Mark Casson, "Brands: Economic Ideology and Consumer Society," in Jones and Morgan (eds.), *Adding Value*: 41–58. Note Casson argues that brands may also accrue rents and distort markets, and that the enormously positive effects of brands reflect "economic ideology" rather than empirical analysis.

[5] Mira Wilkins, "The Neglected Intangible Asset: The Influence of the Trademark on the Rise of the Modern Corporation," *Business History*, Vol. 34, No. 1 (1992): 66–99.

[6] Ronald Coase in his work on the nature of the firm also recognizes the importance of studying industries. Ronald H. Coase, "The Nature of the Firm: Influence?" in Oliver E. Williamson and Sidney G. Winter (eds.), *The Nature of the Firm: Origins, Evolution and Development* (Oxford: Oxford University Press, 1993).

the longevity of firms and the role of families in the successful development of brands.

The chapters are thematic rather than providing a comprehensive history of each firm. The first theme concerns the general patterns that might explain growth and independent survival of multinational firms in alcoholic beverages. Edith Penrose is probably one of the best-known researchers to have written on this topic. Penrose argued that growth was strongly associated with a number of competitive advantages, among which were branding and advertising.[7] In the context of international business, John Dunning created the "eclectic paradigm" to explain international production, but his model has also been applied to services. Dunning suggests that for firms to succeed in international markets they need to have ownership advantages (e.g., brands and superior technology), as well as location and internalization advantages.[8] I present a large amount of evidence to explain which determinants were important for the development of multinationals in alcoholic beverages.

Brands are, nonetheless, considered to be the most important determinant in the growth of firms. Brands explain to a considerable extent the evolution of industry structures. Business historians such as Mira Wilkins and, more recently, Nancy Koehn have drawn attention to these issues in the growth of modern business.[9] The role of brands is even more striking when looking at the number of cases where firms have disappeared but their brands survived, having multiple ownerships and enjoying eternal lives.

A second theme pursued here is why most of the leading multinationals of alcoholic beverages are family owned. The Chandlerian model, based

[7] Edith Penrose, *The Theory of the Growth of the Firm* (Oxford: Blackwell, 1959/1995): 254.
[8] John H. Dunning, "Trade, Location of Economic Activity and the MNE: A Search for an Eclectic Approach," in B. Ohlin, P. O. Hesselborn, and P. M. Wijkman (eds.), *The International Allocation of Economic Activity* (London: Macmillan, 1977): 395–418.
[9] Mira Wilkins, *The Emergence of Multinational Enterprise* (Cambridge, Mass.: Harvard University Press, 1970); idem, *The Maturing of Multinational Enterprise* (Cambridge, Mass.: Harvard University Press, 1974); idem, *The History of Foreign Investment in the United States to 1914* (Cambridge, Mass: Harvard University Press, 1989); idem, *The History of Foreign Investment in the United States 1914–1945* (Cambridge, Mass: Harvard University Press, 2004); Nancy F. Koehn, *Brand New* (Boston, Mass.: Harvard Business School Press, 2001); Geoffrey Jones, *Renewing Unilever: Transformation and Tradition* (Oxford: Oxford University Press, 2005): chapter 5; idem, *Multinationals and Global Capitalism* (Oxford: Oxford University Press, 2005); Roy Church and Christine Clark, "The Origins of Competitive Advantage in the Marketing of Branded Packaged Consumer Goods: Colman's and Reckitt's in Early Victorian Britain," *Journal of Industrial History*, Vol. 3, No. 2 (2000): 98–199. For an analysis of brands in the evolution of firms in the context of alcoholic beverages, see Teresa da Silva Lopes, *Internacionalização e Concentração no Vinho do Porto, 1945–1995* (Porto: GEHVID/ICEP, 1998); Paul Duguid, "Developing the Brand: The Case of Alcohol, 1800–1880," *Enterprise and Society*, Vol. 4, No. 3 (2003): 405–41. See also Paul Duguid (ed.), "Networks in the Trade of Alcohol," *Business History Review*, Vol. 79, No. 3 (2005); "Why Brands Are Good For You," *The Economist* (6 Sept. 2001).

essentially on the world's leading high-tech and capital-intensive firms, suggests that widespread ownership predominates and families can hinder the growth of firms.[10] I offer a case study of the evolution of a global industry, covering different countries and challenging Chandlerian assumptions.

A third theme is concerned with channel management. Transaction cost economists study the motivations for internalization or, alternatively, the conditions that allow cooperation to be the better option.[11] I offer a dynamic story about the changing relationship between producers, wholesalers, and retailers, where competition and cooperation are very common. Again, I challenge Chandlerian studies on the largest U.S. enterprises that claim that beverages such as coffee and soft drinks are better distributed through vertically integrated channels.[12] In the alcoholic beverages industry, alliances between direct competitors in distribution appear to have been very significant in the international expansion strategies of the leading multinational firms.

The fourth theme pursued is the diversification strategies used by the leading multinationals in alcoholic beverages in the face of changing environmental circumstances. I look at why these changes took place, what kind of knowledge the leading multinationals acquired and developed over time that allowed them to follow distinct strategies and yet achieve similar leadership positions by the twenty-first century.[13]

A fifth theme, again a Penrosian topic, looks at the growth of firms through mergers and acquisitions. It focuses, however, on the role of brands and marketing knowledge in that process. In industries like alcoholic beverages, brands are distinctive combinations of cultural characteristics and values. Consequently, they are much more independent of the firms and of the ownership of production than in other industries. Even when they depend on the location of production, brands are often assets that can be easily traded. Indeed, it will be argued below that the acquisition of brands became a strong determinant of concentration in the alcoholic beverages industry.[14]

A final theme pursued is the impact of firms in the life of brands. The alcoholic beverages industry has provided some of the oldest and best-known brands in the world. It is not surprising, then, that some of these brands, like the firms that created them, go far back in time. In some cases brands have remained under the same family ownership throughout their lives; in others,

---

[10] Alfred D. Chandler Jr., *Scale and Scope* (Cambridge, Mass: Harvard University Press, 1990).

[11] Ronald H. Coase, "The Nature of the Firm: Influence?" in Oliver E. Williamson and Sidney G. Winter (eds.), *The Nature of the Firm: Origins, Evolution and Development* (Oxford: Oxford University Press, 1993); Oliver E. Williamson, "The Modern Corporation: Origins, Evolution, Attributes," *Journal of Economic Literature*, Vol. 19 (1981): 1537–68.

[12] Chandler, *Scale and Scope*.

[13] On the theory of multiproduct firms, see David Teece, "Towards an Economic Theory of the Multiproduct Firm," *Journal of Economic Behaviour and Organization*, Vol. 3 (1982): 39–63.

[14] Penrose, *The Theory*: 254.

they outlived the entrepreneurs and firms that created them, having multiple ownerships during their lives. Even though these changes in ownership are often more apparent than real, with licensing deals or alliances transferring effective control to another institution while ownership stays with the original firm, different owners seem to develop brands in different ways. This chapter looks at the evolution of global brands, the distinct roles played by the entrepreneurs and managers who created and developed those brands.

Brands

A brand is defined as a legally defensible proprietary name, recognized by some categories of consumers as signifying a product with dimensions that differentiate it in some way from other products designed to satisfy the same need. A common characteristic of global brands is that even if their sales originate from a small number of markets, they are available in many markets.[15]

Brands may add value to the consumer in multiple ways. They may promote not only the tangible characteristics of a product, but also intangible characteristics, which can either be functional and objective (such as quality, value for money, and consistency) or abstract and emotional (reflecting psychological and social values such as prestige associated with products from a certain region or country and heritage).[16] They may convey information and help simplify decision making for the consumer by giving a sense of security and consistency, and supporting his "fantasies."[17] Furthermore, brands are an important way for firms to communicate with consumers and cultivate their loyalty. They also add value to the firm by sustaining a continuing revenue stream because of the consumer propensity for long-term brand loyalty.[18]

---

[15] For alternative definitions of brands, see Kevin Lane Keller, *Strategic Brand Management* (London: Prentice Hall, 1998): 4; Leslie de Chernatony and Malcom McDonald, *Creating Powerful Brands* (Oxford: Butterworth-Heinemann, 1998); Leslie de Chernatony and G. McWilliam, "The Varying Nature of Brands as Assets," *International Journal of Advertising*, Vol. 8 (1989): 339–49; idem, "Brand Consultants' Perspectives and the Concept of the Brand," *Marketing and Research Today*, Vol. 25, No. 1 (1997): 45–52; G. Michel and Tim Ambler, "Establishing Brand Essence Across Borders," *The Journal of Brand Management*, Vol. 6, No. 5 (1999): 333–45; Kevin Lane Keller, "The Brand Report Card," *Harvard Business Review* (Jan.–Feb., 2000): 147–57; Susannah Hart and John Murphy, *Brands: The New Wealth Creators* (London: Macmillan, 1998).

[16] Leslie de Chernatony, *Brand Management* (Aldershot: Ashgate, 1998); Leslie Chernatony and Francesca Dall'Olmo Riley, "Defining a Brand: Beyond the Literature with Experts' Interpretations," *Journal of Marketing Management*, Vol. 14, No. 5 (1998): 417–43; Steven King, *Developing New Brands* (Bath: Wiley, 1973).

[17] David A. Aaker, *Building Strong Brands* (New York: Free Press, 1996); Peter Doyle, "Building Successful Brands: The Strategic Options," *Journal of Marketing Management*, Vol. 5, No. 11 (1989): 78.

[18] P. Barwise and T. Robertson, "Brand Portfolios," *European Management Journal*, Vol. 10, No. 3 (1992): 277–85.

Several studies have proposed models to analyze the nature of brands, although authors differ in the amount of emphasis they give to the tangible and intangible elements of brands and also to their other aspects.[19] This book focuses on the intangible elements of brands and the value they add to firms. Such intangible elements include the uniqueness of the brand and its "personality," built over time, embedded in a particular culture or associated with a particular set of values (such as heritage or country image), and with an economic value associated with the investments made to build its reputation.[20]

The "personality" of brands in alcoholic beverages is associated with the characteristics of the industry where products tend to have long life-cycles, and brands acquire associations with tradition, heritage, and country of origin.[21] While country of origin is particularly important in wines and spirits (being sometimes perceived as even more than with conventional brands),[22] the ability of the brand to indicate age and tradition is also relevant. Consequently, it is not surprising to see some remarkably old brands in this industry.

In many cases the personality of brands and their longevity also reflect the significance of having been first movers in a particular market. In such cases brands may set the standard against which subsequent entrants in that market are judged and may simultaneously raise the cost of entry for new brands and firms.[23] To be able to sustain the value added by its brands in the face of competition, however, and especially when the product to which they refer is in fact similar (such as the case for whiskies with similar blends carrying different brands), even first movers must invest in marketing to ensure that consumers do not perceive rival brands as acceptable substitutes.[24]

In wines, a different type of branding has been developing in recent years. While old world wines have, to a significant degree, been branded by region,

[19] For a review of the existing models, see Leslie de Chernatony and Francesca Dall'Olmo Riley, "Modelling the Components of the Brand," *European Journal of Marketing*, Vol. 32, No. 11/12 (1998): 1077–90.

[20] V. N. Balasubramanyam and M. A. Salisu, "Brands and the Alcoholic Drinks Industry," in Jones and Morgan (eds.), *Adding Value*; Birger Wernerfelt, "A Resource-based View of the Firm," *Strategic Management Journal*, Vol. 5 (1984): 171–80.

[21] John Kay, *Foundations of Corporate Success* (Oxford: Oxford University Press, 1993): 299; P. Feldwick, "Defining a Brand," in D. Cowley (ed.), *Understanding Brands* (London: Kogan Page, 1991): 19; W. J. Bilkey and E. Nes, "Country-of-Origin Effects on Product Evaluations," *Journal of International Business Studies*, Vol. 13, No. 1 (1982): 89–99.

[22] G. Erickson, R. Jacobson, and J. Johansson, "Competition for Market Share in the Presence of Strategic Invisible Assets," *International Journal of Research in Marketing*, Vol. 9, No. 1 (1992): 23–37; C. K. Kim and J. Y. Chung, "Brand Popularity, Country Image and Market Share: An Empirical Study," *Journal of International Business Studies*, Vol. 28, No. 2 (1997): 367.

[23] R. Schmalensee, "Product Differentiation Advantages of Pioneering Brands," *The American Economic Review*, Vol. 72, No. 3 (1982): 360.

[24] Trevor Watkins, *The Economics of the Brand* (Whitstable: McGraw-Hill, 1986): 3.

de novo wines are branded by individual firms. The former are subject to problems of free riding by low-quality producers who can damage the status of the region as a whole. The latter, by contrast, have more control over the perception of their brand. New branded wines tend to be produced in "new world" countries such as the United States, Chile, Argentina, Australia, and New Zealand. The brands emphasize the grape variety above the region or the date, giving the consumer an alternative (and easier) way of sorting through the wide variety of brands from the old world wines where *terroir* and date are highly important, but highly variable. Private brands are thus the most important part of the strategy used in the marketing of new world wines. These branded wines offer an accessible starting point for new drinkers, providing some sort of guarantee that they will get what they are paying for from one outlet and from one year to the next. For the companies they offer the prospect of creating consumer loyalty and hence higher sales volumes, profit margins, and lower risks from asset specificity.

Marketing Knowledge and Entrepreneurship

Marketing knowledge is considered here to comprise the "intelligence" and the skills that are deployed in the management of firms' activities. This definition draws on evolutionary and neo-Schumpeterian concepts of the role of the entrepreneur.[25] I draw on Penrose's concept of knowledge, which considers the firm to be an evolving collection of resources: the optimal growth of the firm involves a balance between exploitation of existing resources and development of new ones. Following this view, Kogut and Zander contend that the multinational corporation arises out of superior efficiency as an organizational vehicle by which firms transfer knowledge across borders.[26] According to these authors, firms grow on the basis of their ability to create new knowledge and to replicate this knowledge so as to expand their markets. Their advantage lies in being able to understand and carry out this transfer more effectively than other firms. Entrepreneurs discussed in this book coordinate scarce resources in new ways and thus disturb the markets, technologies, and organizational methods. They have the capacity to

---

[25] Richard R. Nelson and Signey G. Winter, *An Evolutionary Theory of Economic Change* (Cambridge, Mass: Harvard University Press, 1982).

[26] Penrose, *The Theory*; Bruce Kogut and Udo Zander, "Knowledge of the Firm and the Evolutionary Theory of the Multinational Corporation," *Journal of International Business Studies*, 24 (1993): 625–45. For an early recognition of Edith Penrose's work in Business History, see Louis Galambos, "Business History and the Theory of the Growth of the Firm," *Explorations in Entrepreneurial History*, Vol. 4, No. 1 (1966): 3–14; William Lazonick, "Understanding Innovative Enterprise – Toward the Integration of Economic Theory and Business History," in Franco Amatori and Geoffrey Jones (eds.), *Business History Around the World* (Cambridge: Cambridge University Press, 2003).

innovate, turning opportunities into new products and services, and are not concerned with the risk of incurring major sunk costs.[27]

Taking into account the above definitions of *marketing knowledge* and *entrepreneur*, I argue here that firms have two types of marketing knowledge. One type is "sticky" to the firm, and is path-dependent (being accumulated within the firm over time).[28] This type of knowledge involves the routines and procedures within the firm designed to harmonize decision taking and to carry out organizational action.[29] It can only be learned through personal experience, in the long term. It is embedded in the firm's routines and structure, and is comparable to Penrose's and Polanyi's definition of implied knowledge, that is, "tacit" and acquired through operating in the market.[30]

The other type of knowledge is "smooth," and is of broader application as it can be applied to the management of different brands and firms in distinct industries. It can be accessed by the firm in the short run, either directly through acquisitions, alliances, and the hiring of consultants or through the appointment of managers with professional experience, training, and marketing skills. These managers focus on enhancing the profitability of the firm by, for example, rejuvenating brands, turning local brands into global brands, and forming alliances in distribution. Indirectly, published studies and academic courses, especially in more recent times, may also provide some of this knowledge about specific countries and the industry.[31] Smooth knowledge is comparable to Penrose's concept of "objective" knowledge.

---

[27] J. A. Schumpeter, *Capitalism, Socialism and Democracy* (London: Unwin University Books, 1943); Mark Casson, *The Entrepreneur* (Oxford: Martin Robertson, 1982); idem, "Entrepreneurship and the Dynamics of Foreign Direct Investment," in P. J. Buckley and M. Casson, *The Economic Theory of the Multinational Enterprise* (London: Macmillan, 1985).

[28] The point of departure for the analysis of stickiness of technical knowledge is Kenneth J. Arrow, "Classification Notes on the Production and Transmission of Technical Knowledge," *American Economic Review*, No. 52 (1969): 29–35. John Seely Brown and Paul Duguid, "Knowledge and Organization: A Social-Practice Perspective," *Organization Science*, Vol. 12, No. 2 (2001): 198–213, explore the issue of sticky and smooth or "leaky" knowledge both within and between firms.

[29] Richard R. Nelson and Sidney G. Winter, *An Evolutionary Theory of Economic Change* (Cambridge, Mass: Harvard University Press, 1982): 4, 14; Sydney G. Winter, "On Coase, Competence and Corporation," in Oliver E. Williamson, Sidney G. Winter (eds.), *The Nature of the Firm: Origins, Evolution and Development* (Oxford: Oxford University Press, 1991): 10, 30, 187; Jos C. N. Raadschelders, "Evolution, Institutional Analysis and Path Dependency: An Administrative-History Perspective on Fashionable Approaches and Concepts," *International Review of Administrative Sciences*, Vol. 64 (1998): 565–82; Kent Eriksson, Anders Majkgard, and D. Deo Sharma, "Path Dependence and Knowledge Development in the Internationalisation Process," *Management International Review*, Vol. 40, No. 4 (2000): 308.

[30] Penrose, *The Theory*; Michael Polanyi, *The Tacit Dimension* (London: Routledge, 1966).

[31] About international marketing knowledge, see also S. Tamer Cavusgil, "Perspectives: Knowledge Development in International Marketing," *Journal of International Marketing*, Vol. 6, No. 2 (1998): 103–12.

Marketing knowledge may either have the characteristics of a public good, such as knowledge about the preferred type of distribution channels to serve a particular market (alliances, wholly owned channels, or simply exports), or of an intangible and legally protected asset, such as the capacity to create and manage successful brands. This concept is used throughout the book to explain, for instance, why some firms are able to merge and acquire other firms and other brands, and also why some firms have the capacity to create and manage successful portfolios of global brands.

The processes by which firms create and acquire sticky and smooth marketing knowledge are not mutually exclusive. On the contrary, by acquiring smooth marketing knowledge, firms are at the same time acquiring sticky marketing knowledge. However, while smooth marketing knowledge may be sufficient to enable firms to grow and survive in domestic or geographically limited and other benign environments, they need to have acquired high levels of sticky marketing knowledge to become leading multinationals and still grow and survive in adverse environments.

Ownership and Corporate Control

Discussion of the separation of ownership and control of firms started early in the twentieth century with the work of Berle and Means (1932).[32] However, comparative analysis of national systems of corporate governance did not gain significance until the 1970s and 1980s, when studies focused on the largest firms in the industrialized countries and used the nation-state as the central reference for making comparative analysis on the evolution of their systems of corporate governance.[33] National systems of corporate governance, in a broad way, include the particular arrangements of hierarchy and market relations that have become institutionalized and relatively successful in particular national contexts. Systems that developed within a particular country reflect not only the formal relations both within firms and between firms and the market, but also the distinctive culture, law, and polity of the country.[34]

---

[32] Adolf A. Berle and Gardiner C. Means, *The Modern Corporation and Private Property* (New York: Harcourt Brace & World, 1932).

[33] Alfred D. Chandler Jr., *The Visible Hand* (Cambridge, Mass: Harvard University Press, 1977); idem, *Scale and Scope*; William Lazonick, *Business Organization and the Myth of the Market Economy* (Cambridge, Mass: Harvard University Press, 1991); Geoffrey Jones, *British Multinational Banking 1830–1990* (Oxford: Clarendon, 1993); John Scott and Catherine Griff, *Directors of Industry: The British Corporate Network 1904–76* (Cambridge: Polity, 1984).

[34] Richard Whitley (ed.), *European Business Systems: Firms and Markets in Their National Contexts* (London: Sage, 1992): 6; Richard Whitley, *Business Systems in East Asia: Firms, Markets and Societies* (London: Sage, 1992); idem, "Eastern Asian Enterprise Structures and the Comparative Analysis of Forms of Business Organization," *Organization Studies*,

In *Scale and Scope*, Chandler looked at the business history of the United States, the United Kingdom, and Germany, setting out an interpretation of the dynamics of industrial capitalism. On the basis of the evolution of the predominantly technology-based leading firms in each country, Chandler distinguished some key characteristics of capitalism, such as the extent to which leading firms established large managerial bureaucracies to coordinate a wide variety of activities and transactions, and the separation of owners from managers. Chandler created two categories for comparing corporate control, which refer to the mechanisms of decision taking by firms between countries. He believed that corporate control can be "personal" or "managerial."[35] It is "personal" when the firm is owner controlled. Chandler emphasized the importance of firms managed by their founders or by members of the founding families. In the absence of a precise definition of "family firms,"[36] this book includes not only firms owned, controlled, and managed by families, but also firms owned by families who run the corporate board, but which are managed entirely by professional managers.[37] In general, such firms lack extensive management hierarchies, but there are exceptions as some "managerial" firms, such as General Electric under Jack Welch, undoubtedly reflect the personality of powerful managers.[38]

In "managerial" enterprises, decisions about current production and distribution and those involving investments in facilities and personnel for future production and distribution are made by a hierarchy of lower-, middle-, and top-level managers governed by a board of directors. Therefore, there is a separation of stock ownership from operating and investment decisions. The United States is characterized by competitive managerial capitalism, the United Kingdom by personal managerial capitalism, and Germany by cooperative managerial capitalism, which combines aspects of US managerial capitalism with concentrated ownership and interfirm cooperation.

Vol. 11, No. 1 (1990): 47–54; Mark S. Granovetter, "Economic Action and Social Structure: The Problem of Embeddedness," *American Journal of Sociology*, Vol. 91, No. 3 (1985): 481–510; R. Levine, "Financial Development and Economic Growth: Views and Agenda," *Journal of Economic Literature*, No. 35 (1997): 688–726.

[35] Alfred D. Chandler Jr., "The Emergence of Managerial Capitalism," *Business History Review*, Vol. 58, (1984): 473–503.

[36] Roy Church, "Family Firm and Managerial Capitalism: The Case of the International Motor Industry," *Business History*, Vol. 28, No. 2 (1986): 165–6; idem, "The Family Firm in Industrial Capitalism: International Perspectives on Hypothesis and History," *Business History*, Vol. 35, No. 4 (1993): 18.

[37] Mary B. Rose, "Family Firm Community and Business Culture: A Comparative Perspective on the British and American Cotton Industries," in Andrew Godley and Oliver Westall (eds.), *Business and Culture* (Manchester: Manchester University Press, 1996); Andrea Colli and Mary B. Rose, "The Culture and Evolution of Family Firms in Britain and Italy," *Scandinavian Economic History Review*, Vol. 47, No. 1 (1999): 24–47; Alfred D. Chandler, "The Enduring Logic of Industrial 'Success," *Harvard Business Review* (March–April, 1990): 132.

[38] More recently, literature has pointed out that communications technology has tended to "flatten" firms, reducing the amount of hierarchy. The examples commonly cited (Federal Express and Wal-Mart) are clearly not particularly personal in their control.

Other authors emphasize the importance of different factors for making a comparative analysis of national systems of corporate governance. For example, Jenkinson and Mayer focus on types of ownership. They classify national business systems as "outsider" and "insider."[39] "Outsider" systems disperse ownership among a large number of individual and institutional investors. Shareholders do not intervene in decision making, which is done by professional managers. In "insider" systems, by contrast, shares are concentrated in the hands of a small number of other firms, financial institutions and families, even when they are publicly quoted. These owners may participate more directly in management decisions. Cross-shareholding between firms is also commonplace in this case.

Jenkinson and Mayer also give considerable importance to external factors such as the political and regulatory environment of countries (e.g., shareholder protection, and development of capital markets). In the beginning of the twenty-first century, countries such as the United Kingdom, the United States, and Canada were considered generally to use "outsider" business systems.[40] Continental European countries and Japan tend to have "insider" business systems. Nonetheless, elements of convergence were discernible between the two.[41]

Both the Chandlerian perspectives and those of Jenkinson and Mayer assume cultural and economic determinism and believe that dominant industries establish the "rules of the game" for all other players in the same country. Therefore, they suggest a strong correlation between the country of origin and the ownership structures or management control systems of firms. For example, if firms are based in the United States, they are expected to have "managerial" corporate control according to Chandler, and to be based on "outsider" systems of corporate governance according to Jenkinson and Mayer. Conversely, if firms are based in countries like France, then corporate control is expected to be "personal," and ownership to be "insider" based. However, these national systems do not necessarily preclude firms in particular global industries from developing distinctive industry-specific capabilities and competitive norms.[42] This is particularly true in pluralist societies, which have a great variety of institutions and a weak cohesion within national boundaries. Indeed, in industries such as alcoholic beverages,

---

[39] Tim Jenkinson and Colin Mayer, "The Assessment: Corporate Governance and Corporate Control," *Oxford Review of Economic Policy*, Vol. 8, No. 3 (1992): 1–10.

[40] P. W. Moreland, "Alternative Disciplinary Mechanisms in Different Corporate Systems," *Journal of Economic Behaviour and Organization*, Vol. 26 (1995): 19.

[41] Geoffrey Jones, "Corporate Governance and British Industry," *Entreprises et Histoire*, No. 21 (1999): 29–43.

[42] Alfred D. Chandler, Franco Amatori, and Takashi Hikino (eds.), *Big Business and the Wealth of Nations* (Cambridge: Cambridge University Press, 1997); Keijo Räsänen and Richard Whipp, "National Business Recipes: A Sector Perspective," and Richard Whitley, "Business Systems, Industrial Sectors and Strategic Choices," both in Whitley (ed.), *European Business Systems*.

cosmetics, or consulting, the national systems perspectives are not sufficient to explain the evolution of their ownership and control.

By bringing ownership and corporate control perspectives together, it is possible to find a wider range of combinations of ownership and control of firms. Apart from technological innovation, other determinants such as brands and marketing knowledge may also have an important impact in the control and ownership structures of multinational firms.

Alliances

There is extensive literature on the growing importance of alliances as alternatives to markets and hierarchies in the evolution of firms that have become global.[43] It shows that a number of these alliances have been formed between firms with similar capabilities and size, aiming to increase efficiencies in various activities such as the procurement of raw materials, research and development, or production. Other alliances are formed between firms of different size with complementary activities, such as production and wholesaling.[44]

Alliances are defined as collaborative agreements between two or more firms involving the exchange of knowledge (technological, marketing, or information about the markets and the customers) and the commitment of resources and capabilities. They include a wide spectrum of modes of organizing the economic activities that lie between single market transactions (involving a buyer and a seller) and hierarchies (wholly owned operations).[45] They can take the form of long-term contractual distribution agreements, joint ventures, minority equity stakes, or licensing agreements and may involve only production or distribution, or a combination of the two.

---

[43] See Mark Casson, *Alternatives to the Multinational Enterprise* (London: Macmillan, 1979); idem, "Contractual Arrangements for Technology Transfer: New Evidence from Business History," *Business History*, Vol. 28, No. 4 (1986): 5–35; Geoffrey Jones (ed.), *Coalitions and Collaboration in International Business* (Aldershot: Elgar, 1993); John H. Dunning, *International Production and Multinational Enterprise* (London: Allen & Unwin, 1981); idem, *Alliance Capitalism and Global Business* (London: Routledge, 1997); J. Farok and Peter Lorange (eds.), *Cooperative Strategies in International Business* (Toronto: Lexington Books, 1988); James C. Anderson and James A. Narus, "A Model of Distributor Firm and Manufacturer Firm Working Partnerships," *Journal of Marketing*, 54 (1990): 42–58; Williamson, "The Modern Corporation."

[44] George B. Richardson, "The Organization of Industry," *Economic Journal*, Vol. 82, No. 327 (1972): 883–96.

[45] Ronald H. Coase, "The Nature of the Firm," *Economica*, NS. 4 (1937): 386–405; Oliver E. Williamson, *Markets and Hierarchies* (New York: Free Press, 1975); idem, *The Economic Institutions of Capitalism* (New York: Free Press, 1985); Stephen H. Hymer, "The Large Multinational Corporation: An Analysis of Some Motives for the International Integration of Business," *Revue Economique*, Vol. 19, No. 6 (1968): 949–73; Peter J. Buckley and Mark Casson, *The Future of the Multinational Enterprise* (London: Macmillan, 1976).

Context

This book is a work of international business history, informed throughout by the application of economic theory, in particular the theory of international business.[46] Focusing on the study of the development of global brands, and the growth of business over time and across borders, the book deals with complex changes in the environment and compares the international evolution of large multinational firms, using empirical research on each one individually. My analysis draws on concepts from the economic theories of international business.

Most frequently, the comparative analysis of institutions and of the environment leads to new generalizations about international business.[47] But sometimes the use of preestablished conceptual frameworks from economic theory can be useful in developing new generalizations,[48] as are general propositions developed by business historians like Alfred Chandler. His ideas about the growth of large firms from different sectors in industrialized countries are extremely useful.[49] And yet, his discussion focuses primarily on manufacturing and other technology-based industries. That is the case even in his discussion on branded and packaged consumer goods in *Scale and Scope*. This book, by contrast, focuses on branded consumer goods in an industry where developments in manufacturing and technology have not had a significant impact, and challenges the applicability of some of Chandler's generalizations to such industries. Here it is argued that rather than technological innovation it is brands, marketing knowledge, and

---

[46] For a discussion of this topic and the scope of business history see Mira Wilkins, "Business History as a Discipline," *Business and Economic History*, Vol. 17 (1988): 1–7; Geoffrey Jones, "Business History: Theory and Concepts," *The University of Reading: Discussion Papers in Economics*, No. 295 (1994); idem, "Company History and Business History in the 1990s," in Wilfried Feldenkirchen and Terry Gourvish (eds.), *European Yearbook of Business History*, 2 (Aldershot: Ashgate 1999); Geoffrey Jones and Tarun Khanna, "Bringing History (Back) Into International Business," *Journal of International Business Studies*, Vol. 37 (2006): 453–68; S. R. H. Jones, "Transaction Costs and the Theory of the Firm: The Scope and Limitations of the New Institutional Approach," *Business History*, Vol. 39, No. 4 (1997): 9–25.

[47] See for instance Alfred D. Chandler Jr., "Comparative Business History," in D. C. Coleman and Peter Mathias, *Enterprise and History: Essays in Honour of Charles Wilson* (Cambridge: Cambridge University Press, 1984).

[48] About theory and business history see also Alan Roberts, "The Very Idea of Theory in Business History," *The University of Reading: Discussion Papers in Accounting and Finance*, Vol. 54 (1998); Terry Gourvish, "Business History: in Defense of the Empirical Approach?" *Accounting Business and Financial History*, Vol. 5, No. 1 (1995): 3–16; T. A. B. Corley, "Firms and Markets: Towards a Theory of Business History," *Business and Economic History*, Vol. 22, No. 1 (1993): 54–66.

[49] On the influence of Alfred Chandler in Business History in general see Louis Galambos, "Identity and the Boundaries of Business History – An Essay on Consensus and Creativity," in Amatori and Jones (eds.), *Business History Around the World*.

distribution channels that are the main determinants in the growth and survival of firms.[50]

Nevertheless, some Chandlerian concepts are of particular relevance to this book. These include the concept of "first-mover advantages," which helps account for the capacity of original firms in an industry to retain their position as industry leaders if they continue to invest in their organizational capabilities; the concept of "economies of scale and scope," which helps explain how firms come to dominate industries; and the concepts of "personal capitalism" and "managerial hierarchies" to describe the predominant governance structures of firms in different countries.[51] The major distinction between this book and other studies that have also drawn on Chandler's work arises from the kind of industry being analyzed – alcoholic beverages – and the scope of activity of the firms – essentially multinationals, originally from multiple countries spread over many continents.

Geoffrey Jones's extensive research on the history of multinationals from various industries is another major influence on the approach followed in this book. Jones's work follows that of Mira Wilkins, who began the historical research on why firms cross borders. Their work is distinct from that of economics as they show the diversity of institutional forms used by firms crossing borders, strong national variations in strategies and propensities to invest, multinational investment in industries other than high-tech manufacturing (such as banking and trading companies), and significant discontinuities. Jones also analyzes the role of brands in consumer goods industries.[52] But it is not only the focus on multinational activity that makes Jones's work so relevant for this book. The methods he uses and the issues that he raises are also very influential.

Jones's work systematically combines empirical international business history and economic theory, looking at a wide array of subjects that have not received much attention in the field of international business history. Of particular relevance to this book is his edited book *Adding Value: Brands and Marketing in Food and Drink*, wherein he looks at the growth of firms in food and drinks. Like Chandler, Jones emphasizes the importance of making

[50] For a discussion of the impact of Chandler's work on the development of business history, see, e.g., Richard R. John, "Elaborations, Revisions, Dissents: Alfred D. Chandler, Jr's, 'The Visible Hand' after Twenty Years," *Business History Review*, 71 (1997): 151–200; Maury Klein, "Coming Full Circle: The Study of Big Business Since 1950," *Enterprise and Society*, Vol. 2, No. 3 (2001): 425–60; Chandler, *Scale and Scope*.

[51] Alfred D. Chandler, *Strategy and Structure* (Cambridge, Mass: The MIT Press, 1962); idem, *The Visible Hand*; idem, *Scale and Scope*.

[52] Mira Wilkins and Frank E. Hill, *American Business Abroad: Ford on Six Continents* (Detroit: Wayne State University Press, 1964); Geoffrey Jones, *Renewing Unilever: Transformation and Tradition* (Oxford: Oxford University Press, 2005); idem, *British Multinational Banking*; Geoffrey Jones et al., "L'Oréal and the Globalization of American Beauty," Harvard Business School Case No. 805-086 (Boston, 2005).

comparative analysis between firms, rather than looking at single firms, as a way to create generalizations.[53]

In his *Multinationals and Global Capitalism,* Jones looks at the international growth of whole sets of firms in such industries as banking and trading. He focuses on industries and firms other than "high-tech manufacturing," stressing the importance of "soft" things like knowledge and information. In his other writings, Jones also examines the importance of alternative organizational forms, including networks or partnerships of merchant houses, rather than just large "Chandlerian" corporations.[54]

Casson's and Dunning's influence on this book goes much beyond the usual application of their theories on the economics of international business and the explanation of the frequent changes in the boundaries of firms.[55] Casson's "systems view" of international business, "internalization theory," and the "theory of the entrepreneur" provide a particularly rich theoretical background for understanding the evolution of multinationals in the alcoholic beverages industry.[56] By relaxing some of the assumptions of neoclassical economics, his theories are able to encompass the extent to which multinationals are integrated in the global economy and are linked by a

---

53 Jones and Morgan, *Adding Value*; Geoffrey Jones, *Merchants to Multinationals* (Oxford: Oxford University Press, 2000); Richard S. Tedlow and Geoffrey Jones (eds.), *The Rise & Fall of Mass Marketing* (London: Routledge, 1993); Geoffrey Jones (ed.), "The Making of the Global Enterprise," *Special Issue: Business History,* Vol. 36, No. 1 (1994); Charles Harvey and Geoffrey Jones (eds.), "Organizational Capability and Competitive Advantage," *Special Issue: Business History,* Vol. 34, No. 1 (1992); Geoffrey Jones and Harm G. Schröter (eds.), *The Rise of Multinationals in Continental Europe* (Aldershot: Elgar, 1993); Geoffrey Jones and Mary B. Rose (eds.), "Family Capitalism," *Special Issue: Business History,* Vol. 35, No. 4 (1993).

54 Geoffrey Jones, *Multinationals and Global Capitalism* (Oxford: Oxford University Press, 2005); idem, *Merchants to Multinationals.*

55 Much of the theoretical discussion draws on Mark Casson and John H. Dunning, whose economic methods and concepts of international business help resolve and generalize different issues about the growth of multinationals being analyzed. See, e.g., Casson, *The Entrepreneur*; idem, *Economics of International Business* (Cheltenham: Elgar, 2000); Buckley and Casson, *The Future of the Multinational Enterprise*; Dunning, "Trade, Location of Economic Activity and the MNE"; idem, *Explaining International Production* (London: Unwin Hyman, 1988); idem, "The Eclectic Paradigm of International Production: A Restatement and Some Possible Extensions," *Journal of International Business Studies,* Vol. 19, No. 1 (1988): 1–31; idem, *Multinational Enterprises.*

56 About the applicability of John Dunning's and Mark Casson's work to international business and business history see, e.g., the special issue of *International Journal of the Economics of Business,* Vol. 8, No. 2 (2001). About Mark Casson and Peter Buckley's work, see the special issue of *Journal of International Business Studies,* Vol. 34, No. 2 (2003); Gordon Boyce, *Information, Mediation and Institutional Development* (Manchester: Manchester University Press, 1995), draws extensively on Casson's concepts. A good illustration of an application of Dunning's Eclectic Paradigm in business history is James Bamberg, "OLI and OIL: BP in the US in Theory and Practice, 1968–98," in Geoffrey Jones and Lina Gálvez-Munõz (eds.), *Foreign Multinationals in the United States* (London: Routledge, 2002).

complex web of product and information flows. Some of the questions he raises deal with the reasons that lead multinationals to internalize activities in the value-added chain and across borders, the costs and benefits of internalization, and the process of reconfiguration of the boundaries of firms driven by entrepreneurs in pursuit of greater efficiency.[57] Casson's analysis takes into consideration firm-specific advantages and can be used as a way to systematize the predominant characteristics of multinational firms.

Casson's work is primarily theoretical. As with all theoretical work, its value must ultimately be proved in terms of its ability to deal with real-world cases. This book brings such real-world examples into Casson's models. In the process, I conclude that an information-based model helps deal with issues raised by the marketing knowledge developed, held, and exploited by firms in their branding and distribution strategies.

Dunning's influence can be seen in the kind of questions this book aims to answer, sometimes without citing Dunning. The Eclectic Paradigm is used throughout as it provides an understanding of multinational growth and survival and also of the changes in boundaries of firms over time. Dunning's work also influenced the levels of institutional analysis here and my take on the dynamic interplay between countries and industries over time.[58]

---

[57] See, e.g., Mark Casson and Mary Rose (eds.), "Institutions and the Evolution of Modern Business," *Special Issue: Business History*, Vol. 39, No. 4 (1997); Mark Casson and Howard Cox, "International Business Networks: Theory and History," *Business and Economic History*, Vol. 22, No. 1 (1993): 42–53; Mark Casson, "General Theories of the Multinational Enterprise: Their Relevance to Business History," in Peter Hertner and Geoffrey Jones (eds.), *Multinationals: Theory and History* (Hants: Gower, 1986); idem, "Institutional Economics and Business History: A Way Forward?" *The University of Reading: Discussion Papers in Economics and Management*, No. 362 (1997/98); idem, "The Nature of the Firm Reconsidered: Information Synthesis and Entrepreneurial Organization," *Management International Review*, Vol. 36, No. 1 (1996): 55–94; idem, "Internalisation Theory and Beyond," in Peter J. Buckley (ed.), *Recent Research on the Multinational Enterprise* (Aldershot: Elgar, 1991): 4–27; idem, *Economics of International Business*; idem, *The Entrepreneur*; idem, *Enterprise and Competitiveness: A Systems View of International Business* (Oxford: Clarendon, 1990); Peter J. Buckley and Mark C. Casson, "Analyzing Foreign Market Entry Strategies: Extending the Internalization Approach," *Journal of International Business Studies*, Vol. 29, No. 3 (1998): 539–62.

[58] John H. Dunning is the pioneer in the development of international business, having produced the first post–World War II academic monograph on international business – *American Investment in British Manufacturing Industry*. In his subsequent publications over four decades, he has unrivalled mastery of empirical evidence in all fields of international business. His concern for the origins and evolution of multinationals, the countries of origin of multinationals, the making of the global enterprise, and the practical methodology he created with his Eclectic Paradigm, based on these and other questions, form an ideal framework for carrying out large-scale research in international business. John H. Dunning, *American Investment in British Manufacturing Industry* (London: Allen & Unwin, 1958).

The firm is the basis of the Eclectic Paradigm (also known as the OLI paradigm: Ownership–Location–Internalization). Dunning argues that to engage in foreign direct investment the firm must possess ownership advantages (O). This is a necessary condition for sustained profitability and growth, and in this book it provides the initial framework for analyzing the growth of multinationals. The country level is incorporated in the location advantages (L) of alternative regions, for undertaking the value-adding activities of multinationals. Dunning uses the term *location* (L) not only to refer to the country or region of destination but also to the country or region of origin. The internalization advantages (I) again relate to the firm and refer to the alternative ways in which firms may organize the creation and exploitation of their core competencies by exploiting locational attractions of different countries and regions. The Eclectic Paradigm further includes a contextual variable that provides the precise configuration of the OLI parameters facing a particular firm. This takes into consideration not only the country or region of origin of the investing firms, and the country or region in which they are seeking to invest, but also the industry and the nature of the value-adding activities in which the firms are engaged.[59]

Like Dunning, I am attempting to assess the pattern of evolution of some of the world's largest multinationals.[60] Dunning tends to focus on nations rather than on the unique characteristics of industries or firms.[61] This book, by looking at one particular industry, takes into consideration three levels of analysis: the uniqueness of firms; the special characteristics of an industry; and the role of the nations in which those firms and the industry are based.

[59] John H. Dunning, "Towards an Eclectic Theory of International Production: Some Empirical Tests," *Journal of International Business Studies*, Vol. 11, No. 1 (1980): 9–31; idem, "Location and the Multinational Enterprise: A Neglected Factor," *Journal of International Business Studies*, Vol. 29, No. 1 (1998): 45–66; idem, "Globalization and the Theory of the MNE Activity," in N. Hood and S. Young (eds.), *The Globalization of Multinational Enterprise Activity* (London: Macmillan, 1999); idem, "The Eclectic Paradigm as an Envelope for Economic and Business Theories of the MNE Activity," *The University of Reading: Discussion Papers in International Investment and Management*, No. 263 (1998/1999).

[60] While it has its own particular value, inevitably the database created for the purpose of this study is not as extensive as Dunning's. See, e.g., Dunning and Pearce, *The World's Largest Industrial Enterprises*; John M. Stopford and John H. Dunning, *Multinationals: Company Performance and Global Trends* (London: Macmillan, 1983); John H. Dunning, *International Production and the Multinational Enterprise* (London: Allen & Unwin, 1981).

[61] Duguid and Lopes make a similar argument about institutional economics, which under the influence of North has focused primarily on organizations within institutions within countries and thus has difficulty in dealing with the evolution of multinational firms. Paul Duguid and Teresa da Silva Lopes, "Institutions and Organizations in the Port Wine Trade, 1814–1834," *Scandinavian Economic History Review*, Vol. 47, No. 1 (1999): 84–102; Douglass C. North, *Institutions, Institutional Change and Economic Performance* (Cambridge: Cambridge University Press, 1990).

Sources and Data Sets

Business history and international business studies very often address the same questions: why do firms exist, grow, survive, and have multiple operations that sprawl across national boundaries, and how do firms deal with the level of complexity and change in the environment? The approaches taken to answer these questions are usually quite distinct. By using essentially the international business history approach and by first establishing the empirical facts, the reliability and validity of the sources used in this book becomes even more important.

Much of the discussion rests on material found in the archives of firms, interviews with top managers and other industry experts, companies' annual reports, and secondary sources. The information on the firms comes primarily from public materials such as annual and other company reports, government publications, articles in periodicals, and also business histories and biographies. Interviews with senior executives and industry experts helped supplement the published record. More detailed information on some of the firms is based primarily on research in company archives.

Although the importance of each of the sources varies according to the purpose and the level of detail and institutional analysis being discussed, their use was constrained by the quality, comparability, and availability of information. The uneven treatment in terms of the amount of space and attention given to firms analyzed in this book reflects essentially the difficulties of research in this area, in particular the availability of sources. The large number of firms studied in this book, the kind of analysis carried out (which focused on strategic moves), and the characteristics of the industry (with leading multinationals spread in all continents of the world) justify the importance of public materials and interviews as sources of information.

The ownership structures of firms in this industry were also an important constraint in the types of sources used. The historical predominance of family-owned firms, which are not obliged to disclose any information about their performance, made access to any confidential information about the company very difficult. To add to this problem the focus on such a recent time period made access to archives even more difficult. In those cases where company archives exist and are open to the public, there is frequently a forty-year embargo, corresponding roughly to the period covered by this book. Therefore, it was only possible to access the archives of a few firms such as Distillers Company, Moët & Chandon, and Seagram, but even in those cases the forty-year embargo applied. Other firms such as Bacardi, Carlsberg, Allied Domecq, Anheuser-Busch, and Hennessy denied access to their archives.

Internal records, which provide the most reliable source about the history of the firms, were used for specialized analysis. Public records were particularly useful as sources of information about strategic events that tend to come into the public domain via company histories, annual reports, or newspaper articles, as were interviews. Despite the changes in the accounting policies between countries and over time, annual reports were a particularly useful source of information on total sales, sales by business activity, sales by geographic region, operating profit, net income, total assets and share-holders capital, corporate governance, brands, and mergers and acquisitions. Companies' histories, where available, were very useful in providing a background on the early evolution of firms, in particular the dates and the facts behind their foundation, incorporation, mergers and acquisitions, and also the creation and disposal of brands.

Because knowledge is fragmented throughout the firm, I interviewed managers from different levels and departments who were involved in taking decisions or implementing changes, as well as industry experts. Interviews were important to understand specific aspects of the recent evolution of firms not documented elsewhere, such as the motivations behind firms' internationalization process, mergers and acquisitions, choice of system of corporate governance, branding policies, views on the use of alternative distribution channels, as well as current developments in the evolution of the industry and deals or decisions that did not succeed. The interviews varied from loosely structured to semistructured, leaving some flexibility so that questions could be geared toward the interviewee's individual background and knowledge. Greater emphasis was given to the firm's historical development mainly when interviewing executives with long service in the corporation. In addition, meetings served as a platform for subsequent interviews with other managers from the same firm or from competitors, and also for accessing other sources of information about the firm such as their company archives. While most of these multiple sources of information complemented and corroborated one another, inevitably there were some cases where they conflicted. In such cases, attempts were made to triangulate the different accounts from alternative sources to resolve such conflicts.

Multiple sources of information were used to create an original database. First, *Fortune* magazine lists of the 500 largest U.S. industrial corporations (in all the benchmark dates), the 100 largest foreign industrial corporations in 1960, the 200 largest foreign industrial corporations in 1970, the 500 largest foreign industrial corporations in 1980, and the 500 largest global corporations in 1990, 2000, and 2005. *Fortune*'s lists, however, are biased toward U.S. firms, which appear in much larger numbers than foreign firms. To address this problem, several additions were made to *Fortune*'s list of alcoholic beverages firms. In particular, I added all the world's largest firms that should have been included had the criteria used for the selection of the U.S. *Fortune 500* been applied to the top 500 companies from other countries like the United Kingdom, France, and Japan. The database also includes firms of smaller size that ended up being acquired by larger firms included in *Fortune*'s list. They often had brands that were fundamental to the growth and survival of these leading multinationals. I also included in the database a third group of large firms that do not publish accounts, owing to their family ownership structure, but that would otherwise rank among the world's largest firms: Bacardi-Martini, E. & J. Gallo, and Pedro Domecq.

A number of reservations should however be noted concerning the selection criteria. First, in some cases the data about the firms in *Fortune* did not agree with the information in the original annual reports (e.g., because *Fortune* only considered the operations of the subsidiary in the United States). In such cases, *Fortune*'s data were corrected using the annual reports. Second, the national differences in market structure and in reporting practices (including exchange rate conversions) lead to different ways of computing and reporting financial data. Third, inflation without strictly equivalent adjustments in the exchange rates (so that the purchasing power parity is kept constant) distorts the rankings of the largest firms and their apparently comparable data. Fourth, many firms were active in other sectors, but these are not always distinguished in performance results. Nevertheless, *Fortune*'s criteria of ranking a firm in a specific sector implies that it has to derive the greatest volume of its turnover from that sector. Fifth, the names of the firms frequently changed over time, as did their managing personnel, their owners, the products they produce, their geographical location, and even their legal form. Yet, in those cases where the identity of the firms remained the same, with alcoholic beverages accounting as the single largest business, they were included in this book. Given these various difficulties, while the upper reaches of the list provided are likely to include the world's largest firms, as one moves downwards in the list, the probability of missing candidates is bound to increase. These same reservations and criteria were used to select other firms to complement *Fortune*'s list.[62] Despite these reservations, the information in this database can be considered to be of relatively high quality as it draws, for the most part, on companies' original annual reports.

As well as offering an original database on the size and performance of the world's largest firms in alcoholic beverages, I also document distinct aspects of the history of the firms, and their process of growth and survival, such as country of origin, date of foundation, and main mergers and acquisitions.

To convert the data into constant U.S. dollars, several indicators were used. First, original currencies were converted into current U.S. dollars, using the average annual exchange rates for Australia, Belgium, Brazil, Canada, Denmark, the European Union, France, Japan, Norway, The Netherlands,

---

[62] See, e.g., *Fortune* (August 2001): F-11.

South Africa, and the United Kingdom. Second, the "export unit values for the industrialized countries" index was used to convert the data from U.S. dollar current prices into U.S. dollar constant prices: unit value (prices) in terms of U.S. dollars of 2000.[63]

Levels of Institutional Analysis

As already noted, this book takes into account three different levels of institutional analysis – the country, the industry, and the firm. These levels are not disjointed but instead overlap and complement each other, with each level providing important determinants to explain the survival and growth of firms.

Country-specific determinants include systems of corporate governance and thus involve the structures, processes, and cultures that engender the successful operation of organizations. They also include the institutional environment, regulation, and the regimes of taxation that have for a long time distinctly affected the countries' industries and their firms.

Industry-specific determinants are predominantly exogenous to the firms and are considered to affect all the firms in the industry equally. Factors such as the way consumption evolved over time according to levels of income and changes in consumers' lifestyles also impact the growth and survival of firms. Industry structure is also a determinant, in the sense that although concentration may first have been determined by some firms, it often determines or at least restricts the choices of all the firms operating in the industry as a whole.

Yet, as I will attempt to show, it is the firm-specific determinants that most influenced the firms' competitive positions. These factors include those that are endogenous to the firms and that differentiate one from another, promoting and limiting individual success. They may refer to firm characteristics or strategic choices. Brands, alliances in distribution networks, and marketing knowledge are some of the factors that have had the most significant impact on survival and growth.

I explore in this inquiry the different forms of corporate governance. In general, studies of this subject tend to oppose family control and ownership and laud professional management. This book, however, draws attention to a form of business system that blended family control and professional management. It shows how, through the kinds of marketing knowledge they generate, family firms are particularly good at creating enduring brands in sectors such as alcoholic beverages, while public companies are more adept at developing these brands.

[63] International Monetary Fund, *International Financial Statistics Yearbook* (Washington, D.C.: IMF, 1990, 2002, 2006).

The last chapter of this book looks deeply into the firm, analyzing the life of brands rather than the life of the firms. This enables me to analyze the role of entrepreneurs as relevant mechanisms for acquiring marketing knowledge. By placing the firm and the brand in an industrial and political context, I hope to advance the study of business history and the analysis of international business in the modern global economy.

2

Leading Firms – The Historical Legacy

Leading Firms Since 1960

I am looking at seventy-five firms, twenty-one from North America, seventeen from the United Kingdom, twenty-one from Continental Europe, six each from Asia and South America, three from Australia and New Zealand, and one from Africa. Several of these firms have ranked among the largest industrial enterprises in the world at different times. For instance, between 2001 and 2004, there were three alcoholic beverage multinationals – Allied Domecq (Allied), Diageo, and Anheuser-Busch – among the top eight multinationals in food and drinks industries, ranked according to total shareholders return.[1]

Table 2.1 provides a list of the world's leading multinationals in alcoholic beverages by 2005, their predecessors, and the firms merged and acquired at six benchmark dates.[2] In addition, it provides information about the dates of foundation or last merger of these firms, the year they were dissolved, merged, or acquired, their country of origin, and their sales volume stated in millions of U.S. dollars.[3]

In 1960, 70 percent of the sales generated by the world's leading alcoholic beverages firms were from North America, 23 percent from the United Kingdom, and 7 percent from other parts of the world. As Figure 2.1 shows, however, over time there was a decline in the importance of North American

---

[1] The other multinationals in this ranking of the top eight in food and drinks were Yum!Brands, Procter & Gamble, Kellogs, Altria, and Unilever. Total shareholder return measures relative return from the movement of share price together with the dividends received. It is measured from 1 July 2001 using the average of the share price from 1 July 2000 to 30 June 2001 as the starting point and using the last months up to 30 June 2004 as the end point. (Source: Diageo).

[2] See Appendix 3 with the annual sales of each of the leading multinationals in alcoholic beverages and their predecessors, from 1960 to 2005. Seagram is an exception. Even though it no longer existed in 2004, its process of growth through mergers and acquisitions of other firms had been very important in shaping the structure of the global alcoholic drinks industry.

[3] More details about this table and how the sample was selected can be found in Appendix 4.

Table 2.1. *The world's largest multinationals in alcoholic beverages and their predecessors, 1960, 1970, 1980, 1990, 2000, and 2005*

Group (firms)*	Country of Origin	Year of Foundation / Last Merger	Year of Merger / Acquisition	1960	1970	1980	1990	2000	2005
Anheuser-Busch	US	1852		1,186	2,696	3,762	10,242	12,499	12,069
Modelo	MEX	1925	1998	n/a	n/a	n/a	2,129	3,911	3,650
Asahi Breweries	JPN	1889		291	533	933	4,452	12,983	10,414
Bacardi	CB/BER	1862		n/a	n/a	n/a	n/a	2,800	2,632
Martini-Rossi	IT	1847	1993	n/a	n/a	n/a	n/a	–	–
Brown Forman	US	1870		392	744	772	1,150	2,146	2,191
Carlsberg	DEN	1847		–	1,021	1,269	2,158	4,272	5,092
Tuborg	DEN	1894	1970	n/a	–	–	–	–	–
Holsten	GER	1879	2004	n/a	n/a	n/a	n/a	1,010	–
Constellation Brands/ Canandaigua	US	1945		n/a	n/a	58	159	2,162	3,281
Diageo	UK	1997		–	–	–	–	17,053	14,506
Grand Metropolitan	UK	1962	1997	–	1,979	6,854	14,713	–	–
Truman	UK	n/a	1971	138	231	–	–	–	–
Watney Mann	UK	1958	1972	n/a	1,290	–	–	–	–
Gilbeys	UK	1872	1962	n/a	–	–	–	–	–
International Distillers & Vintners	UK	1962	1972	–	863	–	–	–	–
Heublein	US	1875	1987	395	1,992	2,194	–	–	–
Liggett & Myers	US	1873	1980	2,085	2,368	–	–	–	–
Guinness	UK	1759	1997	737	1,482	2,079	5,499	–	–
Arthur Bells	UK	1825	1985	54	178	538	–	–	–
Distillers Company	UK	1877	1986	2,512	3,046	2,680	–	–	–
Schenley	US	1920	1971/1987	1,467	2,275	n/a	–	–	–

E. & J. Gallo	US	1933		n/a	n/a	n/a	926	1,650	1,366
Fortune Brands/American Brands/American Tobacco	US	1864		5,068	9,092	7,765	11,444	5,845	5,668
Jim Beam	US	1795	1966	305	–	1,770	–	–	–
National Distillers	US	1924	1986	2,228	3,516	2,860	–	–	–
Foster's Group/Foster's Brewing/Elders IXL	AUS	1888	1983	n/a	2,149	n/a	10,475	1,835	2,436
Carlton United Breweries	AUS	1907		n/a	n/a	n/a	–	–	–
Heineken	NL	1864		117	545	1,855	3,915	7,469	10,778
Amstel	NL	1870	1968	n/a	–	–	–	–	–
Inbev	BEL/BRA	2004		–	–	–	1,485	5,212	11,637
Interbrew	BEL	1988	2004	–	–	–	–	–	–
Artois	BEL	1366/1717	1988	n/a	n/a	n/a	–	–	–
Piedbouef-Interbrew	BEL	1853	1988	n/a	n/a	n/a	–	–	–
John Labbatt	CAN	1847	1995	250	998	1,137	3,539	–	–
Bass	UK	1777	2000	431	2,794	3,351	6,987	–	–
Whitbread	UK	1742	2000	321	1,650	1,959	3,897	6,619	–
Brauerei Beck/Haake Beck-Brauerei	GER	1873	2001	n/a	372	289	928	811	–
Ambev	BRA	2000	2004	–	–	–	–	2,706	–
Companhia Antarctica Paulista	BRA	1885	2000	n/a	n/a	n/a	n/a	–	–
Companhia Cervejeira Brahma	BRA	1888	2000	n/a	n/a	381	–	–	–

(continued)

Table 2.1 (Continued)

Group (firms)*	Country of Origin	Year of Foundation / Last Merger	Year of Merger / Acquisition	1960	1970	1980	1990	2000	2005
Kirin	JPN	1907		806	3,569	4,813	8,636	9,959	8,992
Lion Nathan	NZ	1988	1998	–	–	–	n/a	456	1,237
Moët-Hennessy Louis Vuitton	FR	1987		–	–	–	3,212	10,670	13,887
Moët & Chandon	FR	1743	1971	41	–	–	–	–	–
Moët Hennessy	FR	1971	1987	–	340	790	–	–	–
Molson-Coors	CAN	2004		–	–	–	–	–	4,420
Molson	CAN	1876	2004	n/a	1,018	1,358	1,928	1,181	–
Bavaria	BRA	1877	2000	n/a	n/a	n/a	n/a	–	–
Adolph Coors	US	1873		n/a	n/a	1,014	1,309	2,414	–
Pernod Ricard	FR	1975		–	–	986	2,727	4,037	3,668
Pernod	FR	1805	1975	1	3	–	–	–	–
Ricard	FR	1932	1975	–	–	–	–	–	–
Allied Domecq	UK	1799/1961	2005	–	3,128	5,837	7,410	3,842	–
Showerings	UK	1932/1961	1968	n/a	–	–	–	–	–
Harveys	UK	1871	1966	n/a	–	–	–	–	–
Hiram Walker	CAN	1926	1986	1,742	2,328	2,466	–	–	–
Pedro Domecq	SPN	1730	1994	–	–	–	–	–	–
Teacher	UK	1884	1975	–	–	–	–	–	–
Rémy Cointreau	FR	1991		–	–	–	–	674	797
Rémy Martin	FR	1724	1991	n/a	n/a	n/a	n/a	–	–
Cointreau & Cie	FR	1849	1991	n/a	n/a	n/a	n/a	–	–

Firm	Country	Founded						
San Miguel	PHIL	1890	n/a	n/a	n/a	n/a	1,771	3,579
Sapporo	JPN	1876	509	1,081	1,393	3,127	5,234	4,100
Scottish & Newcastle	UK	1749/1960	n/a	1,094	1,321	1,942	5,419	5,233
Courage	UK	1787	292	940	1,433	–	–	–
SAB Miller / South African Breweries	SA	1895	133	713	2,526	4,517	4,806	10,355
Miller Brewing	US	1855	n/a	675	2,903	3,117	4,375	–
Stroh	US	1850	n/a	n/a	331	n/a	–	–
Schlitz Brewing	US	1858	637	1,572	1,024	–	–	–
G. Heileman Brewing	US	1853	n/a	n/a	824	n/a	–	–
Pabst Brewing	US	1844	576	1,233	974	–	–	–
Seagram	CAN/US	1924	2,950	4,886	3,294	4,923	15,686	–
Suntory	JPN	1899	n/a	1,280	3,469	4,851	7,879	n/a
Tsingtao	CHI	1903	n/a	n/a	n/a	n/a	3,760	n/a

Notes: Amounts stated in millions of constant US dollars (2000 = 100). '–' – not applicable (either was not formed yet or had been merged or acquired); n/a – not available.

* The firms highlighted in bold are those that survived until the beginning of the twenty-first century. The firms below (not highlighted in bold) were merged or acquired.

Source: Database prepared using companies' archives, annual reports, and other published sources.

27

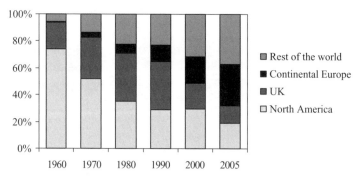

Fig. 2.1. Percentage of sales of the world's largest multinationals by country/continent of origin.
Source: Prepared by the author using companies' annual accounts.

firms and an increase in the importance of firms from the United Kingdom, continental Europe, and the rest of the world.[4]

Over time, the proportion of firms from the United Kingdom and Continental Europe (especially France, the Netherlands, and Denmark) grew in terms of total sales. The proportion of sales generated by firms from the rest of the world, in particular South Africa, South America, and the Far East (especially from Japan) also increased. U.S. firms lost the dominant position they had held in 1960. While most leading U.S. spirits firms disappeared, wines firms such as E. & J. Gallo (Gallo) and Constellation Brands (previously called Canandaigua) flourished, ensuring that the United States continued to be home to a major alcoholic beverages industry.

Apart from having complex histories resulting from multiple mergers, acquisitions, and cross-border network arrangements, the world's leading alcoholic beverages multinationals also diversified into unrelated businesses, from chemicals to entertainment.[5] Of the U.S. firms, only Anheuser-Busch, Brown Forman, Constellation Brands, and Gallo, all family controlled, survived independently until the beginning of the twenty-first century. National Distillers, the world's largest alcoholic beverages firm in 1912,[6] was acquired by American Brands in 1985 (renamed Fortune Brands in 1997), which had owned Jim Beam since 1966. The North American breweries, Stroh, Schlitz, G. Heileman, and Pabst were also of significant size early in the twentieth

---

[4] This figure should, however, be analyzed with caution, as the total sales for each firm often include all their business activities. For example, the data for 2000 for North America and the Rest of the World appears distorted due, respectively, to the high percentage of sales generated by Seagram in the media and entertainment business, and Japanese firms such as Kirin and Asahi, which also have interests in other nonalcoholic beverages businesses.

[5] Appendix 5 provides brief biographies of the world's leading multinationals in alcoholic beverages.

[6] See Table 1 ("Largest Industrials in 1909") in Alfred D. Chandler Jr., *Strategy and Structure* (Cambridge, Mass: The MIT Press, 1962): 5.

century. They survived until the early 1970s, when technological advances increased the minimum efficient scale relative to the size of the market, and greater emphasis was placed on advertising, creating an environment where fewer firms could operate profitably. During the 1980s, these brewers went through several mergers and acquisitions and by 1999 had all become part of Miller Brewing. Miller, traditionally a family firm, was acquired in 1970 by Philip Morris, a tobacco company, as part of its diversification strategy. However, in 2002, Philip Morris sold Miller to South African Breweries, which was renamed SABMiller.

There were other American alcoholic beverages firms that since the mid-1960s had become part of the tobacco conglomerates, which, like Philip Morris, diversified as a result of the litigation over the harmful effects of smoking. Liggett & Myers, originally also a tobacco company, acquired several U.S. wines and spirits distributors. However, it ended up being taken over by Grand Metropolitan from the United Kingdom in 1980. In 1986, Grand Metropolitan bought the American firm Heublein, which owned the famous vodka brand Smirnoff.[7]

The Canadian firms also lost their relative importance in the world's rankings. By the beginning of the twenty-first century, none were surviving independently. The Canadian brewer Molson had merged with U.S. Coors in 2004. Molson's ownership had been shared with Miller and Foster Brewing until 1997 and 1998, respectively, when they sold their stakes. It had again briefly become family owned before merging with Coors in 2004. Seagram, also a family-controlled firm in wines and spirits, which from 1960 had always ranked among the top three alcoholic beverages multinationals in the world, was acquired by the French entertainment and water group Vivendi in 2000. Vivendi kept Seagram's entertainment and media businesses, but sold the alcoholic beverages business to Diageo and Pernod Ricard.[8] Hiram Walker, another Canadian family firm, producer of the whisky brand with the same name, was acquired by Allied Lyons in 1986. Interbrew acquired the Canadian brewer John Labbatt, in 1995.

In South America, two leading brewers, Companhia Cervejeira Brahma and Companhia Antarctica Paulista, merged in 2000 to form Ambev. This new firm, which became the largest brewer in Latin America, continued consolidating its position on this continent, by merging and acquiring breweries in other neighboring countries, for example, Quilmes in Argentina.[9] In 2004, Ambev merged with the old-established Belgium family firm, Interbrew, creating Inbev. Two other large groups from South America are Grupo Modelo

---

7 William J. Reader and Judy Slinn, Grand Metropolitan (unpublished manuscript, 1992).

8 After the joint acquisition of Seagram by Diageo and Pernod-Ricard, Samuel Bronfman II, a family member and former chairman of Seagram, was appointed as chairman of global wine operations at Diageo PLC, which became Seagram's parent company, *The Wall Street Journal* (9 July 2001).

9 "Ambev buys stake in Quilmes for $346m," *Financial Times* (2 May 2002). This acquisition was later opposed by Templeton Emerging Markets Fund.

from Mexico, producer of Corona beer, and Santo Domingo from Colombia, a conglomerate with interests in brewing, owner of Aguila. Anheuser-Busch acquired an interest in Modelo in 1993, and later increased that stake.[10]

Bacardi, originally from Cuba, developed essentially out of its sales of a single product (rum) and a single brand, Bacardi.[11] In 1993, Bacardi acquired Martini-Rossi from Italy, yet another family firm whose sales also relied essentially on a single product and brand – Martini vermouth. Martini had good distribution networks in Europe, a market Bacardi needed to penetrate.[12] Since then, it acquired several independent brands such as Dewar's Scotch whisky, Bombay Sapphire gin, and Grey Goose vodka.

In the United Kingdom the industry concentrated since very early. Grand Metropolitan, which entered the alcoholic beverages business during the late 1960s with the acquisitions of Truman and Watney Mann (Watney had just acquired International Distillers and Vintners [IDV]), became the world's largest multinational in the industry as a result of its aggressive growth strategy during the 1980s and early 1990s. Arthur Bell and Distillers were acquired by Guinness in, respectively, 1983 and 1985 (Distillers' acquisition caused a celebrated corporate scandal).[13] The merger in 1997 between Guinness and Grand Metropolitan, which produced Diageo, represented a major turn in the way competition was played in this global industry: in terms of the scale and scope of the activity of firms and also in the way in which brands were managed internationally. The new world leader in alcoholic beverages became a new force in branded food and drinks, with a truly global scope of operations. Diageo was also able to obtain substantial cost savings due to marketing synergies (such as shared consumer understanding and management skills), reduction of head and regional office overhead

---

[10] Even though this additional stake gave majority of the shares to Anheuser-Busch, the founding family of Modelo and its employees in Mexico retained the voting control of the firm. This investment by Anheuser-Busch, together with the deregulation of the Mexican market and the "peso crisis," led to a rapid increase of exports by Modelo.

[11] See, e.g., the lists provided by *Impact International*, Vol. 13 No. 4 (Feb. 1998): 40, on the world's largest spirits firms in volume.

[12] Interview with José Luis Martin, President Bacardi-Martini Spain, and with Xavier Serra, General Manager Bacardi-Martini, Barcelona, 22 July 1999.

[13] Guinness's takeover of Distillers was helped by a substantial rise in its share price during the period of the acquisition. After the merger, it came out that Guinness's Chairman, Ernest Saunders, had been manipulating the share price. After he was accused of offenses under the Companies Act, Saunders was fired. Then in 1990, along with other senior managers, he was charged and convicted of fraud, false accounting, and theft in a highly public and, for the company, embarrassing trial. Nick Kochan and Hugh Pym, *The Guinness Affair – Anatomy of a Scandal* (London: Christopher Helm, 1987). Christopher Schmitz, "The World's Largest Industrial Companies of 1912," *Business History*, Vol. 37, No. 4 (1995): 89; Leslie Hannah, *The Rise of the Corporate Economy* (London: Methuen, 1976): 102, 189; Ronald Weir, "Managing Decline: Brands and Marketing in Two Mergers, 'The Big Amalgamation' in 1925 and Guinness-DCL 1986," in Geoffrey Jones and Nicholas J. Morgan (eds.), *Adding Value: Brands and Marketing in Food and Drink* (London: Routledge, 1994): 139–61.

expenses, and production and purchasing efficiencies. With the merger, the new multinational Diageo was able to achieve a complementary and broad product and brand range; obtain greater geographic breadth, enhanced marketing capability, greater cost efficiency, and the financial capacity to develop the businesses. The merger was followed by a process of integration, and prioritization, of brands according to their strategic role in the portfolio of the company, and the disposal of those brands that were not strategic.[14] This merger led to a new wave of mergers and acquisitions in the industry that has continued to the present day.

Allied Breweries (Allied), also from the United Kingdom, made several important acquisitions beginning in the 1960s. In 1968, it acquired Showerings, a family firm that owned a famous cider brand, Babycham, and that had also acquired Harveys, another wines merchant and owner of Harveys Bristol Cream (a sherry), which had considerable retail holdings. In the 1990s, Allied made other acquisitions that greatly changed the structure of the industry and the way competition was played. In 1994, despite resistance from the family, it acquired Pedro Domecq, a Spanish family firm and a leading producer of sherry and brandy, and changed its name to Allied Domecq. The acquisition strengthened the links that already existed between Pedro Domecq and Hiram Walker (acquired by Allied in 1986), which had been joint venture partners since 1966.[15] In 2005, Allied Domecq was acquired by Pernod Ricard from France. This acquisition was supported by Fortune Brands, which acquired more than twenty spirits and wines brands that belonged to Allied Domecq. Scottish & Newcastle only started internationalizing from 2000, becoming the largest brewer in the United Kingdom.

The continental European alcoholic beverages firms joined the ranks of the world's largest multinationals only in the 1980s. Heineken and Carlsberg, the two most internationalized brewers in the world, had developed very rapidly, beginning in the 1970s, after merging with their most important domestic competitors, Amstel and Tuborg, respectively.[16] Pernod Ricard was formed in 1975 as a result of the merger of two long-established French family firms, Pernod and Ricard. In the twenty-first century, in addition to the abovementioned acquisition of Allied Domecq, it also acquired Seagram jointly with Diageo, enabling this French multinational to enlarge its portfolio of globally successful brands. Rémy Cointreau was formed in 1991, also as a

---

[14] Interview with Jack Keenan, CEO of Diageo, London, 3 June 2003; "Proposed Merger of Guinness PLC and Grand Metropolitan Public Limited Company," Circular to Guinness Shareholders, 3 November 1997.

[15] Interview with José de Isasi-Isasmendy y Adaro, former President of Pedro Domecq and also a family member, Madrid, 18 July 2000. On Pedro Domecq's acquisition, see also Allied Lyons, Annual Report and Accounts (1994).

[16] M. G. P. A. Jacobs and W. H. G. Mass, *Heineken History* (Amsterdam: De Bussy Ellerman Harms bv., 1992): 302–3; Kristof Glamann, *Jacobsen of Carlsberg – Brewer and Philanthropist* (Copenhagen: Gyldendal, 1991).

result of a merger of two French family firms. In the 1990s, Louis Vuitton Moët Hennessy (LVMH) joined the list of the world's largest multinationals in alcoholic beverages, after the merger in 1987 of two family-controlled French companies, Louis Vuitton and Moët Hennessy.

Interbrew was formed in 1988 as a result of a merger of two Belgian firms, Artois and Piedboeuf-Interbrew (whose constituent companies can be traced back to 1240). Before merging with the Brazilian Ambev in 2003, Interbrew had grown very rapidly.[17] In the 1990s, its major acquisitions were John Labbatt from Canada, Bass and Whitbread from the United Kingdom (which in the 1970s were national leaders in brewing), and also Brauerei Beck from Germany.[18]

Of the Japanese firms, Kirin, the leading brewer since 1954, is the only firm that has always ranked in the list of the world's largest multinationals.[19] Asahi Breweries grew essentially since the mid-1980s, mainly due to its product innovation strategy, and also to the alliances it established with other alcoholic beverages firms (e.g., the German company Löwenbräu), and with soft drinks firms from Europe (e.g., Pripps from Sweden) to bottle and distribute sports beverages in Japan. Suntory, Japan's largest wines and spirits firm and producer of brands such as Midori liqueur, Suntory Malts beer, and Suntory whiskey grew organically for the most part, out of sales in the domestic market. Beginning in the 1980s, it also established important alliances with European and North American alcoholic beverages multinationals.[20]

On the African continent, the leading alcoholic beverages multinational is SABMiller, a Johannesburg-based company quoted on the London Stock Exchange, which for a long time was almost a monopoly. After the end of Apartheid it started making acquisitions internationally, in particular in other African and eastern European countries, and then in the United States (Miller Brewing) in 2002.[21]

In Australia, the leading multinational is Foster's Brewing (which changed its name from Elders IXL in 1990). Formed in 1981 as a result of the merger of very old-established firms, Henry Jones (IXL) and Elders IXL, Foster's

---

[17] Interview with Philippe Spoelberch, Member of the Board of Directors of Interbrew and family member, Brussels, 5 July 2004.

[18] In January 2001 the UK Monopolies Commission ordered the sale of Bass, claiming the purchase gave Interbrew an unfair advantage in the marketplace. However, a UK High Court overturned the order in May, leaving competition issues unresolved. Later this dispute was solved with the sale of the brand Carling by Interbrew to Coors in 2002.

[19] Kirin, Annual Report and Accounts (1966, 2000).

[20] Interview with Yoshi Kunimoto, Executive Vice President of Suntory-Allied and with Kunimasa Himeno, Manager International Division of Suntory, Tokyo, 16 September 1999.

[21] "SAB mulls $5bn bid for Miller Brewing," *Financial Times* (24 May 2002); "SAB bid buy Miller raises eyebrows," *Financial Times* (25 May 2002); "It's Miller time for South Africans," *Evening Standard* (30 May 2002).

Brewing has grown rapidly as a result of mergers and acquisitions of other large brewers.[22] The success of this firm's most well-known brand, Foster's, is linked with the long-lasting alliance made with Scottish & Newcastle in the mid-1990s, which gave the latter the license to produce and distribute the brand across Europe.[23]

An interesting feature of this industry is that during the period of analysis, German firms were not among the world's largest multinationals and held few significant brands.[24] Brauerei Beck (formerly called Haake Beck – Brauerei), acquired Interbrew in 2001, is one of the few German firms that own a global beer brand. Its surprising absence from the list of multinationals is essentially due to the remarkably local character of its domestic market. Even though Germany is the country with the largest per capita consumption of beer in the world, it is characterized by a very localized system of distribution. This country exhibits high but very fragmented consumption, with patterns deeply entrenched in regional loyalties. As a result, the industry is disaggregated and dominated by family firms. The restrictive legislation that for a long time protected domestic firms from foreign competition also led German firms to limit their activities to the national market, as they could grow and survive just by expanding in line with population growth and changes in consumer preferences.[25] More generally, Germany chose to internationalize in those industries that were innovation- and technology-intensive, leaving the branded packaged products to countries like the United Kingdom.[26]

Historical Legacy

Prior to the 1960s, habits of alcoholic consumption were heavily resource- and culture-specific. Wine producing and drinking nations such as France, Italy, and Portugal developed mainly wine firms, while beer and spirits

---

[22] John Cavanagh, Frederick Clairmonte and Robi Room, *The World Alcohol Industry With Special Reference to Australia, New Zealand and the Pacific Islands* (Sydney: Transnational Corporations Research Project – University of Sydney, 1985): 45; Tim Hewat, *The Elders Explosion – One Hundred and Fifty Years of Progress from Elder to Elliot* (Sydney: Bay Books, 1988).

[23] Interview with Tony Frogatt, CEO of Scottish & Newcastle, Edinburgh, 11 July 2004.

[24] In the last quarter of the nineteenth century and early twentieth century, some German brewers had internationalized into the United States, but when compared with British brewers their foreign direct investment was not substantial. Mira Wilkins, *The History of Foreign Investment in the United States to 1914* (Cambridge, Mass: Harvard University Press, 1989): 324–31.

[25] In 1987 the European court declared invalid the Reinheitsgebot Law, which established that only 100 percent malt beer could be sold.

[26] Alfred D. Chandler Jr., *The Visible Hand* (Cambridge, Mass: Harvard University Press, 1977).

producing and drinking countries such as United Kingdom, the United States, Germany, and Holland developed mainly spirits producers and brewers.[27] These are all countries where traditions of alcohol consumption date back centuries.[28] As in Northern Europe, in the United States production and consumption were essentially of spirits and beer, although its traditions and habits are inevitably younger. South America had similar characteristics to Europe, but like the United States was a recent market, traditionally emphasizing beer and also some spirits.

Although European wine producers had been exporting wines since ancient times, the industry remained very fragmented until the 1960s. Competition was played at a domestic level, the growth of firms was mostly organic, and the few mergers and acquisitions that took place aimed at increasing the firms' presence in new markets. Rather they aimed at widening their portfolios of products to serve existing markets. Nonetheless, in some cases firms grew quickly as they started branding and selling their beverages internationally very early. The timing of growth and internationalization during this early period depended to a great extent on the type of beverages the expanding firms produced and where they were based. Whisky and gin firms were internationalized since the nineteenth century, whereas brewers still operated within very limited regional areas by the end of the twentieth century. Yet, a few beer firms, originally from small countries, such as Heineken from the Netherlands and Carlsberg from Denmark, had a very rapid process of internationalization from the 1930s.

There seems to be a correlation with the origins of the first multinationals in alcoholic beverages and the level of development of their countries of origin. A global economy was first created between the late nineteenth century and 1914,[29] and Western Europe and North America were the home regions of the multinationals of this era. They had the most advanced technologies, most skilled labor, highest per capita incomes, and most sophisticated distribution structures.[30] It is not surprising that until 1960 the United Kingdom, Ireland, the United States, and Canada had the largest alcoholic beverages

---

[27] As Adam Smith noted, even Scotland is actually capable of producing wine. However, he suggested it would be unwise to compete in the wine market and foolish to raise barriers to protect a nascent wine industry. Adam Smith, *An Enquiry Into the Nature and Causes of the Wealth of Nations* (New York: Modern Library, 1776/1937).

[28] Tim Unwin, *The Wine and the Vine* (London: Routledge, 1991).

[29] John H. Dunning, *Multinational Enterprises and the Global Economy* (Wokingham, Berkshire: Addison Wesley, 1993); Geoffrey Jones, *Multinationals and Global Capitalism – From the Nineteenth to the Twenty First Century* (Oxford: Oxford University Press, 2005).

[30] Chandler, *The Visible Hand*; Richard Tedlow, "The Fourth Phase of Marketing: Marketing History and the Business World Today," in Richard Tedlow and Geoffrey Jones (eds.), *The Rise and Fall of Mass Marketing* (London: Routledge, 1993); A. Maddison, *L'Économie Mondiale 1820–1992* (Paris: OCDE, 1995): 206–9; Glenn Porter and Harold C. Livesay, *Merchants and Manufacturers* (Baltimore: Johns Hopkins Press, 1971): 12.

firms worldwide, namely Guinness, Distillers Company, Distillers' Securities, and Seagram.[31]

United Kingdom and Ireland

The United Kingdom had one of the largest markets in Europe and possessed a wide domestic resource base in the production of beer and spirits. It also had an extensive import and reexport business in other alcoholic beverages stemming from a colonial heritage that encouraged many firms to internationalize very early through exports and foreign direct investment.[32]

Guinness, a brewery founded in Ireland in 1759, was exporting a branded product into Britain by the 1820s with great success, leading the firm to open agencies in that market soon after. It was incorporated in 1886, the same year it was floated on the London Stock Exchange.[33] By 1912, Guinness ranked as the largest alcoholic beverages firm worldwide and among the one hundred leading industrial companies in the world.[34]

Distillers Company Limited (Distillers hereafter), a producer of whisky and gin founded in 1877 in Scotland, merged and acquired several firms in the same and other businesses to become a world leader in scotch whisky and gin. In 1925, after its last big amalgamation with Buchannan and Dewar, it even surpassed Guinness in size.[35]

Another leading domestic alcoholic beverages firm before 1960 is Bass. Founded in 1777 in the United Kingdom, it was already selling branded beer by the early nineteenth century. Bass was, in fact, one of the earliest firms to register a trademark following the English legislation of 1875. However, its scope of operations always remained essentially domestic. Unlike the

---

[31] Schmitz, "The World's Largest Industrial Companies of 1912," 87; Leslie Hannah, "La Evolución de las Grandes Empresas en el Siglo XX: Un Análisis Comparativo," *Revista de História Industrial*, No. 10 (1996): 118.

[32] On wine imports see Pierre Spahni, *The International Wine Trade* (Cambridge: Woodhead, 1995): 104, 189–200. On imports of spirits and beer, see Wendy Hurst, Eg Gregory, and Thomas Gussman, *Alcoholic Beverages Taxation and Control Policies* (Ottawa: Brewers Association of Canada, 1997): 536–42.

[33] Andy Bielenberg, "The Irish Brewing Industry and the Rise of Guinness 1790–1914," in Richard G. Wilson and Terry Gourvish (eds.), *The Dynamics of the International Brewing since 1800* (London: Routledge, 1998): 114, 118; S. R. Dennison and Oliver MacDonagh, *Guinness 1886–1939: From Incorporation to the Second World War* (Dublin: Cork University Press, 1998): chapter 2.

[34] Schmitz, "The World's Largest Industrial Companies of 1912": 87; Hannah, "La Evolución de las Grandes Empresas en el Siglo XX": 118. In 1912 Guinness had a market capitalization of $19 million, and ranked as the nineteenth largest firm worldwide (according to Schmitz estimates) or twentieth (according to Hannah estimates).

[35] This account of Distillers is based on Ronald B. Weir, *The History of the Distillers Company 1877–1939* (Oxford: Oxford University Press, 1995), chapter 13; Hannah, *The Rise*, Table 8.1. By 1930, Distillers had an estimated market value of capital of £45.5 million while Guinness's was of £43 million.

other leading British alcoholic beverages firms, Bass was vertically integrated into distribution, reflecting UK's licensing legislation (which made special provisions for "on-license" sales), and the perishable character of beer. Bass relied heavily on the distribution of bottled ales via an agency network and operated several retail outlets (stores owned or rented and run by the brewery itself). It also used agents – independent traders operating on a commission basis – who often also traded wines and spirits.[36]

The other British brewers included Whitbread and Scottish & Newcastle (formed in 1960 as a result of an amalgamation of several brewers from the North of England and Scotland), which were not multinational and their growth has been essentially through mergers and acquisitions of other domestic brewers. Whitbread divested from alcoholic beverages, selling the brewing business to Interbrew. Scottish & Newcastle remained independent until the twenty-first century. Its leadership position in the beginning of the twenty-first century was, to a great extent, related to mergers and acquisitions of leading domestic brewers in Continental Europe.

United States and Canada

The North American companies, with an even larger market than those from the United Kingdom, grew very rapidly in the period prior to 1960 in absolute terms. This growth was, however, constrained by the nation's unfortunate experience with national Prohibition. Although the industry had developed relatively large firms prior to this period, antialcohol movements with deep roots in nineteenth-century America, and power following the creation of The Woman's Christian Temperance Union in 1874, had a significant impact in restraining its development. This resulted in the Eighteenth Amendment, which passed into law in 1920, and was not repealed until 1933.[37]

The leading U.S. firm before World War I was Distillers' Securities.[38] Distillers' Securities Corporation was formed in 1902 as an outgrowth of the Whiskey Trust of the 1880s and 1890s.[39] In 1920, under Prohibition, the

---

[36] Hannah, *The Rise*: 102–3, 189, 190; Colin C. Ownen, *The Greatest Brewery in the World: A History of Bass, Ratcliff & Gretton* (Chesterfield: Derbyshire Record Society, 1992): 5, 164; Terry Gourvish and Richard G. Wilson, *The British Brewing Industry, 1830–1980* (Cambridge: Cambridge University Press, 1994): 438–39. Bass was the first trademark registered after the after the First Trademark Act in 1875. "Trademark Registration," BT82–1, entry number 1 and 2, 1 January, Public Record Office.

[37] See, e.g., K. Austin Kerr, *Organized for Prohibition: A New History of the Anti-Saloon League* (New Haven: Yale University Press, 1985); Laurence Spinelli, *Dry Diplomacy: The United States, Great Britain and Prohibition* (Wilmington, Del: S.R. Books, 1989).

[38] Schmitz, "The World's Largest Industrial Companies of 1912," 89.

[39] Werner Troesken, "Exclusive Dealing and the Whiskey Trust, 1890–1895," *Journal of Economic History*, Vol. 58, No. 3 (1998): 755–78.

company changed its name as well as its activity, producing yeast, vinegar, and cereal products. In 1924, it was reorganized and renamed National Distillers Corporation.[40]

Other U.S. alcoholic beverages firms that survived to the repeal of Prohibition in 1933 included Brown Forman, Heublein, Anheuser-Busch, Coors, and Miller. While most had diversified into other businesses, a few such as Brown Forman managed to continue producing alcoholic beverages. Brown Forman, a family firm founded in 1870 to produce bourbon, had been licensed by the Federal Government to sell medicinal whiskey to druggists for use only by prescription from physicians.[41]

After repeal, most firms quickly returned to the production of alcoholic beverages, selling essentially in the domestic market. As they lacked scale and scope in their activities, most formed multiple alliances with competitors to market their products domestically, using a variety of mechanisms such as the exchange of stocks, distribution agreements, or production and distribution joint ventures. The firms they formed alliances with were then still distant competitors, as they were primarily from Europe and Canada.[42]

Schenley developed very rapidly on the basis of acquisitions of U.S. whiskey firms and the stocks of firms that had closed down due to Prohibition. Subsequently, it developed by using alliances formed with foreign firms to import and distribute their wines and spirits in the domestic market, for example, the successful alliance formed in 1936 with Distillers Company to distribute Dewar's White Label scotch whisky. Despite also engaging in various other nonalcoholic beverages activities (such as the production and sale of cooperage and farm feeds since the 1940s), the firm was primarily in the alcohol market. By the 1960s, around half of Schenley's alcoholic beverages business related to the distribution of imported brands.[43]

By restraining growth of domestic alcoholic beverage firms, Prohibition had created new opportunities for foreign firms to enter the U.S. market not only through alliances but also through direct investment. Canadian firms took greatest advantage as they were culturally and geographically

---

[40] William L. Downar, *Dictionary of the History of the American Brewing and Distilling Industries* (London: Greenwood, 1980): 128–9.

[41] William F. Lucas, *Nothing Better in the Market: Brown Forman Century of Quality 1870–1970* (New York: Newcomen Society, 1970).

[42] One example is the alliance between Gilbey's and National Distillers to produce and sell gin in the American market – W & A. Gilbey Ltd of Delaware – in 1933. Another example is the alliance between De Kuyper & Zoon (a geneva from the Netherlands) and National Distillers, where the latter was licensed to produce geneva in the United States. Richard McGowan, *Government Regulation of the Alcohol Industry* (Westport, Conn: Quorum Books, 1997): 3–4; Gilbey 1945 GE-GK 31 (London-Guildhall Library); for details, see Alec Waugh, *Merchants of Wine* (London: Cassell, 1957): 91–4; K. E. Sluyterman and H. H. Vleesenbeek, *Three Centuries of De Kuyper 1695–1995* (Shiedam: Prepress Canter Assen 1995): 48–9.

[43] Schenley, Annual Report and Accounts (1963, 1965, 1969).

closer and had never stopped producing alcohol during Prohibition. The largest Canadian firms investing in the United States in this period were Hiram Walker-Gooderham & Worts, Canadian Industrial Alcohol Co. Ltd., and Distillers Corporation-Seagram Ltd (DC-SL), but it was the latter that grew most rapidly from the new opportunities offered by the U.S. market.[44] DC-SL entered the American market on its own by merging and acquiring local distilleries, and by forming Joseph E. Seagram & Sons Inc. as the U.S. subsidiary of this Canadian firm. DC-SL developed initially out of sales in the United States, which soon became more important than the home country. It made several important acquisitions during the late 1940s and early 1950s in the United Kingdom (of Chivas Brothers and Strathisla-Glenlivet Malt Distillers), France (of G. H. Mumm), and in Latin America and the Caribbean (of, e.g., Captain Morgan and Myer's rum). These acquisitions gave Seagram a wider portfolio of products to be sold in the U.S. and Canadian markets.[45] The company then sold its brands through a vast, longstanding network of distributors around the country.[46]

Bacardi was another firm that grew out of its sales in the U.S. market after repeal of Prohibition. It was established in Cuba in 1862, with production operations in Spain since 1910, and in Mexico since 1931. Because Bacardi had become well known during Prohibition through smuggling and from Americans visiting Cuba, it was among the most sought after brands following repeal.[47]

Other firms that were leading players in the United States, despite not ranking at this stage in the rankings of the world's largest industrials, were Anheuser-Busch, Brown Forman and Heublein. Anheuser-Busch became the world's leading brewer in 1957. Like most U.S. alcoholic beverages firms during Prohibition, the company survived by producing a near-beer called Bevo, malt syrup, cane sugar, yeast, ice cream, commercial refrigeration units and truck bodies, and non-alcoholic beverages. It became nationally dominant in the 1950s, when most brewers were locally and regionally oriented. In this period it already combined national advertising, and regional distribution strategies. Although vertically integrated, it also used wholesale agencies and

[44] About foreign investment by these alcoholic beverages firms during this period, see Mira Wilkins, *The History of Foreign Investment in the United States 1914–1945* (Cambridge, Mass.: Harvard University Press, 2004).

[45] The Distillers Corporation – Seagram Ltd., Annual Report and Accounts (1971); "Corporate Documentation by Company," *Records of the Seagram Collection*, Accession 2126, Box 20, Hagley Museum and Library.

[46] Seagram Collection, Record Group 2; Series VI: Sales and Distribution, Hagley Museum and Library; DC-SL, *Annual Reports and Accounts* (various years); Graham D. Taylor and Peter A. Baskerville, *A Concise History of Business in Canada* (Toronto: Oxford University Press, 1994); Michael R. Marrus, *Samuel Bronfman: The Life and Times of Seagram's Mr. Sam* (London: Brandley University Press, 1991).

[47] Peter Foster, *Family Spirits: The Bacardi Saga* (Toronto: MacFarlane Walter & Ross, 1990): 23, 43, 54–5.

salaried men, depending upon the size of the business in a particular sales territory, and also on the availability of competent men and the ease of access.[48] It was also the first national producer to offer a diversified line of brands, and the first major brewer to invest in marketing research. During the 1950s, Anheuser-Busch also built breweries near the major urban centers, as a way to reduce transportation costs. The firm never competed based on prices and discounts, and instead, chose to charge higher prices and emphasize in its marketing campaigns the quality of the beverage.[49]

In the United States, as in the United Kingdom, some firms that emerged in the late nineteenth century specialized in the distribution of alcoholic beverages. Heublein was established in 1875 as a food importer and distributor. It started to integrate vertically into production before the end of the nineteenth century. During Prohibition, it diversified into the production of sauce. With repeal, Heublein re-entered the alcoholic beverages business and in 1939, acquired the sole rights to produce and distribute in the United States, Smirnoff, a Russian vodka brand which had established its reputation in the late nineteenth century among the Russian aristocracy.[50] Meanwhile, companies that were predominantly wine producers such as Gallo, Constellation Brands (previously called Canandaigua) were still growing organically and selling only within the domestic market before the 1960s.

Continental Europe

Heineken, although not on *Fortune*'s list of the world's leading firms, had already internationalized its brand with great success before the 1960s. The firm's early internationalization resulted to a great extent from the quasi-monopolistic position it established in the Netherlands and also from the characteristics of the beer, which was light and could therefore travel better. The initial international success of the brand can also be attributed to its performance in the United States and the way it was marketed. Heineken had initiated its exports to the United States before World War I, but it was after repeal that sales started growing rapidly. At first, Heineken appointed Van Munching as its official agent in the United States, but in 1935, Austin Nichols & Co, a large New York wholesaler of fruit and vegetables that acted as an agent for a variety of other firms (including those in alcoholic beverages), became the official distributor of Heineken (employing Van Munching

[48] Downar, *Dictionary*: 9–10; Ronald Jan Plavchan, *A History of Anheuser-Busch, 1853–1933* (New York: ARNO Press, 1976): 84–5, 87.

[49] David John Collis, "The Value Added Structure and Competition Within Industries" (Harvard University Ph.D., 1986): 160, 527–8; Martin Stack, "Local and Regional Breweries in America's Brewing Industry, 1865 to 1920," *Business History Review*, Vol. 74, No. 3 (2000): 535–63.

[50] Agreements between G. F. Heublein & Bro and Ste. Pierre Smirnoff (13 January 1939; 6 March 1939; 31 March 1939), Heublein Archive, Diageo.

to run Heineken affairs). This arrangement was not, however, successful. The distributor's representatives did not pay much attention to the Heineken brand, as they represented a multitude of other brands. The recognition that all the growth in sales in that market was due to Van Munching's commitment, led the management of Heineken in 1945 to appoint the newly formed firm Van Munching & Co. to become the sole importer of Heineken.[51] Since then, the U.S. market proved to be very important for the growth of Heineken.

Heineken was also internationalized into other parts of the world. After 1945, it had substantial production and distribution facilities in British West Africa (Ghana, Nigeria and Sierra Leone) through joint ventures with United Africa Company, a subsidiary of Unilever, and with the French trading company, "Companie Française de l'Afrique Occidentalle."[52]

Government intervention also played an important part in the development of firms from Continental Europe prior to 1960.[53] An example is Moët & Chandon from France, which ultimately became part of the multinational LVMH. Founded in 1743, it is one of the oldest champagne houses. Because champagnes were exempt from British customs regulations forbidding imports in bottles, Moët & Chandon and other French wines houses, including Cliquot, were able to bottle wine domestically and, unlike wine exporters from other countries, they distributed under their own brand names in Britain, their major overseas market. This gave them a significant advantage over other wine exporters, whose wine was generally bottled and sold under the name of British retailers, and enabled them to develop an early expertise in the management of brands.[54]

Remainder of the World

In Japan, alcoholic beverages firms only developed major proportions in the period following World War II, as a result of the rapid economic and social transformations that took place. Most of today's industry leaders from Japan were established in the late nineteenth century and early twentieth century. For instance, Suntory, the largest Japanese firm in wines and spirits, was founded in 1899 to produce sweet red wine, and it diversified into other businesses including Japanese whiskey beginning in 1923. Until World War Two, however, the activity of the leading Japanese firms was essentially

[51] This account of Heineken is based on Jacobs and Mass, *Heineken History*: 256–60.

[52] D. K. Fieldhouse, *Merchant Capital and Economic Decolonization* (Oxford: Clarendon Press, 1994): 306–7; Geoffrey Jones, *Transforming Unilever: Transformation and Tradition* (Oxford: Oxford University Press, 2005).

[53] Interbrew and Pernod Ricard did not yet exist in 1960, and, even though the scope of activities of their predecessors' was large, it was still essentially domestic.

[54] Paul Duguid, "Developing the Brand: The Case of Alcohol, 1800–1880," *Enterprise and Society*, Vol. 4, No. 3 (2003): 405–41.

regional and their growth was organic. Apart from investing in alcoholic beverages, they diversified into other business activities including soft drinks. By 1960, the most important firms were Asahi Breweries, Kirin, and Sapporo in beer, and in wines and spirits, Suntory. In 1954, Kirin already ranked among the largest breweries in the world.[55]

In Australia, there had been some concentration in brewing in the early part of the twentieth century. This was a result of the temperance movements, which had started in the late nineteenth century, and of the contraction of the market caused by the depression of the 1930s. Large brewers, such as Carlton & United Breweries (Carlton), were formed in 1907 as the result of a merger of six major metropolitan breweries. Even though Carlton was among the top 100 Australian firms throughout the twentieth century, and developed an export market in the East, most of its activity was concentrated domestically.[56] In New Zealand, similar developments took place, leading to the creation of two leading firms – New Zealand Breweries (renamed as Lion Brewery in 1979) and Dominion Breweries, both created in the 1920s. They also remained essentially domestic firms until the 1960s, with some geographical diversification within Australia.[57]

Conclusion

The companies analyzed in this book have, at one time or another, ranked among the world's leading multinationals in alcoholic beverages. Prior to 1960s, the world industry was still fragmented, consumption was culture-specific and competition was played at a domestic level. Country-specific determinants, such as the level of economic development, the resource base and regulations (including Prohibition and licensing laws), clearly had an impact on the early development of these firms. The U.S. was the most developed economy in the world and produced the largest firms in alcoholic beverages. However, during this period it saw the growth of its firms constrained by Prohibition. This forced companies to create multiple alliances with foreign competitors after repeal as a way to expand and meet rapidly

---

55 Kirin, Annual Report and Accounts (1954, 1961–1969).

56 It is only from 1983, when it was acquired by Elders IXL (the predecessor of Foster's Brewing) that Carlton became a multinational firm. David T. Merrett, "Stability and Change in the Australian Brewing Industry, 1920–94," in R. G. Wilson and T. T. Gourvish (eds.), *The Dynamics of the International Brewing Industry since 1800* (London: Routledge, 1998); Simon Ville and David D. T. Merrett, "The Development of Large Scale Enterprise in Australia, 1910–64," in David Merrett (ed.), *Business Institutions and Behaviour in Australia* (London: Frank Cass, 2000).

57 In the late twentieth century that these firms diversify into wines, taking advantage of the competitive advantages that these countries had developed in this business. S. R. H. Jones, "The New Zealand Brewing Industry, 1840–1995," in Wilson and Gourvish (eds.), *The Dynamic*.

growing demand, thus overcoming limitations of scale and scope. The end of Prohibition also created opportunities for foreign firms, particularly from Canada, to enter the United States. Several distributors that survived Prohibition also integrated vertically into production.

As a result of regulation and other constraints (such as religious beliefs), concentration came more slowly to this industry than it did to many other consumer goods industries. Moreover, very few firms were internationalized before the 1960s. There were, nonetheless, some exceptions. National leaders from Continental Europe such as Heineken, Carlsberg and Moët & Chandon were among the first to internationalize their businesses.

As we have seen, however, several of the world's leading firms in alcoholic beverages or their predecessors at the beginning of the twenty first century, already ranked amongst the world's largest industrials by the 1960s. While in this decade the world's largest firms remained North American, by the beginning of the twenty-first century, British and continental European firms that had become multinational, often surpassed U.S. firms in their size and the geographic scope of their activities. Most of these firms had developed through multiple mergers, acquisitions and cross-border network arrangements. The impact of all this history on the post-1960 era and how these and not other firms became leading multinationals, will be discussed in the forthcoming chapters.

3

Growth and Survival

Introduction

What, then, are the general patterns that explain the independent survival and growth of multinational firms in the global alcoholic beverages industry since 1960? The term *growth* is used to mean "increase in size as a result of a process of development" either organically or through merger and acquisition, and "size is a by-product of the process of growth."[1] *Survival* is used to mean the maintenance of the firm's autonomy of action.[2] In this respect, non-survivals or "exits" include firms that have either been liquidated, dissolved, discontinued, or absorbed, as well as firms that were merged or acquired by other firms, even if they were able to retain their corporate identity and continuity of existence for a significant period of time.

Two questions are being asked: What principles will determine firm growth? How fast and for how long can they grow? The next section examines the main determinants in the growth and survival of firms, giving some examples to illustrate their changing relevance over time. The following section provides a general framework to explain the different patterns of growth and survival, illustrating each of these patterns with some examples. The final section provides a summary of the preliminary findings that are analyzed in more detail in the following chapters.

---

[1] Edith Penrose, *The Theory of the Growth of the Firm* (Oxford: Oxford University Press, 1959/1995): 1–2.

[2] Alfred D. Chandler Jr., *The Visible Hand* (Cambridge, Mass: Harvard University Press, 1977): 371, talks about the survival of managerial hierarchies. See also Leslie Hannah, "Scale and Scope: Towards a European Visible Hand?" *Business History*, Vol. 33, No. 2 (1991): 298–99, for a critical analysis of the definition of survival used by Chandler. Neil M. Kay, *Pattern in Corporate Evolution* (Oxford: Oxford University Press, 1997): 78–81, offers a broader definition of survival, also including firms that were merged or acquired and were able to keep their corporate identity. M. T. Hannan and J. Freeman, "The Population Ecology of Organisations," *American Journal of Sociology*, 82 (1977): 929–64; idem, *Organizational Ecology* (Cambridge, Mass: Harvard University Press, 1989): 150–52.

Determinants

Although there is no "secret recipe" that explains survival and sustained growth, it is possible to monitor the evolution of firms by making systematic comparisons between the largest multinationals from different countries and assessing the type of relationship, such as cooperation and competition, they established among themselves.[3] The distinctive nature of studying the evolution of multinationals is that beyond the multiproduct and multiplant firm dimensions, they also need to possess other ownership advantages over competing indigenous firms when dealing with different economies and cultures.[4]

Figure 3.1 provides a general framework to analyze the determinants of growth and independent survival of firms in this industry.[5] They are divided into three groups: country-specific, industry-specific and firm-specific determinants. The focus is on the firm.[6]

The country- and industry-specific determinants, which are predominantly exogenous and affect the whole industry equally, include the national systems of corporate governance in which firms are based, and the institutional environment in which they operate (such as the countries' regimes of taxation and regulation). The industry-specific determinants refer to the predictability of demand/consumption and the level of competition. Industry structure, associated with its level of concentration, is also an industry-specific determinant in the sense that although it first emerged as a result of the activity of some firms, it then encouraged and restricted the choices of all the firms operating in the industry.[7]

---

[3] Peter E. Hart and Robert D. Pearce, "Growth Patterns of the World's Largest Firms 1962–1982," The University of Reading: Discussion Papers in International Investment and Business Studies, No. 83 (1984).

[4] John H. Dunning, "Trade, Location of Economic Activity and the MNE: A Search for an Eclectic Approach," in B. Ohlin, P. O. Hesselborn, and P. M. Wijkam (eds.), *The International Allocation of Economic Activity* (London: Macmillan, 1977); idem, *International Production and the Multinational Enterprise* (London: Allen & Unwin, 1958); Richard E. Caves, *Multinational Enterprise and Economic Analysis* (Cambridge: Cambridge University Press, 1982).

[5] It draws on several theoretical strands and in particular on John Dunning's Eclectic Paradigm. His concepts of "location advantages" and "ownership advantages" provided a fundamental theoretical background in the construction of this framework. Concepts from other scholars were also considered, such as Chandler's claim that structure follows strategy, the importance of the entrepreneur, economies of scale and scope, and first-mover advantages.

[6] Ronald H. Coase, "The Nature of the Firm," *Economica*, NS 4 (1937): 386–87.

[7] This process reflects Giddens's notion of "structuration." Giddens argues that in their actions people create social structures that then determine and restrict the choices of those who created them. This process is similar to the one described here. Anthony Giddens, *The Constitution of Society: Outline of the Theory of Structuration* (Cambridge: Cambridge University Press, 1984).

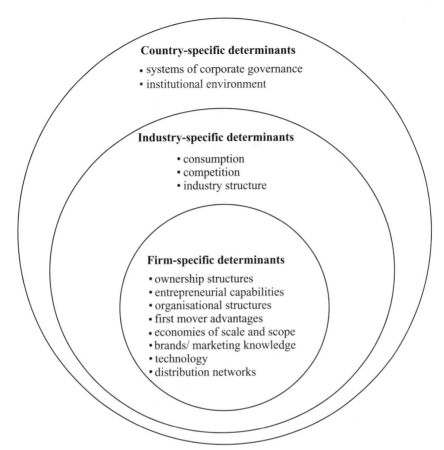

Fig. 3.1. The determinants of growth and survival of firms in alcoholic beverages.

The firm-specific determinants encompass those factors that are endogenous to the firms and differentiate them from one another, promoting and limiting their success.[8] They include firm-specific characteristics or strategic choices, such as brands and marketing knowledge, distribution networks, ownership structures, entrepreneurial capabilities, organizational structures, first-mover advantages, economies of scale and scope, and technology. These

---

[8] Stephen Hymer, "On Multinational Corporations and Foreign Direct Investment," selected by John Dunning from "The International Operations of National Firms: A Study of Foreign Direct Investment" (PhD Dissertation, MIT, 1960, in Christos N. Pitelis and Roger Sugden (eds.), *The Nature of the Transnational Firm* (London: Routledge, 1991): 23–43; Richard R. Nelson, "Why do Firms Differ and How Does it Matter," *Strategic Management Journal*, Vol. 14 (1991): 61–74.

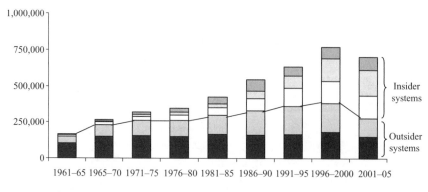

Fig. 3.2. Cumulative sales of firms from different systems of corporate governance. Values stated in millions of constant US dollars (2000 = 100).
Sources: The author, based on companies' annual reports. (All subsequent figures and tables without a source are the author's).

are fundamental to explaining the growth and independent survival of firms.[9] The remainder of this section lays out briefly these three specific determinants of growth and survival, the most relevant of which will be analyzed in more detail in the next chapters.

Country-Specific Determinants

Systems of Corporate Governance

There is evidence that in recent years, systems of corporate governance have been converging, yet there are large differences between countries that may influence companies' goals and behavior as well as their performance over time.[10] Studies tend to distinguish the systems by which firms are governed into two types: the "outsider" system and the "insider" system.

Figure 3.2 takes into consideration the concepts of "outsider" and "insider" systems of corporate governance and aggregates the sales volume of the world's largest multinationals in alcoholic beverages by decade.[11] Until

---

[9] Alfred D. Chandler Jr., "Managerial Enterprise and Competitive Capabilities," *Business History*, Vol. 34, No. 1 (1992): 39; William Lazonick and William Mass (eds.), *Organizational Capability and Competitive Advantage* (Aldershot: Elgar, 1995): xi.

[10] Mary O'Sullivan, *Contests for Corporate Control* (Oxford: Oxford University Press, 2000); Steen Thomsen and Torben Pedersen, "Industry and Ownership Structure," *International Review of Law and Economics*, Vol. 18 (1999): 385–402; Steve Toms and John Wilson, "Scale, Scope and Accountability: Towards a New Paradigm of British Business History," *Business History*, Vol. 45, No. 4 (2003), 1–23.

[11] See Chapter 1 for concepts of "outsider" and "insider" business systems of corporate governance.

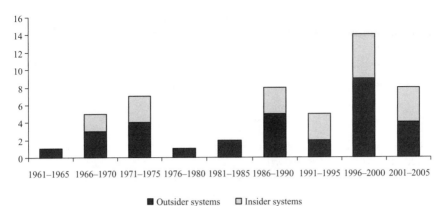

Fig. 3.3. Main mergers and acquisitions by the world's largest multinationals in alcoholic beverages.

the 1980s, the firms originally from countries where "outsider" systems of corporate governance predominated, such as the United States, United Kingdom, and Canada, always accounted for a higher volume of sales in the industry.

Since the 1980s the relative importance of firms originally from "insider" systems of corporate governance increased, in particular those from Continental Europe – France, Denmark, and the Netherlands. Firms started to grow faster following the mergers and acquisitions that took place between domestic leaders from different countries. During this period, firms from "outsider" systems of corporate governance were more likely to merge and acquire or be merged or acquired. This outcome reflected the increasing attention firms from these countries gave to short-term performance, as well as the pressure that financial institutions (as intermediaries to shareholders) were putting on firms to keep high share prices.

Figure 3.3 shows the number of firms merged or acquired by the world's largest multinationals in alcoholic beverages. It includes the list of firms from Table 2.1 (in Chapter 2), and shows the number of firms in that list that were merged or acquired by other large firms from the same list in each decade, distinguishing the systems of corporate governance on which they were based.

By the beginning of the twenty-first century, following pressures toward harmonization and integration within the European Union, mergers and, in particular, acquisitions were as common between firms based on "insider" systems as between firms from "outsider" systems of corporate governance.[12] As a result, the systems of corporate governance that were standard

---

[12] Richard Whittington and Michael Mayer, *The European Corporation: Strategy, Structure and Social Science* (Oxford: Oxford University Press, 2000): 90.

in the nations in which firms were based began to converge. For instance, firms within outsider systems of corporate governance often have ownership structures more typical of firms from insider systems. The mismatches that emerged from this convergence will be analyzed in more depth in Chapter 4.

Institutional Environment

The institutional environment, an industry-specific determinant, both facilitated and inhibited the growth and survival of firms. Among the facilitators were developments in technologies, in infrastructures, in global communications, and in logistics. These reduced the costs of distribution of products and improved their availability to consumers, allowing firms to obtain economies of scale and scope (these also facilitated the globalization of marketing and managerial decision making). These changes began in the 1960s, but increased very rapidly from the mid-1980s, in particular with the emergence of cheap international telecommunications, first the telephone and fax, and then the Internet and intra-firm networks. Among other things, they allowed firms to centralize decision making.[13]

The most important inhibitors were laws and governmental campaigns in most Western countries, such as those on drinking and driving. These aimed at restricting alcohol consumption in order to minimize its harmful effects, and shifting consumption away from higher to lower alcohol content beverages.[14]

The barriers to entry imposed by certain governments to protect their domestic industries were also important inhibitors.[15] In the United Kingdom, for example, licensing laws, which existed since the nineteenth century, restricted the sale of alcoholic beverages to specific outlets, predetermined the hours at which outlets could open, and fixed prices. The Licensing Act of 1961 ended resale price maintenance and enabled off-license shops to open during normal shop hours. These changes significantly affected the growth of firms in this industry. The monopoly created in the Scandinavian countries and in Canada from the 1930s, where trade became completely controlled by

---

[13] John Seely Brown and Paul Duguid, *The Social Life of Information* (Boston, Mass: Harvard Business School Press, 2000); Harold Innis, *The Bias of Communication* (Toronto: University of Toronto Press, 1991); Andrew Odlyzko, "The Internet and Other Networks: Utilizations Rates and Their Implications," *Information Economics Policy*, Vol. 12, No. 4 (2000): 341–65.

[14] However, there are cases of beverages of high alcoholic content whose consumption increased over time. For example, the sales of the famous Swedish vodka brand Absolut rose in the United States by an annual rate of 8.4 percent between 1990 and 1999, because of a very strong marketing strategy by its U.S. distributor.

[15] John Cavanagh and Frederick Clairmonte, *Alcoholic Beverages: Dimensions of Corporate Power* (London: Croom & Helm, 1985): 152.

government institutions, is another example.[16] In Norway and Sweden, alcohol retailing is a near government monopoly, with sales taking place through the Systembolaget or state liquor chain in Sweden, or the Vinmonopolet in Norway. In Denmark, there are no such limitations anymore, and retailers can sell what they like.

By the beginning of the twenty-first century, restrictions imposed by different countries (such as taxes and controls on prices) had become less distinct. For example, the increased membership within the European Union in 1995 was an important countertrend. There was a movement of harmonization of prices and taxes on alcoholic beverages between member states, a change that indirectly encouraged alcohol consumption in many countries.[17] This had the effect of dramatically reducing the prices of wines, bringing countries in Northern Europe into line with the lower-priced south. For example, in Portugal the abolition of trade barriers led to an increase of whisky consumption of 400 percent from 1980 to 1991, corresponding to an increase from 7 to 33.5 percent of the Portuguese spirits market.[18] However, this harmonization of taxes was not uniformly introduced in all countries in the European Union. In Finland, in the beginning of the twenty-first century, the government still intervened to restrict alcohol trade and consumption.[19]

Industry-Specific Determinants

Consumption

World consumption of alcoholic beverages increased during the 1960s and 1970s, and showed a tendency to level off and even decrease in some regions from the 1980s. Figure 3.4 illustrates the evolution of alcohol consumption by region of the world from the 1960s.

Overall, alcohol consumption grew at an average rate of 1.5 percent per year from 1961. During the 1960s and 1970s, there was an increase in

---

[16] About the impact of Prohibition in the alcoholic beverages industry see, e.g., A. M. McGahan, "The Emergence of the National Brewing Oligopoly: Competition in the American Market, 1933–1958," *Business History Review*, Vol. 65 (1991): 229–84. On the UK Licensing Acts, see Terry Gourvish and Richard Wilson, *The British Brewing Industry, 1830–1980* (Cambridge: Cambridge University Press, 1994): chapter 1; and Asa Briggs, *Wine for Sale* (London: Bastford, 1985): 160. On the Temperance Acts and monopoly regimes in Scandinavia, see Jette Schramm-Nielsen, Peter Laurence, and Karl Henrik Sivesind, *Management in Scandinavia – Culture, Context and Change* (Cheltenham: Elgar, 2004).

[17] D. E. Smith and H. S. Solgaard, "The Dynamics of Shifts in European Alcoholic Drinks Consumption," *Journal of International Consumer Marketing*, Vol. 12, No. 3 (2000): 107.

[18] "O Mercado Nacional – O Whisky Domina o Mercado de Bebidas Espirituosas em toda a Europa do Sul," *Revista dos Vinhos* (Novembro 1998).

[19] Pierre Spahni, *The International Wine Trade* (Cambridge: Woodhead, 1995): 204–14; Hurst et al., "Swedish Government Ready to Relax Alcohol Restrictions," *Alcoholic Beverage Taxation*; *Drinks International Bulletin* (6 March 2000).

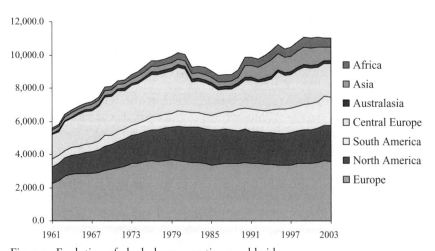

Fig. 3.4. Evolution of alcohol consumption worldwide
(Amounts stated in millions of liters).
Source: Per capita consumption, *World Drink Trends* (Henley-on-Thames: NTC Publications, 2005); Estimates of midyear population by country, United Nations, *Demographic Yearbook* (New York: UN, 2005).

consumption, at least in the industrialized world. Several changes took place,
including rising incomes, changes in lifestyles and tastes of consumers, and
the "re-creation" of a global economy.[20] As in other industries, these changes
led to an increase in the consumption of alcoholic beverages, and had a strong
impact on the development of multinational activity, in particular the growth
and survival of firms.[21]

In the 1980s and 1990s, per capita consumption of alcoholic beverages leveled off in the Western world. The rise of consumption in emerging markets
such as India, China, Thailand, and South America partially compensated
for this. For example, in Thailand, where either water or beer was normally
consumed with meals, the economic boom of the early 1990s led to a very fast
growth in wine consumption (although this fell away following the financial
crisis that began in 1997). These countries are not considered in Figure 3.4,
however, because of the lack of systematic data from 1961.

While between 1988 and 1996, consumption of alcoholic beverages in
the forty-six countries considered in Figure 3.4 grew at an average rate of
0.8 percent, in those emerging markets not included, consumption increased at an average of 6 percent a year.[22] The maturing of markets in the

---

[20] Sydney Pollard, *The International Economy Since 1945* (London: Routledge, 1997).
[21] Teresa da Silva Lopes, "The Impact of Multinational Investment on Alcoholic Consump-
    tion," *Business and Economic History*, Vol. 28, No. 2 (1999): 109–22.
[22] Compound average annual growth rates estimated using per capita consumption by coun-
    try, *World Drink Trends* (Henley-on-Thames: NTC Publications, 2005); and estimates of
    midyear population by country, United Nations, *Demographic Yearbook* (New York: United
    Nations, 2005).

Western world was associated with changes in the legislation on drinking and driving and also with the higher levels of education by consumers, who became more concerned with the quality of the beverages they were drinking, with their own fitness, and with other side effects related to addiction and health.

In the emerging markets, several factors contributed to the rise in consumption from the mid-1980s. Stagnation of consumption in the Western world had led the leading multinationals to internationalize – that is, to intensify their investments in those markets, increasing the availability and diversity of branded drinks. In many of these emerging markets, statistics on consumption and production only started to be reliable after these investments by multinationals. Rapid technological strides in transportation and telecommunications also led to an unprecedented migration from rural areas to urban regions, particularly in former colonies and other developing countries. People living in the cities acquired more westernized lifestyles, owing to the growth of elites with high purchasing power.[23]

Although countries such as the United States and Canada figure among the largest absolute consumers of alcohol in the world, the biggest markets in per capita terms are found in a cluster of Western European countries. Figure 3.5 illustrates this situation for some of the most important markets from 1961 as well as their evolution. I distinguish two periods: 1960–1969 and 1980–2003.

This figure shows a trend away from culture-specific consumption patterns. In Northern Europe, where people traditionally consumed beer, there was an increase in wine consumption. For example, in the United Kingdom, wine consumption grew progressively from the 1960s. This growth reflected evolving social trends, such as the increase in holidays abroad and the globalization of tastes, the growth of eating out as a leisure activity, the increase in home-based entertainment, and also the increasing economic participation of women as consumers, as they started to learn more about wines and developed new habits.

The slower, but ultimately similar, evolution of beer trade in Southern Europe emphasizes the overall trend toward homogenization and globalization proposed here. Although by the beginning of the twenty-first century, wine still accounted for the majority of alcohol consumption in France, Italy, Portugal and Spain, beer consumption had increased very rapidly from the 1970s. The previously mentioned increase in travel, the rise of foreign direct investment, and alliances in distribution formed between competing alcoholic beverages firms, explain this trend. These changes led to the emergence of a more pan-European cultural identity associated with the growing strength of the European Community and more homogenized patterns of consumption.[24]

[23] Cavanagh, Clairmonte, and Room, *The World Alcohol*: 4–5, 10; Lopes, "The Impact."
[24] Tim Unwin, *The Wine and the Vine* (London: Routledge, 1991): 359.

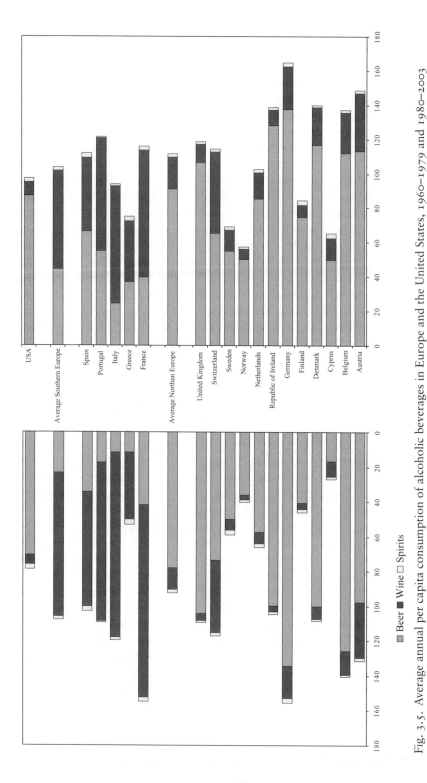

Fig. 3.5. Average annual per capita consumption of alcoholic beverages in Europe and the United States, 1960–1979 and 1980–2003 (Amounts stated in liters of pure alcohol).

Source: Based on data from Wendy Hurst, Ed Gregory, and Thomas Gussman, *Alcoholic Beverage Taxation and Control Policies* (Ottawa: Brewers Association of Canada, 1997); *World Drink Trends* (Henley-on-Thames: NTC Publications, 2004).

The level and patterns of consumption were particularly important in the growth and survival of firms before the 1980s, when they were still culturally specific. For example, in the United States the relatively low level of per capita consumption can in part be traced to Prohibition and the temperance mindset that has always existed among a significant part of the population. Combined with the large size of the country, this indicated there was potential demand that firms could create, giving them the possibility of growing very large by concentrating essentially on the domestic market.

The need for firms to create ownership advantages before going abroad explains in part the low level of foreign direct investment by alcoholic beverages firms and, consequently, their lack of international experience. This became crucial for their survival from the 1980s. In the United Kingdom, the changing drinking patterns from the 1960s, where beer consumption started to stagnate and spirits consumption increased, also illustrate the transformations that were affecting the growth and survival of firms. Brewers such as Allied Breweries and Grand Metropolitan were forced to diversify into spirits to meet consumers' preferences, offering a greater choice of drinks sold through a wider variety of outlets.[25]

Consumption patterns are also reflected in the type of beverage business that served as the basis for the development of the world's largest multinationals of alcoholic beverages. It is in countries such as Denmark, the Netherlands, the United States, Japan, and the United Kingdom where beer was the most important alcoholic beverage and the level of per capita consumption was high that the world's largest beer firms developed.[26] From the 1980s, in order to survive, firms had to be able to stimulate consumption. Those firms with the most "portable" products tended to internationalize first. Consequently, spirits firms tended to be the first to become multinational and wines firms the last.[27]

International Competition

International competition, another industry-specific determinant, increased in the 1960s, after the economic health of the European nations was fully restored and Japan started to undergo rapid economic growth.[28] The changes in the political and economic environment during that period were distinctive

---

[25] Tony Millns, "The British Brewing Industry, 1945–1995," in Richard Wilson and Terry Gourvish (eds.), *The Dynamics of the International Brewing Industry Since 1800* (London: Routledge, 1998): 154.

[26] This situation should not however be overgeneralized. Germany had the highest consumption of beer in the world and yet did not develop leading multinationals.

[27] Again this situation should not be overgeneralized. Only some spirits firms were able to internationalize and become large.

[28] Alfred D. Chandler Jr., "Organizational Capabilities and the Economic History of the Industrial Enterprise," *Journal of Economic Perspectives*, Vol. 6, No. 3 (1992): 98.

from those seen in the late nineteenth century in several ways. These included an increase in the propensity to spend on consumer products in the Western world, deeper cross-border transactions, and the dissemination of electronic information systems. With the globalization of economies from the 1980s, competition intensified even further, and was now played out at a multimarket level.

Diageo and Its Predecessors

Table 3.1 below illustrates for the case of Diageo and its most important predecessors – Guinness, Grand Metropolitan, International Distillers and Vintners (IDV), and Distillers – and the tendency for firms to become increasingly committed to international markets and simultaneously to compete and collaborate. Several indicators are used to measure this pattern of evolution in each decade: percentage of sales by markets (where sales in the country of origin are separated from sales in the major continents), percentage of foreign to total mergers and acquisitions, and the number of international alliances in production or distribution (which include joint ventures, distribution agreements and licensing agreements, among others).

This table illustrates the general patterns and directions of growth followed by each of the major firms that preceded the formation of Diageo. There was a very fast rise in the average sales from one decade to another. Most firms grew through mergers and acquisitions rather than organically, with Grand Metropolitan being the most striking case. This rise in the number of mergers and acquisitions reflected to a great extent the internationalization strategies of firms. The total number of mergers and acquisitions in production and distribution by alcoholic beverages multinationals reached its peak in the 1980s and decreased in the 1990s. While by the end of the twentieth century and early twenty-first century these mergers and acquisitions tended to be across countries, in the 1960s and 1970s, they essentially involved domestic firms, signaling strategies of consolidation in the home markets.

Over time, there was also a trend toward diversification in terms of geographical markets. Until the 1980s, the predecessor firms of Diageo tended to sell essentially in their countries of origin or in the United States and the British Commonwealth. This high concentration of sales can in part be explained by fairly distinctive national consumption patterns in the other countries of the Western world (especially in Continental Europe) and also by barriers to trade. From the 1980s, there was a dispersion of sales to Continental Europe and to markets in other continents that had not been part of the British Commonwealth.

Alliances in the form of joint ventures, distribution agreements, licensing agreements, and also minority investments in production and distribution were always an important alternative for growth. This approach reached a peak in the 1990s. Those firms that did not follow these patterns of growth

Table 3.1. *International evolution of Diageo and its major predecessors, 1960–2000*

| Firm/Decade | Total Average Sales | Sales by Markets | | | | Total Number of New Mergers and Acquisitions | % of Foreign to Total New Mergers and Acquisitions | Total Number of Alliances With International Partners |
		UK Country of Origin (%)	North America (%)	Continental Europe (%)	Other (%)			
Grand Metropolitan								
1962–1969	332	92	2	6	0	0	0	0
1970–1979	4.553	91	1	5	2	3	33	4
1980–1989	9.182	64	27	5	4	13	77	15
1990–1996	12.076	20	55	17	8	15	100	18
IDV								
1963–1969	517	29	56	4	12	6	50	32
1970–1974	962	72	8	4	16	5	60	0
Guinness								
1960–1969	1.049	n/a	n/a	n/a	n/a	1	100	17
1970–1979*	1.551	78	4	3	15	0	0	13
1980–1989*	3.100	66	10	8	16	16	88	22
1990–1996	6.212	40	16	35	9	7	100	31
Distillers Company								
1960–1969	3.146	57	28	0	14	3	67	0
1970–1979	2.721	53	13	7	24	3	33	0
1980–1985	2.261	43	17	12	28	4	100	0
Diageo								
1997–1999	18.533	14	41	21	25	1	100	0
2000–2004	15.649	14	26	15	48	5	100	1
Total								
1960s	1.261	59	29	3	9	10	54	49
1970s	2.447	73	6	5	14	11	32	17
1980s	4.848	58	18	8	16	33	88	37
1990s	12.274	25	37	24	14	23	100	49
2000s	15.649	14	26	15	48	5	100	2

Note: Sales values stated in millions of constant US dollars (2000 = 100). n/a – not available.

* Sales by geographical region for Guinness from 1970 to 1979 only include data from 1979 as the information for the years 1970–1978 is not available. Information on mergers and acquisitions and alliances by Guinness during the period 1970 and 1989 was only available for the years 1970–1975 and 1983–1989.

Sources: The information in table 3.1 and 3.2 draws on the companies' archives and annual reports. The data on total number of mergers and acquisitions only include firms merged or acquired within the alcoholic beverages industry. New companies formed and new offices or warehouses acquired or built are excluded. Minority interests are considered as alliances, apart from joint ventures, licensing agreements, and distribution agreements. Alliances with international partners include both alliances in the United Kingdom and abroad.

were restricted in their process of growth and less likely to survive. Distillers Company had become one of the most internationalized firms in the world since its last big amalgamation in 1925. However, its number of new foreign direct investments and alliances (both in production and distribution) from the 1960s was very low when compared with that of other leading firms such as Grand Metropolitan.[29] This evolution in part explains the failure of this firm to survive independently from the 1980s.

Schenley is yet another case of a firm that did not follow the general pattern that made for growth and survival. This U.S. firm relied almost exclusively on the domestic market. A large number of the brands in its portfolio were obtained through alliances (in the form of distribution contracts). Its lack of international experience, as well as limited ownership of successful brands, is to a great extent associated with Prohibition, which led it to diversify into other businesses such as chemicals and biochemicals; this impeded the firm from acquiring new marketing knowledge in alcoholic beverages.

The average growth rate in sales for Schenley, which was slower than that of leading multinationals such as Guinness and Grand Metropolitan, also reflects the firm's passive strategy in a period of concentration and globalization. Failing to grow, this firm became vulnerable to a takeover by Guinness in 1987.

Table 3.2 provides a detail of one of the columns from Table 3.1 about the total number of alliances. It distinguishes alliances by type of activity (distribution only or production and distribution) and by type of partner (direct competitor, or partner with a complementary activity).[30]

There is an apparent correlation between the type of alliances formed by firms and the type of beverages they produced. For example, gin and beer firms tended to form more alliances in production and distribution. These beverages, such as whisky, are not dependent on specific natural resources available only in certain locations. Hence, International Distillers and Vintners (IDV), with a major interest in gin, formed many alliances involving both production and distribution. Similarly, Guinness, before the mid-1980s, when it was still essentially a beer business, found multiple alliances, a strategy suited to a business with high transportation costs.

Table 3.2 also makes clear the importance of alliances with competitors. The alliances recorded there involve firms operating within the same business activity (wine, spirits, beer, or a combination of the three). The firms included are leading multinationals or at least leading players in their domestic

[29] Ronald B. Weir, *The History of the Distillers Company, 1877–1939* (Oxford: Oxford University Press, 1995); idem, "D.C.L.: Acquisitions and Major Shareholdings, 1877–1940" (mimeo, 1990); idem, "D.C.L. Acquisitions, 1940–1986" (mimeo, 1999).

[30] Diageo had no new alliances until between 1997 and 2000 owing to the fact that it had just been formed and because it was in the process of rationalizing its operations. At the end of 2000, however, it made a major acquisition with Pernod Ricard of the alcoholic beverages business of Seagram.

Table 3.2. *Number of alliances formed by Diageo and its predecessors, 1960–2000*

Firm/Decade	Type of Activity		Type of Partner		Total Number of Alliances
	Distribution Only	Production and Distribution	Competitor	Complementary Activity	
Grand Metropolitan					
1962–1969	0	0	0	0	0
1970–1979	3	1	3	1	4
1980–1989	11	4	15	0	15
1990–1996	15	5	4	14	18
IDV					
1963–1969	4	28	32	0	32
1970–1974	0	0	0	0	0
Guinness					
1960–1969	3	14	15	2	17
1970–1979*	7	6	8	5	13
1980–1989*	22	0	17	5	22
1990–1996	5	26	29	2	31
Distillers Company					
1960–1969	0	0	0	0	0
1970–1979	0	0	0	0	0
1980–1985	0	0	0	0	0
Diageo					
1997–1999	0	0	0	0	0
2000–2004	1	0	1	0	1
Total					
1960s	7	42	47	2	49
1970s	10	7	11	6	17
1980s	33	4	32	5	37
1990s	20	31	33	16	49
2000s	2	0	2	0	2

markets. The complementary partners, by contrast, are firms that produce alcoholic beverages but are of small size and do not have a leading position internationally or domestically. They can also refer to firms that operate in the alcoholic beverages industry but specialize in distinct activities such as distribution, or to firms specializing in unrelated activities such as the distribution of all sorts of other products.

The high number of alliances in distribution formed by Guinness in the 1980s reflects the firm's wide-ranging alliance with Moët Hennessy. The two multinationals formed seventeen distribution alliances covering markets all over the world, some of which also included other partners, such as Jardine Wines and Spirits in Japan and Irish Distillers in Eire.

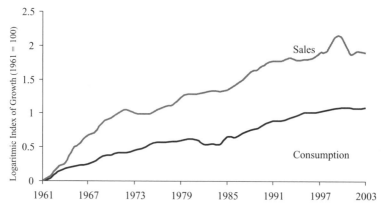

Fig. 3.6. Indexes of growth in consumption of alcoholic beverages and in sales by the world's largest multinationals in 1960.
Source: Database; *World Drink Trends* (Henley-on-Thames: NTC Publications, 2005); and population by country – United Nations, *Demographic Yearbook* (New York: United Nations, 2005) – estimates of midyear population.

Industry Structure

A third industry-specific determinant is industry structure. The patterns of growth of the world's largest firms in alcoholic beverages from 1960 (through mergers and acquisitions, alliances, or organic expansion), in particular those in the beer and spirits businesses, led to the concentration of the industry by a small group of large firms.[31] As there are no robust estimates on the size of the industry, Figures 3.6 and 3.7 provide alternative approaches to analyzing the evolution of industry structure. Showing the world's largest firms in 1961, and assuming that in the long run the evolution of consumption corresponds to that of sales in the entire industry, Figure 3.6 illustrates that there was a rise in the index of growth in sales at constant prices by the world's largest firms. The increase was higher than the index of growth in consumption of alcoholic beverages, indicating a higher level of concentration in the industry.[32]

Figure 3.7 illustrates the evolution in the volume of sales by the world's largest firms between 1960 and 2004, and the total number of firms considered in the database in each year. It also confirms the trend toward a higher degree of concentration in the industry. In particular, it illustrates that during

---

[31] Terry Gourvish, "Economics of Brewing, Theory and Practice: Concentration and Technological Change in the United States, United Kingdom and Germany Since 1945," *Business and Economic History*, Vol. 33, No. 1 (1994): 256; idem, "Concentration, Diversity and the Firm Strategy in European Brewing, 1945–90," in Wilson and Gourvish (eds.), *The Dynamics of the International Brewing Industry*, 81, 85.

[32] Statistics on the evolution of the number of firms in the global industry and of trade and consumption of alcoholic beverages are not very robust.

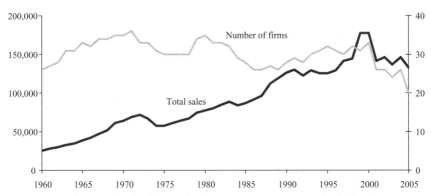

Fig. 3.7. Evolution of sales by the leading multinationals in alcoholic beverages.[33] Sales in millions of constant US dollars (2000 = 100)

the 1960s, new large firms developed but their sales rose slowly. In the 1970s, sales started to rise at a faster rate and the number of firms decreased. From the 1980s, when competition became global, there was a sharp rise in the volume of sales and at the same time the number of firms decreased and then leveled off.

These four sets of factors – consumption, competition, institutional environment, and industry structure – were very distinct among countries before the 1960s, having an important impact on the growth and independent survival of firms, especially when the resulting environment was adverse. By the beginning of the twenty-first century, they had become less significant. With the globalization of the industry, the capacity of firms to deal with country- and industry-specific factors had become a necessary, but not sufficient, determinant in their growth and survival.

Nonetheless, industry-specific determinants still had a very important impact in the wines business. By the beginning of the twenty-first century, it was still fragmented, and the performance of the firms was strongly influenced by the institutional environment of their country of origin. Consumption was still culture specific, and competition was essentially played at a domestic level. There were, however, some signs that the industry was starting to concentrate and globalize. Technological developments had allowed firms to improve the quality and predictability of their products. That is why many multinationals, like Foster's Brewing from Australia, changed the nature of their businesses. From 1996, Foster's Brewing embarked on a series of acquisitions of wines firms and became more than a multinational brewer.[34] Allied Domecq's acquisitions of leading wine firms in

---

[33] This figure only takes into account those alcoholic beverages firms from the database for which there exist consistent and systematic data for every year from 1960 to 2005.

[34] In 2001, after acquiring International Wine Accessories, the firm changed its name from Foster's Brewing Group to Foster's Group Limited; *Financial Times* (3 and 5 July, 2001).

New Zealand, Argentina, and California in 2001 provide another illustration of a leading multinational seeking a large presence in the global wines business.[35] This pattern of concentration was not only occurring in the wine regions of the new world but also in the old world.[36]

Firm-Specific Determinants

This set of determinants looks inside the firms and establishes what led to their different patterns of evolution over time. Each of the isolated determinants is insufficient to ensure growth and long-term survival of firms, and at each moment in time some determinants are more important than others. Firm-specific advantages also have to be constantly created or rebuilt, adapted to the economic needs and opportunities in the environment.[37] Of particular importance in assessing firm-specific capabilities are brands, distribution networks, the capacity of firms to acquire and transfer marketing knowledge, ownership structures, and the entrepreneurial capabilities of management. Given the importance that each of these factors had in the growth and long-term survival of firms, they will be analyzed in more detail in the following chapters. In addition, there were other firm-specific determinants, including organizational structures, economies of scale and scope at various levels of activity, first-mover advantages, and firm technology.[38]

Chandler and Nelson and Winter suggest inverse relationships of causality between the organizational structure of the firm and its strategy. Chandler proposes that structure follows strategy, and Nelson and Winter that strategy follows from structure.[39] Both deal with the issue of how firms explore economies of scale and scope, given the existence of bounded rationality.[40]

The evidence from the alcoholic beverages industry seems to support both cases. However, when competition accelerated beginning in the 1980s, firms most frequently adapted their organizational structures to their new strategies, a la Chandler. An example is Allied Lyons, which changed its

---

[35] 'Lion Nathan Wine bid hit by NZ Watchdog Ruling', *Financial Times* (17 July 2001); 'Allied Buys Argentina Winemakers', *The Independent* (5 July 2001).

[36] Interview with John de Lucca, President of the California Wine Institute, San Francisco, 20 March 2001; Interview with Colin Campbell, Director at Moët-Hennessy, Paris, 22 November 1999; Cavanagh, Clairmonte, and Room, *The World*, 54. Tony Spawton, "Development in the Global Alcoholic Drinks Industry and its Implications for the Future Marketing of Wine," *European Journal of Marketing*, Vol. 24, No. 4 (1990): 49.

[37] Alfred D. Chandler Jr., *Scale and Scope: The Dynamics of Industrial Capitalism* (Cambridge, Mass: Harvard University Press): 35.

[38] Chandler, *The Visible Hand*, 8. For a definition of economies of scale and scope, see Chandler, *Scale and Scope*: 17–18.

[39] Alfred D. Chandler Jr., *Strategy and Structure* (Cambridge Mass: The MIT Press, 1962); Richard R. Nelson and Sidney G. Winter, *An Evolutionary Theory of Economic Change* (Cambridge, Mass: Harvard University Press, 1982).

[40] Oliver Williamson, *The Economic Institutions of Capitalism* (New York: Free Press, 1985): 45.

organizational structure in the early 1980s due to transformations in its strategy.[41] As a result, while in 1985 Allied sold US$6,431 million (at constant prices 2000 = 100), 27 percent of those sales being generated by subsidiaries operating in seven different, essentially European, countries, in 1990 sales had risen to US$8,878 million, 40 percent being generated by subsidiaries based in twenty countries from different continents.[42] Allied Lyons, now renamed, was by this time a truly global multinational.

As most of the world's largest multinationals were long-established, they tended to have been first movers in their markets of origin and in their beverages categories. There were, however, some "challengers," who relied on the management of successful brands that they had obtained through mergers with or acquisitions of long-established firms. In all cases, these firms had created cost advantages related to learning, reputation, and brand image.[43] However, since during the period of analysis most beverages had long achieved maturity in their life-cycles, first-mover advantages were no longer sufficient to sustain growth and secure independent survival. For instance, Distillers and Arthur Bell, two firms that had been first movers in scotch whisky, had not rebuilt new firm-specific advantages after the 1960s, and ended up being acquired in the 1980s.

Technology had been an important firm-specific determinant in the beer sector until the 1960s. Since then, it had become less important. Some general technological developments, such as refrigeration and containerization, allowed firms to obtain economies of scale and scope, which translated into more effective distribution across regions.[44] Improvements in information systems and logistics were also important in increasing the availability of beer to consumers and enhancing communications and decision taking by the firms in this part of the industry.

In wines, some of the major innovations included improvements in the quality of grape varietals, new systems of mechanization, the creation of pressure tanks and coolers, better control of the temperature of fermentation, and a new ability to fit grape varieties to the climate. These scientific methods and techniques in wine production allowed firms to make consistent, high quality wines and permitted mass branding strategies.[45] Branded

[41] Interview with Michael Jackaman, former Chairman of the Wines Spirits and Soft Drinks Division, and also former Chairman of Allied Domecq, Somerset, 8 December 1998.
[42] Allied Lyons, *Annual Reports and Accounts* (1985, 1990).
[43] Glenn R. Carroll and Michael T. Hannan, *The Demography of Corporations and Industries* (Princeton: Princeton University Press, 2000).
[44] Gourvish, "Economics of Brewing": 255.
[45] David John Collis, "The Value Added Structure and Competition Within Industries" (PhD dissertation, Harvard University, 1986); James Espey, "A Multinational Approach to New Product Development," *European Journal of Marketing*, Vol. 19, No. 2 (1985): 5–18; David Merrett and Greg Whitwell, "The Empire Strikes Back: Marketing Australian Beer and Wine in the United Kingdom," in Geoffrey Jones and Nicholas J. Morgan (eds.), *Adding Value: Brands and Marketing in Food and Drink* (London: Routledge, 1994).

wines also offered an accessible starting point for new drinkers, providing some sort of guarantee that they would get what they paid for from different outlets and from one year to the next. For the companies, they offered the prospect of creating consumer loyalty and hence higher sales volumes and profit margins, and lower risks (such as those associated with unexpected changes in climate).

Analytical Framework: Patterns of Growth and Survival

Although no two firms can ever be exactly alike, it is possible to identify some general patterns in their processes of growth, particularly among those which tended to focus their activities in the distilled spirits and brewing businesses.[46] Table 3.3 provides an analytical framework for the patterns of growth and survival of the world's largest multinationals. It considers three different phases between 1960 and the beginning of the twenty-first century. In each phase, some firms survived independently and others merged or were acquired. The table also reflects three levels of analysis – country, industry, and firm – related to three sets of determinants. At the level of country-specific determinants, which affect all the firms operating in a given system of corporate governance equally, conditions are always adverse for firms operating in "outsider" systems of corporate governance. This is due to the characteristics of capital markets and the high likelihood that firms will be subject to takeovers. In contrast, conditions in "insider" systems of corporate governance are considered to be benign at an initial phase, as capital markets are not as developed, and firms are not publicly quoted, and therefore not subject in the same way to mergers and acquisitions.

Like country-specific determinants, industry-specific determinants are considered to affect growth and survival of firms depending on whether they are benign (+) or adverse (–). In Table 3.3, country- and industry-specific determinants are considered to be adverse (–), either when both determinants are adverse, or in situations where only one is adverse (e.g., when the firm is from an "outsider" system of corporate governance, but the industry-specific determinants are benign). Firm-specific determinants vary in their relative importance in determining the firms'-specific advantages.

As Table 3.3 shows, in Phase 1, in the 1960s, consumption was culture-specific, the relevant level of competition for firms and the institutional environments that affected their activities were local, and the industry was still fragmented. So, as long as industry-specific determinants were relatively

---

[46] As already mentioned, the world wines business, by contrast, remained relatively fragmented until the beginning of the twenty-first century. There are some exceptions, including Moët-Hennessy, Gallo, and Constellation Brands, which developed from their beginnings in the sparkling wines and still wines businesses.

Table 3.3. *Patterns of growth and survival of firms in the alcoholic beverages industry*

		Phase 1	Phase 2	Phase 3
Country	System of corporate governance	Outsider: (−) adverse Insider: (+) benign	Outsider: (−) adverse Insider: (−) benign	Outsider: (−) adverse Insider: (−) benign
Industry	- Consumption - Competition/Inst. Environ. - Industry structure	Culture specific Local/Regional Fragmented benign: (−) adverse	Culture spec./homogenised Regional/Global Transitory Period (−) adverse only	Homogenised Global Concentrated (−) adverse only
Firm	Patterns of growth and survival			

Firm specific advantages?
Country/Industry specific determinants?

Phase 1:
- Yes → + Survival / − Survival
- No → + Survival / − Exit

Phase 2 / Phase 3:
Firm specific advantages?
- Yes → Survival / No → Exit (repeated three sets)

benign, it was possible for firms to grow and survive independently even without constantly rebuilding their firm-specific advantages. An example is Distillers Company, which had built firm-specific capabilities before the 1960s by achieving economies of scale and scope in production. It also developed a complex and heavily bureaucratic organization structure, with lots of duplication of activities (which obviously increased costs); it was not sufficiently internationalized when compared to its competition, and also was not adequately investing in marketing. So long as the environment was relatively benign, Distillers Company was able to survive independently. From the 1980s on, as competition became global and the industry concentrated, Distillers Company, by not rebuilding firm-specific capabilities, was not able to survive independently.[47]

Phase 2 is a transitional period (a shakeout period around the 1980s) when firms started to become global and became used to dealing with a multitude of institutional environments, competitors, and consumers.[48] Consumption patterns across markets became more homogenized and the industry concentrated. Firms were able to grow and survive only if they created or rebuilt firm-specific advantages.[49] An example is Moët Hennessy, which was able to rebuild the necessary capabilities by remaining a family-controlled firm after merging with another family firm and hiring a professional manager to run the business.

Finally, in Phase 3, in the 1990s, the industry became very concentrated and truly global. Here, firms could only survive as long as they created or continued to rebuild their firm-specific advantages. The merger between Guinness and Grand Metropolitan in 1997, which led to the creation of Diageo, is an example. This merger allowed the new firm to obtain economies of scale and scope at various levels of activity and, in particular, in marketing and distribution.

These phases differed according to the type of alcoholic beverages business, whether wines, spirits, or beer. For beer and spirits firms, benign industry-specific determinants had a significant impact on the growth and survival of firms until the 1980s, at which point businesses encountered more adverse conditions related to the globalization of the industry. They then had to summon new firm-specific capabilities to grow and survive. In the wines business,

---

[47] Chandler, *Scale and Scope*: 378; Ronald B. Weir, "Managing Decline: Brands and Marketing in Two Mergers 'The Big Amalgamation' 1925 and Guinness DCL 1986," in Jones and Morgan (eds.), *Adding Value*.

[48] Steven Klepper and Kenneth L. Simons, "Innovation and Industry Shakeouts," *Business and Economic History*, Vol. 25, No. 1 (1996): 81–89; Richard N. Foster and Sarah Kaplan, *Creative Destruction* (London: Doubleday, 2001): 54.

[49] Alfred D. Chandler Jr., "The Enduring Logic of Industrial Success," *Harvard Business Review* (March–April 1990): 140.

due to its asset-specific nature, industry-specific factors still determined firms' growth and survival at the beginning of the twenty-first century.

Conclusion

This chapter has sought to cover a wide range of issues related to the growth and survival of the world's largest multinationals in the alcoholic beverages industry. Several of these issues will be analyzed in more detail in the following chapters. Here I developed data on three sets of determinants: country-specific, industry-specific, and firm-specific. Although they were always important in the growth and survival of firms, their relative significance varied over time and also differed for the various beverages.

When country- and industry-specific factors were benign – that is, when consumption patterns were culture-specific, competition and the institutional environment were principally domestic and the industry was fragmented – it was possible for firms to grow and survive without constantly rebuilding their firm-specific advantages. Once these country- and industry-specific factors became adverse, however, it was no longer possible for firms to grow and survive without constantly creating or rebuilding firm-specific advantages.

An adverse setting does not necessarily prevent growth and survival. Indeed, globalization merely demands that firms learn to deal with multiple markets. Such a multiplicity of markets can make the industry-specific determinants under which firms operate adverse, even if they are benign at the level of particular market conditions. In such circumstances, country- and industry-specific determinants become a necessary but not sufficient condition for firms to grow and survive. At this stage firm-specific factors become increasingly important. These include brands and marketing knowledge, ownership structures, and distribution networks, among other firm-specific factors.

The different patterns of growth followed by leading firms from these different sectors were heavily dependent on product category (wine, beer, or spirits). In beer and spirits, benign industry-specific determinants significantly determined the growth and survival of firms until the 1980s. At that point they encountered more adverse conditions related to the globalization of the industry and had to summon new firm-specific capabilities to grow and survive. In the wines business, which is less global due to its asset-specific nature, industry-specific factors still determined firms' growth and survival at the beginning of the twenty-first century.

By deepening the level of analysis from Chapter 1, this chapter shows that the study of this industry needs to be disaggregated. It remains to be seen whether these findings about the impact of the country-, industry-, and firm-specific determinants on the patterns of growth and survival of firms over time can also be applied to the study of smaller firms in the alcoholic beverages industry that operate at a global level. Such a study would require more rigorous analysis, but it would also indicate the possible generality of my argument with regards to the evolution of other non–science-based industries that, like alcoholic beverages, are characterized by a high level of competition, concentration, and globalization, and produce globally branded products with long life cycles.

4

Family Ownership and Managerial Control

Introduction

When we look at corporate governance of firms a number of questions come to mind. Does the country of origin matter? Has the level of concentration of ownership influenced the growth and survival of firms? Who manages these firms? How has their ownership and control evolved over time? This chapter analyzes these questions, focusing on the evolution of the predominant governance structures of the leading multinationals in alcoholic beverages.

Country of Origin

As we noted before, the leading firms in the world originate both from "outsider" and "insider" systems of corporate governance. Table 4.1 uses this classification to aggregate those firms with published accounts into these two groups. The United States, United Kingdom, Canada, Australia, and South Africa are grouped as "outsider" systems. Continental Europe, Japan, and South America are grouped as "insider" systems of corporate governance.[1] This Table provides, for each firm, the average sales in each decade: 1961–1970, 1971–1980, 1981–1990, 1991–2000, and 2001–2005.[2]

In the 1960s, the number and size (measured by sales volume) of firms originally from the outsider systems was much higher than that of firms from insider systems. This is what one might expect from a neoclassical perspective. Open systems should make for more competitive firms. In contrast, by 2004 the number of firms from outsider systems was similar to that of firms from insider systems. Firms like National Distillers (which had been

---

[1] Tim Jenkinson and Colin Mayer, "The Assessment: Corporate Governance and Corporate Control," *Oxford Review of Economic Policy*, Vol. 8, No. 3 (1992): 1–10.

[2] Amounts stated in U.S. dollars (2000 = 100). To convert the data into constant US dollars, several indicators were used. First, original currencies were converted into current US dollars, using the average annual exchange rates for Australia, Belgium, Canada, Denmark, the European Union, France, Japan, the Netherlands, South Africa, and the United Kingdom. Second, the export unit values for the industrial countries' index was used to convert the data from US dollar current prices into US dollar constant prices: unit value prices in terms of US dollars of 2000.

Table 4.1. *Average annual sales by decade for the world's leading firms in alcoholic beverages, 1960–2005[a]*

	Year of Foundation / Last Merger	Year of Merger / Acquisition	1960–1969	1970–1979	1980–1989	1990–1999	2000–2005
Outsider Systems							
United States and Canada							
Anheuser-Busch	1852		1.634	2.973	7.410	10.389	12.864
Brown Forman	1870		513	699	1.225	1.482	2.200
Constellation Brands/ Canandaigua	1945		n/a	55	128	651	2.646
E. & J. Gallo	1933		n/a	n/a	n/a	1.057	1.284
Fortune Brands	1864		5.824	7.985	8.765	7.418	5.646
John Labbatt	1847	1995	356	1.084	2.471	3.340	–
Heublein	1875	1987	857	2.464	2.488	–	–
Hiram Walker	1926	1986	1.861	1.804	3.005	–	–
Liggett & Myers	1873	1980	2.045	1.763	–	–	–
Molson-Coors	2004		–	–	–	–	4.019
National Distillers	1924	1986	3.083	2.953	1.983	–	–
Schenley	1920	1971/1987	1.703	2.176	–	–	–
Seagram	1924	2001	3.695	4.008	3.401	7.210	–
Average			2.157	2.542	3.431	4.507	4.776
Standard deviation			1.663	2.124	2.832	3.822	4.245
United Kingdom							
Allied Domecq	1799/1961	2005	1.956	3.502	5.700	7.336	4.578
Arthur Bells	1825	1985	164	303	501	–	–
Bass	1777	2000	1.390	2.852	4.533	6.655	–
Diageo	1997		–	–	–	18.533	15.615
Distillers Company	1877	1986	3.146	2.721	2.261	–	–
Grand Metropolitan	1962	1997	234	4.553	9.182	12.076	–
Guinness	1759	1997	1.049	1.551	3.100	6.212	–
International Distillers & Vintners	1962	1972	517	962	–	–	–

Scottish & Newcastle	1749/1960		978	1.094	1.338	3.289	5.986
Truman	n/a	1971	191	239	–	–	–
Watney Mann	1958	1972	1.197	1.338	–	–	–
Whitbread	1742	2000	922	1.554	2.335	5.195	–
Average			1.067	1.879	3.619	8.471	8.726
Standard deviation			886	1.363	2.798	5.188	6.007
Australia and South Africa							
Foster's Group / Foster's Brewery / Elders IXL	1888		1.731	2.352	6.442	4.364	2.357
SABMiller / South Africa Breweries	1895		266	1.663	3.509	5.666	6.824
Average			998	2.007	4.976	5.015	4.591
Standard deviation			1.036	487	2.074	921	3.158
Average (US, Canada, UK, Australia, and South Africa)			1.354	1.991	3.444	6.437	6.039
Standard deviation (US, Canada, UK, Australia, and South Africa)			1.359	1.700	2.658	4.537	4.552
Insider Systems							
Japan							
Asahi Breweries	1889		550	626	1.644	7.120	11.497
Kirin	1907		1.694	3.100	6.799	7.761	9.371
Sapporo	1876		888	1298	2457	4646	4339
Suntory	1899		631	2.395	4.454	5.858	6.402
Average			1.071	2.264	3.838	6.346	7.902
Standard deviation			523	1.105	2.300	1.382	3.164
Continental Europe							
Carlsberg	1847		911	1.336	1.595	2.697	4.678
Inbev	2004		–	–	–	–	10.288
Interbrew	1988/2004		–	–	1.265	2.072	5.212
Heineken	1864		252	1.390	2.785	5.620	8.793
Moët & Chandon	1743	1971	69	–	–	–	–

(continued)

Table 4.1 (Continued)

	Year of Foundation / Last Merger	Year of Merger / Acquisition	1960–1969	1970–1979	1980–1989	1990–1999	2000–2005
Moët-Hennessy	1971	1987	–	502	1.168	–	–
Moët-Hennessy Louis Vuitton	1987		–	–	2.785	5.181	12.254
Pernod Ricard	1805/1975		–	933	1.512	4.783	3.989
Rémy Cointreau	1724/1991		–	–	–	1.031	858
Average			411	1.040	1.852	3.564	6.582
Standard deviation			443	413	740	1.883	3.996
South America							
Ambev	2000	2004					2.706
Bacardi	1862		n/a	n/a	n/a	2.294	2.779
Companhia Antarctica Paulista	1885		n/a	n/a	877	863	–
Companhia Cervejeira Brahma	1888		n/a	n/a	n/a	1.724	–
Modelo	1925	1998	n/a	n/a	2.622	2.751	3.860
Average			n/a	n/a	1.750	1.908	3.115
Standard deviation			n/a	n/a	1.234	813	646
Average (Japan, Continental Europe, and South America)			684	1.285	2.000	3.240	5.732
Standard Deviation (Japan, Continental Europe, and South America)			576	1.025	2.001	2.925	4.390

Note: Amounts stated in millions of constant U.S. dollars (2000 = 100).

Source: Based on companies' archives, annual reports, and other published sources.

[a] To create this table, annual reports that were available of all the firms cited in the table were used. For those where annual reports were not available, other sources such as the Hoovers.com database were utilized. n/a – not available. For some firms such as Constellation Brands, Heublein, Hiram Walker, Schenley, Grand Metropolitan, Scottish & Newcastle, Whitbread, Foster's Group, Asahi Breweries, Suntory, Moët et Chandon and Rémy Cointreau annual data is sometimes not available for the whole period covered. See Appendix 3 with Annual Sales in for Each Firm.

the world leader in the industry at the beginning of the twentieth century),[3] and Schenley (another leading U.S. spirits firm) had disappeared, having been acquired by, respectively, American Brands in 1986 (renamed Fortune Brands in 1997) and by Guinness in 1987. Other firms listed in the table, such as Seagram, disappeared. Large multinationals from insider systems such as Pernod Ricard and Inbev continued to expand during this period.

Early Development of Leading Alcoholic Beverages

There are two arguments that explain the faster development of leading alcoholic beverages firms in the United States, the United Kingdom, and Canada. One is specific to the industry and concerns the type of alcoholic beverages produced and consumed in each country. The other is of a more general scope and is consistent with the national systems perspective, and the Chandlerian explanations focused on the emergence and development of large industrial firms.

The Anglo-Saxon countries were the first to develop large firms despite the temperance movements and high tax restrictions that have affected production and consumption of alcoholic beverages since the late nineteenth century. These firms mainly produced beer or spirits, two types of beverages where it is possible to industrialize production and yet maintain the desirable characteristics of the beverage. Consequently, in such firms it was relatively easy to obtain economies of scale and scope in production and also to create branded products.[4]

In Continental Europe, in particular in the south, the trend was, by contrast, for wine production to develop first. And yet, in countries such as France, Italy, or Spain, where wine is the most popular alcoholic beverage, large wine firms, if they developed at all, only developed recently. This is due to the characteristics of wine, for which it is difficult to obtain homogeneous quality in quantity and which has been traditionally branded by region.

The firms from these Southern European countries that developed as leading multinationals had their original base in the production of processed wines or spirits based on wine, such as cognac or champagne. In France, the creation of Moët Hennessy in 1971 is a good illustration of this pattern. In Spain, a processed wine (sherry) and spirits (brandy and tequila) allowed Pedro Domecq to develop into a relatively large firm, with brands such as Don Pedro, Presidente, and Fundador. By processing wine, firms were able

---

3 Alfred D. Chandler Jr., *Strategy and Structure* (Cambridge, Mass: MIT Press, 1962).

4 This capacity of beer and spirits to be easily branded, and allow the firm to obtain economies of scale and scope, has not always existed. For a historical analysis of the evolution of pasteurization in beer and how it revolutionized trade, see, e.g., Terry Gourvish and Richard G. Wilson, *The British Brewing Industry, 1830–1980* (Cambridge: Cambridge University Press, 1994).

to mix wines from several producers and so overcome some of the limits of *terroir*.

The emphasis on the region nonetheless makes the development and expansion of branded wines difficult, due to limitations to production related to climate and the crop, as well as to the geography. Firms have more difficulty obtaining economies of scale and scope at various levels of their activity. Nonetheless, Moët Hennessy has been very good at overcoming these limitations, acquiring since 1960 vineyards in countries such as Argentina, Brazil, Germany, Austria, United States, Spain, Australia, and New Zealand. The firm does not use the word *champagne* for these products as that name is legally protected and can only be used for wines produced in the demarcated region of Champagne. Instead, its subsidiaries produce and market their sparkling wines from different countries using brand extensions such as Domaine Chandon, very similar to that of the famous champagne brand Moët & Chandon.[5]

Other explanations for the early development of these firms fit with Chandler's arguments about big business in the United States, the United Kingdom, and Canada. These countries were early industrializers, were the first to make widespread use of modern management practices (such as the disclosure of accounts), and were the first to create markets for corporate control. The large size of their markets compensated for the relatively low levels of per capita consumption of alcohol in relation to many Continental European countries.[6] The management practices and disclosure of accounts that firms in the United States and United Kingdom were required to follow, and the ways by which the information was passed between market participants, greatly improved the allocation of economic resources and the development of large multinationals in these countries.[7]

Government regulation and the procedures for mergers and acquisitions was another distinctive characteristic of these countries. The United States instituted active anti-trust measures at an early date, only a few years after the adoption of the Sherman Act in 1890. The United Kingdom took longer to adopt a monopoly policy and did not converge on the American pattern until

---

[5] "Moët-Hennessy's Strategy" (14 November 1987), Moët et Chandon, "Moët et Chandon Australia" (March 1989); "The Case of Domaine Chandon: California Wine Experience" (May 1984), all from Moët & ChandonArchive, LVMH.

[6] Chandler, *Strategy and Structure*; Leslie Hannah, *The Rise of the Corporate Economy* (London: Methuen, 1976): 102, 189; Christopher Schmitz, "The World's Largest Industrial Companies," *Business History*, Vol. 37, No. 4 (1995): 85–96; *Fortune Magazine: The Largest Industrials* (1961, 1971, 1981, 1991, 2001, 2005); Wendy Hurst, Ed Gregory, and Thomas Gussman, *Alcoholic Beverage Taxation and Control Policies* (Ottawa: Brewers Association of Canada, 1997).

[7] Eugene F. Fama, "Efficient Capital Markets II," *Journal of Finance*, Vol. 46, No. 5 (1991): 1575–617; Matthias Kipping and Ove Bjarnar, *The Americanisation of European Business: The Marshall Plan and the Transfer of US Management Models* (London: Routledge, 1998).

after World War II. Then, in 1948 the United Kingdom created the Monopolies and Restrictive Practices Commission, which was reinforced in 1956 by the Restrictive Trade Practices Act. In continental European countries and Japan, these changes only developed in the late 1950s and early 1960s, and were, in the case of Japan, of little practical significance in changing the legal setting.

Differences in Performance

There are clear differences between family and managerial firms in terms of their economic and financial performance over time. Table 4.2 shows, by decade, these differences. It indicates the evolution of several indicators of economic and financial performance of the world's largest multinationals: total sales, profitability ratio (measured as the ratio of operating profit to total sales), and return on equity (ROE) (calculated as the ratio between net earnings and equity). This table also includes an indicator of independent survival that shows, for a population of seventy-five firms analyzed, fifty-one were merged or acquired by other firms.

In the beginning of the 1960s, family firms had on average a similar level of sales to that of managerial firms and had higher profitability and lower return on equity. From the 1980s, this situation was reversed, with family firms showing on average a higher return on equity, although a lower sales volume and lower profitability. This evolution suggests that the basic goal of the managerial enterprise was growth and short-term performance. Such a finding contradicts Chandler's view about large industrial firms that have an advantage over family firms because of their long-term orientation, which contrasts with families' demands for short-term income.[8]

The evolution of the indicators shown in Table 4.2 can also be connected to the strategies followed by firms. Family firms tended to use more conservative financing policies, relying essentially on internal funds, and for that reason grew more slowly than managerial firms. They also tended to acquire firms of smaller size, usually also family owned. Nonetheless, this strategy generated on average more income for shareholders (family members) in the long term, confirming that they were not forces for conservatism and backwardness, but rather that they could compete successfully on an international basis.[9]

There were more family firms than managerial firms that did not survive. Of the total number of firms analyzed – twenty-six managerial firms and forty-nine family firms – 54 percent of managerial firms and 75 percent for

---

[8] Alfred D. Chandler Jr., "The Enduring Logic of Industrial Success," *Harvard Business Review* (March–April 1990): 138.

[9] Roy Church, "The Family Firm in Industrial Capitalism: International Perspectives on Hypothesis and History," *Business History*, Vol. 35, No. 4 (1993): 17–43; Geoffrey Jones and Mary Rose, "Family Capitalism," *Business History*, Vol. 35, No. 4 (1993): 2.

Table 4.2. *Economic and financial performance ratios of the world's largest multinationals in alcoholic beverages*[a]

Decade	Average Sales		Average Profitability		Average ROE		Merged or Acquired Firms		
	Managerial Firms	Family Firms	Managerial Firms	Family Firms	Managerial Firms	Family Firms	Managerial Firms	Family Firms	Firms Total
1960–1969	1.260	1.117	0.12	0.12	0.07	0.12	0	6	6
1970–1979	1.979	1.646	0.09	0.11	0.08	0.13	4	4	8
1980–1989	3.165	2.581	0.08	0.11	0.06	0.11	4	6	10
1990–1999	6.189	3.678	0.19	0.10	0.04	0.11	5	14	19
2000–2005	6.523	5.459	0.16	0,12	0,11	0.16	1	7	8
							14	37	51
Independent survival							12	12	24
Total firms							26	49	75

Note: Amounts stated in millions of constant U.S. dollars (2000 = 100). Profitability ratio = operating profit / sales; ROE = return on equity = net earnings / equity.

Source: Based on companies' archives, annual reports, and other published sources.

[a] The use of economic and financial indicators has the advantage of providing a clear view of the actual performance of firms and consequently of their evolution over time. However, considerable care should be taken, as these results might be distorted due to differences in accounting systems, exchange rate variations, inflation rates in the countries concerned as well as considerable currency movements.

family firms did not survive. This is in great part related to the nature of the industry, where family ownership has always predominated.

There is another apparent contradiction between the evidence provided here, where family firms predominate, and Chandler's argument about their lack of sufficient managerial resources and talent to manage the large complex enterprises of the twentieth century. Chandler believed that the failure to hand over control to professional managers inhibited both the growth and the development of organizational structures and capabilities.[10] The main explanation for this apparent contradiction lies in the industry being analyzed. Chandler was looking essentially at capital-intensive industries, where the rationale for managing firms is very different when compared to non–science-based industries such as alcoholic beverages. In the alcoholic beverages industry, which is not based on scientific advantages and where products have very long life cycles, although family members frequently keep their position as CEO and chairman of the firm, in fact their role is essentially nominal and marketing-oriented, reflecting the character of the industry.

There are several differences between capital-intensive industries and non–science-based industries, the strategic focus of firms being the most important. While in the capital-intensive industries the focus tends to be on the short run because products have very short life cycles, in non–science-based industries relying on heritage and tradition, the focus tends to be on the long run.[11]

When competition accelerated and became global, family firms that later became leaders in the industry tended to hire new entrepreneurs with wider horizons and capabilities in marketing and management of brands, executives who were able to rebuild the firms' capabilities, especially in adverse periods of stagnation and rationalization. Frequently, as a result of globalization and of competition, firms also merged with other family firms. In this process they often became publicly quoted, but families retained control of the ownership. This allowed them to raise capital and still impose their own priorities on managers, such as keeping a long-term perspective. This situation was not possible in managerial firms, where the dispersion of shares allowed managers to pursue their own objectives while protecting their positions by striving for higher sales and profitability and also a high return on investment in the short term.

The tradition of entrepreneurship and trading skills established and nourished by family firms laid the foundation for the growth of modern-day

[10] Roy Church, "The Limitation of the Personal Capitalism Paradigm," in Roy Church, Albert Fishlow, Neil Fligstein, Thomas Hughes, Jürgen Kocka, Hidemasa Morikawa, and Frederic M. Scherer, "Scale and Scope: A Review Colloquium," *Business History Review*, Vol. 64, No. 3 (1990): 704.

[11] Alfred D. Chandler Jr., *Scale and Scope: The Dynamics of Industrial Capitalism* (Cambridge, Mass: Harvard University Press, 1990): 236–94.

Management Control Systems

Ownership Structures	Personal	Managerial
Insider	Entrepreneurial based	Marketing based
Outsider	Information based	Technology based

Fig. 4.1. Industry systems of corporate governance.

managerial techniques in the food and drinks business.[12] However, the professional managers and the agents representing the shareholders hired by these firms had a fundamental role in changing the recent mindset in the industry, which increasingly became oriented toward financial performance.[13]

Combining Ownership With Corporate Control

Given the higher number and larger size of alcoholic beverages firms from the United States, United Kingdom, and Canada in the period 1961–1970, one would expect the predominant governance structures of the leading multinationals in alcoholic beverages in those countries to reflect the national systems of corporate governance. Intriguingly, the predominant governance structures in this industry were characterized in that period by insider ownership and personal control. By the beginning of the twenty-first century, however, while insider ownership still predominated, corporate control had become "managerial."

To explain this apparent contradiction, I analyze two dimensions – management control systems and ownership structures – to look at the predominant systems of corporate governance in global industries. Each of the four quadrants of the matrix in Figure 4.1 offers an alternative combination between management control systems and ownership structures.

[12] V. N. Balasubramanyam, "Entrepreneurship and the Growth of the Firm: The Case of the British Food and Drink Industries in the 1980s," in Jonathan Brown and Mary B. Rose (eds.), *Entrepreneurship, Networks and Modern Business* (Manchester: Manchester University Press, 1993).

[13] Interview with Michael Jackaman, former Chairman of Allied Domecq, Somerset, 19 June 2000; Interview with James Espey, former Chairman of Seagram Distillers and former Chairman of IDV-UK, Wimbledon, 23 February 2000.

Industries are considered to be "entrepreneurial based" when "personal" control and "insider" ownership characterize the predominant forms of governance. They tend to rely on the capabilities of the entrepreneurs, who simultaneously own and manage the firms. The entrepreneurs have superior judgment, which enables them to exploit new economic opportunities.[14]

The predominant governance structures of firms in the alcoholic beverages in the 1960s, when the industry was still fragmented and family firms predominated, was entrepreneurial. It is also possible to find other entrepreneurial global industries that are highly concentrated with a small number of very large firms. The consultancy industry is an example. Multinational firms such as McKinsey, which ranks among the world's leaders in its industry, are in fact owned by the entrepreneurial partners that simultaneously manage and control the business.

Industries are considered to be "technology based" when their predominant governance structures are characterized by "managerial" control and "outsider" ownership structures. Firms operating in this type of industry commonly appear in the rankings of the world's leading industrials such as those in the *Fortune 500* and are widely studied in business history. Chandler in *Scale and Scope* traces the management control systems and ownership structures of this kind of firms to technological innovation. Examples of leading industries that fit in this category are the chemical and automotive industries, where Ford might be characterized as the exception to the rule.

Industries are considered to be "information based" when their predominant governance structures rely on "personal" control and have "outsider" ownership structures. An example is the high-tech industry, where the founders of the firms are often their managers and have control over decision taking. However, as a result of their process of growth, the firms become publicly quoted and the entrepreneurs lose control over the ownership of shares, which become spread among a large number of shareholders. Nonetheless, as the most important input is human capital, the ability of the founders to inspire loyalty and commitment has remained important well after they surrendered financial control. For example, Apple and Microsoft are each still led by some of the members who founded the companies. The Apple case suggests that these are not simply first-generation effects in young industries. Apple tried to go for a purely managerial system when Steve Jobs, the founder, was replaced by John Scully as CEO. The subsequent collapse of Apple's fortunes, even when Scully was replaced, suggests the importance

---

[14] Mark Casson, *The Entrepreneur: An Economic Theory* (Oxford: Martin Robertson, 1982); idem, "The Entrepreneur as Coordinator," in Martin Carter, Mark Casson, and Vivek Suneja (eds.), *The Economics of Marketing* (Cheltenham: Elgar, 1998).

of the entrepreneur's vision. Apple returned to prosperity only when Jobs returned as CEO.[15]

Industries are classified as being "marketing based" when the predominant governance structures are characterized by "managerial" control and yet have "insider" ownership structures. The alcoholic beverages and cosmetics industries at the beginning of the twenty-first century where brands are often linked with family ownership are good illustrations.

Figure 4.1 provides an essentially static picture as it categorizes the predominant systems of corporate governance of industries at a particular moment in time. This figure can, however, be used in comparative statistics if applied to the study of particular industries at different periods. For example, the alcoholic beverages industry from 1960 to the beginning of the twenty-first century evolved from being "entrepreneurial based" to "marketing based."[16]

Most industries that are "technology based," "marketing based," or "information based" are usually in advanced stages in their evolution, having started by being "entrepreneurial based." However, as already mentioned, "entrepreneurial based" industries may also correspond to advanced stages in their development. These processes of evolution of corporate governance do not, therefore, necessarily converge on one particular type, but reflect adaptations to the different requirements in these industries.

Industries that became "information based" were able to grow by keeping "personal" management control systems characterized by simple organization structures and centralization of decision taking. They changed their ownership structures into "outsider" based, when they required high capital investments. In contrast, the industries that moved from being "entrepreneurial based" to "marketing based" developed complex organization structures as a result of their expansion in terms of business activities and geographical scope of operations. They became "managerial based," but required relatively low capital investments when compared with "technology based" industries. They were, however, able to keep "insider" ownership as shares remained in the hands of a small number of investors.

Marketing-Based Industries

Despite the extensive literature, there are no systematic accounts of the wide range of combinations of ownership and control that corporations are increasingly forming, perhaps because the Chandlerian model tends to assume all governance is converging. By focusing on "marketing based"

---

[15] William Gates, *The Road Ahead* (London: Viking, 1996); Jim Carleton, *Apple: The Insider Story of Intrigue, Egomania and Business Blunders* (New York: Times Business Books, 1997).

[16] A similar analysis could be made for the predominant governance structures of other industries over time, but that is beyond the reach of this study.

systems of corporate governance, this book associates the evolution of ownership and control in the alcoholic beverages industry with the increasing impact of marketing knowledge in the growth and survival of firms.

At the early stages of the life of a firm, marketing knowledge is essentially "sticky."[17] For example, when the entrepreneur (or founder) has an idea such as a new brand, the routines and procedures that he creates for its implementation are "sticky" to the firm. It is important to distinguish between the concept of "sticky" marketing knowledge from that of procedures. While procedures embody the perception of the business problems and strategic solutions of the entrepreneur, knowledge resides in the minds of particular individuals (such as marketing managers or the CEO of the firm). In contrast to procedures, knowledge is not as easily shared with other people in the organization. Procedures and routines monitor and cope with short-term volatility and enhance decision taking and organizational actions.[18] Knowledge represents a strategic response to long-term challenges.

As time passes, some of the routines become obsolete and if not abandoned may threaten the brand. If the brand succeeds, it is necessary to acquire marketing knowledge to keep the brand alive and rejuvenate it. The manager needs to have the capabilities to update such routines, to adapt the brand to changing consumer preferences. While the firm is still small, it is possible for the entrepreneur to centralize the management, ownership, and control of the firm.

Once organizational complexity and diversity increases, the entrepreneur needs to acquire "smooth" marketing knowledge by hiring professional managers. These professional managers have the credentials that will allow them to update the routines and procedures developed by the entrepreneur, and also deal with short-term volatility. On the other hand, the entrepreneur can concentrate on long-term issues, such as building new routines if exogenous shocks occur, making existing knowledge obsolete.[19] He also has more availability for valuing brands and looking at their future earnings.

Corporate Control

National systems perspectives tend to explain family control on the basis of the existence of illiquid markets, and vulnerable businesses, especially in adverse economic environments. However, in the global alcoholic beverages industry, none of these reasons explains the predominance of family businesses even in countries such as the United States. There are other reasons not

---

[17] See Chapter 1 for a definition of "sticky" and "smooth" marketing knowledge.

[18] They may include procedures for the procurement of raw materials, production process, bottling, ageing distribution system, and sales and marketing of the brand.

[19] Christiansen Clayton, *The Innovator's Dilemma* (Cambridge, Mass: Harvard University Press, 1996).

directly connected with financial interests that seem to explain such trends. They include "private benefits" such as the pursuit of dominance, the ambition to perpetuate the family name, and the search for recognition, honor, and prestige rather than performance-related pay, factors usually mentioned in studies on the endurance of firms.[20]

These family firms succeed in separating ownership from control by keeping a position on the boards, where decisions that have long-term implications in the evolution of firms are taken. This is evident in firms such as Bacardi and Heineken, which in the beginning of the twenty-first century remained owned by families. However, they had switched from using family members as managers to hiring professional managers to run their businesses, while the families nonetheless retained ultimate control. In Bacardi, this switch took place in 1996 with the appointment of a professional manager as CEO to replace the great-great-grandson of the founder. Initially this change in management caused some friction among shareholders (around 500 heirs of Don Facundo Bacardi, the founder of the firm), not only because the newly appointed CEO was the first not to be a family member, but also because he had been previously a mergers and acquisitions specialist in a Washington law firm with no operating experience in the consumer goods industry.[21]

At Heineken, this switch took place in 1989 with the retirement of A. H. Heineken. The chairmanship passed to a professional manager who had been working for the company for his whole career. However, like Bacardi, Heineken remained a family-controlled firm, with Mr. Heineken (and after his death, his daughter) owning 50.5 percent of the shares of Heineken's holding company, which controlled 50.5 percent of the Heineken brewery.[22]

The switch from personal control systems to managerial control is not, however, always so straightforward. In some cases, family members remain as top executives of the firms, sharing the day-to-day management with hired professionals. In other cases, they delegate the day-to-day management totally to professionals and become nonexecutive top managers. Anheuser-Busch, Brown Forman, and Pernod Ricard, are illustrations of the distinct nature that family control may have.

[20] Colin Mayer, "Firm Control," Inaugural Lecture delivered to the University of Oxford, 18 February 1999.
[21] Mr. Reid had been an adviser in the creation of a single global holding company in 1992 to unify five separate operations of Bacardi in 1992, and had advised Bacardi on the $2 billion acquisition in 1993 of Martini & Rossi, the Italian-owned drinks group. In 2000 he resigned, after the company decided not to proceed with a planned initial public offering. He was replaced by Ruben Rodriguez, another hired professional manager who became CEO and chairman of the group. "A Spirited Strategist," *Financial Times* (8 March 1999).
[22] Interview with Jan Beijerinck, former Worldwide Client Services Director of Heineken, Utrecht, 10 March 2001; Heineken, Annual Reports and Accounts (1989); "Head of Heineken Brewing Family Dies Aged 78," *Financial Times* (4 January 2002).

At the end of the twentieth century, August A. Busch III served as chairman of Anheuser-Busch. However, in the year 2000, the firm appointed a professional manager as CEO and president. He had been working for Anheuser-Busch for thirty-one years and had a wide knowledge of the firm and the industry (being involved in building the company's global leadership position). However, August A. Busch III remained as chairman.[23]

At Brown Forman, the chairman and CEO – Owsley Brown II – was also a family member. But, like Augustus Busch III, in 2000 Mr. Brown II appointed a graduate from Princeton and Harvard Business School, who had been working for the company since 1963, as president of Brown Forman.[24]

Since the merger in 1975, Pernod Ricard was run by a professional manager who married into the Pernod family, playing a key role in the creation of the group Pernod Ricard. In 2000, after his retirement as president, Mr. Jacquillat became vice-chairman, and Patrick Ricard, another family member, became the chairman and CEO of the firm. In addition, two joint managing directors were hired to run the business, neither of whom was a family member. One had previously served as chairman of Irish Distillers, and the other had been chairman of Pernod Europe.[25]

Seagram hired professional managers to run the business after the death of the founder, Samuel Bronfman, in 1971. One of the managers, Phillip Beekam, who had previously been president of Colgate International, played an important role in the introduction of marketing techniques at Seagram during the 1970s. Throughout this period, Edgar and Charles Bronfman, the two sons of the founder, kept their positions as chairman and CEO, thus ensuring tight control of decision taking.[26] Seagram reversed the trend toward independent management in 1990, when Edgar Bronfman Jr., the grandson of the founder, took over the management of the firm, until it was sold to Vivendi in 2001.[27]

Concentrated Ownership: Does It Matter?

This raises the question of whether it matters if ownership is dispersed or controlled by a family, provided that there is professional management running the firm. The evidence provided by the alcoholic beverages industry indicates that having ownership concentrated in the hands of a small number of

[23] "St. Louis-based Anheuser-Busch announces new CEO," *St. Louis Post-Dispatch* (30 July 2000).
[24] "Brown Forman Names Street President of the corporation," *PR Newswire* (15 November 2000).
[25] Pernod-Ricard, Annual Report and Accounts (2000).
[26] "Records of the Seagram Company Ltd.," Record Group 2, Accession 2126, Hagley Museum and Library; Edgar M. Bronfman, *Good Spirits: The Making of a Businessman* (New York: Putman's, 1998); The Seagram Company Ltd, Annual Report and Accounts (1971, 1977).
[27] The Seagram Company Ltd., Annual Report and Accounts (1989, 1990).

shareholders, in particular families, has had important implications in the growth and survival of firms and the evolution of the industry in general.

There are two arguments supporting this. One is of broader application, and concerns the capacity of firms to overcome the free-rider problems that afflict capital markets with dispersed ownership, and also regulation systems (e.g., such as investor protection).[28]

The most important reasons are, however, specific to the global alcoholic beverages industry. In some sectors, such as whisky, port wine or sherry, brand image is often associated with heritage. Having family members who also represent the living icons of the brands enhances the heritage image of those brands. A more important reason concerns the longevity of brands. Families tend to take more long-term views than professional managers in their investment decisions. However, the strategies may differ, and depend on the cultural environment of those firms.[29] Similar reasoning may be applied to the lives of brands. The evidence provided by the world's most successful alcoholic beverages brands shows that most are long established, and some go as far back as the eighteenth and nineteenth centuries.[30]

A final reason why family ownership predominates in this industry relates to the private interests of the entrepreneurs, such as ambition to build an empire, or preserve the family name, which can be achieved because the capital required for investment is primarily for marketing, and can be obtained from retained profits, without the firm having to recur to capital markets.

The Case of LVMH

Despite the waves of mergers and acquisitions that occurred in the alcoholic beverages industry from the 1960s, family members often remained as shareholders of the acquiring firms, taking nonexecutive positions on the boards. The ownership structure of LVMH after the 1987 merger of Moët Hennessy with Louis Vuitton is a good illustration of this situation.

The merger between Moët & Chandon and Hennessy in 1971 united France's biggest exporters of champagne and cognac, respectively, allowing the two companies to take advantage of their similarities in terms of the "personalities" of their brands and the geographical scope of operations, as well as to economize on costs of, for example, distribution.[31]

---

[28] A. Schleifer and R. W. Vishny, "Large Shareholders and Corporate Control," *Journal of Political Economy*, Vol. 94 (1986): 461–88; R. La Porta, F. Lopez-de-Silanes, A. Schleifer, and R. Vishny, "Legal Determinants of External Finance," *Journal of Finance*, No. 52 (1997): 1131–50.

[29] Jones and Rose, "Family Capitalism"; Church, "The Family."

[30] Paul Duguid, "Developing the Brand: The Case of Alcohol, 1800–1880," *Enterprise & Society*, Vol. 4, No. 3 (2003): 405–41.

[31] "Records of Moët et Chandon, 1971," LVMH; Moët-Hennessy, Annual Report and Accounts (1971).

In 1987, the families of the newly merged multinational hired a professional manager, Bernard Arnault, who had graduated from the elite École Polytechnique, worked for his family firm dealing in real estate, and lived in New York, where he had learned about the aggressiveness of the stock market. When he took over the management of LVMH, he embarked on a fast and aggressive process of mergers and acquisitions of other alcoholic beverages firms, and other French luxury businesses as well, showing an enormous capacity to detect opportunities and deal with adversity. In this process, he also became the major shareholder of this French multinational.[32]

By 1988, there were four groups of shareholders: 32 percent of the capital was held by the consortium Financière Agache and Guinness headed by Bernard Arnault; 14 percent was held by the Chandon, Moët, Mercier, and Hennessy families; 23 percent by the Vuitton family, and 31 percent by the public. The board comprised twelve members, four from the Agache/Guinness group, four from the Vuitton family, and four from the Moët Hennessy family.[33] The tight links established between the majority shareholders and the board of directors reduced the risk of opportunistic behavior by the management of the firm (a risk considered to exist when the shares are widely dispersed among a large number of shareholders, and no single shareholder is in a position to control the affairs of the firm). Minority shareholders had no representation on the board at that time, even though the firm was publicly quoted.

The case of LVMH also illustrates another trend in the corporate governance of alcoholic beverages firms, the creation of interlocking shareholdings. The British whisky and gin producer Distillers Company had a profound role in the foundation and rise of Distillers Corporation, later renamed Seagram. With the formation of LVMH, Guinness became a shareholder together with Financière Agache through a holding company called Jacques Rober (60 percent owned by Financière Agache and 40 percent by Guinness). Conversely, LVMH acquired Guinness's shares, obtaining a 12 percent ownership in that firm. Despite Bernard Arnault's initial opposition to the merger of Guinness with Grand Metropolitan to form Diageo in 1997, this interlocking shareholding between the two firms remained until the beginning of the twenty-first century, and there have been only a few changes in the percentages of the interlocked shareholdings.[34]

Together with interlocking shareholdings, it is common for firms to have interlocking directorships. For example, at the time of the LVMH merger, Bernard Arnault, who became the company's chairman, also had a position

[32] Michel Refait, *Moët & Chandon: de Claude Moët à Bernard Arnault* (Saints-Geosmes: Dominique Guéniot, 1998).
[33] Barclays de Zoete Wedd, LVMH (1988).
[34] "Cognac Threat to Diageo Deal," *The Independent on Sunday* (23 July 2000).

on Guinness's board of directors. Conversely, Anthony Tennant, Guinness's chairman, had a position on LVMH supervisory board.[35]

But multiple directorships may also exist independently of interlocking shareholdings. For example, by 2000, Bernard Arnault was also on the board of directors of other firms, including Vivendi.[36] These multiple directorships, which usually occur among large firms, are thought not only to bring prestige to the directors and the firms they manage, but also to reduce transaction costs, when the firms involved have transactions among themselves. In this sense, multiple directorships can be considered as a hybrid mode for organizing transactions, which lies midway between markets and hierarchies.[37] The case of Bernard Arnault's participation in Vivendi's board of directors provides, however, an additional insight into the mixture of cooperation and competition that interlocking directorships may create in the alcoholic beverages industry. He would have had an interesting view of the fate of Seagram, which, as mentioned earlier, was first bought by Vivendi, before its alcoholic beverages business was sold to Diageo (which owns a substantial share of Arnault's LVMH) and Pernod Ricard, an important French competitor.

Other Sources of Concentration of Shareholdings

It is not only families that concentrate ownership of firms. Financial intermediaries such as banks, insurance companies and pension funds have also contributed to a reconcentration of corporate power in the global alcoholic beverages industry. Even when families control the firms, these institutions tend to have a substantial number of shares traded through the capital markets. An example is Pernod Ricard, in which the French bank Société Générale has an indirect ownership corresponding to 5.6 percent.[38]

Carlsberg, the leading Danish brewer is yet another case. It is controlled by a foundation formed by the founder in 1906. In 2000, the Carlsberg Foundation owned 55 percent of the shares, other Danish investors such as banks, insurance companies, and pension funds controlled 28.5 percent, and foreign institutional investors controlled 16.5 percent.[39] This association with other institutions through their investment in the capital of alcoholic beverages firms may bring several benefits for firms, such as obtaining better

---

[35] Guinness, Annual Report and Accounts (1988); LVMH, Annual Report and Accounts (1988).

[36] Vivendi, Annual Report and Accounts (2000).

[37] Oliver E. Williamson, *Markets and Hierarchies* (New York: Free Press, 1975); Frans N. Stockman, Rolf Ziegler, and John Scott, *Networks of Corporate Power: A Comparative Analysis of Ten Countries* (Cambridge: Polity, 1985): 274.

[38] Pernod Ricard, Annual Report and Accounts (2001).

[39] Carlsberg, Annual Report and Accounts (1999/2000).

banks loans, as these tend to accept a higher risk in financing their own entrepreneurial ventures.[40]

Conclusion

The United States and United Kingdom tended to develop large firms earlier than Continental Europe and Japan. However, by the beginning of the twenty-first century, Continental Europe and Japan had also developed leading multinationals. Regardless of national systems of corporate governance, family ownership remained predominant in alcoholic beverages, even though certain managerial firms (such as Diageo and SABMiller) had also become very important as the industry consolidated internationally.

Initially firms were entrepreneurial based, with ownership and corporate control concentrated in the hands of a small group of investors, mainly families. Over time, they developed distinct institutional arrangements, becoming marketing based. Ownership tended to remain concentrated in the hands of families or restricted groups of investors, but corporate control was now in the hands of professional managers.

There are several reasons behind the apparent discordance between the existing literature on national systems of corporate governance, and the actual institutional arrangements that predominate in the global alcoholic beverages industry by the beginning of the twenty-first century. The first is that those studies tend to make generalizations based on industries and firms that are dominant in their countries' economies. The second is that different industries require distinct corporate capabilities. It is the way in which these capabilities evolved over time that leads firms to adapt their ownership and control structures.

In some industries such as automotive or pharmaceuticals, which are technology based, the predominant governance structures of firms adapted by having dispersed ownership of shares and managerial corporate control. In other industries such as alcoholic beverages or cosmetics, where the distinctive capabilities required by firms are marketing knowledge, systems adapted by keeping insider ownership structures but switched to managerial control. This knowledge, which basically relates to the management of brands, has two main parts. One part is "sticky" to the firm, and is accumulated over time. Another part is "smooth," and may be acquired in the short run by hiring professional managers. As a result of their growth, most firms tended to acquire "smooth" knowledge, and to switch from "personal" to "managerial" control. In this process, it was possible for ownership to remain concentrated due to the characteristics of the businesses, where the main investments are in marketing and brand management, and where the cash

---

[40] Naomi R. Lamoreaux, *Insider Lending* (Cambridge: Cambridge University Press, 1994): 9.

flows generated by the operations of firms tend to be sufficient to cover those investments.

This study shows that as we move from looking at countries to looking at industries and firms, the picture is quite different from that claimed in the literature on the evolution of systems of corporate governance. In global industries that are not dominant in any single country's economy, the predominant systems of corporate governance may evolve into a wide range of combinations of ownership and control.

5

Channel Management

Introduction

Over time, the manner in which finished products were handled and delivered to the final consumers of alcoholic beverages changed substantially. While in many countries the wholesaler was traditionally the major intermediary between the producer and the retailer, in some countries other modes of distribution also developed. Interestingly, a number of direct competitors have created distribution alliances. This chapter explores the rationale behind the creation and evolution of different modes of distribution, and, in particular, of alliances that involved only producers, or producers and distributors (mainly wholesalers). I analyze the different levels of commitment by multinationals and provide an overview of the long-term patterns in the global distribution of this product.

Differing Levels of Commitment, 1960s

During the 1960s, alcoholic beverages firms from different parts of the world had distinct forms of distribution. In the United States, wholesalers were starting to concentrate at a regional or state level.[1] In Europe, retailers entered into direct marketing relationships with producers, increasingly bypassing the wholesalers. As distributors grew in size and power, they reduced the number of purchasing channels and suppliers lost bargaining power. Many were at the mercy of retailers. The development of large-scale supermarkets and hypermarkets made it very difficult for beverage producers to integrate vertically into retailing (either outright or through contractual agreements) and remain competitive, as that would have entailed disposing of brands and other kinds of products from competing firms.[2] Large retailers, such as Sainsbury (in the United Kingdom) and Carrefour (in France) sold a wide range of consumer goods, often under their own private label.

---

[1] Richard S. Tedlow, *New and Improved – The Story of Mass Marketing in America* (Oxford: Heinemann, 1990); Erdener Kaynak (ed.), *Trans-National Retailing* (New York: Walter de Gruyter, 1988); Luca Pellegrini and Srinivas K. Reddy (eds.), *Retail and Marketing Channels* (London: Routledge, 1989).

[2] Pellegrini and Reddy (eds.), *Retail and Marketing Channels*:18.

Cooperating directly with the producers, they eliminated the role of the wholesaler and sold products at great discount.[3]

This was also a period when in the United Kingdom there was a widespread growth of specialist outlets, such as "off-licenses," that sold only alcoholic beverages. The end of resale price maintenance and the development of large retail units such as supermarkets in the 1960s meant that distributors could now cover wider regions and even neighboring countries.[4]

The structure of distribution was also greatly affected by the use of new systems of storage, stockholding, and warehousing, including the development of stainless steel casks and aluminum containers. These developments allowed better cleaning and refrigeration, which, with the advent of pasteurization, helped stabilize the products in containers and reduce maintenance. Major changes in logistics, especially with the growth of large-scale computerized warehouses, allowed firms to centralize their stockholding and obtain economies of scale.[5]

While alliances between direct competitors in alcoholic beverages had developed in the United Kingdom and the United States since Prohibition in the 1930s,[6] in Europe they were still very unusual as late as the 1960s. These alliances provided economies of scale and scope in distribution and also minimized risk and the uncertainty related to their operations in foreign markets. In other parts of the world such as Japan, however, the industries were still very closed to foreign direct investment and alliances were nonexistent.

United Kingdom – Development of Alliances Between Competitors

The United Kingdom was the first to develop distribution alliances between direct competitors. The growth of incomes in the 1960s was accompanied by a liberalization of prices. Changes in the taxation of alcoholic beverages and licensing laws allowed "off-licenses" to keep shops open for long

---

[3] Peter Jones, Colin Clarke-Hill, David Hillier, and Peter Shears, "A Case of Bargain Booze," *British Food Journal*, Vol. 103, No. 7 (2001): 453–59; Asa Briggs, *Wine for Sale: Victoria Wine and the Liquor Trade, 1860–1984* (London: Bastford, 1985): 160; Frederick F. Clairmonte and John Cavanagh, *Merchants of Drink: Transnational Control of World Beverages* (Penang: Third World Network, 1988): 176.

[4] See Appendix 6 for a definition of *distributors*, *supermarkets*, and *hypermarkets*.

[5] Tim Unwin, *The Wine and the Vine* (London: Routledge, 1992): 546.

[6] For example, Distillers from the United Kingdom formed several alliances in the United States and Canada after Prohibition with companies such as National Distillers, and Distillers Corporation (later renamed as Seagram). Ronald B. Weir, *The History of Distillers Company 1877–1939* (Oxford: Oxford University Press, 1995): 261, 271–72, 277–78; Peter Foster, *Family Spirits: The Bacardi Saga* (Toronto: MacFarlane Walter & Ross, 1990): 53; "Agreement Between Distillers Company Ltd (in the United Kingdom) and Distillers Corporation (in Canada)," 1927, Box 93 (Seagram Collection, Hagley Museum and Library).

hours and made it much easier for restaurants to obtain liquor licenses. The growth and geographical dissemination of supermarkets and hypermarkets that could sell wine all day at cheaper prices played a very important role in stimulating wine consumption and in ending the elite image of wine. By offering information about how to combine wine with food, these markets encouraged an increasing number of consumers in this traditionally beer and spirit drinking nation to acquire wine drinking habits.[7] Internationally, most firms relied on third parties to distribute their beverages.

Distillers Company ranked as the largest alcoholic beverages firm in sales volume until the late 1960s. Foreign sales accounted for nearly 50 percent of its activity, with whisky and gin corresponding to around 80 percent of total sales (the remaining 20 percent came from chemicals and plastics). Essentially, its strategy was based on high volume, low prices, and international distribution. Its foreign direct investment, in France, Australia, Brazil, Canada, the United States, and South Africa, was primarily in the production of gin. Distillers Company also had a few investments in distribution. For example, in 1958 it opened a warehouse and bottling unit in New Zealand in order to overcome progressive restrictions to imports. In 1967 it acquired a 70 percent share in the French company Simon Frères Ltd., which had been the distributor for Johnnie Walker & Sons, Ltd. In the domestic market, Distillers Company acquired several old scotch whisky brokers such as Messrs. Ross & Coulter Ltd. in 1954. Nonetheless, for most of its sales in foreign markets, Distillers Company relied on independent distributors.[8]

Allied Breweries was the second largest British firm in sales volume during the 1960s. It concentrated on the production of beer for the domestic market and the sale of alcoholic beverages through a vast chain of licensed houses (pubs and inns). It owned Victoria Wine, a large wine and spirits retail chain, which had been taken over by Ind. Coope in 1959.[9] The acquisition in 1966 of Showerings, a leading British wine merchant (which had itself acquired Harveys), allowed Allied Breweries to gain control of the distribution of its beverages in the United Kingdom. It was also able to acquire marketing knowledge about the domestic market, and the management of brands in the wines and spirits business in general.

Guinness was the third largest firm operating in the United Kingdom during this period. The firm had some production operations in developing countries of the Commonwealth. In Nigeria, for instance, Guinness had a joint venture operation with the Anglo-Dutch consumer goods multinational

[7] Unwin, *The Wine and the Vine*: 341.

[8] The Distillers Company Limited, *Annual Report and Accounts* (1961–1970); *D.C.L. Gazette*, Winter (1967): 209–11; Ronald Weir, "List of DCL Acquisitions, 1940–1986" (York, 1999, mimeo).

[9] Allied Breweries, Annual Reports and Accounts (1961); Briggs, *Wine for Sale*: 134.

Unilever,[10] allowing the company to acquire market knowledge about the operation without incurring much risk.

The other large British firms, Bass, Scottish & Newcastle, Truman, Watney Mann, and Whitbread, were all in the brewing business. They tended to have essentially national coverage, distributing either through their own subsidiary companies, independent bottling companies (traditionally very important in the case of beer), or through reciprocal trade agreements that provided economies of scale and scope in distribution. Reciprocal trade agreements had the additional advantage of giving the owners of the brands national coverage without the costs of acquiring and managing a national chain of public houses. Whitbread was the leading practitioner of this strategy. The firm frequently cemented these arrangements by acquiring a small but significant share of the trading partner's equity.[11]

North America – Domestic Distributors of Foreign Brands

In the United States, the firms that had developed very rapidly during this period were Anheuser-Busch, Seagram, Hiram Walker, Heublein, Schenley and National Distillers.[12] National Distillers, the leading alcoholic beverages firm in the 1960s, had an important import business that involved several alliances (long-term distribution agreements) with producers of successful brands from Europe, Canada, and the Caribbean. These alliances were in part the result of attempts by foreign firms to overcome the high barriers to entry imposed by the U.S. three-tier distribution system. This system had emerged after Prohibition to prevent a repeat of the pre-Prohibition "tied house evils," where saloons were controlled by distillers and brewers and therefore had a vested interest in encouraging excessive drinking. The new distribution system, which still applies today, did not permit firms to be vertically integrated, and required that the channels used for the distribution of alcoholic beverages be distinct according to their type and level of alcohol content. Thus, beer is usually distributed through different channels from wines and spirits. Under the three-tier system producers are prohibited from shipping directly to retailers and consumers, as goods have to pass physically through the hands of at least one intermediary. A similar situation applies to importers of alcoholic beverages, where wholesaling

---

[10] Terry Gourvish and Richard G. Wilson, *The British Brewing Industry, 1830–1980* (Cambridge: Cambridge University Press, 1994): 453; S. R. Dennisson and Oliver MacDonagh, *Guinness 1886–1939: From Incorporation to the Second World War* (Dublin: Cork University Press, 1998): 202.

[11] K. H. Hawkins and C. L. Pass, *The Brewing Industry* (London: Heinemann, 1979): 53, 57. See, e.g., Whitbread, Annual Reports and Accounts (1961): 8–9.

[12] Although Seagram and Hiram Walker were two Canadian firms, they were running most of their operations in the United States.

(usually handled at a state level) and retailing have to be performed by distinct parties.[13]

During this period, National Distillers started to consolidate its position in the domestic market by acquiring distributors/importers. In 1962, it bought Peel Richards Ltd., a company that for the previous twelve years had been responsible for the distribution in New York of most of National Distillers' brands. In 1963, it acquired another wholesaler, Munson G. Shaw Co. Inc., which added well-accepted imported brands such as Cockburn port, Cossart-Gordon madeira, Bertolli Italian wines, and the wines of Baron Philippe de Rothschild to its portfolio. The acquisition also expanded the sales force of the firm.[14]

Schenley was another firm with a very large imports business and sales organization in the United States. Brands imported by Schenley through distribution agreements included Dewar's Scotch whisky and Mateus Rosé, a Portuguese wine. Although it also owned sales organizations in foreign markets, by 1970 exports only accounted for 6.6 percent of total sales (distributed essentially through sales organizations in eleven countries).[15]

Heublein developed very rapidly in the 1960s, mainly as a result of its activity in the domestic market, and, in particular, the success achieved with the vodka brand Smirnoff. It also distributed other beverages as a result of the alliances formed with leading European beverage brand owners. These included Harveys Bristol Cream (beginning in 1959), Lancers Vin Rose, a Portuguese wine (that became the largest selling imported wine of its type in the United States from 1965), Gilbey's Black Velvet, and McMaster Canadian whiskeys (from 1967). Several of the alliances involved reciprocal transactions. For example, Heublein's alliance with Gilbey's also involved the license for the latter to produce Smirnoff vodka in several markets including Ireland and the United Kingdom. As a result of its successful growth, Heublein appeared among the top 500 U.S. corporations in 1966 for the first time. In 1967, it became the largest U.S. importer of wines and spirits, with a sales force spread throughout the country.[16] Heublein acquired several distributors and formed strategic alliances in production. For example, in 1968 it acquired Don Q Imports Inc., the U.S. distributor of Puerto Rico's leading brand of rum. In the same year, it also formed an alliance with José Maria da Fonseca in Portugal to set up a plant that would more than double production of Lancers.[17]

The changing nature of alliances and the role and level of control of each partner over the management of the brand also led to the termination of some

[13] Brian Newkirk and Rob Atkinson, "Buying Wine Online – Rethinking the 21st Amendment for the 21st Century," *Policy Report* (January 2003).

[14] National Distillers, Annual Reports and Accounts (1962, 1963).

[15] Schenley, Annual Report and Accounts (1963, 1970).

[16] Heublein, Annual Report and Accounts (various years).   [17] Ibid.

alliances. For instance, in 1965, Heublein terminated the arrangements with Guinness and L. Rose & Co. for Guinness Stout and Rose's Lime Juice, respectively. This was the result of disagreements concerning the marketing of the brands in the United States, where the producing firms wanted to have more control over their management than Heublein would allow.[18]

U.S. firms tended to use different modes for distributing their own and their partner's brands. Brown Forman, for instance, used a separate sales force to distribute imported brands. Some of the imported brands they distributed during the 1960s were Veuve Cliquot champagne; Usher's Green Stripe Scotch; Bols liqueurs, brandies, and gin; Ambassador Scotch; Old Bushmills Irish whiskey, and Martell.[19]

There were two leading Canadian alcoholic beverages firms, Hiram Walker and Seagram, that had an important position in the U.S. market during this period. They had their own distribution channels that dealt with the wholesalers in various regions of the country. Apart from selling in the United States, Seagram was doing business in several other parts of the world. It had invested in wholly owned operations in countries such as Belgium, Argentina, and Venezuela.[20]

Continental Europe – In Strategic Markets

There were many differences between the development of firms in Continental European countries and those from the United States and the United Kingdom. Leading Continental European firms, for instance, tended to have a high ratio of exports to total sales, whereas only a few Anglo-Saxon firms (such as Distillers Company) generated a significant part of their sales in foreign markets.[21] Continental European firms were smaller in size, remained family owned and controlled, and were part of distribution systems that were much more fragmented.[22] The firms tended to concentrate their sales among a smaller number of distributors. In some cases, they integrated vertically into distribution in their domestic markets and in foreign markets considered to

---

[18] Heublein, Annual Reports and Accounts (1965).

[19] Brown Forman, Annual Reports and Accounts (various years); William F. Lucas, "Nothing Better in the Market: Brown Forman's Century of Quality 1870–1970," *The Newcomen Society in North America* (New York: Newcomen Society, 1970).

[20] Distillers Corporation – Seagrams Ltd., Annual Report and Accounts (1960–1970); Seagram, Annual Report and Accounts (1984); Samuel Bronfman, "...From Little Acorns...," in Distillers Corporation – Seagrams Ltd., Annual Report and Accounts (1970): 73.

[21] For example, Moët & Chandon in 1960 exported 49 percent of its sales, to 113 countries (Moët & Chandon, Annual Report and Accounts, 1960). Distillers Corporation, Annual Report and Accounts (1961–1970).

[22] James B. Jeffreys and Derek Knee, *Retailing in Europe: Present Structure and Future Trends* (London: Macmillan, 1962): 25. For example, in 1955 the number of retail establishments in France was 755,000 and in the United Kingdom was 596,000, corresponding respectively to 57 and 86 inhabitants per retail establishment.

be strategic.[23] For example, in 1957, Moët & Chandon acquired its former agent in the United Kingdom, Simon Brothers & Co. At the time of this acquisition, that market represented 20 percent of the firm's total exports, in a period when the total number of markets of destination for their champagne was 108.[24]

It is also during the 1960s that continental European firms started to form distribution alliances with direct competitors, sometimes from different countries, at other times from the same country. For example, by 1967, Moët & Chandon had alliances with leading alcoholic beverages firms such as Heineken and Distillers Company. Through its sales organization, S.A. France Champagne, which consisted of eighteen agents each working a given region and using subagents and representatives, Moët & Chandon sold Heineken beer, J&B Rare Scotch whisky, and the liqueur Erven Lucas Bols.[25] Another example was the alliance created in 1967 between the French firms Cointreau, Izarra, and Rémy Martin, which were direct competitors. This alliance led to the creation of Rivière Distribution, which sold their products in both the domestic and foreign markets, particularly in Europe.[26]

In the Netherlands, there were several firms that by the 1960s were already highly internationalized. Heineken, for example, had been managed in the United States by a distributor, Van Munching, since 1945. In 1992, Heineken acquired this distributor, as Van Munching's heirs had no interest in the business and also because this family firm was losing its competitiveness given the changes that were occurring in distribution. In the United States, this brand was positioned as a beer for special occasions, consumed primarily in the on-premise market. This helps explain why Heineken's management decided never to produce locally.[27] The firm formed alliances in other foreign markets to overcome entry barriers such as high import duties and high transportation costs associated with large geographical distances. In the United Kingdom, Heineken had an alliance with Whitbread during the 1960s. This permitted the firm to penetrate that market in a period in which distribution was dominated by breweries, most of whom owned pubs.[28] The early alliances established by Heineken in France to overcome the ceilings established by the

---

[23] See, e.g., Philippe Roudié, "Une Vénérable Entreprise Bordelaise de Liqueurs Marie Brizard et Roger," in Alain Huetz de Lemps and Philippe Roudié (eds.), *Eaux-de-Vie et Spiritueux* (Paris: Centre National de Recherche Scientifique, 1985): 295–300.

[24] Moët & Chandon, Annual Report and Accounts (1957).   [25] Ibid (1968).

[26] Jacques Jeanneau, "La Société Cointreau, D'Angers au Marché Mondial," and Pierre Laborde, "*La Société Izarra de Bayonne*," both in Huetz de Lemps and Roudié, *Eaux-de-Vie*: 307–20.

[27] Interview with Jan Beijerinck, former Worldwide Client Services Director of Heineken, Utrecht, 10 March 2001.

[28] Heineken, Annual Reports and Accounts (1960–1961); M. G. P. A. Jacobs and W. H. G. Mass, *Heineken History* (Amsterdam: De Bussy Ellerman Harms bv., 1992): 264, 270, 287–88.

local government on imports of alcoholic beverages after World War II were not very successful. It was only after 1961 when Heineken appointed Moët & Chandon as its general importer that sales started to develop. Moët & Chandon had a powerful, countrywide, modern sales organization and distribution network and could obtain a higher level of economies of scale and scope in distribution, selling different brands.[29] This alliance ended in 1972, when Heineken acquired a majority interest in Alsaciène de Brasserie group (Albra), owner of the Mützig beer brand.[30] De Kuyper, another Dutch firm that before the War had been relatively large and had an internationalized Genever and liqueurs business, did not profit as much as it could have from the economic prosperity of the 1960s. However, it kept its old established alliances with companies such as National Distillers.[31]

The Danish brewers, Carlsberg and Tuborg, held almost a monopoly position in Denmark in the 1960s. There, they used exclusive distributors, which were only allowed to carry brands of a single brewery. In foreign markets they used local distributors, which handled competing beer brands. These distinct strategies matched the different objectives the firm had for each market. In Denmark, the aim was to remain a leader in the industry and extract as much rent as possible, drawing to a great extent on their reputation and image; in foreign markets, minimization of risk and uncertainty were the main concerns. Often, the distributors in foreign markets were leading local alcoholic beverages firms. For instance, in the United Kingdom, Carlsberg had a distribution agreement with Grand Metropolitan that enabled its beers to be distributed through the latter's pubs and retail outlets.[32]

Japan – Focus on Distribution of Domestic Beverages

Distribution in Japan also evolved after World War II, following the changing habits of consumption and the transformation in the structure of the alcoholic beverages industry. Rapid economic growth and remarkable economic changes took place. Concentration within both the manufacturing and retailing sides forced changes in the traditional distribution structure.[33] Although Asahi Breweries, Kirin, Sapporo, and Suntory developed during this period,

[29] Interview with Jan Beijerink, former Worldwide Client Services Director, Utrecht, 10 March 2001; Jacobs and Mass, *Heineken*: 294–96.

[30] Heineken, Annual Reports and Accounts (1972–1973).

[31] K. E. Sluyterman and H. H. Vleesenbeek, *Three Centuries of De Kuyper 1695–1995* (Shiedam: Prepress Center Assen, 1995): 69, 79.

[32] Hans Chr. Johansen, "Marketing and Competition in Danish Brewing," in Geoffrey Jones and Nicholas J. Morgan (eds.), *Adding Value: Brands and Marketing in Food and Drink* (London: Routledge, 1994): 126–38.

[33] Kazutoshi Maeda, "The Evolution of Retailing Industries in Japan," in Akio Okochi and Koichi Shimokawa (eds.), *Development of Mass Marketing: The International Conference on Business History*, 7 (1981): 265–89.

Japanese firms had no incentive to form alliances with leading multinationals of alcoholic beverages to distribute their brands locally because there was still no demand for international brands, and consumption of alcohol was growing slowly.

By 1954, Kirin had become an industry leader, ranking among the largest breweries in the world. Kirin's activities focused essentially on the Japanese brewing and soft drinks businesses, but it also had some international activity, the United States being its most important market. In Japan, Kirin distributed its beer through retailing companies, and also through wholly owned vending machines.[34] Distribution to foreign markets was essentially carried out by subsidiary companies engaged in various transport operations.

Suntory's spirits business took off after the War, because Suntory whisky had built a reputation in the U.S. military officers' clubs in Japan. The success with the military forces gave the brand an association with the American lifestyle. The firm took advantage of this association in aggressive marketing campaigns. Distribution of Suntory whisky spread to every part of Japan. The launching of Suntory bars in 1955 played an important part in this subsequent success. In 1963, Suntory expanded into brewing, using its wide distribution network in the food and drinks industries to sell a variety of products.[35]

Globalization, Vertical Integration, and Joint Venture Formation, 1970s–1980s

The convergence of strategies in the 1970s and 1980s did not entail only mergers and acquisitions of firms that owned brands with the potential to become global. In the 1970s, it also involved firms that owned distribution channels. And in the 1980s, it involved the creation of distribution joint ventures between leading multinationals to cover multiple markets, including Japan. The trend toward concentration in the off-premise market by supermarkets and hypermarkets created a danger of cartel formation.[36]

Vertical Integration

In the United Kingdom, where brewers had traditionally been vertically integrated, there was a trend toward disintegration, with brewers concentrating on production and branding. On the other hand, there was a tendency for

[34] Kirin, Annual Report and Accounts (1954, and 1961–1969).

[35] Interview with Kunimasa Himeno, Manager International Division of Suntory and Yoshi Kunimoto, Executive Vice President of Suntory-Allied, Tokyo, 16 September 1999; Christopher Fielden, *A Drink Dynasty: The Suntory Story* (Throwbride: Wine Source, 1996): 29–32.

[36] Indeed, some believe that has already happened in the United Kingdom, where Tesco, Sainsbury's, Asda and Safeway are often accused of bringing down the prices paid to suppliers without passing these savings onto consumers.

wines and spirits firms to create wholly owned distribution channels. There was a perception that leading firms needed to control strong distribution networks either on their own or through alliances. Ownership of distribution also aimed at overcoming the problem of the so-called parallel distribution, whereby brands were sold in the same market at different prices. Networks would enable firms to increase control over the marketing of their brands and acquire thorough knowledge about their markets. Simultaneously, they would minimize the risk of distributors or agents switching to a competitor. Firms, therefore, needed to have sales and marketing teams as well as wide portfolios of brands in order to be able to control their marketing. This vertical integration into distribution took the form of acquisitions of small family-owned distributors. These distributors usually had carried the acquiring firm's brands and thus had played an important role in the creation of their success in particular markets. In this period of high competition, the acquisitions prevented competitors from taking over these distributors and acquiring the valuable knowledge they possessed.

In the United States, despite the three-tier system of distribution, a similar trend toward vertical integration emerged. Leading multinationals from Europe acquired their former importers, which until then had acted as sales agents handling the local advertising and marketing of the brands. This activity, which only required a small number of employees, provided very good margins. These margins were much higher in the United States than in Europe, where importers and distributors were usually the same entity and distribution was much more fragmented.[37]

Beginning in the 1980s when demand started to stagnate in the West, the largest multinationals of alcoholic beverages made their biggest investments in distribution. Only a few of the leading North American firms survived independently. Seagram, which had invested strongly in Europe and also in the Far East, was one of the few exceptions. Many North American firms with strong distribution channels in the domestic market were acquired by European firms. As previously mentioned, the major acquisitions by European firms in North America were Hiram Walker by Allied Lyons in 1986, Schenley by Guinness in 1987, Liggett & Myers by Grand Metropolitan in 1982, and Heublein also by Grand Metropolitan in 1987. The family-controlled U.S. firms of Anheuser-Busch, Brown Forman, and Coors remained independent, while Miller Brewing fell under the control of the acquisitive U.S. tobacco company Philip Morris.[38]

Grand Metropolitan's acquisition of Liggett brought with it two important marketing companies in the United States, Carillon Importers and

[37] Interview with James Espey, former Chairman of Seagram Distillers PLC, former Managing Director of United Distillers/Guinness Plc and former Chairman of IDV-UK, Wimbledon, 4 September 2000.
[38] Miller was subsequently acquired by South African Breweries in 2001.

Paddington Corp. Paddington Corp. had helped develop the U.S. market for European spirits, in particular whisky brands such as Grand Metropolitan's J&B Rare.[39] The hostile acquisition of Liggett & Myers allowed Grand Metropolitan to gain control of the management of its own brand, J&B Rare, in a market where it was very successful. In the early 1980s, Grand Metropolitan's own distribution channels were selling about half of the total volume of their major brands.

There are other examples of European multinationals that during this period integrated vertically by acquiring North American distribution companies. Pernod Ricard's acquisition of Austin Nichols in 1980, which was also part of Liggett & Myers, is one case. Austin Nichols owned the bourbon Wild Turkey, and was a major importer of European brands such as Baileys Irish Cream and Campari, as well as French wines. Initially, the management of Austin Nichols resisted being acquired by Pernod Ricard, and as a gesture of goodwill, the two parties agreed that Austin Nichols would be the importer of Pernod in the United States. When the threat of a hostile takeover by Grand Metropolitan appeared, however, the management of the U.S. distribution firm finally agreed to sell the business to Pernod Ricard.[40] Another case is Schieffelin & Co., which had been the U.S. distributor for Moët Hennessy since 1945 and was acquired by Moët Hennessy in 1980. At the time of the acquisition, Schieffelin accounted for roughly 40 percent of Hennessy's and close to 15 percent of the champagne Moët & Chandon's sales.[41]

Guinness only started to integrate vertically very late, after the acquisition of Distillers Company in 1986. The company chose vertical integration to create new wholly owned distribution channels. But there were problems with that strategy as it could lead to parallel pricing. Selling brands through existing distribution channels as well as through new wholly owned channels might imply that the beverages would reach the final customer at higher prices than if the distribution was controlled by the firm. This concern led Guinness to buy out its own distributors. Guinness's sales through its own distribution channels moved from 25 percent at the outset of 1987 to more than 70 percent in 1988.[42] The ownership of distribution channels gave Guinness a margin available on distribution as well as critical control of the marketing activity of its brands at the local level.

[39] Interview with Sir John Bull, former Chairman of Grand Metropolitan and Diageo, London, 19 November 2003; interview with Tim Ambler, former consultant for Grand Metropolitan, London, 12 July 2000.
[40] Interview with Thierry Jacquillat, former CEO of Pernod Ricard, London, 20 January 2004, "The Austin Nichols Story," Accession 2126, Box 773, Seagram Collection.
[41] Moët & Chandon, Annual Report and Accounts (31 July 1946); Moët Hennessy, Annual Report and Accounts (1980).
[42] James Capel & Co. Ltd., "United Distillers Group'" (November 1988): 1, 25; Distillers Archive, Diageo.

With the move to wholly owned distribution, Guinness rationalized its list of third-party distributors. It went from a situation of 1,304 agents/distributors worldwide and zero owned distribution channels in 1986, to a situation of 470 agents and thirty-seven owned distribution channels in 1989. However, despite this move into distribution, Guinness often used different channels to serve the same market. In Asia, for example, the firm had two joint venture alliances with distinct partners and also used wholly owned distribution channels, with each arrangement covering different regions and brands.[43]

Seagram followed a similar strategy. In order to gain control over the distribution of its beverages, Seagram acquired several leading family firms that, apart from having well-established channels of distribution in certain markets, also owned successful brands. One illustration is Sandeman, a leading port and sherry producer with a very strong distribution network in Europe, which was acquired in 1979. Another is Martell, acquired in 1989, which apart from the very successful cognac brand also owned a strong distribution network in France.[44] In 1984, Seagram integrated into retailing in the United Kingdom and France by acquiring two retail outlet chains, Oddbins Limited, and Gough Brothers from Scottish & Newcastle brewery.[45] Specialist distributors such as Oddbins played an important role in weaning middle-class British customers off consumption of French and German wines by introducing them to new world and other wines.[46]

Despite its investments in foreign markets, Seagram still relied extensively on third-party distributors in the 1970s and 1980s. Important independent channels of distribution were the worldwide Duty Free Stores and other special markets such as military bases, where the firm was one of the largest suppliers in the industry. In the United States, Seagram had several sales organizations (each one specializing in a particular set of brands and markets) and a network of independent distributors most of which had been working for the firm since the repeal of Prohibition or at least since World War II.[47] Some Japanese firms also established wholly owned subsidiaries in the U.S. market during this period. One example was Kirin, which formed "The Cherry Company Ltd." in 1981, the sole importer of Kirin beer in the United States.

[43] Ibid.
[44] Interview with George Sandeman, Chairman of the House of Sandeman, and Managing Director of Seagram Iberia, Oporto, 19 January, 2000; Teresa da Silva Lopes, "A Evolução das Estruturas Internacionais de Comercialização de Vinho do Porto no século XX," *Revista de História Económica e Social*, Série 2, No. 1 (2001): 91–132; Seagram, Annual Report and Accounts (1980, 1989).
[45] Seagram, Annual Report and Accounts (1985).
[46] In 2001 Seagram disposed of its drinks business, and in 2002 Oddbins was sold to Castle Frères, a giant French wholesaler, wine merchant, and wine producer.
[47] Seagram, Annual Report and Accounts (1972).

Spread of Joint Ventures With Local Partners

During the 1970s and 1980s, alliances were also an important mode through which firms distributed their brands worldwide. Leading multinationals continued to form alliances with local partners, but there was also a proliferation of alliances between direct competitors – such as large multinationals and leading local partners in emerging markets of Asia and South America – to produce, bottle, and distribute locally.

During this period, consumption of alcoholic beverages increased in Japan. Japanese firms formed multiple alliances with firms from other countries both to produce beer and spirits locally and also to sell imported beverages locally. These alliances provided Japanese firms with the opportunity to acquire marketing knowledge while simultaneously obtaining economies of scale and scope in various levels of activity, especially distribution. Foreign firms were able to minimize the risk associated with entering such a different cultural and geographical market as Japan. Japanese firms also started to internationalize their alcoholic beverages businesses (mainly through exports and licensing agreements), but overall they remained essentially domestic firms up until the beginning of the twenty-first century.

Kirin and Seagram formed one of the first joint ventures in Asia in 1972, at a time when firms wanted to consolidate their positions in their domestic markets and maximize market share. Kirin owned 50 percent, Seagram 45 percent, and Chivas Brothers 5, and they planned to produce whiskey at the foot of Mount Fuji, famous for its fresh water and clean air. Seagram brought its manufacturing techniques and Kirin its sales network and market knowledge. Apart from selling locally produced whiskey, Kirin also sold the Seagram's brands Robert Brown, Dunbar, Emblem, Burnett's Gin, and Nikolai vodka in Japan. This joint venture, which relied on both a long-term relationship based on a contract and on mutual trust, became part of Diageo, after its joint acquisition with Pernod Ricard of the Seagram alcoholic beverages business worldwide in 2002.[48]

Suntory also began to form alliances with Western partners in the 1970s. Its first distribution agreement was with Brown Forman in 1970. In the 1980s, it allied with other leading multinationals, including Seagram for the local distribution of the brand Martell, and Guinness for the brand Haig Scotch. However, the instability associated with these short-term agreements led to the creation of a joint venture with Allied Lyons in 1988. For Suntory, this new alliance brought the reputation and profitability of a leading British multinational in a period when demand for imported brands was

---

[48] Kirin, Annual Report and Accounts (1973), 13; Seagram, Annual Report and Accounts (1972). For a detailed analysis of different modes of coordinating international activities by multinationals, and for a discussion of long-term close trading relationships based on trust in Japan see also Mari Sako, *Prices, Quality and Trust – Inter-Firm Relationships in Britain and Japan* (Cambridge: Cambridge University Press, 1992).

starting to expand very rapidly. In addition, Suntory gained access to a wide distribution network of alcoholic beverages in Europe and North America. For Allied Lyons, it provided the opportunity to enter a new market where consumption of alcoholic beverages was growing very fast. Suntory took Allied Lyons's brands in Japan, and Hiram Walker took Suntory's brands in the United States. This agreement also involved cross-shareholding, with Suntory investing £89 million to acquire 2.5 percent of Allied's share capital and Allied Lyons investing £28 million to become Suntory's first outside shareholder.[49]

The joint venture formed in 1986 between Guinness and Moët-Hennessy was a landmark agreement. It covered multiple markets including Japan, Hong Kong, Singapore, Malaysia, Thailand, France, Eire, and the United States. This global alliance between two leading multinationals became a model in the industry owing to the benefits it brought to the firms involved. It permitted a careful marketing of limited volumes of deluxe and premium quality brands for high margins and status positioning. The complementarity of these brands in terms of their beverage type (champagne, cognac, scotch whisky, and gin) permitted them to be sold in the same markets, using a single sales force, with complete cost sharing, thereby obtaining economies of scale and scope and flexibility in distribution. In the United States, this joint venture brought together Schieffelin & Co. Importers (acquired by Moët Hennessy) and Somerset Importers (acquired by Guinness). Apart from the cost benefits, this alliance gave Moët Hennessy access to an operation with superior marketing skills and Guinness/Distillers a very good sales team.

This alliance soon created a general trend in the industry, especially among the leading multinationals, but the geographical focus on the Far East and South American markets was quite clear. Brewers and spirits firms with complementary brands formed alliances, relying essentially on distinct positioning of the beers in the markets. Some examples are the alliances formed in the 1980s between Kirin and Heineken (to market Dutch beer in Japan), Asahi Breweries and Löwenbräu (to market its specialty German beer in Japan), Pripps of Sweden and Asahi (to bottle and sell Swedish beer in Japan), Sapporo and both Miller Brewing and Guinness, and also Suntory and Anheuser-Busch (to produce Budweiser beer in Japan). In the spirits business, examples of alliances in emerging markets during this period include Guinness and Jinro in South Korea, Seagram and China Distillery Shanghai in China, and the joint venture involving Moët-Hennessy, Cinzano, Monteiro, and Aranha in Brazil.

---

49 Interview with Mr. Kozo Chiji, Manager of the Corporate Planning Department of Suntory, Tokyo, 16 September 1999; Interview with Yoshi Kunimoto, Executive Vice President of Suntory-Allied, and Kunimasa Himeno, Manager of the International Division of Suntory, both in Tokyo, 16 September 1999; Allied Lyons, Annual Report and Accounts (1989): 8; Canadean Ltd, "Suntory" (Hants, 1999).

In Europe, there was a proliferation of alliances in distribution between leading multinationals. They also aimed at developing greater control over distribution and obtaining economies that would otherwise not have been available. For example, Guinness created joint ventures with Bacardi (in Spain and Germany), Uderberg (in Germany), Codorniu (in Spain), Boutari (in Greece), and Real Companhia Velha (in Portugal). By allying its substantial scotch whisky and gin interests with those of major local operators, scale and scope economies were achieved much more quickly than would have otherwise been the case.[50]

In 1988, Grand Metropolitan also had joint ventures in France, Germany, the Benelux, Japan, and Australia. Allied Lyons and Whitbread had created a jointly owned European Worldwide Cellars in 1985, with the aim of merging the wine interests of both companies in the United Kingdom and worldwide, and Brown Forman formed an agreement with Martell for the distribution of Jack Daniels in France. The arrangement in 1984 between American Brands and Grand Metropolitan, whereby the latter undertook the selling of Whyte & Mackay whiskies in the "on-license" trade and in "cash-and-carry" outlets in the United Kingdom, is yet another illustration.[51]

Alliances Between Competing Partners From the 1990s

In the beginning of the 1990s, consolidation in the retailing and wholesaling businesses accelerated. Large retailers and wholesalers demanded wider portfolios of brands of wines, spirits, and beer from different geographical origins, sourced from just a few distribution networks at low costs and in short periods of time.[52]

In countries such as the United States where each state has its own laws about distribution, labeling, packaging, and retailing, there were very few companies with national distribution channels. The distribution of wines, spirits, and beer is still dominated by family businesses such as Southern Wine & Spirits of America, Charmer-Sunbelt Group, and National Distributing. These wholesalers have regional coverage (either one- or multistate) and often handle competing brands.

By the beginning of the twenty-first century, there were very few wines and spirits firms integrated vertically into retailing. LVMH is one of the few leading multinationals vertically integrated into retailing through its international chain Duty Free Stores, aimed especially at tourists. The concentration by firms on one activity in the value added chain rather than in

[50] James Capel, "United Distillers Group": 25, Distillers Archive, Diageo.
[51] Grand Metropolitan, Annual Reports and Accounts (various years).
[52] Teresa da Silva Lopes, *Internacionalização e Concentração no Vinho do Porto, 1945–1995* (Porto: GEHVID/ICEP, 1998); Nirmalya Kumar, "The Power of Trust in Manufacturer-Retailer Relationships'" in *Harvard Business Review on Managing the Value Chain* (Boston, Mass: Harvard Business School Press, 2000): 92–93.

vertical integration into retailing is due in part to the very high overhead costs of distribution and the distinct kinds of capabilities necessary to run such businesses.

E-commerce also started to develop at the beginning of the twenty-first century, even though this channel still did not account for a substantial amount of trade in alcoholic beverages.[53] Nevertheless, this activity was expanding as companies and retailers sought to increase the scope of their businesses, transmit the imagery of their brands to their customers, and position themselves strategically for future modes of competition.

During this period, the way business was conducted had changed, and logistics in distribution had gained increasing importance as firms had to manage larger stocks of different brands and deal with larger retailers. Technology had improved logistics, integrating information systems to provide quicker and easier mechanisms for decision taking within multinationals.

By the end of the 1990s, however, many firms had failed to achieve their aims and had begun to disintegrate vertically. Distribution operations often involved high fixed costs, which were not always covered by the gains obtained from sales. The maturation of product categories also led firms to disintegrate vertically.[54] Many firms had overexpanded, offering very wide portfolios of brands. Their distribution channels caused them to face the basic conflict of being both in the distribution business and in the management of brands. The sale by Seagram of its wholly owned distribution channels in Austria, Scandinavia, and Australia (in, respectively, 1997, 1998, and 1999), for which alliances with local partners were subsequently substituted, demonstrates this trend.

Leading multinationals such as Diageo, Allied Domecq, Seagram, Bacardi, and Pernod-Ricard, which were traditionally vertically integrated, started to rationalize their operations in existing markets, covering new regions with interlocking alliances. One of the major aims in the formation of Diageo in 1997 was the creation of new efficiencies at the distribution level. Putting Guinness and Grand Metropolitan together produced a stronger brand portfolio and provided £300–400 million ($495–660 million) in annual cost savings, some for the bottom line and some for investing in brands.[55] After the acquisition of Seagram's brands in 2002, Diageo concentrated its distribution

---

[53] For example, the Internet business accounted for 33.5 million pounds of Bass worldwide sales, but that figure was expected to treble in 2000 [Interview given by Sir Ian Prosser, Bass's chairman to Lucy Killgrem in "Bass put £5m into last minute," *Financial Times* (4 February 2000)].

[54] Seagram, *Annual Report and Accounts* (1997, 1998, 1999). For a theoretical analysis of the advantages and disadvantages of wholly owned distribution channels, see Erin Anderson and Anne T. Coughlan, "International Market Entry and Expansion via Independent or Integrated Channels of Distribution," *Journal of Marketing*, Vol. 51 (1997): 72.

[55] Interview with Jack Keenan, Chairman of Diageo, London, 3 June 2003; Diageo, Annual Report and Accounts (1998).

on fewer wholesalers, with whom they formed long-term distribution agreements.[56]

The creation of Maxxium in 1999, a distribution joint venture formed between Rémy Cointreau, Highland Distillers, and Fortune Brands, and later extended to Vin & Sprit, was in part a reaction to the creation of Diageo. Maxxium sought to form a global distribution company for premium wines and spirits that would operate in fifty markets outside the United States. This move cemented some long-standing business relationships, and helped the firms to obtain lower costs and greater effectiveness and thus to grow their brands into many major overseas markets where they did not have a presence.

Alliances in distribution among smaller firms owning different types of alcoholic beverages brands (in wines, beer, or spirits) became even more common than in previous decades. These alliances permitted smaller firms to explore the complementarities between the products of several companies. They also allowed them to achieve strategic objectives (such as filling country and portfolio gaps in demand), to obtain a higher control of the marketing of their brands, and to achieve economies of scale and scope in distribution. Some examples are Brown Forman and the old Swedish Liquor Monopoly, which owned the famous vodka brand Absolut produced by Vin & Sprit.

The close ties between the two family businesses Bacardi-Martini and Brown Forman led to the creation of Gemini, a distribution alliance that covered different markets. Through this alliance, Bacardi distributed Brown Forman's Jack Daniels whiskey in Europe where it had a strong distribution network, especially after the acquisition of Martini Rossi in 1993. Prior to that, the two family-controlled companies had also collaborated, partnering in an on-premise distribution initiative.

By the beginning of the twenty-first century, most of the top brewers still relied on their home countries for the bulk of their sales. However, with trade barriers falling within regions such as Europe and Latin America, and with production synergies becoming possible, pressure increased for local giants to expand outside their home markets. There had been a similar process in the United States twenty years earlier when domestic consolidation occurred very rapidly. These changes in the external environment suggested two possible ways for brewers to develop. One was through mergers and acquisitions of brewers in other countries. The other was through the creation of alliances. For instance, after the late 1990s many companies entered the Asian market. South African Breweries was the first multinational brewer to enter China, taking a 49 percent stake in a joint venture with the second leading brewer in China, China Resource Beverage Ltd. Anheuser-Busch followed by forming

---

[56] While the cost of distributing a case of spirits is about $16.25, a box of soft drinks costs on average $5.3 and beer $6.25. "Diageo aims to outstrip the market with its new distribution model," *Impact International*, Vol. 33, Nos. 3 and 4 (2003).

a joint venture with Tsingao Breweries, the leading Chinese brewer (with a market share of around 10 percent).

Alliances also provided important learning experiences for wines firms. For example, the Californian wines producer Mondavi started making efforts to become a global company in the 1970s through the 1990s by producing California wines and selling them globally. But it was through a joint venture with French wine maker Baron Philippe de Rothschild that Mondavi learned what it took to succeed on a global scale. The managers of the firm realized that to be a global wine business they not only had to produce and sell wines from California on a global basis, but they also had to produce wines in many of the great countries of the world. They had to market those wines by emphasizing a unique style and character that represented the cultures and people from those places.[57]

Long-Term Patterns in Distribution

The alcoholic beverages industry thus changed decisively in the years following the 1960s, consumption was country-specific, distribution was fragmented, competition was essentially domestic, and firms had little marketing knowledge about the management of brands and distribution or the markets and their social and cultural specificities. The most frequent modes through which firms distributed their beverages were those that minimized risk and uncertainty. Their lack of experience in international distribution meant that firms had no control over the logistics or the marketing of their brands and therefore could hardly acquire any marketing knowledge about the performance of their brands in different markets. Therefore, they tended to sell their brands primarily through agents and distributors. These provided a quick entry into markets and allowed firms to economize on information costs associated with the risk of exposure to uncertainty.[58] Only when contracts with distributors were well formulated could firms acquire some knowledge of those markets.

In the 1960s, communication and transportation costs decreased, markets opened to foreign direct investment, competition intensified and became global, and as the distribution activity of consumer goods started to consolidate, new imperfections in intermediate product markets emerged. Control became an important incentive for internalization, leading to the creation of long-term alliances or hierarchical relations in distribution. At that stage, several alcoholic beverages firms acquired marketing knowledge either from their operations in their domestic markets or internationally. This allowed

[57] Interview with Robert Mondavi, *Impact International* (2002).

[58] Mark Casson, "The Organisation and Evolution of the Multinational Enterprise: An Information Cost Approach," *Management International Review*, Vol. 39 (1999): 119; Oliver E. Williamson, *The Economic Institutions of Capitalism* (New York: Free Press, 1985): 57.

them to change the modes through which they distributed their beverages, finding better combinations of risk and control for the marketing of their brands. This also provided new economies of scale and scope in their operations, including distribution in different regions of the world. They were able to obtain reliable feedback and better information about the preferences of consumers and the performance of their brands.

The joint ventures formed between Western multinationals and partners in geographically and culturally distant markets of the Far East from the 1980s allowed firms to acquire marketing knowledge about the distribution systems and social habits in those markets. They could simultaneously overcome tariff or other types of constraints imposed by the institutional environment.

Later in the 1980s, the economies of scale and scope in distribution provided by long-term alliances became increasingly important. Consumption stagnated, distribution was concentrated, competition was played at a multimarket level, and the costs and benefits of the alternative channel designs became very different, threatening the independent survival of nonefficient firms.[59] By aggregating different beverages and brands and targeting distinct market segments, it was possible to obtain declining average costs associated with increasing output of a single line of commerce. At the same time it was possible to reduce the risk and uncertainty associated with distribution, thereby lowering the cost of market entry to the internationalizing companies. Appendix 7 offers a schematic representation of the main types of alliances used by alcoholic beverages firms over time.

Overall, it is possible to identify four significant trends in distribution of alcoholic beverages. First, in the initial part of the twentieth century the modes of distribution of alcoholic beverages were similar to those used in other consumer products in general.[60] One striking difference about this industry, however, is that, despite the high risk of failure of alliances, they remained an important alternative governance structure used for distribution even in periods such as the 1980s when firms were integrating vertically by merging and acquiring their distributors.[61] While the types of alliances formed by firms may have changed over time, this did not necessarily imply that the existing ownership structures were wrong, but that these structures often represented transitional circumstances.

---

[59] About multimarket competition see, e.g., Satish Jayachadran, Javier Gimeno, and P. Rajan Varadarajan, "The Theory of Multimarket Competition: A Synthesis and Implication for Marketing Strategy," *Journal of Marketing*, Vol. 63 (1999): 49–66.

[60] See, e.g., Geoffrey Jones, *Merchants to Multinationals* (Oxford: Oxford University Press, 2000).

[61] For an analysis of failure in alliances see, e.g., Bruce Kogut, "A Study of the Life Cycle of Joint Ventures," in F. J. Contractor and P. Lorange (eds.), *Cooperative Strategies*; and Andrew C. Inkpen and Paul W. Beamish, "Knowledge, Bargaining Power, and the Instability of International Ventures," *Academy of Management Review*, Vol. 22, No. 1 (1997): 177–202.

A second trend involves the tendency of firms to use several types of governance structures simultaneously to distribute their brands, each one adapted to the strategy of a particular market or region, to the product being traded (wines, beer, or spirits), or the specific brand being marketed. A third trend is that alliances in distribution tended at first to involve one large firm that owned brands that were leaders in specific market segments and types of beverages. But early in the twenty-first century, it was common for alliances to be formed between firms of all sizes, including leading multinationals that were direct competitors.

A fourth trend relates to the apparent correlation between the country of origin and the main geographical scope of activities of the largest firms, and the governance structures used to distribute their products. In countries such as the United States and the United Kingdom, which developed capital markets where shares of most of the large firms could be publicly quoted (even when families kept control of the shares), alliances in distribution developed very early in the century. In continental Europe and Japan, by contrast, this type of alliances became popular only later. Here, shares tended to be concentrated in the hands of a small number of investors; often families, banks, and governments, and interlocking shareholdings were common.

Cross-border alliances in distribution developed beginning in the 1930s between firms from Anglo-Saxon countries, in particular from the United Kingdom, United States, and Canada. In the 1970s and 1980s they spread to firms from European countries and Japan. Volume and profitability seemed to have been the main determinants for firms to integrate vertically through wholly owned distribution units. Nonetheless, by the beginning of the twenty-first century, alliances were very common in the industry and were used even between firms of smaller size and those from emerging markets. It is in this period that a convergence of strategies occurred in the industry (even though sometimes these did not result in the most efficient decisions or appear to reflect genuine economies), especially between the world's largest multinationals. Publicly quoted large firms, which did not follow these convergent strategies, were often acquired by others that did. Only firms in which families controlled the shares were able to remain independent while following distinct strategies. Alliances in distribution focused essentially on obtaining economies of scale and scope in logistics, as firms sought to retain control over their marketing operations and minimize externality costs.

In addition, in a world where smooth marketing knowledge is becoming more important for growth and survival, the creation of alliances rather than hierarchies facilitates the acquisition of vital knowledge. The frequency of global alliances between competitors in alcoholic beverages also shows the increasingly strategic role of distribution in the value-added chain of firms.

6

Diversification Strategies

Introduction

The vulnerability of the specialized firm to fast and unexpected changes in the environment in the last half of the twentieth century meant that firms in many industries chose to diversify as a way to grow and survive.[1] The development of the multiproduct firm is often considered to be related to factors such as excess capacity and its creation, market imperfections, and the peculiarities of organizational knowledge, particularly its fungibility and tacit character.[2] This chapter explores the role of marketing knowledge and brands as underutilized resources. I want to explain how despite following apparently different strategies of related and unrelated diversification, a group of multinational firms from different countries achieved similar global leadership positions.

It is very difficult to classify firms' strategies over long periods of time as involving only related or unrelated diversification. Nonetheless, despite the unique ways through which firms respond to imperfections in markets and other factors,[3] it is possible to find common patterns in their diversification strategies. Commonalities exist not only in the products and geographical markets they selected, but also in their vertical integration strategies and

[1] See, e.g., H. I. Ansoff, "Strategies for Diversification," *Harvard Business Review*, Vol. 35, No. 5 (1957): 113–24; idem, "A Model for Diversification," *Management Science*, Vol. 4 (1958): 392–414; Edith Penrose, *The Theory of the Growth of the Firm* (Oxford: Oxford University Press, 1959/1995): 111–12; Robin Marris, *The Economic Theory of Managerial Capitalism* (London: Macmillan, 1964); M. Gort, *Diversification and Integration in American Industry* (Princeton, NJ: Princeton University Press, 1962); Richard Whittington and Michael Mayer, *The European Corporation* (Oxford: Oxford University Press, 2000). In business history, the seminal work of Alfred Chandler in *Strategy and Structure* highlighted the importance of the diversified firm in the development of modern economy. Alfred D. Chandler Jr., *Strategy and Structure* (Cambridge, Mass: The MIT Press, 1962).

[2] Penrose, *The Theory*; Alfred D. Chandler Jr., *The Visible Hand* (Cambridge, Mass: Harvard University Press, 1977); David J. Teece, "Towards and Economic Theory of the Multiproduct Firm," *Journal of Economic Behaviour and Organization*, Vol. 3 (1982): 39–63; Michael E. Porter, "From Competitive Advantage to Corporate Strategy," *Harvard Business Review*, Vol. 65, No. 3 (1987): 43–59.

[3] Richard R. Nelson, "Why Do Firms Differ, and How Does it Matter?" *Strategic Management Journal*, No. 14 (1991): 61–74.

the physical and knowledge linkages they created. Some firms even adopted strategies of double diversification, engaging simultaneously in geographical and industrial diversification.[4]

In this chapter, I provide empirical evidence on the imperfections in alcoholic beverages firms and markets that led firms to diversify into related and unrelated areas over time and to create different kinds of physical and knowledge linkages.[5] I also explain the cycles of diversification of firms within the industry. Finally, I highlight the increasing role played by brand management in creating the knowledge linkages required for successful diversification.

Shifts in Diversification Strategies Over Time

The changes in the imperfections generated in markets and in firms create costs that affect firms' efficient operations in multiple ways and ultimately may lead them to reassess their diversification strategies.[6] Imperfections in markets are created by changes in the external environment. They include declining demand, competitive shocks, country barriers, and policy distortions such as tax and antitrust policy. These prevent firms from economically exploiting ownership advantages in any way other than by internalizing the market.[7] To minimize these costs and simultaneously take advantage of the benefits that the internalization of new linkages might provide, firms often substitute market transactions for a hierarchy or for hybrid governance structures.[8]

Imperfections in firms are created by changes that occur inside the firms. They include the development of excess resources (tangible, intangible, or

---

[4] Robert D. Pearce, "The Internationalisation of Sales by Leading Enterprises: Some Firm, Industry and Country Determinants," *The University of Reading: Discussion Papers in International Investment and Business Studies*, No.101 (1987).

[5] This chapter draws to a great extent on concepts from Peter J. Buckley and Mark Casson, *The Future of the Multinational Enterprise* (London: Macmillan, 1976); and from Mark Casson, *Enterprise and Competitiveness: A Systems View of International Business* (Oxford: Clarendon, 1990); idem, "Internalisation Theory and Beyond," in Peter J. Buckley (ed.), *Recent Research of Multinational Enterprise* (Aldershot: Elgar, 1991); idem, *Economics of International Business* (Cheltenham: Elgar, 2000): chapter 3.

[6] Robert D. Pearce, *The Growth and Evolution of Multinational Enterprise* (Aldershot: Elgar, 1993).

[7] Oliver E. Williamson, *Markets and Hierarchies* (New York: Free Press, 1975); idem, "Transaction-Cost Economics: The Governance of Contractual Relations," *Journal of Law and Economics*, Vol. 22 (1979): 3–61; Benjamin Klein, Robert Crawford, and Armen Alchian, "Vertical Integration, Appropriable Rents and the Competitive Contracting Process," *Journal of Law and Economics*, No. 21 (1978): 297–326; Buckley and Casson, *The Future of the Multinational*.

[8] David Teece, "Economies of Scale and Scope of the Enterprise," *Journal of Economic Behaviour and Organisation*, Vol. 1, No. 3 (1980): 223–47.

financial), or shifts in managerial motives and shareholder interests.[9] They may lead firms to internalize physical or knowledge linkages that had not previously existed, not even through the market.[10] The costs they generate may be of two types – transfer costs or information costs. In this discussion only transfer costs are analyzed.[11]

Transfer costs are the costs of actually moving the resources from one location to another. In the case of physical resources in alcoholic beverages, transfer costs include transportation costs, tariffs, and costs of overcoming nontariff barriers. In the case of knowledge resources in alcoholic beverages, transfer costs include costs of training. The linkages that result from the attempt to reduce these costs are of two kinds – physical or knowledge linkages.

Physical linkages involve tangible assets, and are characterized by one-way product flows (inputs or outputs) that run from the supplier to the consumer of those products. Plant capacity and the equipment necessary to manufacture a product are examples of such linkages. Tangible assets such as specialized manufacturing equipment are not very flexible in facilitating diversification because of their indivisibility and the likelihood of creating excess capacity.[12] Often, the excess assets (plant and equipment) can only be used for very closely related products, especially those requiring similar manufacturing technology. Another limitation relates to the fact that these types of assets eventually become physically exhausted.

Knowledge linkages relate to the firms' human capital, its expertise such as marketing knowledge, or a knowledge of the technologies that can improve the business assets of a new domain being considered for investment. This knowledge accrues to the firm over time and involves intangible linkages. These linkages flow from the supplier to the customer but may also be acquired by the supplier due to its linkage with its customer.[13] Knowledge is easily transferred between separate activities, is less imitable than physical assets, and can be repeatedly used in different products with little cost in the effectiveness of the original operations. It is this fungible character of knowledge assets and the excess resources that the firm may generate that

---

[9] See, e.g., Richard P. Rumelt, *Strategy, Structure and Economic Performance* (Cambridge Mass: Harvard University Press, 1974).

[10] The two different imperfections that may lead to diversification are not mutually exclusive. In fact change may simultaneously produce imperfections in markets and in firms.

[11] Information costs may take the form of communication costs (which are costs of agreeing on the price and quantity of the resource to be transferred, assuming honesty), or of assurance or transaction costs (which are costs incurred in dealing with misinformation or dishonesty). Mark Casson, *Information and Organization: A New Perspective on the Theory of the Firm* (Oxford: Clarendon, 1997).

[12] Penrose, *The Theory*; Robert E. Hoskisson and Michael A. Hitt, "Antecedents and Performance Outcomes of Diversification: A Review and Critique of Theoretical Perspectives," *Journal of Management*, Vol. 16, No. 2 (1990): 461–509.

[13] Casson, *Information and Organization*.

are critical in the understanding of a firms' diversification into new as well as existing lines of business. As mentioned before, marketing knowledge is the knowledge within the firm about marketing methods, branding, and distribution. Smooth marketing knowledge can be shared among different industries; and sticky marketing knowledge is more limited in scope – it is relevant in the operation of particular geographical markets or in the industry for which it was developed, and is not easily shared with other business activities.

From Physical Linkages to Knowledge Linkages

In the beginning of the 1960s, physical linkages were more important than knowledge linkages in determining the diversification strategies of firms. Most of the world's largest alcoholic beverages firms were either not diversified at all, or had low levels of diversification.[14] Over time, as the size of firms expanded and professional managers took on a larger role, knowledge linkages gained increasing importance. Many firms evolved into medium or highly diversified businesses. By the beginning of the twenty-first century, firms were refocusing in areas where they could obtain cost efficiencies through both physical and knowledge linkages. Appendix 8 provides the ratio of sales in alcoholic beverages to total sales between 1960 and 2005 for a group of firms.[15]

In each decade, the incentives for internalization were created by different imperfections in markets and in firms. As previously mentioned, in the 1960s, consumption was growing in the Western world and competition was still largely local. There were no incentives for firms such as Seagram and IDV to diversify into other businesses rather than spirits and wines. For Distillers, the alcoholic beverages business accounted for between 80 and 91 percent of its annual sales during the 1960s, with the remaining sales

---

[14] For a more detailed analysis of diversification of multinationals in wines and spirits, see Alfredo Coelho and António de Sousa, "Stratégies de Développement des Groupes Multinationaux des Vins et Spiritueux," *Économies et Sociétés*, Vol. 10–11, No. 24 (2000): 257–70.

[15] This Appendix provides an illustrative sample of firms with high levels of diversification and internationalization. There were nonetheless other firms with similar levels of diversification that are not included in Appendix 8. For example, the U.S. firms Schenley and Heublein had diversified into other businesses as a consequence of Prohibition. The governmental restrictions imposed on consumption and on production during that period left firms with excess resources (such as production capacity and human capital). While many firms closed down and sold their stocks to others, some, especially those that had flexible resources, were able to survive by diversifying into other areas, running high levels of risk. Heublein, for instance, developed a food business during the time of Prohibition. The firm started producing a steak sauce from an operation acquired in 1918, which turned out to be very successful. It was still an important business by the 1960s. William L. Downar, *Dictionary of the History of American Brewing and Distilling Industries* (London: Greenwood, 1980): 90.

coming from investments in chemicals and biochemicals. It had diversified into these businesses almost since its foundation in 1877, as some of the firms that merged to form Distillers Company already produced alcohol for industrial use. This available knowledge served as the basis for investments in the manufacture of organic chemicals and in biochemicals. By the end of the 1960s, following the litigation over the sleeping pill thalidomide (which caused birth defects when taken by pregnant women), Distillers Company begun to divest from these nonalcoholic beverages businesses. The poor performance of the chemicals businesses ultimately led to their sale to the oil group British Petroleum (BP) in 1969.[16]

Firms such as Guinness in the United Kingdom were already diversified, but like Distillers Company, had low levels of product diversification. Guinness essentially produced beer. It also had small investments in other businesses such as confectioneries (butterscotch, nougat), pharmaceuticals, and property, and was vertically integrated in the British market, where it had marketing and distribution activities. However, unlike British brewers such as Allied Breweries, Bass, and Whitbread, Guinness was able to grow without diversifying into the ownership of pubs.[17]

During the 1970s, three different kinds of shifts took place in the diversification strategies of firms in alcoholic beverages. One involved the diversification into other industries by firms originally focused on alcoholic beverages. A second strategy adopted by owners of successful brands involved growing in size while remaining in alcoholic beverages. This group merged or acquired other firms from the same industry, consolidating their positions in the domestic market. A third strategy was adopted by well-established firms operating in other industries that entered the alcoholic beverages business through the acquisition of existing firms.

Allied Breweries' acquisition in 1978 of J. Lyons & Co., a leading food specialist, is an example of the first strategy. With this large investment in another industry, Allied Breweries hoped to ensure a steady cash flow and to spread risk.[18] J. Lyons & Co. had a vast array of businesses in cakes, cookies, and other confectionery, as well as groceries and frozen and refrigerated food. In addition, it had services and leisure businesses in Africa, where it owned Embassy Hotels, J. Lyons Catering Ltd., and Lyons Brooke Bond (in Zambia and Zimbabwe). In the United States, J. Lyons & Co. owned major firms in different food sectors: Baskin & Robbins ice cream, DCA Foods (cereal mixes), and Tetley Inc. (a leading tea, coffee, and frozen foods producer).

---

[16] Ronald B. Weir, *The History of the Distillers Company, 1877–1939* (Oxford: Oxford University Press, 1995); James Bamberg, *British Petroleum Global Oil, 1950–1975* (Cambridge: Cambridge University Press, 2000).

[17] Terry Gourvish and Richard G. Wilson, *The British Brewing Industry, 1830–1980* (Cambridge: Cambridge University Press, 1994).

[18] Interview with Michael Jackaman, former Chairman of Allied-Domecq, Somerset, 8 December 1998.

In 1991, after the company incurred a £147 million loss caused by currency portfolio mishandling and low returns on investment, Allied Lyons sold the Lyons business.[19] Since then the firm has refocused its activities on its core businesses in wines and spirits.

Within the group of alcoholic beverages firms that diversified into other businesses, different strategies of diversification were adopted. While some firms, such as Allied, sought to diversify risk by merging and acquiring other firms and exercising control over their management, others sought only financial investments in other firms. In both instances, firms attempted to substitute markets by spreading their portfolios of investments indirectly. The argument was that if investors recognized this service, then the benefit would be reflected in the stock price of the firms.[20] In those cases where diversification meant financial investments only, the linkages (either in terms of physical assets or knowledge) tended to be very low or nonexistent. The acquisition in 1980 of Home Oil Company by Hiram Walker, a leading Canadian bourbon producer, is an example. Apart from spreading risk, this acquisition also prevented HCI Holdings from taking over Hiram Walker. Another example of unrelated diversification where there was no control of the management or share of physical or knowledge linkages, is Seagram's acquisition in 1981 of a 21 percent interest in DuPont.[21] The lack of physical or knowledge linkages between the oil, gas, and chemicals businesses and the alcoholic beverages business, however, led the management of the firms to realize that it was too costly to keep these financial investments. In the case of Hiram Walker, the oil business was sold right after the firm was acquired by Allied Domecq in 1986. In the case of Seagram, the financial investment in DuPont was sold in 1995 when the firm entered the entertainment and leisure industry, which its managers believed was more closely related.

A second group of firms diversified in the 1970s by merging with direct competitors originally from the same domestic markets. The creation of Pernod Ricard in 1975 is an example of this strategy. Ricard's diversification into tea and coffee had not been successful, and Pernod had not succeeded in its efforts to diversify into bio-products. The merger between Pernod and Ricard created a large national alcoholic beverages company that would diversify internationally into spirits other than anis. As a result of the merger, the firm became a leading producer of anis pastis, as well as major exporter of Australian wines and producer of Irish whiskey. In 1973, Pernod Ricard

[19] Allied Lyons, Annual Report and Accounts (1991).

[20] Williamson, *Markets and Hierarchies*, chapter 9; Alan K. Severn, "Investor Evaluation of Foreign and Domestic Risk," *Journal of Finance*, Vol. 29 (1974): 545–50; Richard E. Caves, *Multinational Enterprise and Economic Analysis* (Cambridge: Cambridge University Press, 1982).

[21] However, this interest of Seagram in the oil and gas business dated as far back as 1947. Hiram Walker, *Annual Report and Accounts* (1980); Edgar M. Bronfman, *Good Spirits: The Making of a Businessman* (New York: Putman's, 1998): chapter 1.

acquired JAF juices. This business was later expanded with the acquisition in 1982 of the SIAS-MPA fruit preparation business and, in 1984, of Orangina, a soda maker.[22] This diversification into soft drinks was a reaction to the changes that were taking place in the alcoholic beverages industry: consumers were becoming more health conscious. These investments were, however, not cost-efficient, as it was very difficult to compete with companies such as Coca Cola. The firm ended up selling these soft drinks businesses in 2001 and 2002 to Schweppes and refocusing on alcoholic beverages.[23]

Grand Metropolitan and Philip Morris are examples of the third strategy mentioned above. Each entered the alcoholic beverages industry during the 1970s. Grand Metropolitan, a hotel and real estate firm, gradually increased its investments in the alcoholic beverages industry by merging and acquiring firms already established in that industry. This ultimately led to its divestment from real estate, its original business. Philip Morris, a tobacco firm, acquired the brewing firm Miller and kept it in its wide portfolio of businesses, with tobacco remaining as its main activity. Philip Morris eventually sold Miller in May 2002. Liggett & Myers, another U.S. tobacco company, also entered the alcoholic beverages business. In this case, the alcoholic beverages business became increasingly important in the total activity of the firm. Its diversification into alcoholic beverages started in 1964 after Liggett & Myers had suffered a decade of declining sales in the tobacco business.

The 1970s was also a period during which many leading firms did not survive independently. In the United States, as a result of the changes that were starting to take place in distribution (with a high concentration of wholesaling and retailing), the alcoholic beverages firms were not able to keep efficient wholly owned distribution channels. Many disappearances can be explained by the small size of portfolios of successful brands and inadequate marketing knowledge acquired from managing their own brands internationally. For example, in 1971, Schenley was sold to Glen Alden Corporation, a conglomerate operating in a multitude of businesses from consumer products to textiles, construction materials, and motion pictures.

The 1980s saw the rise in the Western world of new market and firm imperfections that created excess capacity in the industry. This led firms with adequate resources to diversify further into new geographical regions and new industries. In Japan, alcoholic beverages firms increased the number of alliances with Western firms while simultaneously starting to internationalize in alcoholic and nonalcoholic beverages (even though the level of that internationalization always remained low). Japanese firms also intensified their investments in the soft drinks industry (in particular in the health

[22] "Will Pernod mix its drinks?" *The Independent on Sunday* (17 October 1999).
[23] Interview with Thierry Jacquillat, family member and former CEO of Pernod Ricard, London, 22 October 2003; Pernod Ricard, Annual Report and Accounts (1991); *Financial Times* (11 January 2002).

and "fitness" supplement beverages) and also in the food business. All the major Japanese alcoholic beverages firms – Kirin, Asahi Breweries, Suntory and Sapporo – followed this trend because of the growth potential of the soft drinks industry. Economies of scale and scope in distribution were also important since soft drinks used the same distribution channels as alcoholic beverages, in particular beer. In addition, many firms in Japan started investing in industries related to health, such as pharmaceuticals.

Following the strategies of diversification into soft drinks by Pernod Ricard and the Japanese firms, Seagram acquired Tropicana, a fruit juices company, in 1988. Despite the potential linkages in marketing knowledge and distribution between the alcoholic and nonalcoholic drinks businesses, Seagram never took advantage of these linkages and ended up divesting from soft drinks in 1993.

Other firms followed a different rationale for diversification during this period: when Moët Hennessy, for example, joined with Louis Vuitton to form LVMH (1987). The merger brought together two French firms, producers of high-prestige premium-priced brands where there was clearly a high potential for sharing marketing knowledge in the management of brands and in international distribution.

The U.S. spirits firm Brown Forman, the owner of the successful bourbon brands Jack Daniels and Southern Comfort, diversified into the consumer durables industry, acquiring Lenox china, crystal, and giftware and Hartmann luggage in 1983, and Dansk table and giftware and Gorham silver in 1991. Unlike the successful merger that created LVMH, this strategic move did not turn out to be cost-efficient.[24] The linkages between the management of brands in bourbon, tableware, and luggage products were weak, and there were no economies of scale and scope in distribution. In 2005 Brown Forman sold Lenox (which by then also included other businesses such as Dansk contemporary tableware and giftware, and Gorham silver).

Grand Metropolitan remained highly diversified until it merged with Guinness in 1996, when it shed its hotel and real estate interests. During the 1980s, it had become the world's largest multinational in alcoholic beverages as a result of its mergers and acquisitions of firms such as Liggett & Myers in 1980 and Heublein in 1987. In its growth strategy, Grand Metropolitan combined geographical and product diversification, focusing not only on the drinks sector but also on food, taking advantage of the physical and knowledge linkages that exist between the two businesses.

While firms in the 1990s tended to refocus on related activities, some leading firms either focused more on alcoholic beverages or definitively abandoned that business and concentrated operations in other industries. In other cases, alcoholic beverages became just part of their wide portfolio

[24] Hoovers Directory of World Business, "Brown Forman," (Austin, Tex: Reference Press, 2002).

of businesses. The high level of competition and stagnation of consumption in many product categories influenced this trend. Most important, this was a way for firms to eliminate costs associated with investments where both the physical and knowledge linkages were weak or nonexistent.

Examples of firms that during the 1990s increased their investments in other businesses are Louis Vuitton Moët Hennessy (LVMH), Seagram, Whitbread, and Bass. Of all these firms, LVMH was the only one that by the beginning of the twenty-first century still operated independently in the alcoholic beverages industry. Since the late 1980s, it had intensified its investments in the perfumes, leather goods, and fashion industries. In 1996, it acquired DFS (Duty Free Stores), the U.S.-based world leader in the sale of luxury goods to international travelers, which then became a major distributor of LVMH products. Here the linkages involved not only marketing knowledge in terms of the general management of brands and distribution, but also knowledge about specific markets, such as the Far East. The strength of the linkages in the distribution of such apparently different products is related to the fact that the beverages produced by LVMH are premium priced. LVMH can, therefore, use the same distribution channels and address the same kind of customers in all of their businesses (e.g., through Duty Free Stores).

In the 1980s, when the beer market was sluggish, many brewers diversified into other leisure and related activities. For example, traditionally a brewing and pubs retailing business, Bass Brewery entered the hotel and restaurants business with the acquisitions of Crest Hotels. Later in the 1980s, they sold this business and acquired instead Holiday Inns International. Bass also invested in biotechnology, bar developments, and the leisure business with the acquisition of Coral Social Clubs, and British American Bingo Inc. Whitbread, traditionally a brewing and wholesaling business, in the 1980s diversified into the restaurant sector by building a chain of Beefeater Steak Houses and forming a joint venture with Pepsi Co.–Pizza Hut. It also had a small wines, spirits, and soft drinks business that was sold to Allied (Hiram Walker) in 1992.

Seagram had made major investments in the film and entertainment industry in the 1990s, after which the alcoholic beverages business lost importance in its overall activity. Although one of the CEOs had a personal interest in this area since 1967 when Seagram acquired Sagittarius Productions (an investment that did not turn out to be very successful), it was only in the 1990s with the acquisition of MCA in 1995 and the investment in the share capital of Time Warner that the entertainment business became the major source of this firm's revenue.[25] Seagram ended up being acquired by Vivendi, which in 2002 sold the alcoholic beverages business to Diageo and Pernod Ricard.

---

[25] Bronfman, *Good Spirits*: chapter 6.

Geographical Markets

In addition to growth in size, firms were also increasingly involved in foreign markets.[26] Table A8.2 in Appendix 8 provides a ratio of geographical diversification for some of those firms between 1960 and 2005. This ratio includes the percentage of sales generated outside the continent of origin of the firms.[27]

Despite the fragmentation of the industry, many leading multinationals were already in advanced stages of internationalization during the 1960s and 1970s, generating more than 30 percent of their sales in foreign markets. Examples are the firms Distillers Company, International Distillers and Vintners, and Guinness, each of which set up operations on other continents in former colonies of the British empire.

Despite having their production operations based in their domestic markets or continents of origin, many firms had high levels of exports. Moët & Chandon and Hennessy internationalized as early as the eighteenth century.[28] However, the foreign direct investment of the newly merged firm essentially began in the 1970s in response to problems of asset specificity associated with the geographic limits on champagne production, the need to target lower segments of the market with sparkling wines, and the tariff barriers imposed on trade in countries such as Argentina and Brazil.

Most spirits firms and producers of still wines, for example, Distillers, Moët & Chandon, and Hennessy, internationalized earlier than the beer firms, with the exception of Heineken (see Table A8.2 in Appendix 8). Two main factors explain the earlier internationalization of spirits and processed wine firms. On the one hand, they had products that were easily branded and that did not change their characteristics significantly when traveling to different places. On the other hand, spirits and processed wines firms had beverages that were drunk by consumers who tended to have higher levels of income and a greater tendency to have more "global" tastes. By internationalizing very early, these firms played an important role in creating habits of alcohol consumption and in educating consumers in markets like the Far East, which were traditionally negligible.[29]

---

[26] Pearce, "The Internationalisation of Sales by Leading Enterprises."

[27] This was the best proxy found to determine the level of internationalization of firms, as there is no systematic data available on the sales level in their country of origin. For that reason this table does not illuminate the initial steps of internationalization of firms, which usually tend to take place in markets that are closer both geographically and culturally.

[28] Paul Butel and Alain Huetz de Lemps, *Hennessy: Histoire de la Société et de la Famille, 1765–1990* (Cognac: Hennessy, 1999); L. M. Cullen, *The Brandy Trade Under the Ancien Régime* (Cambridge: Cambridge University Press, 1998); Claire Desbois-Thibault, *L'Extraordinaire Aventure du Champagne: Moët & Chandon: Une Affaire de Famille, 1792–1914* (Paris: PUF, 2003).

[29] Teresa da Silva Lopes, "The Impact of Multinational Investment on Alcohol Consumption Since the 1960s," *Business and Economic History*, Vol. 28, No. 2 (1999): 109–22.

In contrast, although easily branded, beer was for a long time perishable and very expensive to transport. That is why companies such as Heineken set up production operations abroad. Wine producers (at least the European firms) had difficulties branding their beverages until recently due to their high grape variety and the fluctuations in the quality of the crops; this made it difficult to produce beverages with the same characteristics every year. Consequently, consumers could not rely on the brand name on the bottle but had to take into account the year of the crop in assessing the quality of the wine.

The 1980s saw a clear shift in the diversification strategies of firms. The percentage of sales generated in markets inside the continent of origin of the firm decreased even further. As analyzed in other chapters, the internationalization of firms during this period not only included mergers and acquisitions of other firms, producers of alcoholic beverages, but also of former distributors. These investments were directed at the European market and at emerging markets such as Asia, South America and central Europe where there existed a potential for further growth of consumption of alcoholic beverages. By making these investments in foreign markets, firms were able to use their excess production capacity and marketing knowledge.

One firm that actually increased its percentage of sales in the continent of origin is Heineken (see Table A8.2). While the European market in 1990 accounted for 76 percent of the total sales of the firm, by 2000 it corresponded to around 90 percent.[30] Although Heineken had invested in different European countries after World War II, it entered actively in this market essentially beginning in the 1990s, acquiring large local brewers in different countries. In 1996, it acquired Fischer and Saint-Arnault in France, thereby entering a market that by the beginning of the twenty-first century had become Heineken's largest. Its acquisition of Birra Moretti in Italy also made Heineken Italia a local market leader.[31]

The largest U.S. and Japanese beer and spirits firms remained focused on their local markets.[32] For example, Brown Forman's very low level of internationalization is partly related to the large size of the U.S. market and also to the firm's strategy of owning very few distribution channels outside its domestic market.[33] Brown Forman's overseas sales relied instead on alliances with multiple partners, in particular with other leading alcoholic beverages multinationals, to distribute their brands in different markets. For instance, in the early 1990s it had distribution alliances with the spirits business of Guinness (United Distillers & Vintners [UDV]) and LVMH to distribute its beverages in Italy, Denmark, Hong Kong, Malaysia, Singapore,

[30] Heineken, Annual Reports and Accounts (1990, 2000).
[31] Heineken, Annual Report and Accounts (1996).
[32] For lack of systematic data these firms are not included in Appendix 8.
[33] Brown Forman is not included in Table 5.2 owing to lack of systematic data.

and South Korea. It had a separate alliance with Seagram to distribute in France and Singapore. In the United Kingdom, it had an alliance with IDV; in Portugal, with Martini; and in Germany, it used Bacardi's distribution channels.[34]

The Role of Marketing Knowledge Linkages

In addition to looking at firms through products and geographical markets, it is also possible to analyze firms as portfolios of resources such as marketing knowledge. Although all these approaches have many similarities (such as those related to the management of the firms' portfolios of products or resources), they highlight different growth avenues.[35]

Marketing knowledge can be easily transferred across different activities within the firm even if the products involved are technically unrelated and have completely different requirements on the production side. For that reason, marketing knowledge may provide a fundamental explanation of the linkages between businesses that operate in distinct industries and where there seems to be no apparent relatedness in terms of products, geographical markets, or complementarity of activities (such as vertical integration).

Several different patterns emerge. The first concerns the diversification strategies followed by firms within the alcoholic beverages business (beer, spirits, and wines). The second is related to the types of nonalcoholic beverages businesses into which they diversified. The third relates to the countries of origin and operation of these nonalcoholic beverages businesses.

Within alcoholic beverages, the strategies of the world's largest multinationals varied. Some only operated in a single business, producing and distributing either beer, spirits, or wine. Others produced different types of beverages, such as wines and spirits, and distributed all three categories of alcoholic beverages, including beer. Of all the possible combinations between these beverages and their production and distribution, the least common is the one that involves firms producing spirits and beer simultaneously. Diageo, which produces Guinness beer and also spirits brands such as Smirnoff vodka, and Johnnie Walker and J&B Rare Scotch whiskies, is an example. But Guinness, unlike other beer brands, is managed and sold in the same way as spirits.[36] Another example is Suntory, which is famous for its whiskies Hibiki and Yamasaki and also sells Suntory beer. This issue of the diversification within alcoholic beverages is analyzed in more detail in the next section of this chapter.

---

[34] International Wine and Spirit Record, "Mergers and Acquisitions 1992" (London, 3 December, 1992).

[35] Birger Wernerfelt, "A Resource-Based View of the Firm," *Strategic Management Journal*, No. 5 (1984): 171–80.

[36] Interview with John Potter, Guinness Brand Manager, London, 21 January 2004.

Table 6.1. *Valued-added chain relatedness between the businesses of the world's largest MNEs in alcoholic beverages*

Standard Industrial Classification: Other Businesses	Beer	Spirits	Wine
SIC 20 Food and Beverages			
Beer	+++	++	+++/++
Spirits	++	+++	+++/++
Wines	+++/++	+++/++	+++
Quick-service restaurants	+	+	+/o
Packaged foods	++	+	+
Soft drinks	+++	++	+
Other SIC codes			
Fashion and leather goods	+/o	++/+	++/+
Home and office products	o	o	o
Leisure – music, films	+/o	+/o	+/o
Perfumes	+	++/+	++/+
Watches	+/o	+	+
Tableware and glassware	o	o	o
Pharmaceuticals and biochemicals	++/+	+/o	+/o
Golf products	+	+	+
Tobacco	+/o	+/o	+/o

Legend: +++ – strong linkage; ++ – medium linkage; + – weak linkage; o – no linkage; +++/++, ++/+, +/o – depends.

The second major pattern that emerges (see Table A8.3 in Appendix 8) involves a split between those firms adopting no or low diversification strategies, and those opting for high diversification. Firms were either refocusing on alcoholic beverages and taking advantage of both product and knowledge linkages or were internalizing essentially knowledge linkages (and in some cases also physical linkages in distribution, depending on the market of operation of the firm). Physical and knowledge linkages of firms with no diversification or low diversification are easy to trace as they tend to occur at all levels of the value-added chain in alcoholic beverages. In highly diversified firms the efficiency rationale is much less easy to access. Sometimes linkages do not even exist, demonstrating the presence of conglomerates rather than diversified firms.

Table 6.1 provides a summarized analysis of the diversification linkages between the alcoholic beverages industry and the other businesses in 2005. In order to avoid bogus quantification, this table identifies four types of linkages: strong linkages (+++), medium linkages (++), weak linkages

(+), or nonexistent linkages (o). When the strength of the linkages created between firms through internalization is not clear, depending on the situation of the firm, this is illustrated in the table as a succession of alternative signs (+++/++), (++/+) or (+/o).

The classification of the linkages between businesses into four categories draws on the analysis of various activities that form the value-added chains of different industries. Basically, these value-added chains are compared in terms of possible physical or knowledge linkages in research and development, production, marketing and branding, and logistics of distribution. For example, if two businesses share the same principles and methods of advertising, benefit from the same market research, rely on the same marketing department, and use the same warehouses and trucks to transport products, as well as sales force, and also target the same kind of customers, then businesses are considered to have strong linkages (+++). On the other hand, if two businesses share none of these kinds of physical or knowledge linkages, then they are considered to have nonexistent linkages (o). It is the nature and incidence of the linkages that may exist between firms that explains the internalization of intermediate product markets and consequently the boundaries of alcoholic beverages firms.[37]

From the analysis of this table, it is clear that despite being apparently unrelated and belonging to different industries, most of the businesses tend to have linkages with the alcoholic beverages industry, even if they are weak (+) or uncertain (+/o). Those linkages tend, however, to be stronger between businesses within the same Standard Industrial Classification (SIC)[38] class. This numerical system developed by the Federal Government for classifying all types of activity within the U.S. economy is very useful for illustrating product relatedness, as it relies essentially on the outputs produced by firms. However, it does not account for those situations where linkages may exist at other levels of the value-added chain of industries such as in marketing or distribution.

The characteristics of the other businesses into which alcoholic beverages firms diversified – essentially related to lifestyle and leisure – point to one common linkage with the alcoholic beverages industry, which is marketing knowledge, since the particular competencies of firms are roughly the same as those required in alcoholic beverages.[39] This is why these businesses to which alcoholic beverages firms diversified offer potential economies of scale and scope in marketing, such as those in the branding of products or the distribution costs of the final products to customers.

---

[37] Neil M. Kay, *Pattern in Corporate Evolution* (Oxford: Oxford University Press, 1997).

[38] Office of Management and Budget, *Standard Industrial Classification Manual* (Washington: U.S. Government Printing Office, 1972).

[39] Praveen R. Nayar, "On the Measurement of Corporate Diversification Strategy: Evidence from Large U.S. Service Firms," *Strategic Management Journal*, Vol. 13 (1992): 219–35.

While marketing knowledge may explain most areas of diversification, production knowledge and common inputs may explain diversification into businesses such as pharmaceuticals and biotechnology. It is possible to apply the expertise and knowledge used in the brewing and distilling applications in those industries.

There are still some other cases of firms where neither physical nor knowledge linkages seem to exist between alcoholic beverages and the businesses into which firms diversified. For example, Fortune Brands diversified in 1970 into home and office products, which include respectively kitchen and bath cabinets, and binders, report covers, labels, and storage boxes (among other items). Despite the firm's claim that marketing linkages exist between all these businesses as they are all branded products, the image transmitted by those brands is completely different. The lack of linkages between the businesses explains, in part, the low value the nonalcoholic beverages business adds to the total profitability of the firm.[40] Another business into which several alcoholic beverages firms diversified but in which the level of physical and knowledge relatedness is very low, is tableware and glassware. The two leading Danish brewers, Carlsberg and Tuborg (acquired by Carlsberg in 1970), have had interests in this industry since the beginning of their operations in the nineteenth century.

In those cases where firms' strategies lack coherence, or where there are no linkages, it is cost-efficient for firms to dispose of these businesses.[41] Some studies argue, however, that such strategies may have been financially motivated, either because the management of the firm thought they had the necessary knowledge to turn the business around and subsequently sell it for a profit, or because they envisaged stock market acceptance of the firm.[42] In other cases conglomerate diversification may also be connected with managerial incentives for diversification (such as managerial risk reduction, and desire for increased compensation), and the lack of adequate corporate governance mechanisms to minimize agency costs where managers are the agents and shareholders the owners.[43] However, evidence suggests that governance structure mechanisms such as boards of directors, ownership monitoring, executive compensation, and the market for corporate control may limit managerial tendencies to overdiversify over the long term.[44]

---

[40] Fortune Brands, Annual Report and Accounts (2000).
[41] G. Dosi, David Teece, and S. Winter, "Toward a Theory of Corporate Coherence: Preliminary Remarks," in G. Dosi, R. Gianetti, and P. A. Toninelli (eds.), *Technology and Enterprise in an Historical Perspective* (Oxford: Clarendon, 1992).
[42] J. Ditrichsen, "The Development of Diversified and Conglomerate Firms in the U.S., 1920–1970," *Business History Review*, Vol. 46, No. 2 (1972): 202–19.
[43] Michael Jensen and William H. Meckling, "Theory of the Firm: Managerial Behavior, Agency Costs and Ownership Structure," *Journal of Financial Economics*, Vol. 3 (1976): 305–60.
[44] Hoskisson and Hitt, "Antecedents and Performance."

The kind of businesses into which firms diversified and the strength of the linkages formed with the alcoholic beverages businesses are also related to the country of origin and operation of those nonalcoholic beverages businesses. As illustrated in Table 6.1, while diversification into food and beverages (in the same SIC class as alcoholic beverages) may have a global scope, in the other SIC classes the scope of diversification tends to be essentially domestic. Food and drink are among the most highly branded sectors in the consumer goods industry.

The evidence provided about the diversification strategies of the world's largest firms in alcoholic beverages by the beginning of the twenty-first century points to the fact that the weaker the linkages between the firm and the businesses into which they chose to diversify, the more domestic these investments tend to be. The presence of high transfer and communication costs associated with risk and uncertainty helps explain such a pattern of diversification.

Cycles of Diversification Within Alcoholic Beverages

Despite the vast array of paths followed by the world's largest firms in alcoholic beverages from 1960, it is possible to find common patterns and the presence of cycles of diversification in their evolution. The origins of wines, spirits, and beer leaders, their distinct cost structures and path-dependent processes in the acquisition of marketing knowledge provide an important base for understanding these cycles. Appendix 9 identifies the different paths of diversification. In this table, the firms are categorized into four groups according to their overall diversification strategies at the beginning of the twenty-first century. In the case of leading firms that did not survive, categorization was based on the type of diversification strategies at the time of merger or acquisition. The four categories used are no diversification/low diversification, medium diversification, high diversification, and conglomerate or unrelated diversification.

For each firm the table in Appendix 9 highlights the types of alcoholic beverages (beer, spirits, and wines) they operated during the period of analysis. The addition of new types of beverages to the portfolio of products appears highlighted on a time line. Investments in production and distribution are also distinguished from investments in distribution alone. While production and distribution activities appear symbolized as wines, spirits, or beer, investments exclusively in distribution appear symbolized in the same way with an added "(d)" for "distribution" after the type of beverage.

There were a relatively high number of brewers that by the beginning of the twenty-first century had not diversified or had a low level of diversification. The firms that originally operated in the spirits business tended to invest in wines (see, e.g., Rémy Cointreau and Bacardi). A similar trend occurred with wines firms. Over time they invested in spirits, with the wines business remaining the dominant activity.

The brewers remained concentrated. This strategy is in part related to the high level of vertical integration and to government regulations concerning the different activities of the firms (including regulations restricting what beverages can be distributed and what channels of distribution can be used).[45] The increasing government regulations of alcoholic beverages in the 1980s and 1990s led the large brewers to make the decisive commitment to stay in the beer industry and divest themselves of non-beer-related businesses. For example, in the early 1990s Anheuser-Busch divested from businesses such as the St. Louis Cardinals Baseball Team Inc., Eagle Snacks, and Campbell Taggart.[46]

The trend toward globalization of the industry enabled firms to grow, either by setting up greenfield investments, forming alliances, or merging and acquiring other firms in foreign markets. Heineken, for example, moved from beer production and distribution to include wines and spirits distribution in the 1970s when it acquired Bokma Distillery, the producer of one of Holland's most popular gins.[47] Other examples are the Japanese firms Kirin and Asahi Breweries, companies that were traditionally brewers that diversified to spirits and wines. Kirin first entered the hard liquor business through its joint venture with Seagram for the production of Japanese whiskey and also distribution of Seagram's spirits. In 1989, Kirin invested in the wine business with the acquisition of Napa Valley Raymond Vineyards in California. In the 1990s, it expanded its interests in the wine business with other acquisitions such as that of Lion Nathan, an Australian brewer that had large interests in the wines business, in 1998.

Allied is a particular case of a firm that between 1960 and the beginning of the twenty-first century operated a full range of alcoholic beverages businesses. When formed in 1961, it was a vertically integrated British brewer. During the 1960s, it moved into processed wines, with the acquisition of Showerings in 1968 (which owned Babycham and Harveys Bristol Cream). In 1976, Allied Breweries entered the spirits business with the acquisition of Teacher's, a scotch whisky producer. By the 1980s, the spirits business had become so important in the total activity of the firm that Allied started to divest itself from the beer business; the last brewing interest sold was the Carlsberg–Tetley joint venture in the United Kingdom, disposed of in 1996.

Firms with medium diversification include brewers that diversified into the wines and spirits businesses, in some cases producing and distributing the beverages, in others engaging in only one activity. The Brazilian firm Ambev, formed in 2000, concentrated on the beer business. However, it also diversified into soft drinks. In 2004, this group merged with Interbrew to form Inbev. The newly merged multinational adhered to a similar strategy.

[45] Richard McGowan, *Government Regulation of the Alcohol Industry: The Search for Revenue and the Common Good* (Westport, Conn: Quorum Books, 1997).

[46] *Business Week* (4 March 1996).

[47] Heineken, Annual Report and Accounts (1970, 1988).

Brown Forman, another medium-diversified firm, moved from the production and distribution of spirits, to the distribution of wines in the late 1960s with the acquisition of the distribution rights for the California sparkling wines Korbel and Bolla & Cella. It was only in 1991, with the acquisition of premium California wine maker Jekel Vineyards and the alliance with Fontanafredda, a producer of Italian wines that licensed the rights to market and distribute their wines, that Brown Forman became a major player in the wine industry.

The firms classified as being highly diversified also tended to be those that diversified the most within the alcoholic beverages industry. In some cases they kept their original business as their core activity. In other cases, the original alcoholic beverages business lost importance to another alcoholic beverages business; for example, in the case of Grand Metropolitan the beer business was discontinued in favor of wines and spirits.

The only brewer that by the end of the twentieth century was part of a conglomerate was Miller Brewing, which belonged to Philip Morris. However, that situation changed in May 2002, when South African Breweries acquired Miller. Figure 6.1 summarizes the alternative cycles of diversification within alcoholic beverages followed by firms originally producers of beer, wines, and spirits from 1960.

Two main patterns emerge from the analysis of this figure. First, while beer firms expanded into wines and spirits (in some cases even divesting from beer), spirits firms only invested in wines and wines firms only invested in spirits. The exceptions are Diageo and Suntory, which operated simultaneously in wines, spirits, and beer. For Diageo this exceptional cycle may be explained by the characteristics of its beer business: Guinness relied essentially on marketing knowledge linkages rather than physical linkages. For Suntory, the linkages between the three businesses were also based on economies of scope in distribution (in Japan, wines, beer, and spirits share the same channels of distribution). However, having been a late entrant to the brewing industry, it took a long time for this business to become profitable. The rationale for keeping it initially was more related to the need for Japanese firms to own wide portfolios of brands, in order to obtain economies of scale and scope in distribution, and also to avoid creating holes in the market that would otherwise be filled by competitors.[48]

Figure 6.1 illustrates another interesting feature in the sequences of diversification followed within the industry. The first firms to diversify were the brewers. They initially moved into processed wines such as port and champagne, then invested in spirits, and finally in wines. One explanation for this

---

[48] Interviews with Yoshi Kunimoto, Executive Vice President of Suntory Allied, and Kunimasa Himeno, Manager of International Division of Suntory; both in Tokyo, 16 September 1999; and interview with Kozo Chiji, Manager of the Corporate Planning Department, Tokyo, 16 September 1999.

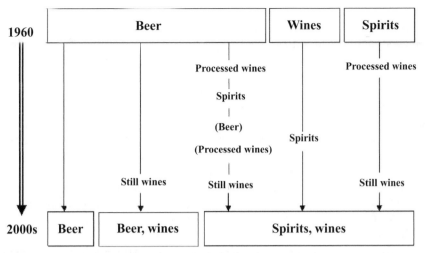

Fig. 6.1. Cycles of diversification in alcoholic beverages.
Notes: Wines – includes investments in both still wines and in processed wines; (Beer) and (Processed wines) – mean divestments from beer and from processed wines businesses.

cycle lies in the knowledge required for managing and branding beer, spirits, and wines. Although branded wine beverages have existed since at least the mid–nineteenth century,[49] beer and cognac were among the first branded and standardized alcoholic beverages. Bass, of England, was the first firm to use the Trade Mark Registration Act of 1875 to protect its red pyramid trademark.[50] Spirits are also easily branded beverages, since in most cases the industrial processes of distillation make standardized products possible. This was not easy with regionally produced wines. Hence, until recently, beer and spirits firms with their strong brands were able to diversify into wines with relative ease, while wine firms with their weaker brands were unable to diversify into beer and spirits.

The marketing knowledge acquired in the management of beer brands allowed brewers to move into other beverages businesses. In contrast, firms originally producing wines tended to remain focused on that business since they had more difficulties in acquiring marketing knowledge that could be transferred to the management of other types of beverages. Those that diversified from wines into other alcoholic beverages entered into spirits production or beer distribution, but wines remained their core business.

By the beginning of the twenty-first century, as the practice of branding wines became more frequent, many large multinationals started making

[49] Paul Duguid, "Developing the Brand: The Case of Alcohol, 1800–1880," *Enterprise & Society*, Vol. 4, No. 3 (2003): 405–41.
[50] Janice Jorgensen (ed.), *Encyclopedia of Consumer Brands* (London: St James Press, 1994): 43.

significant investments in the wines business. This trend occurred not only among brewers but also among large spirits firms with excess resources to be applied in new ventures. The Foster's Group, for example, acquired premium wines companies in Australia (Mildara Blass and Rothbury Wines in, respectively, 1995 and 1996), New Zealand (Montana Wines in 2001), United States (Beringer Wine Estates in 2000), and Italy. Allied Domecq made investments in wines and spirits, enlarging its portfolio of premium brands. In table wines, it created a premium wine portfolio through the acquisition of firms such as Montana in New Zealand, Buena Vista Winery in the United States, Graffigna in Argentina, and Kuemmerling in Germany. Diageo continued pursuing a strategy of creating a restricted portfolio of successful global brands, including table wines. The acquisition of The Chalone Wine Group from the United States in 2004 enhanced the range of premium brands of Diageo in the North American market.

The cycles of diversification in alcoholic beverages are to a certain extent also visible in the level of globalization and concentration of the three drinks sectors. While the spirits industry became global after the 1980s, the wine industry only began to concentrate and globalize at the beginning of the twenty-first century. Owing to the high level of distribution costs that characterized the physical handling of the product, the beer industry remained until recently concentrated only at a regional level despite producing and trading the most easily branded alcoholic beverage. As with wines, it was only in the late 1990s that the brewing industry started to globalize and concentrate on an international scale.

Another explanation for the cycles of diversification can be found in the need for firms to obtain economies of scale and scope in production and distribution. These economies are not as relevant in wines and spirits as in beer, where value addition generated in the production process is low. That is why it is cost-efficient for firms to be in the beer business only if they are able to obtain economies of scale and scope in production as well as marketing.

The major differences between the value-added chains of these three drinks sectors helps to explain not only the cycles of diversification in the alcoholic beverages industry, but also the timing in which they took place.[51] From the 1960s, despite the major transformations in production and in R&D, it was in marketing (in particular in the management of brands) and in distribution that those changes were most significant.[52]

---

[51] Even within the same sector there exist high differences in the cost structure of beverages. For example, the production costs of a Bordeaux wine such as Chateau d'Yquem (one of the world's most expensive wines owned by Bernard Arnault who is also the major shareholder of LVMH) are certainly much higher than those of a standard wine like Ernest & Julio Gallo. Even within the same firm it is possible to find great differences in terms of the cost structure of the different beverages.

[52] See Teresa da Silva Lopes, "Brands and the Evolution of Multinationals in Alcoholic Beverages," *Business History*, Vol. 44, No. 3 (2002): 1–30; James Espey, "A Multinational Approach to New Product Development," *European Journal of Marketing*, Vol. 19,

Historically, beer traveled on average less than spirits or wines as transport costs as a percentage of its unit value were substantial (due to its high level of water content of over 90 percent), and also because it was easily perishable.[53] Over time, as new technologies developed, transportation costs decreased and firms were able to achieve economies of scale and scope. There was also a reduction in distribution costs in spirits and wines, but that depended on the type of beverage.[54] For example, in spirits such as gin that can be produced anywhere and are not asset specific (e.g., on soil or climate), it was possible for firms to lower their distribution costs by investing in production facilities in foreign markets.

The revolution in distribution that took place during the late 1970s and the globalization of markets led to a convergence of distribution systems for beer, wines, and spirits. Many large multinationals created central warehouses from where they managed the logistics for distributing their products. The acquisition of warehouses also created incentives to diversify into other alcoholic beverages businesses. In sophisticated markets such as those in western Europe, stockholding and distribution frequently appeared together as the same function since firms were able to send the beer to the outlets straight away without any stockholding. Apart from the cost advantages, these changes made it possible for firms to get the beer to the final consumer in fresher and better condition. Despite this trend toward convergence in distribution systems for beer, wines, and spirits, in some countries like the United States, regulations did not allow beer to be distributed through the same channels as spirits and wine. For that reason there were no incentives for brewers to diversify into the wines and spirits business.[55]

Diversification and Branding

It is the combination of physical and knowledge linkages that explains the diversification strategies of the leading multinational firms in the alcoholic beverages industry from the 1960s until the present day. This diversification included not only investments made by firms in products similar to those they were already operating, but also investments in new geographical markets, in complementary activities (through vertical integration), and in

No. 3 (1985): 5–18; Tim Craig, "Achieving Innovation Through Bureaucracy: Lessons From the Japanese Brewing Industry," *California Management Review*, Vol. 38, No. 1 (1995): 8–36.

[53] Federal Trade Commission: Bureau of Economics, *The Brewing Industry* (Dec. 1978).

[54] For examples of cost structures per bottle in spirits and wines, see: for spirits, ABN AMRO, "The Sting Is in the Tail" (London, 1999): 23; for wines, Harper Trade Journals, *The Harpers Handbook to the Wine Trade* (London: Harper Trade Journals, 1997); "Conseil Interprofessionnel des Vins du Languedoc et Syndicat des Vins de Pays d'Oc, 'Réflexion sur la Valeur Ajoutée des Vins de Pays d'Oc et des A.O.C. du Languedoc" (Languedoc, 2001).

[55] Interview with John de Lucca, President of the California Wine Institute, San Francisco, 20 March 2001.

businesses that though not sharing the same physical resources, required similar knowledge, in particular, knowledge about the management of brands and distribution channels.

In the 1960s, most firms were focused on their core businesses. Diversification was most frequently based on linkages in physical assets such as similar raw materials and means of production or distribution. As firms grew in size and acquired marketing knowledge, they often diversified into nonalcoholic beverages businesses, taking advantage of efficiencies related to those knowledge linkages. By the beginning of the twenty-first century, the high number of low-diversified alcoholic beverages firms reflected the importance that both physical and knowledge linkages had in the efficient operation of firms and thus on their long-term survival.

Diversification strategies also included geographical expansion. Internationalization tended to take place essentially within alcoholic beverages. This contrasted with diversification into nonalcoholic beverages businesses, which tended to focus on the domestic markets of the investing firms. The lack of strong physical and knowledge linkages and the higher risk involved in international investment explain why firms did not combine strategies of unrelated diversification with geographical diversification. Exceptions were the investments in the food and soft drinks industry, which in some cases were globalized.

Within the alcoholic beverages industry, the diversification strategies of multinationals tended to evolve in cycles. While brewers expanded into wines and spirits, spirits firms only invested in wines, and wines firms invested in spirits but modestly. Another interesting feature of these cycles concerns the sequences of diversification followed by firms, where the last kind of beverage to become the target of multinational investment was wine. There were also some differences in terms of the timing in which these cycles took place in different countries. British firms started to diversify into other alcoholic beverages businesses prior to firms from continental Europe, the United States, and Japan.

Overall, the origins of firms in wines, spirits, and beer and their distinct cost structures and path-dependent processes in the acquisition of marketing knowledge provide an important base for understanding the diversification cycles within alcoholic beverages. Again this reflects the importance that the marketing knowledge acquired by multinationals in alcoholic beverages in the management of brands and distribution channels has in their growth and survival.

7

Acquiring Brands

Introduction

There were four merger waves between the early 1960s and 2005. These broadly paralleled the more general trends in the world economy during this period.[1] Whereas in industries such as those analyzed by Alfred Chandler these waves tended to be related to the technological development of firms, fluctuations in the stock market, and the search for economies of scale and scope;[2] however, in industries such as alcoholic beverages and cosmetics other determinants played a predominant role. Firms domiciled in the United Kingdom seem to have engaged in higher levels of mergers and acquisitions at an earlier time than firms from continental Europe, the United States, and Japan, which for a long time had quite distinct systems of corporate governance.

This chapter focuses on analyzing the impact of brands on firm decisions to merge with or acquire others, and how this influenced the nature and scope of the successive merger waves that have transformed the industry. I provide a summary of the main mergers and acquisitions from 1960 to 2005 and analyze the different merger waves, providing empirical evidence for each one. Finally, I highlight the increasing role of brands in shaping the growth and survival strategies of multinationals in this industry.

Mergers and Acquisitions Waves

The mergers and acquisitions that took place beginning in the 1960s were not a new phenomenon in the industry. While prior to this period, they tended to be sporadic and involve small interests,[3] they now became very

---

[1] Appendix 10 provides a schematic representation of the process of growth of multinationals in alcoholic beverages over time.

[2] See, e.g., Alfred D. Chandler Jr., *Scale and Scope* (Cambridge, Mass: Harvard University Press, 1990); M. Bishop and John Kay (eds.), *European Mergers and Merger Policy* (Oxford: Oxford University Press, 1993).

[3] There are some exceptions of large amalgamations before 1960s such as those that led to the creation of Distillers in 1925. R. Weir, *The History of the Distillers Company, 1877–1939* (Oxford: Oxford University Press, 1995).

frequent, and involved large investments and leading alcoholic beverages firms from different geographical regions. Mergers and acquisitions became much more important than greenfield investments during this period because firms wanted to enlarge their portfolios of beverages by adding brands that had proven successful in specific markets and that had the potential to become global. Apart from providing the possibility of quicker growth, these mergers and acquisitions involved less risk since established brands already had portfolios of customers.

Even though brands have always played an important role in determining mergers and acquisitions in this industry, there were other factors involved in those decisions, especially in the first merger waves. Moreover, distinct countries and alcoholic beverages businesses were affected by these factors at different time periods. This time lag in part reflects the structure of the alcoholic beverages industry in those countries as well as the legal and corporate governance systems.

In the last wave from 1997, firms from emerging markets were also drawn into the process, either as acquirers or acquired firms. Although this merger wave also concerned global brands, firms now aimed at rationalizing costs, leading to a major consolidation of the global industry.

The group of giant multinationals that emerged from this evolutionary process, Diageo, LVMH, Inbev, Fortune Brands, SabMiller, and Pernod Ricard, now look very different from their initial profile as small, locally focused companies. The new firms hold portfolios of multiple global brands involving different types of alcoholic beverages. As a consequence of both horizontal and vertical integration, their activities reach around the world. Table 7.1 identifies some of the major mergers and acquisitions that, from the late 1950s, marked the waves of concentration in this industry.[4] The amounts stated in Table 7.1 include all the business activities of the companies that were merged or acquired. Often, these include other activities besides alcoholic beverages. Caution, therefore, needs to be exercised regarding the analysis of the financial data. Nevertheless, in the absence of satisfactory quantitative means of measuring concentration in the alcoholic beverages industry, the increase in the volume of the transactions in real terms using 2000 prices provides a reasonable proxy.[5]

Mergers and acquisitions gave firms fast market access and increased their probability of success, whereas creating new brands was a slower process

---

[4] See, e.g., for the acquisition of Showerings: Allied Breweries Limited, Annual Report and Accounts (1968), 7; for the acquisition of Martell: Seagram, Annual Report and Accounts (1987); and for the acquisition of Hiram Walker, Allied Lyons, Annual Report and Accounts (1986). "Domecq Adds Spanish Winemaker to Its Stock," *Financial Times* (8/9 September 2001).

[5] Robert D. Pearce, "Concentration, Diversification and Penetration: Some Dimensions of Industry Structure and Interaction," *The University of Reading: Discussion Papers in Industrial Economics*, No. 13 (1989).

Table 7.1. *Major mergers and acquisitions in the alcoholic beverages industry, 1958–2005*

Merger Wave	Year	Companies Involved	Amount (current) in Millions	Amount (2000 = 100)
1958–1962	1958	Watney Mann – merger between Watney Combe Reid and Mann (UK), Crossman (UK) & Paulin (UK)	n/a	n/a
	1961	Allied Breweries – merger between Ind Coope (UK), Tetley Walker (UK), and Ansells Brewery (UK)	n/a	n/a
	1961	Showerings – merger of Showerings (UK), Vine Products (UK), Whiteways (UK)	n/a	n/a
	1962	International Distillers and Vintners – merger between Gilbey (UK) and United Wine Traders (UK)	n/a	n/a
1968–1975	1968	Allied Breweries (UK) acquires Showerings (UK)	239	860
	1968	Heineken (NL) acquires Amstel (NL)	n/a	n/a
	1970	Carlsberg – merger between Carlsberg (DEN) and Tuborg (DEN)	n/a	n/a
	1971	Grand Metropolitan (UK) acquires Truman (UK)	95	310
	1971	Moët-Hennessy – merger between Moët & Chandon (FR) and Hennessy (FR)	n/a	n/a
	1972	Watney Mann (UK) acquires International Distillers and Vintners (UK)	193	578
	1972	Grand Metropolitan (UK) acquires Watney Mann (UK)	946	2.834
	1975	Pernod Ricard – merger between Pernod (FR) and Ricard (FR)	n/a	n/a
1985–1988	1985	Guinness (UK) acquires Arthur Bells (UK)	430	443
	1985	Miller Brewing (US) acquires Pabst Brewing (US)	63	81
	1986	Guinness (UK) acquires Distillers Company (UK)	2.148	2.432

(continued)

Table 7.1 *(Continued)*

Merger Wave	Year	Companies Involved	Amount (current) in Millions	Amount (2000 = 100)
	1986	Allied Lyons (UK) acquires Hiram Walker (CAN)	1.760	1.992
	1986	American Brands (US) acquires National Distillers (US)	663	751
	1987	LVMH – merger between Moët-Hennessy (FR) and Louis Vuitton (FR)	n/a	n/a
	1987	Grand Metropolitan (UK) acquires Heublein (US)	1.616	1.643
	1987	Guinness (UK) acquires Schenley (US)	787	800
	1988	Seagram (CAN) acquires Martell (FR)	36	41
	1988	Interbrew – Artois (BEL) merges with Piedboueuf Interbrew (BEL)	n/a	n/a
1997–2005	1997	Diageo – merger between Guinness (UK) and Grand Metropolitan (UK)	n/a	n/a
	2000	Interbrew (BEL) acquires Whitbread (UK)	400	400
	2000	Interbrew (BEL) acquires Bass (UK)	2.300	2300
	2000	Diageo (UK) and Pernod Ricard (FR) acquire Seagram's (CAN) alcoholic beverages business	5.500	5.500
	2000	Scottish & Newcastle (UK) acquires Kronenbourg (FRA)	3.550	3.550
	2000	Ambev – merger between Companhia Antarctica Paulista (BRA) and Companhia Cervejeira Brahma (BRA)	n/a	n/a
	2001	Allied Domecq (UK) acquired Montana (NZ)	523	537
	2001	Interbrew (BEL) acquires Brauerei Beck (GER)	1.570	1.612
	2001	Aldolph Coors (USA) acquires Carling (UK)	1.700	1.745
	2002	SABMiller – South African Breweries (SA) acquires Miller (US)	5.600	5.697
	2003	Heineken (NL) acquired BBAG (Austria)	2.130	1.940

Merger Wave	Year	Companies Involved	Amount (current) in Millions	Amount (2000 = 100)
	2003	South African Breweries (SA) acquires Peroni (ITA)	5.600	5.100
	2004	Inbev – Merger between Interbrew (BEL) and Ambev (BRA)	n/a	n/a
	2004	Carlsberg (DEN) acquires Holsten (GER)	1.370	1.202
	2005	SABMiller (SA) acquires Grupo Empresarial Bavaria (COL)	7.800	6.724
	2005	Pernod Ricard (FR) acquires Allied Domecq (UK)	14.200	12.241
	2005	Fortune Brands (US) acquires Allied Domecq's brands (UK) from Pernod Ricard (FR)	5.300	4.569

Note: Amounts stated in millions of current and constant U.S. dollars for 2000. n/a – not available or not applicable.

Sources: The Times 1000 (various issues); other secondary sources. For the exchange rates and U.S. price index for 2000, see Export Unit Values – Industrial Countries, *International Statistics Yearbook CD ROM* (Washington, D.C.: International Monetary Fund, 2005).

and the costs involved were high.[6] Consequently, brands with the potential to become global made the firms that owned them attractive targets for mergers and acquisitions and led to both the survival of some firms and the disappearance of many others. Those firms that moved decisively from familiar to geographically and culturally distant markets were able to achieve continuous growth and long-term survival.

Consolidation in the United Kingdom

The first merger wave, from 1958 to 1962, included distillers and brewers from the United Kingdom who fought over tied houses in an effort to obtain national coverage with their brands. Factors such as shifts in consumption, legislation, distribution systems, and competition also had a major influence on merger activity. Mergers primarily involved brewers who sought relief from a scarcity of resources available to re-equip their plants and refurbish their outlets; they were concerned as well about stagnation in per capita consumption of draught beer despite a general increase in consumption of

---

[6] P. Barwise and T. Robertson, "Brand Portfolios," *European Management Journal*, Vol. 10, No. 3 (1992): 277–85.

alcoholic beverages in the Western world. Firms sought to diversify their portfolios of brands available in each market, expand sales to new geographical regions, and reach distinct types of customers (with different ages, genders, and levels of income). The mergers involved a large number of regional leaders, although many companies were left out.[7]

One of the most important creations of this period was Allied Breweries, which became Britain's second largest brewer. Allied Breweries operated at a national level and managed a wide portfolio of successful regional brands such as Double Diamond, Skol, and Long Life. This allowed the firm to acquire marketing knowledge and obtain economies of scale and scope. Its major competitors at the time were other British brewers that produced a limited range of beverages (beer, wines, or spirits) such as Bass, Scottish & Newcastle, Whitbread, and Watney Mann.[8]

Other alcoholic beverages were also involved in this first merger wave. International Distillers and Vintners (IDV) was another important creation during this period. Formed in 1962 as a result of a merger between the spirits and wine merchants United Wine Traders Limited and the vodka and gin distiller Gilbey's Limited, IDV became a major U.K.-based wines and spirits company, producer and distributor of brands with long history such as Gilbey's Black Velvet gin, J&B rare scotch whisky and Croft port.[9]

Although this merger wave was mainly a British phenomenon, there were echoes in other countries such as the Netherlands. There, too, concentration was associated with rising production costs, resulting from (among other things) increases in wages and the desire among a variety of firms to diversify their activities.[10]

Domestic Leaders

A second period of consolidation followed in 1968–1975. Then, firms beyond the United Kingdom, in particular from other European countries, were involved. The worldwide growth in spirits consumption, related in part to the liberalization of retail prices in a number of countries and changes in consumer tastes, affected mergers and acquisitions in this era as did brands. In the United Kingdom, Allied Breweries acquired several wines and spirits firms that owned successful brands. Nonetheless, despite its size, Allied

[7] In 1960, there existed 358 breweries registered in Britain. T. R. Gourvish and R. G. Wilson, *The British Brewing Industry 1830–1980* (Cambridge: Cambridge University Press, 1994), Table 11.1.

[8] Ind Coope Tetley Ansell Limited, Annual Report and Accounts (1961).

[9] International Distillers and Vintners Limited, Annual Report and Accounts (1962).

[10] K. E. Sluyterman and H. H. Vleesenbeek, *Three Centuries of De Kuyper 1695–1995* (Shiedam: Prepress Center Assen, 1995): 63; Commission of the European Communities, "A Study of the Evolution of Concentration in the Dutch Beverages Industry" (1976).

remained a vertically integrated firm selling essentially in the domestic market until the 1970s. Its international activity was limited to targeting the production and sourcing of beverages that could be sold in the domestic market.

The stagnation of beer sales and the expansion of consumption in wines and spirits in the United Kingdom led Allied Breweries to acquire Showerings in 1968 (which brought with it three very successful domestic brands: Harveys Bristol Cream, Babycham, and Cockburn's port). Harveys Bristol Cream, a brand that goes back at least to 1882 (even if not in its present form) was, by the early 1960s, a very successful brand of sherry consumed in Britain before meals on special occasions. After Showerings acquired Harveys in 1966, an aggressive marketing strategy successfully positioned the brand as something to be drunk by younger people in pubs. This proved a temporary phenomenon. The age profile of the population had changed as the "baby boomers" reached drinking age and sought to sample new products, different from those associated with their parents. After acquiring the brand, Allied Breweries reduced investment, focusing instead on brands such as Cockburn's port and Babycham. This also contributed to the decline of Harveys Bristol Cream. Yet, Showerings' sherry (Harveys Bristol Cream) and port wine (Cockburn) brands brought considerable cash flow to Allied Breweries for a long time.[11]

Babycham, a cider brand created in 1953,[12] became the popular new drink of the 1950s due to television advertising and to the way the product was positioned as "mill girls' champagne." Alcohol consumption by women in Western countries such as the United Kingdom had increased significantly during this period as growing numbers of women pursued careers outside their homes and consequently had greater spending power. While traditionally only men (or, at least, no respectable "ladies") had gone to pubs or bars, from the late 1950s, it became normal for women to be seen socializing in pubs. But women didn't buy the same drinks as men. This was crucial to the development of branding strategies of beverages such as Babycham,[13] which was distributed in the domestic market and sold in pubs to young women. Showerings even provided special glasses that looked like champagne glasses for drinking Babycham, making women feel very distinct. However, its consumption decreased sharply in the 1970s due to changes in tastes and fashions and to the competition

[11] Interview with Michael Jackaman, former Chairman of Allied Domecq, Somerset, 19 June 2000; Thomas Henry, *Harveys of Bristol* (London: Good Books, 1986), 10; Tim Unwin, *The Wine and the Vine* (London: Routledge, 1991), 330; Allied Breweries, Annual Report and Accounts (1968, 1969).

[12] Asa Briggs, *Wine for Sale* (London: Bastford, 1985): 130–32.

[13] James Espey, "A Multinational Approach to New Product Development," *European Journal of Marketing*, Vol. 19, No. 3 (1985): 12.

of other drinks brands targeting women, such as Martini and beer with lime.[14]

Grand Metropolitan, formerly a hotel and leisure services firm, was another company that developed very rapidly in the alcoholic beverages business during this period. In 1971, it acquired a small regional brewer – Truman, followed one year later by Watney Mann, which had just acquired IDV. At the time of the acquisition, IDV was drifting: direction from top management was often lacking, there was no marketing strategy, no investments in innovation, and practically no coordination of activities. IDV was nothing more than a collection of different operating companies bound together essentially by history and brands.[15]

With its acquisitions, Grand Metropolitan aimed at expanding in real estate, catering businesses, management of pubs, and at developing retail and distribution networks. Grand Metropolitan had initially hoped to dispose of IDV after completing the acquisition of Watney Mann. After some failed attempts to sell the business, in the beginning of the 1970s Grand Metropolitan realized that the wines and spirits businesses had promising prospects. The company also responded to the problems created by the collapse of the property market and the lagging hotel and tourism industry.[16] This acquisition changed the nature of Grand Metropolitan's business forever. Until its merger with Guinness in 1997, Grand Metropolitan continued to diversify into many different businesses, ranging from consumer services to foods, and even to betting and gaming.[17]

In the Netherlands, the growth of the beer market had attracted foreign direct investment. Foreign firms such as Allied Breweries and Artois from Belgium entered the Dutch market by acquiring local brewers.[18] This competition from abroad and the threat of foreign takeover of Amstel led to the merger in 1968 of the two leading Dutch brewers Heineken and Amstel.[19] In Denmark, the two leading brewers also merged in 1970 to form United Breweries (renamed Carlsberg in 1987). This merger followed many years of collaboration between Carlsberg and Tuborg, which in the years after World

[14] Interview with Michael Jackaman, former Chairman of Allied Domecq, Somerset, 19 June 2000.

[15] This is discussed in detail in James Espey, "The Development of a Worldwide Strategy for International Distillers and Vintners Limited" (Unpublished Ph.D. thesis, Kensington University, 1981).

[16] Interview with Sir George Bull, former CEO of Grand Metropolitan and Diageo, London, 19 November 2003; William J. Reader and Judy Slinn, "Grand Metropolitan" (unpublished manuscript, 1992): 51, 62, 73, 76.

[17] Reader and Slinn, "Grand Metropolitan": 62, 73, 76; Grand Metropolitan, Annual Reports and Accounts (1960–1995).

[18] Allied Breweries, Annual Reports and Accounts (1969); M. G. P. A. Jacobs and W. H. G. Mass, *Heineken History* (Amsterdam: De Bussy Ellerman Harms bv., 1992).

[19] Interview with Jan Beijerinck, former Worldwide Client Service Director of Heineken, Utrecht, 10 March 2000.

War II had worked as a cartel.[20] By the time of the merger, Tuborg was not doing so well, due to its focus on the domestic market.[21]

In France, the merger between Moët & Chandon and Hennessy in 1971 united France's biggest exporters of champagne and cognac, respectively, allowing the two companies to take advantage of the similarities in the "personalities" of their brands and their geographical scope of operations, as well as to economize on distribution costs.[22] At the time of the merger, their main competitors were other champagne houses like Perrier Jouët and G. H. Mumm, and cognac houses like Martell and Courvoisier, all of which were later merged or acquired by firms that became leaders in the global industry.

In 1975, another major French merger formed Pernod Ricard, bringing together the family firms Pernod and Ricard. These firms had already made some unsuccessful attempts to diversify into other business such as tea and coffee. The merger was a natural outgrowth of the alliances they had formed in distribution. The aim was to become a large national company and to diversify within alcoholic beverages, developing an international business.[23]

Another striking merger attempt in 1968 involved Allied Breweries and Unilever, Europe's largest consumer goods company. Unilever had made large investments in brewing in West Africa since 1945 through its joint venture (United Africa Company) with Heineken and Guinness.[24] When it was approached by Allied Breweries, which was seeking access to its wide international distribution network, it responded positively as this proposal fitted with its efforts at that time to develop branded wines.[25] Because of its size and potential impact on industrial concentration, this merger proposal was referred to Britain's Monopolies Commission. Few saw the logic of such a merger, including Allied Breweries' own merchant bankers and other advisors. If the merger between Allied Breweries and Unilever had gone ahead, it would have certainly changed the structure of the industry in the late 1960s. Even though the two companies were related functionally at the production

[20] Kristof Glamann, *Jacobsen of Carlsberg – Brewer and Philanthropist* (Copenhagen: Gyldendal, 1991).

[21] United Breweries, Annual Reports and Accounts (1971); Kristof Glamann, "Voresool – Og Hele Verdens" (Copenhagen: Carlsberg, 1997); Keetie E. Sluyterman, *Dutch Enterprise in the Twentieth Century – Business Strategies in a Small Open Economy* (London: Routledge, 2005): 157–58.

[22] Interview with Colin Campbell, Director of Moët-Hennessy, Paris, 22 November 1999; Moët-Hennessy, Annual Report and Accounts (1971); M. Refait, *Moët Chandon: De Claude Moët à Bernard Arnault* (Saints Geosmes: Dominique Guéniot, 1998): 172.

[23] Interview with Thierry Jacquillat, former CEO of Pernod Ricard, London, 22 October 2003.

[24] Geoffrey Jones, *Merchants to Multinationals* (Oxford: Oxford University Press, 2000), 316; Jacobs and Mass, *Heineken History*: 231–42.

[25] Unilever made several investments in branding and marketing standard wines for mass consumption from 1963 to 1975, but it never succeeded in achieving significant profits. Geoffrey Jones, *Renewing Unilever: Transformation and Tradition* (Oxford: Oxford University Press, 2005).

and the marketing level, the main purpose of the merger, which was to distribute wines, had lost its attractiveness because of the rapid developments in distribution that were taking place in the 1960s. Large hypermarkets had emerged in developed countries, and the distribution channels used for food were quite distinct from those used in alcoholic beverages in many markets. By the time regulatory approval was gained, Unilever's share price was too low for the merger to be considered viable.[26] In 1994, Unilever sold most of its residual stake in United Africa Company in Nigeria, but retained its holdings in some West African businesses. In 1996, Unilever sold its 25 percent stake in Kumasi Brewery of Ghana and its 15 percent stake in Nigerian Breweries.[27] The evidence provided by one of Unilever's competitors, Danone, which held a brewing business until 2000 (Kronenbourg), when it was sold to Scottish & Newcastle, illustrates that in the long run there were no real synergies for food companies in alcoholic beverages.

Acquiring Brands with the Potential to Become Global

The third stage, between 1985 and 1988, was the most significant in terms of the effect on the structure of the global industry. It involved cross-border mergers and acquisitions of firms that owned leading domestic brands with the potential to become global. European firms also bought U.S. companies and brands, although of significantly smaller size, especially when compared with other industries. In contrast to previous decades, where the strategies of the leading firms in alcoholic beverages were distinct and their scale of operations was essentially regional, beginning in the 1970s and 1980s strategies of leading firms from different countries converged. This did not entail a unique best strategy, but rather reflected the changes that were occurring in the industry: multimarket competition between a small group of large multinational firms with high levels of marketing knowledge that were now striving to obtain efficiencies in the various areas of their business.

In the Western world, consumption slowed down in the 1980s as a consequence of recessions in the previous decade, harmonization of taxes among countries, and new concerns about the health consequences of excessive drinking. These issues prompted firms to seek to acquire existing brands that would enable them to rapidly obtain market share while maintaining high levels of control over implementation in terms of costs and time. However, this route of expansion had both advantages and disadvantages. On the one hand, firms acquired large portfolios of complementary brands. On the other hand, problems of brand rationalization arose due to the acquisition of brands that competed with the ones already in the existing portfolios.

[26] Ibid, Monopolies Commission, *Unilever Ltd. and Allied Breweries Ltd. A Report on the Proposed Merger*, PP (1968–69, LX, HC297) (9 June 1969).
[27] Unilever, Annual Report and Accounts (1994, 1996).

During this period, new opportunities appeared in some emerging markets in Africa, Latin America, and Asia, where rising incomes stimulated an interest in Western lifestyles and brands.

The largest multinationals in alcoholic beverages firms now competed at a multimarket level. Firms were involved in foreign direct investment and international alliances rather than just exports. Foreign direct investment was directed to emerging markets such as Africa and Latin America, and leading alcoholic beverages firms achieved international expansion essentially through alliances with local partners. While in the previous two merger waves, firms essentially became domestic leaders and gained an international presence by acquiring foreign brands in their domestic markets, from the 1980s they became truly global multinationals by targeting consumers in foreign markets as well as firms with the similar portfolios of brands. The new strategies reversed the 1970s trend in which firms diversified beyond alcoholic beverages. Firms now followed the general tendency in all industries to own brands with global potential and to build scale in "core" businesses, owning successful brands and appropriating the margins of those activities in the value added chain that added most value.

The larger firms tried to reach new cultural, political, or geographic markets and to appropriate more value added by acquiring firms that owned successful brands. These would form part of a wider array of brands that could provide access to multiple market segments, allowing firms to respond to the increasing power of having a position in the channels of distribution and to take advantage of scale and scope economies in marketing and physical distribution. Those firms that were not able to pursue these strategies of globalization in production and distribution during this period did not survive independently, even if they had previously ranked among the largest worldwide.

Edith Penrose and other researchers on the growth and survival of firms argue that firms behave like species in biology, where only the "fittest" are able to adapt to changing environments.[28] In the late twentieth century, significant changes took place in the corporate environment. Those firms whose control remained in the hands of families were safe from takeover and survived independently, still following distinctive strategies. Anheuser-Busch, Bacardi, Heineken, Martini, Moët-Hennessy, Pernod Ricard, all privately held firms, and also Carlsberg, owned by a charitable foundation, tended either to focus on their domestic markets or to internationalize, specializing in particular products, such as champagne, rum, or beer alone.

The rapid growth of sales in dollar terms of the Japanese firms Asahi Breweries, Kirin, and Suntory during this period was in part illusory, caused by the rapid appreciation of the yen after 1971. However, the growth in

---

[28] Edith Tilton Penrose, "Biological Analysis in the Theory of the Firm," *American Economic Review*, Vol. 42, No. 5 (1952): 804–19.

incomes and the steady spread of western consumption patterns in Japan, combined with strong investment in the development of new and prestige brands by firms (some through alliances with foreign multinational competitors), led to fast "real" growth as well.

While larger multinationals grew by merging and acquiring firms in different parts of the world, smaller firms specialized in niche markets, offering a single brand and relying on other companies to distribute their products. Vin & Sprit from Sweden is a classic example of a smaller firm that developed a survival strategy focused on a niche market, with a single brand – Absolut vodka.[29]

Guinness, Grand Metropolitan, Moët-Hennessy, American Brands, Allied Lyons, Seagram, and Bacardi exemplify the larger-firm strategy during this period. Beginning in the 1980s, financial analysts and advisers, who played a very important role as intermediaries between the stockholders and the firms and in the negotiations for mergers and acquisitions, had a large influence on the strategies of the publicly quoted U.K. firms. They believed that alcoholic beverages firms, in order to remain competitive, should integrate vertically into distribution and shift their management focus from marketing to finance.[30]

In the 1980s, Guinness disposed of all its nonrelated businesses and acquired several firms, gaining the size necessary to compete with the world's largest firms, that is, Grand Metropolitan, Allied Lyons, and Seagram. Guinness first bought Arthur Bell's (owner of the scotch whisky brand of the same name), followed by Distillers. In 1987, Guinness acquired Schenley, which had an old established alliance with Distillers Company for the distribution of Dewar's scotch whisky in that market.[31] This acquisition, along with Grand Metropolitan's acquisition of Smirnoff, illustrates another aspect of the merger wave from 1985 to 1988. Often, firms aimed at gaining access to distribution channels or production rights to successful brands that were being produced or distributed under license by direct competitors in strategic markets.

Heublein was a very attractive target for takeover in the early 1980s owing in great part to its ownership of Smirnoff and its distribution subsidiaries. In an effort to remain independent, it reinforced its portfolio of imported brands in the United States through its distribution companies. Pernod Ricard's

[29] Susannah Hart and John Murphy, *Brands: The New Wealth Creators* (London: Macmillan, 1998), 129; M. Troester, "Absolut Vodka," in Janice Jorgensen (ed.), *Encyclopaedia of Consumer Brands* (London: St James Press, 1994): 4–7; C. Hamilton, *Absolut: Biography of a Bottle* (London: Texere, 2000); Interview with James Espey, former Chairman of Seagram Distillers and former Chairman of IDV-UK, Wimbledon, 3 December 1999.
[30] Interview with Michael Jackaman, former chairman of Allied Domecq, Somerset, 19 June 2000.
[31] Schenley, "Annual Meeting of Stockholders" (21 May 1971), HBS, Historical Collections; Schenley, Annual Report and Accounts (1963).

Wild Turkey is an example of a brand that was newly imported during that period. Despite having just acquired Austin Nichols, Pernod Ricard agreed to form an alliance with Heublein, in which it would have 30 percent of Heublein's business and rights to distribution of Smirnoff in Brazil and Japan. Heublein, on the other hand, would acquire 30 percent of the production and distribution of Wild Turkey in the United States.[32]

During this period, General Cinema began purchasing stock in Heublein. In order to avoid a takeover, the management of Heublein approached Pernod Ricard, asking the latter to consider the acquisition of Heublein. At that stage, however, Pernod Ricard was only prepared to pay a small amount of cash. Heublein ended up being bought by J. R. Reynolds, which later sold the business to Grand Metropolitan.[33] The alliance created between Heublein and Pernod Ricard lasted in its majority (except for the right for Pernod Ricard to distribute Smirnoff in Europe) until 2000, when Diageo formed a consortium with Pernod Ricard for the acquisition of Seagram.[34]

In 1986, Allied Lyons (the successor to Allied Breweries following the acquisition of the foods and retailing company J. Lyons & Co. in 1978) acquired Hiram Walker, owner of several successful brands such as Canadian Club, Ballantines, Courvoisier, and Kahlua. Hiram Walker was also well networked in terms of distribution in the North American market. Seagram had challenged the acquisition, but although outbidding Allied, did not succeed in acquiring the firm.[35] In 1994, Allied sold the Lyons business as part of the firm's strategy to focus on its core activity.[36] It then acquired Pedro Domecq, a leading Spanish brandy and tequila family firm that had a long-standing joint venture with Hiram Walker, a large market share in Latin America, and owned the successful brands Don Pedro, Presidente, Fundador, and Sauza. Allied was interested in Domecq's brandy and tequila brands and its business in South America. It also wanted to appropriate the rest of the joint venture network in Spain to correct tax inefficiencies that did not allow the profits to be repatriated to Britain. This deal, which the Domecq family resisted for some time, was finally agreed on by the widely dispersed shareholders.[37]

North American firms that had largely stood aside from major acquisitions (except in a passive way) also started concentrating by merging and acquiring

[32] Interview with Thierry Jacquillat, former CEO of Pernod Ricard, London, 22 October 2003; "Pernod Ricard Buys Liggett Liquor Unit," *New York Times* (5 June 1980).

[33] Interview with Sir George Bull, former CEO of Grand Metropolitan and Diageo, London, 19 November 2003; Reader and Slinn, "Grand Metropolitan."

[34] Interview with Thierry Jacquillat, CEO of Pernod Ricard, London, 22 October 2003.

[35] Seagram Archive, Accession 2126/ Box 774.   [36] See chapter 6.

[37] Interview with Michael Jackaman, former chairman of Allied Domecq, Sussex, 19 June 2000; Interview with José Isasi-Isasmendi y Adario, former President of Pedro Domecq and also a family member, Madrid, 18 July 2000.

other firms from the 1980s. American Brands acquired two leading U.S. spirits firms. In 1985, the firm took over Jim Beam, owner of the bourbon brand with the same name, and in 1987, National Distillers. Besides Windsor Canadian Supreme whisky, National's portfolio included the American rights for Gilbey's Black Velvet gin (since 1956), as well as De Kuyper's liquor, which had been a very fashionable cocktail in the 1980s.[38]

Seagram, despite its many acquisitions of small firms before 1960, had essentially grown organically. In 1987, it made a major takeover of the French cognac firm Martell, which had a significant market share in the Far East. Seagram was then able to globalize some of its successful brands with international reputations for quality and prestige.

The mergers and acquisitions into foreign markets were mainly by firms that in previous merger waves had already consolidated leading positions in their domestic markets. There were also some mergers between firms that had not participated in the previous merger waves. In 1987, LVMH was formed as a result of the merger between Moët Hennessy, which had interests in the luxury industry (having acquired Christian Dior in 1971), and Louis Vuitton, which owned champagne houses such as Veuve Cliquot and Canard Duchêne. The merger resulted from Christian Dior shareholders' desire to diversify into a business that was French and had a similar image. Moët Hennessy acquired the management knowledge of the Vuitton family, in particular with regard to the management of luxury brands, and made the company a truly global competitor.[39]

In 1988, Interbrew was also formed as a result of the merger between two Belgian brewers Artois and Piedboeuf-Interbrew. The two leading brands had very distinctive positioning and were sold in different kinds of distribution channels. Artois was an old established brand associated with peasants. It had a reputation for creating headaches and was distributed mainly on-trade. Piedboeuf was a comparatively new brand symbolizing youth, virility, and sports and was distributed off-trade.[40] Artois was a leading brand in Belgium until the 1960s when volume began to grow, and Piedboeuf brands such Jupiler started to gain visibility. The alliance between the two firms took place in 1971. It allowed Piedboeuf to have better access to the Belgium market and Artois to improve its market share.

---

[38] Interview with Barry M. Beisch, president and CEO of James B. Beam Distilling Company, *Impact International* (October 1987); National Distillers, Annual Report and Accounts (1973); K. E. Sluyterman and H. H. Vleesenbeek, *Three Centuries of De Kuyper 1695–1995* (Shiedam: Prepress Center Assen, 1995).

[39] Interview with Colin Campbell, Director General of Moët Hennessy (Paris, 22 November 1999).

[40] Interview with Charles Adrianssen, Member of the Board of Directors of Interbrew, and family member, London, 11 June 2004.

Rationalizing Portfolios of Brands

The last merger wave occurred between 1997 and 2005. In this phase, leading global alcoholic beverages firms sought not only to buy successful brands, but also to rationalize costs and obtain other operating efficiencies in maturing markets. Very few new brands were now developing successfully into global brands, and the threat of new entries into the industry had diminished as a result of high concentration. Firms realized that the internalization of intermediate product markets, such as distribution, produced higher transaction costs than using the market, so they kept their wholly owned channels of distribution only in markets that were strategic in the total activity of the firm. There was an increase in mergers and acquisitions of close competitors, along with vertical disintegration, even in markets culturally and geographically close.

This merger wave was initiated by Guinness and Grand Metropolitan, which combined in 1997 to form Diageo. At the time the merger talks started, there were four leading multinationals in the wines and spirits industry – Guinness, Grand Metropolitan, Allied Domecq, and Seagram. None was significantly large in relation to the size of the industry, leaving scope for further mergers between large firms. There were several attempts at mergers between these firms. For example, prior to merging with Guinness, the top management of Grand Metropolitan had approached Seagram. The lack of interest of Seagram's shareholders thwarted a merger. Guinness was a good alternative. It had well-established distribution networks for its spirits brands in the emerging markets of Asia and Latin America, while Grand Metropolitan's business was strong in central Europe. The spirits brands' portfolios were also complementary: Guinness was strong in scotch whisky and gin, whereas Grand Metropolitan was strong in vodka, liqueurs, and tequila. Other synergies related to logistics at several levels of the value-added chain (such as with raw materials and glass purchasing).[41]

When the merger was announced, it was clear that the combined company had a very high share of scotch whisky in both the United States and in several European countries since it owned successful global brands such as Johnnie Walker, J&B Rare and Dewar's. The European Union antitrust authorities forced Diageo to sell Dewar's, as Johnnie Walker and J&B had a broader international presence. Bombay Sapphire was another brand sold in order to allow the merger. The European authorities did not raise any concerns over the combined gin share of the merged group, but the U.S. Federal Trade Commission constructed a market subsegment for imported gin and noted that the two leading gin brands of Diageo, Tanqueray and Bombay Sapphire,

[41] Interview with Jack Keenan, Executive Director of Diageo and Deputy Chief Executive of Guinness/UDV, Cambridge, 14 May 2003; "Analysing the Impact of the UD/IDV Merger," *Spiritscan*, Vol. 10 (November, 1997): 2; ABN AMRO, *Spirits Consolidation* (20 March 1998).

had virtually the entire U.S. market for premium imported gin. Even though Diageo contested this decision, countering that their subsegment was not relevant to consumers in economic terms, they ended up selling Bombay Sapphire, the smallest of the two brands, to avoid any more delays with the merger.[42]

The early twenty-first century saw the start of the international consolidation of the brewing industry that until then had remained essentially regional. Pressure had increased on local giants to expand outside their home markets, with trade barriers falling in Europe and Latin America. Exports and imports of beer were no longer cost-effective, creating new incentives for firms to merge and acquire other brewers in order to have production platforms in key markets and also to create alliances with direct competitors.

In 2001, Belgian Interbrew acquired the brewing business of Bass and Whitbread, in a deal that was subject to an antitrust investigation.[43] Prior to being acquired by Interbrew, Bass and Whitbread had made a few mergers and acquisitions, such as Bass's acquisition of Charrington United Breweries in 1967. However, Whitbread relied essentially on organic growth, and its acquisitions within the alcoholic beverages business did not provide control of the management of the breweries. Unlike its major competitors, Whitbread and Bass remained vertically integrated into retailing for most of the period of analysis. This became a disadvantage once new forms of distribution, in particular supermarkets and hypermarkets, developed.

Artois and Whitbread had a long-established licensing agreement that allowed Whitbread to develop the brand Artois in the United Kingdom for about twenty years with no interference from the Artois family. By the time of Whitbread's sale, the main assets of the firm were the brands produced under license to Stella (positioned as a top-of-the-market beer), and Heineken (positioned as a core lager). Heineken bought back the rights for the Heineken brand, and Interbrew bought the rest of the brewing business.[44]

At the same time, Bass was also coming up for sale. Already strongly positioned in its home market, Interbrew decided to buy Bass as a way to get an important share in the British market.[45] Interbrew thus acquired 34 percent of the market share in Britain, raising antitrust concerns at the Office of Fair Trading. As a result, Interbrew was only able to keep Bass brewers

[42] Interview with Jack Keenan, Executive Director of Diageo and Deputy Chief Executive of Guinness/UDV, Oxford, 5 August 2003; Circular to Shareholders, "Proposed Merger of Guinness Plc and Grand Metropolitan Plc" (3 November 1997).
[43] See, e.g., "Interbrew Attacks UK Over Bass Hangover," *Financial Times* (15 March 2001); K. H. Hawkins and C. L. Pass, *The Brewing Industry* (London: Heinemann, 1979), chapter 3.
[44] Interview with Philippe Spoelberch, member of the Board of Directors of Interbrew and family member, Brussels, 5 July 2004.
[45] Interview with Charles Adrianssen, member of the Board of Directors of Interbrew and Inbev, and family member, London, 6 June 2004.

by disposing of Carling, Britain's best-selling lager, to Coors of the United States at the end of 2001. In the same year, Interbrew continued its strategy of international growth by acquiring Brauerei Beck, the third largest brewer in Germany.[46] Brauerei Beck's main brand, Becks, was a German beer with very high visibility in the United States. In 2004, Interbrew merged with the Brazilian leader, Ambev, to form a world-leading brewer with a global platform. This merger brought successful regional brands – Stella, Artois, Becks, and Brahma – together with the aim of transforming them into global brands.

Scottish & Newcastle, which always focused on the British market and had become the largest brewer in the country after the acquisition of Courage in 1995, started expanding abroad in 2000. Its strategy was to acquire leading domestic brewers in various European countries, such as Brasseries Kronenbourg in France, Hartwall in Finland, and Central de Cervejas in Portugal. In addition, it added stakes in brewers in Italy, Russia, and India. Even though the main aim was to grow in foreign markets by selling existing local brands, Scottish & Newcastle also turned some brands such as Kronenbourg and Foster's (for which the company had a long-term license to produce and market in Europe) into international brands.[47]

Anheuser-Busch, which had always concentrated on producing and selling for the U.S. market, also took part in this last merger wave. In 2000, it acquired a controlling share of Grupo Modelo, the largest Mexican brewer, producer of the brand Corona. In 2002, it also became the second major shareholder after the Chinese government of Tsingtao, the largest of the four Chinese brewers. Other major North American mergers took place, including one between the two family firms Molson, from Canada, and Coors, from the United States, in the beginning of 2005.[48]

In South America, there were also several major mergers and acquisitions in the brewing industry. The most important was between Companhia Antarctica Paulista and Companhia Cervejeira Brahma in 2000, to form Ambev, thus acquiring a 70 percent share of the Brazilian market. This is the company that in 2002 merged with Interbrew to become Inbev. The rationale behind Interbrew was a desire to overcome the barrier created by the Brazilian government to foreign takeovers in brewing. For its part, Ambev wanted to be connected with a leading multinational brewer with a family structure.[49]

The acquisition in 2002 by South African Breweries (SAB) of U.S. Miller brewing from the tobacco and food group Philip Morris gave SAB a major

[46] *World Reporter* (17 August 2001); idem (4 September 2001).
[47] Interview with Tony Froggatt, CEO of Scottish & Newcastle, Edinburgh, 11 July 2003.
[48] Molson Coors, Press Release (9 February 2005).
[49] Interview with Charles Adrianssen, Member of the Board of Directors of Interbrew and family member, London, 11 June 2005.

step into the developed world. Until then, SAB had mainly acquired local brewers in African countries and in central Europe. Protection by the South African government had allowed the company to grow and develop its capabilities at managing firms in a monopoly environment. Shareholders initially viewed the acquisition with anxiety, feeling that the company had not acquired sufficient marketing knowledge to operate in an environment where competition over branding and marketing was intense. Although this acquisition did not create huge efficiencies for SAB, which had a limited presence in the United States, it reduced the firm's dependence on the depreciating South African currency, provided the firm with a source of hard currency, protected it from a possible takeover from Interbrew, and gave a broad U.S. distribution network for its brands, including Castle and Pilsner Urquell.[50]

In 2005, Pernod Ricard acquired Allied Domecq, becoming the second largest multinational in the world in wines and spirits. Fortune Brands supported this acquisition by buying more than twenty spirits and wines brands.

Conclusion

Between the 1960s and the beginning of the twenty-first century, brands played a major part in the concentration of the alcoholic beverages industry through mergers and acquisitions. Despite the significant role of technological innovation in the industry, the reputation associated with brands increasingly shaped the trends and fashions of alcohol consumption. As the main source of competitive advantage in this industry, brands turned the firms that owned them into strategic targets for mergers and acquisitions in an environment characterized by constant changes in consumption patterns, competition, and government and taxation policies.

There were four merger waves from the late 1950s: 1958–1962, 1968–1972, 1985–1988, and 1997–2005. Despite their similarities, each one had some distinguishing characteristics. The first was mainly concerned with the British market. A group of old established firms, in particular in the brewing industry, merged to become national leaders. The second was similar but involved firms from other countries, in particular from Europe, which merged in their domestic markets becoming national leaders in their particular products. During these two first waves, firms widened their portfolios of brands in their domestic markets and entered new markets (other regions within the same country or other countries), different from where these brands originated. The targets were mainly beer and wines firms (in particular producers of processed wines such as port, champagne, and sherry). At this stage, the levels of marketing knowledge acquired by the firms were still relatively low.

50 "SAB's bid to Miller raises eyebrows," *Financial Times* (26 May 2002); "SAB mulls $5bn bid for Miller Brewing," *Financial Times* (24 May 2002).

The third merger wave had quite distinct characteristics, basically giving the industry the shape it has today. Leading multinationals with widespread geographic activities emerged, and successful brands developed to become global. As firms acquired high levels of marketing knowledge, they entered markets more culturally, politically, and geographically distant and acquired firms that owned brands with the potential to be sold globally. Mergers and acquisitions during this period targeted essentially spirits firms and firms that owned distribution channels.

The fourth wave aimed at rationalizing costs and taking advantage of synergies at various levels of the value-added chain. The trend toward vertical integration that had taken place during the 1980s was reversed. Instead, there were widespread alliances between leading multinationals and local partners with complementary activities, or between direct competitors with complementary brand portfolios. This consolidation took place in beer, spirits, and wines, where technological changes had made global brands and distribution viable strategies, in particular with wines from the new world. For the first time, the industry aroused significant antitrust concern in the United Kingdom and the United States. Even this did not, however, stop the trend toward global organizations and global brands.

8

The Life of Brands

Introduction

Many of the world's top brands in wines, spirits, and beer that we know today are originally from diverse countries. They exchanged ownership multiple times, outliving the entrepreneurs and the firms that created them. As shown in previous chapters, most of these brands were added to companies' portfolios after the 1960s. Nevertheless, some multinationals have grown by remaining focused on particular kinds of beverages, such as Heineken and Carlsberg on beer, or E. & J. Gallo on wine. Their brands tend to have the same names as the firms.[1] This chapter focuses on the life of brands in alcoholic beverages from 1960, taking the reverse view from previous chapters. I analyze the origins of today's leading brands and look at the processes through which firms build and grow portfolios of successful brands. I also provide a detailed analysis of how LVMH built its portfolio of brands over time and how firms extend brands. I explain the role of firms in the rationalization and globalization of portfolios of brands and highlight the tendency of firms to trade brands almost as pieces of intellectual property, to rationalize their portfolios of brands, and to standardize the marketing of those brands remaining in their portfolios. I discuss the increasing role of brands in firms' everyday lives, and why and how brands may achieve independent and eternal lives. Detailed empirical examples on successful and unsuccessful branding strategies accompany the central discussion. Finally, I highlight the role of the entrepreneur in explaining the life of brands.

The Origins of Leading Brands

The origin of brands in alcoholic beverages varied widely over time.[2] Before the 1960s, while markets were fragmented and the industry was developing, it was possible for brands to grow and flourish as long as they had some distinctive characteristics such as original recipes or innovative modes of

---

[1] Appendix 1 lists leading multinationals and their brands by 2005.
[2] Paul Duguid, "Developing the Brand: the Case of Alcohol, 1800–1880," *Enterprise and Society*, Vol. 4, No. 3 (2003): 405–41.

distribution. The increase in global competition, the professionalization of management, and the pressure for firms to obtain short-term results, either for shareholders' interests or for performance-related pay, changed the success rate and the life expectancy of brands. A much smaller number of brands launched in recent years became leaders in the industry.

The launching of new brands involves more risk than the management of existing brands. From the 1960s, innovations thus tend to focus instead on the creation of line extensions (using existing well-established and successful brands) and on other investments in the marketing mix of existing successful brands, such as the packaging of the beverages. The increase in competition means that innovation involves very extensive consumer research to position the brands in specific market niches. Consumer research becomes even more important once firms create global brands that require appealing to similar tangible and intangible benefits sought by consumers worldwide.

The most successful brands in wines, spirits, and beer at the beginning of the twenty-first century had a good deal in common.[3] Many were first-movers in their beverage categories. Most relied on family names and were owned by leading multinationals. There were also similarities in terms of the countries where they had been launched. Appendixes 11.1, 11.2, and 11.3, respectively provide detailed information on the evolution of the world's leading brands in wines, spirits, and beer in 2002.

A large number of brands are long-established and were created by entrepreneurs whose businesses were focused on the production of one type of beverage and one brand. They usually built brand identity by relying on the reputation and commitment of their creators: Bacardi in rum, Gallo in table wines, Heineken in beer, Ricard in anis, and Suntory in Japanese wines. Brand identity was particularly important when brands were sold in restricted geographical regions where it was possible for customers to have contact with the entrepreneurs or members of their families working in the business. In the present day, giving family names to brands is still important to the success of the brands. The association of the brand with a history and an entrepreneur provides the customer an assurance about the authenticity and reliability of the product. To the families that own the brands, they are a way to perpetuate the family name, even after the creator of the firm has died. Brands are also an important marketing tool, especially when the family members with the same name as the brand are involved in the marketing activities of the firms.

---

[3] For the purpose of this study "successful brands" are considered to be those that have the largest volume of sales worldwide in their beverage type. Other factors, such as the importance of the volume of sales of the brand in relation to the total activity of the firm and the margins it provides, would have also been very useful in defining what successful brands are. However, the lack of systematic and detailed information led to their not being considered.

Brands may owe their original success to the efforts of different kinds of entrepreneurs. In most cases, the original entrepreneurs who created the brands were responsible for building their imagery and first making them successful. For example, Budweiser from the United States, the world's top beer brand, was always owned by the same family. It was first produced in 1876 through an alliance between Anheuser & Co. and Carl Conrad, a St. Louis wine merchant. When Carl Conrad went bankrupt in 1883, Anheuser formed a partnership with Busch. In addition to producing beer, the new partnership started bottling and marketing it, transforming Budweiser into the first U.S. brand to be distributed nationally. This strategy was supported by innovation in the production of a pasteurized beer that could travel long distances without losing its flavor and also in the creation of an effective distribution network in which Busch got directly involved.[4]

But brands may also become successful due to the role of entrepreneurs within the firm who were not its original creators. These can be other family members, descendents of the creators of the brands, or distributors. The leading scotch whisky brand, Glenfiddich, owned by the family firm William Grant is an example. Launched in 1887, the brand remained a regional one exclusively sold in Scotland until the early 1960s.[5] It was essentially drunk by local consumers involved in sports such as shooting, hunting, and fishing, as malt scotch whisky was considered to be unsuited for people living in southern climates with sedentary occupations.[6]

The increase in competition in the early 1960s, however, led two members of the Grant family to seek new arenas for the growth of their business. One involved launching Glenfiddich outside Scotland under the slogan: "Now you know your Scotch, taste what came before." The first market targeted in 1964 was England and, subsequently, Continental Europe in 1966.[7] Being the prime movers in this market segment of pure malt whiskies gave William Grant an enormous advantage over companies such as Distillers Company that until then only marketed blended whiskies.

Another example of a brand whose success cannot be attributed to its original creator is Absolut vodka, which was principally developed by its distributor. Absolut was launched in 1879, and was owned by the Swedish state monopoly Vin & Sprit. In 1980, Absolut was still a tiny brand. Research conducted at that time in the United States had pointed out a number of liabilities for the brand. The name was seen as too gimmicky; the bottle

[4] Ronald Jan Plavchan, *A History of Anheuser-Busch, 1853–1933* (New York: ARNO Press, 1976).

[5] Francis Collinson, *The Life and Times of William Grant* (Dufftown: The Firm, 1979).

[6] However, the trademark registration of Greenless Brothers Malt Whisky suggests that at least some malt whisky was sold in England in the late nineteenth century. Board of Trade, Trademark Registrations, 1876, volume 1, numbers 102, January 3 [PRO 82/1].

[7] Interview with David Grant, family member of William Grant and Marketing Director, London, 7 January 2004; Collinson, *The Life and Times of William Grant*.

shape was ugly and bartenders found it hard to pour; its appeal was limited as there was no credibility for a vodka made in Sweden.[8] But in the early 1980s, Michel Roux, President of Carillon Importers (then owned by IDV) became the importer and distributor of Absolut in the United States, and TBWA from New York became Absolut's advertising agency. Fortuitously, this happened when America was boycotting Russian products, including vodka. Despite coming from a country not recognized for its vodka, and the trend toward drinks with lower alcohol content, Vin & Spirit jointly with Carillon built a marketing strategy that used the oddities of the brand – its quirky name and odd bottle shape – to create a "personality" relying on quality and style in a series of creative print ads. Each ad in the campaign visually depicted the product in an unusual fashion and verbally reinforced the brand image with a simple headline using few words. For example, the first ad showed the bottle prominently displayed, crowned by an angel's halo, with the headline: "Absolut Perfection" appearing at the bottom of the page. Follow-up ads explored various themes (such as seasonal, geographical, celebrity artists), but always attempted to put forward a fashionable, sophisticated, and contemporary image. By 1991, even though Russian vodkas were available again, Absolut had become the market leader of the imported vodka sector in the United States, with sales of 3.7 million cases.[9]

Like Absolut, many successful brand names created in the twentieth century have origins other than the name of the original founder. They invoked special occasions or dates, or created associations with specific meanings, being in that way evocative.[10] For example, the bourbon Crown Royal (owned by Diageo) was launched by Seagram in 1934 to celebrate the visit of King George VI and Queen Elizabeth, the first visit of a reigning monarch to Canada.[11] The Mexican brandy, Presidente was created by the Spanish firm Pedro Domecq (later part of Allied Domecq) for the Mexican market to acknowledge the importance the president has in Mexico.[12]

A leading brand that relied on evocative imagery is the rum Captain Morgan. Produced in Puerto Rico by Destileria Serralves, it was first launched in 1944 in Canada by Seagram. Seagram named this rum after an old pirate who had sailed to the Caribbean and become the Governor of Jamaica in 1673. Seagram was seeking to take advantage of a segment

---

[8] C. Hamilton, *Absolut: Biography of a Bottle* (London: Texere, 2000).

[9] Ibid; *Impact International Database*.

[10] This was actually a very frequent form of branding in the nineteenth and beginning of the twentieth century. See, e.g., Roy Church and Christine Clark, "The Origins of Competitive Advantage in the Marketing of Branded Packaged Consumer Goods: Colman's and Reckitt's in Early Victorian Britain," *Journal of Industrial History*, Vol. 3, No. 2 (2000): 98–119; François Guichard, *Rótulos e Cartazes no Vinho do Porto* (Lisboa: INAPA, 2001).

[11] Seagram Collection, Hagley Museum and Library.

[12] Interview with José Isasi-Isasmendi, former chairman of Pedro Domecq and family member, Madrid, 17 July 2000.

of the Canadian alcoholic beverages market at a time when it was expanding very rapidly and had very few competitors, Bacardi being clearly the leader.[13] Despite its success in North America, Captain Morgan remained essentially a local brand until 1983, when Seagram introduced the line extension, Captain Morgan Original Spiced Rum, which became more successful than the original brand. Being both very easy to drink and very masculine were the keys to its almost instant success. Even though the combination of rum and cola make it the sort of very sweet drink that is usually associated with women, the brand imagery that associated the beverage with Captain Morgan made it a very masculine beverage. Another reason for the success of Captain Morgan Spiced Rum is its unpretentious imagery in the United States, its major market. This is related to the location where the brand first became successful. Unlike most premium brands that in the United States tend to have been launched in the most sophisticated markets of the East and West Coast, Captain Morgan Spiced Rum first became successful in Chicago, in the middle of the United States.[14]

Kahlua, a coffee liqueur launched in 1937, is another evocative brand that built its personality by associating the beverage with the Pre-Columbian era. Produced by Kahlua SA, a Mexican firm, its growth dates from 1951, when Berman, a Southern Californian distributor, bought the rights to bottle and import the liqueur. Berman built the personality of the brand using Pre-Columbian terra cotta statues to advertise it. The beverage was initially marketed as a highly mixable product, pushing recipe ideas such as Kahlua over ice cream and Kahlua and coffee. In 1965, Berman sold the brand and its production facilities in Mexico to Hiram Walker, which was later acquired by Allied Lyons, the predecessor of Allied Domecq.[15]

Some brands use emblems as a way of differentiating and personalizing themselves according to the aesthetic ideals of consumers. The world of whisky is filled with wild, rare, untameable animals used to symbolize the natural, pure, and authentic character of this alcohol. An example is the red grouse, symbol of Scotland and a rare bird known for its noble gait and carriage, chosen as the emblem of Highland Distillers' Famous Grouse whisky. Another similar example is the Wild Turkey bourbon brand. The wild turkey is a stubborn and clever bird that symbolizes the independence of the United States. Both symbols appeal to a culture of hunting, and The Famous Grouse adds an aristocratic tone to this (because aristocrats are

---

[13] "Seagram Correspondence," Seagram Collection, Hagley Museum and Library.

[14] Interview with Andy Fennell, President of Global Marketing for Smirnoff and Captain Morgan, Connecticut, 13 January 2004.

[15] "Hiram Walker Past and Present," *Ambassador* (Canada: The Company, 1982), Seagram Collection, Hagley Museum and Library; Allied Lyons, Annual Report and Account (1986).

traditionally the hunters in Britain, whereas the common man is in the United States).

Brand names can also be evocative of special locations that do not coincide with the real origin of the brand. An example is the liqueur brand Malibu created by IDV, the wines and spirits division of Grand Metropolitan in 1980.[16] When the brand was first launched it was produced in the United Kingdom. However, the advertisements associated it with the surfer world of Southern California beach culture.

There are yet other cases where brands build their imagery around the country of origin or region where the beverage was actually produced. Jack Daniel's owes much of its success to imagery associations with rural Kentucky where it is distilled. The image focuses on the authenticity and credibility of the beverage. Almost since its acquisition by Brown Forman in 1956, Jack Daniels was managed as a global brand, appealing to U.S. ideals of Jeffersonian agricultural individualism and to nostalgic views of the 1950s American lifestyle. This global strategy was particularly innovative in a period when markets were still perceived as being different and therefore requiring distinct marketing strategies.[17]

Historically beer, too, was closely associated with the place where it was brewed. Bass, for example, was once closely associated with Burton-on-Trent, where it was made. Although global brands often lose such connections, as had been the case with Bass, the U.S. beer Coors has retained a connection with the Rocky Mountains. Of course, some beer brands do draw on national associations for global marketing. Foster's beer, for instance, is very popular in Western Europe due to its image as an authentic product and its associations with Australian masculinity in campaigns such as: "He who drinks Australian, thinks Australian!"[18]

The world's leading brands in wines tend to ignore the region of origin or *terroir*, as illustrated in Table A11.1 in Appendix 11. Whereas old wines to a significant degree are branded by the region, de novo wines are branded by individual firms. The former are subject to problems of free riding by low-quality producers who can damage the status of the region as a whole. The latter, by contrast, have more control over the perception of their brand. New branded wines tend to be produced in new world countries such as the United States, Chile, Argentina, Australia, and New Zealand. The brands emphasize the grape variety above the region or the date, giving the consumer an alternative (and easier) way of sorting through the wide variety of brands. With the old world wines, *terroir* and date are highly important but highly

[16] Grand Metropolitan, Annual Reports and Accounts (1980).
[17] Interview with Ian Kennedy, former brand manager of Jack Daniel's in the United Kingdom, through the agency contract Brown Forman had with IDV, London, 4 February 2004.
[18] "Foster's Enviable Spread," *Impact International* (1 July, 1992).

variable. Private brands are thus the most important part of the strategy used in the marketing of new world wines. These branded wines offer an accessible starting point for new drinkers, offering some sort of guarantee that they will get what they are paying for from one outlet and from one year to the next. For the companies, they offer the prospect of creating consumer loyalty and hence higher sales volumes and profit margins, and lower risks from asset specificity.

An example of a successful de novo brand is Jacobs Creek, an Australian wine produced since the nineteenth century, acquired by Pernod Ricard in 1989 when the brand was just beginning to be exported to the United Kingdom. Pernod Ricard's high levels of marketing knowledge and skill at creating an imagery for the brand, combined with the vertical integration into production, allowed a successful domestic brand to become a successful global brand.

By the beginning of the twenty-first century, the country of origin of the brands and the country of origin of their owners often did not coincide. The brands had either changed ownership or had first been launched and developed outside the country of origin of the owner.[19] The initial development of the brands in foreign markets was often achieved through alliances with local partners or through the creation of wholly owned subsidiaries. A large number of the world's most successful brands were now owned by the leading multinationals in alcoholic beverages. For example in 2002, five of those top multinationals owned fifty-one of the leading hundred premium spirits brands, corresponding to 62 percent of the sales volume in that year (see Table 8.1). This number had, however, decreased as compared to 1990 when these same multinationals (or their predecessors) had a share of about 64 percent. The development of equally successful brands by competitors largely accounted for this decline in brand concentration.

Sales of the world's leading brands in wines, spirits, and beer grew at very high rates between 1990 and 2002, despite the trends toward stagnation of alcohol consumption from the 1980s and the increase in competition. This is particularly evident in table wines and ready-to-drink beverages due to the growing concern with healthier drinking.

In alcoholic beverages, brands coexist with other quality signs. Beverages with certification of origin (such as scotch whisky or port wine) provide quality assurance by protecting a branch of agriculture and the goods produced in a particular area according to a certain tradition, while at the same time enhancing the product image by providing a touch of mystery and a sense of the area's unique character.

The predominance of long-established brands is related to several characteristics of the industry. One concerns the corporate governance of firms. Brands that remain in family hands and are not leaders in their product

---

[19] See Appendix 11.

Table 8.1. Leading multinationals' share of the world's top 100 spirits in 1990, 1997, 2002, and 2005

Multinational	2005 Number of Brands	2005 Sales (Millions of 9-L Cases)	2005 Share of Top 100 Spirits	2002 Number of Brands	2002 Sales (Millions of 9-L Cases)	2002 Share of Top 100 Spirits	1997 Number of Brands	1997 Sales (Millions of 9-L Cases)	1997 Share of Top 100 Spirits	1990 Number of Brands	1990 Sales (Millions of 9-L Cases)	1990 Share of Top 100 Spirits
Diageo (Grand Metropolitan/ Guinness)	17	76.7	26.7	17	67.9	25.8	19	69.8	17.5	9	32.8	12.6
										9	29.7	11.4
Pernod Ricard	16	42.8	14.9	13	28.2	10.7	6	15.8	4	4	12.4	4.8
Allied Domecq	–	–	–	12	27.4	10.4	11	26.9	6.7	12	30.6	11.8
Seagram	–	–	–	–	–	–	9	22.3	5.6	9	22.6	8.7
Bacardi	7	31.8	11.1	5	27.1	10.3	3	21.9	5.5	2	24.7	9.5
Brown Forman	3	12.8	4.5	4	12.2	4.6	4	11.5	2.9	4	12.4	4.6
Total	43	164.1	57.2	51	162.7	62.0	52	168.2	42.2	49	165.2	63.4

Sources: Based on data from *Impact International* and *Drinks International Bulletin*.

categories tend to survive longer because families are willing to sacrifice short-term profitability for long-term survival.[20] Another reason relates to the fact that consumers of alcoholic beverages place tradition and heritage among the main criteria for expressing a preference for a particular brand.[21] Old, established brands that were first movers in particular product segments and performed satisfactorily usually created product differentiation advantages of provenance and heritage. They consequently became the standard against which subsequent entrants were judged.[22] Yet, another reason involves financial issues. The historical low success rates attained with launches of new brands, the high investment costs they require, and the increasing pressure on firms to achieve short-term financial results, in particular publicly quoted ones, explains why so few of the leading brands were launched in recent years.

Recently Launched Successful Brands

There are, however, a few cases of brands launched in the last quarter of the twentieth century that became the leaders in their beverage categories. Baileys Irish Cream and Malibu are two classic examples. Other successful brands launched in this period include Piat D'Or, a French wine, and Croft Original, a sherry. All these brands were launched in the 1970s by International Distillers and Vintners, after it was acquired by Grand Metropolitan. In the 1970s, Grand Metropolitan was a publicly quoted company, operating mainly in the real estate business. Therefore, the attention from shareholders and financial analysts was focused on that business, putting less pressure on the wines and spirits business to generate short-term results. This made it possible for the top management of the wines and spirits subsidiary of Grand Metropolitan to encourage innovation among its employees and even to allow some mistakes.[23] Each of these four brands has its own story.

Baileys Irish Cream was launched in 1974 by Gilbey's Limited of Ireland, not as a direct response to a consumer opportunity, but as a business

[20] Geoffrey Jones and Mary B. Rose, "Family Capitalism," *Business History*, Vol. 35, No. 4 (1993): 1–16; Jonathan Brown and Mary B. Rose (eds.), *Entrepreneurship, Networks and Modern Business* (Manchester: Manchester University Press, 1993); Mark Casson, *Enterprise and Leadership: Studies on Firms, Markets and Networks* (Cheltenham: Elgar, 2000); Andrea Colli, *The History of the Family Firm* (Cambridge: Cambridge University Press, 2003).

[21] "Global Brand Essence and Positioning" (2002), Diageo Archives.

[22] R. Schmalensee, "Product Differentiation Advantages of Pioneering Brands," *American Economic Review*, Vol. 72, No. 3 (1982): 349–65; G. S. Urban, T. Carter Gaskin, and Z. Mucha, "Market Share Reward of Pioneering Brands," *Management Science*, Vol. 32 (1984): 645–59.

[23] Interview with Chris Nadin, former Marketing Manager at Grand Metropolitan, London, 10 December 2003.

opportunity. This was a period when the Irish government was encouraging exports and when, simultaneously, traditional market segments in alcoholic beverages such as gin, whisky, and vodka were maturing rapidly in the Western world. Consumption was moving toward lighter alcohol products, and there was an increase in the number of women drinking alcohol. Coincidently, Grand Metropolitan had two interests in Ireland. It owned Gilbey's Limited Ireland, a small and successful wines and spirits business, and also Express Dairies, which produced dairy products and had excess milk production arising from Common Market subsidies and high tariff barriers. To a large extent, Gilbey's Limited of Ireland controlled the wines and spirits business in that market with brands such as Gilbey's Black Velvet gin, Smirnoff vodka (produced under license for Heublein), Red Breast Irish whiskey, and a range of wines. This very strong position in the Irish market together with the incentives for exports by the Irish government created the need to develop alternative uses for cream, and an opportunity for Gilbey's Limited to develop a new export brand that mixed milk with a spirit.

In addition, the biggest alcoholic beverages brand exported out of Ireland at that time was Irish Mist, which was a liqueur whisky produced by D. E. Williams. The performance of this brand gave Gilbey's Limited managers the idea of moving into the liqueurs business, which was then diverse and relatively underdeveloped, with no really strong brands. Hence, liqueur promised to be an easy and inexpensive kind of product to introduce. Moreover, most existing liqueurs had a low use up rate (which is the speed at which a product is consumed), were high proof, and difficult to drink and therefore took a long time to finish.

Baileys Irish Cream took several years to develop, but when launched became almost an immediate success. It was an instantly palatable liqueur that invited rapid consumption. Being a first-mover in its market segment and having developed a patented process that involved a revolutionary technology for mixing milk with alcohol, it created a very strong barrier to entry by competitors for several years.[24]

Malibu liqueur is another success story. It was first launched in the 1970s by Grand Metropolitan in South Africa under the brand name Coco Rico, and was aimed at competing with a local brand, Coco Ribe. In 1980, Grand Metropolitan decided to launch the brand in the United Kingdom, changing its name from Coco Rico to Malibu (the trademark Coco Rico was already registered by another firm), and the level of alcohol content lowered (to respond to local consumer preferences). The new brand name conveyed the image of "a product that came from paradise and tasted like heaven," which

[24] Interview with Peter O'Connor, Brand Manager of Baileys Irish Cream, London, 22 January 2004.

was believed to appeal to the public's expectations and social and cultural fads at the time.[25]

Piat D'Or, a very successful red wine launched in the early 1970s was the result of thorough consumer research. Grand Metropolitan owned a business called Piat de Beaujolais, based in France, specializing in Beaujolais wines. There was an opportunity in the market to sell to nonspecialists, as consumption of wine had started to grow very rapidly. IDV (then the wines and spirits subsidiary of Grand Metropolitan) found that people loved the sophistication of drinking red wine, but preferred the taste of white wine. Diageo created a wine that tasted like white wine, but was red in color.[26] It was marketed as a relatively cheap wine, using an established icon of quality – the famous Piat. The marketing strategy led to the creation of a distinctive brand. The proposition was strong, the bottle was distinctive, the wine was blended, and the retail price was low. The advertising campaign underlined the heritage of the proposition "the French Adore le Piat D'Or," suggesting the French drank this beverage (even though the brand was never sold in France), and providing a guarantee for those people that were starting to drink wine that it was good value for money.[27]

The wine branded as Piat D'Or was acquired from local French producers and then blended, bottled, and branded by IDV and sold in markets outside France. It became the number one wine in the United Kingdom in its product category. It was subsequently launched in other markets outside the United Kingdom, in particular in Canada and Japan, but never had the same level of success. This was a period of great competition, as other firms such as Paul Masson and Barton & Guestier had recognized the same opportunity and entered this market segment. Over time, as British consumers became more knowledgeable about wines, they started drinking other brands that had come into the market and proved to have a preferred combination of price and quality.[28]

In recent years, Diageo has relaunched Piat D'Or, introducing different wine varieties, new labels, and different bottle shapes. The relaunched brand did not achieve the same success as previously, mainly because the way in which firms compete in the standard quality wines segment had changed. Brand recognition in standard wines is less important than in quality wines, as other factors come into play, for example, price, special deals, mood, point of purchase, shopping channel, and time pressure at point of purchase.[29]

[25] Interview with James Espey, Brand Manager responsible for launching the brand internationally, London, 2 February 2004.

[26] Interview with Steve Wilson, former Brand Innovation Manager at IDV, London, 17 February 2004.

[27] Interview with Chris Searle, Brand Manager who launched Piat D'Or, London, 22 January 2004.

[28] Ibid.

[29] BNP Paribas, "Global Wine Industry" (January 2003).

This is why supermarkets' own brands and promotions have become major competitors of standard wines such as Piat D'Or.

Croft Original was another successful innovation by IDV during this period. It was based on thorough consumer research that detected a whole new niche in the drinks market. At that time, the vodka brand Smirnoff had achieved a high level of success in the United Kingdom, being particularly popular with young people. The British sherry market was also very large, but was populated by an ageing market segment. This market was dominated by sherry brands such as Harveys Bristol Cream and Domecq's Century. Croft Original was distinctive, as it was light in color and looked like a dry sherry, but tasted like a sweet sherry. Young consumers could enjoy the beverage and still look cool and different from their parents, who drank brands such as Harveys Bristol Cream. Over time, the brand started to fade in part due to changing consumer tastes and to the very strong competition of suppliers' own brands. The brand was sold in 2002 to the Spanish family firm Gonzalez Byass.

There are also some examples of very young brands, innovations that focus on very particular niches. Ciroc is a premium vodka brand launched by Diageo in 2003 in the United States to meet customers' growing interest in more healthy products. Being the first vodka made from grapes, the imagery associated with the brand relied extensively on provenance and heritage, considered to give credibility to the brand. For that purpose, it used the provenance from the wine business and grapes from the Champagne region in France.[30]

Building Portfolios of Successful Brands

The number of brands in the portfolios of the world's largest multinationals in alcoholic beverages varied substantially during the last forty years of the twentieth century. From the early 1960s to the late 1980s, these portfolios tended to grow very rapidly. This was mainly achieved through mergers and acquisitions of firms, the creation of line extensions, and the inclusion of agency brands in those portfolios that were the result of alliances with competitors. The merged or acquired target firms tended to own successful brands and cover types of alcoholic beverages in which the acquiring firm yet had no presence. They could also involve competing brands in the same product category, which were successful in different market segments. Alliances with competitors involved low risk and enabled firms to enlarge their portfolios of brands in the short term. Through these alliances, firms were able to produce and market the brands in particular markets for established periods of time. Line extensions were a distinct way of enlarging the

[30] Interview with Steve Wilson, Global Brand Innovation Manager, Diageo, London, 17 February 2004.

portfolios of brands as they used existing brand names and applied them to other beverages.

From the 1990s, the number of brands in firms' portfolios has stagnated if not decreased. Firms started to concentrate on those brands that were most successful and offered the highest profit. With these brands, firms widened further the geographical scope of their operations, using global marketing strategies. The very high success of a few brands led to the development of a new form of transaction in this industry, which involved the acquisition of brands independently from the firms that owned them, almost as if they were pieces of intellectual property.

The Case of LVMH

Louis Vuitton Moët-Hennesy (LVMH; formed in 1987) and its predecessors in alcoholic beverages, Moët Hennessy and Moët & Chandon, provide a good illustration of how multinationals build their portfolio of brands over time.[31] Table 8.2 lists the portfolio of wholly owned brands by these firms in 1977, 1987, 1997, and 2002. It does not consider, however, agency brands obtained through alliances.

In 1997, Moët & Chandon owned 18 brands. Some of these brands had been obtained through the acquisition and absorption of direct competitors, other champagne houses such as Mercier in 1970 and Ruinard in 1973. Others resulted from investments in different kinds of sparkling wines such as Proviar in Argentina 1960, Chandon Munich 1970, Domaine Chandon winery in Nappa Valley, California, in 1973, and acquisitions such as Provifin in Brazil in 1974. Moët Hennessy also invested in other beverage types such as Rozés in 1978, which owned successful brands in champagne and port wine.

The merger between Moët Hennessy and Louis Vuitton in 1987 meant that the portfolio of brands owned by the firm expanded even faster, now involving not only new types of beverages but also more brands in each type. New firms that owned successful brands were merged and acquired; new alliances with competitors, producers of complementary beverages, were formed; and new line extensions were created. Examples of important acquisitions are the champagne houses Pommery in 1990 and Veuve Cliquot in 1994, owners of successful brands.

LVMH only started systematically using line extensions to grow its portfolio of brands in the 1990s. These line extensions were essentially new products (beverages with different characteristics) that demonstrated the contemporary relevance of the brand, meeting modern expectations and matching new consumer needs. The line extensions took advantage of the

---

[31] Hennessy was not included in this table as there was no information available about the number of brands owned by the firm prior to the merger with Moët & Chandon.

Table 8.2. *Portfolio of wholly owned brands of LVMH and its predecessors in 1977, 1987, 1997, and 2002*

	1977	1987	1997	2002
Total number of Brands	18	34	126	57
⇨By Type of Beverage				
Champagne	4	7	42	11
Other sparkling wines.	2	3	13	17
Cognac	7	11	35	17
Still wine	–	1	18	14
Port wine	2	1	6	0
Other fortified wines.	1	–	1	0
Brandy	2	2	2	1
Vodka	1	1	1	1
Gin	1	1	1	0
Liqueur	1	2	1	0
Whisky	–	–	–	1
Other spirits	–	–	6	1
Of which total line extensions (excluding the original brand)	5	10	72	38
⇨By Type of Beverage				
Champagne	–	–	26	2
Other sparkling wines.	–	3	5	16
Cognac	5	7	28	10
Table wine	–	–	5	8
Port wine	–	–	5	–
Other fortified wines.	–	–	1	–
Brandy	–	–	–	1
Vodka	–	–	–	–
Gin	–	–	–	–
Liqueur	–	–	–	–
Whisky	–	–	–	1
Other spirits	–	–	2	–

Sources: Based on *Annual Report and Account Moët-Hennessy* (1977, 1987, 1997, 2002); *Canadean*; Barclays de Zoete Wedd, LVMH (1988).

reputation and personality of already successful brands. For example, in the 1970s, Moët Hennessy developed the brand M. Chandon, used in sparkling wines produced in Brazil and Germany. Despite having a different country of origin, these sparkling wines benefited from the association with the champagne brand name Moët & Chandon, its heritage and imagery of luxury. M. Chandon wines targeted new market segments, notably young people with lower incomes than the typical Moët & Chandon customer, but who had the potential to later become consumers of the main brand.

director of Heublein's, who thought he could teach Americans to use vodka in mixed drinks. Moscow Mule eventually became a very popular beverage in bars all over the United States. The launch in 1992 of Smirnoff Mule in the United Kingdom as a ready-to-drink beverage was aimed at responding to the problems cocktails raised by taking preparation time at the bar and by varying according to the capacities of the bartender. This frequently led consumers to drink beer instead. However, Smirnoff Mule was unsuccessful. It did not have sufficient appeal to the target market, and the bottle, which was too sophisticated, did not correspond to the content of the beverage.

This was in fact IDV's second unsuccessful attempt to enter the ready-to-drink market. It had previously launched Saint Leger, a California Wine Cooler, an alternative to wine and beer. The product failed because the company had not transferred the knowledge from its wine and spirits business to the beer market, and had not done sufficient consumer research.[38]

These unsuccessful ventures were, nonetheless, very useful as learning experiences for the subsequent launch in 2002 of Smirnoff Ice, which turned out to be very successful. Smirnoff Ice's imagery was very different from that of Smirnoff Mule, being much less sophisticated and more connected with the spirits brand. The success of Smirnoff Ice was such that it regenerated consumer interest in the core brand.

The third possible path of line extension occurs when brands are used in different types of beverages. An illustration is Gilbey's Green Label, which was extended from gin to Indian whiskey in 1995. Grand Metropolitan was a late entrant in the Indian whiskey market, which was already quite large. As part of its marketing strategy, the firm used a renowned brand name, Gilbey's, which relied on the imagery and heritage of the original brand. The brand took the name of an importer of wines and spirits from England in the nineteenth century. The success achieved with the brand helped Gilbey's Green Label whiskey become a leading brand in the Indian market.[39] The brand was subsequently sold to UB Group (a leading Indian alcoholic beverages firm) as part of Diageo's strategy of focusing on a small group of global brands.

In the process of creating line extensions, the new rejuvenated brands often become more important than the original brands, surpassing them in their contribution to the total turnover of the firm. In some cases where the firm used an umbrella brand name for all its products, the difference between launching new brands and line extensions is not clear. One example is the beer brand Asahi Super Dry, which succeeded Asahi Draft beer. It was launched in 1987 by Asahi Breweries, during a period when the Japanese beer

[38] Interview with Chris Nadin, former Marketing Manager at Grand Metropolitan, London, 10 December 2003.
[39] *Impact International*; Interview with Richard Watling, Scotch Whisky Global Marketing Director for Diageo, London, 8 March 2004.

industry was suffering a variety of demographic, dietary, social, economic, and distribution changes that affected the demand for beer. Whereas consumers traditionally exhibited strong brand loyalty and conservative taste, the modern drinkers were eager to try new types of beer.[40] This was also a difficult period for the firm, which was on the edge of bankruptcy and was therefore sufficiently desperate to risk a frontal attack on the industry leader, Kirin. Asahi Super Dry targeted an unexploited niche of the Japanese market *koku-kire*, "rich in taste and yet also sharp and refreshing." The level of sales not only surpassed those of any other brand owned by the firm but led Asahi Breweries in 2002 to become Japan's largest beer supplier for the first time since 1954.[41]

Launching line extensions may be easier and less risky than launching completely new brands, but it nonetheless requires very careful consumer research and planning, even when the extension refers to the same kind of product as the original brand. J&B Rare Jet is an example of a line extension launched in 1996 that, despite relying on a top whisky brand J&B Rare, only achieved limited success. The aim of this 12-year-old whisky was to compete with Johnnie Walker Black, just as J&B Rare competes with Johnnie Walker Red. However, there were several problems with the launch. First, the 12-year-old scotch category was not very large, and there was considerable consumer loyalty toward existing brands. Second, in order to compete with Johnnie Walker Black and Chivas Regal (then owned by Seagram), very high investments in marketing were required. And third, the investments in maturing stock were very high. The brand was progressively withdrawn from most of the markets beginning in 1999, except for South Korea, where it was a huge success.[42]

In the brewing industry, line extensions have become the most common way for firms to innovate. The success of many long-established brands means that it is difficult for new firms and new brands to enter the market. In recent years, new opportunities appeared in market segments such as women and light beer consumers. Line extensions provide a way for rejuvenating brands and keeping them "forever young."

Brand Portfolios

From the early 1990s, the globalization of the industry accelerated. Trade in brands independent of firms increased. Multinational firms rationalized

---

[40] Asahi Brewery, Annual Report and Accounts (1988); Tim Craig, "The Japanese Beer Wars: Initiating and Responding to Hyper-Competition in New Product Development," *Organization Science*, Vol. 7, No. 3 (1996): 302–21.

[41] Kirin, Annual Report and Accounts (1966); "Asahi Pushes Kirin out of Pole Position," *Financial Times* (21 February 2002).

[42] *Impact International*.

their brand portfolios focused on those that were most successful and easiest to turn into global brands. The aim was to achieve economies of scale and scope at various levels of the value-added chain, including advertising and distribution. Turning renowned domestic brands with a history of past success into global brands assured consumers of the universal quality and reliability of the beverages. Table 8.3 lists the top brands at the beginning of the twenty-first century for five leading multinationals in premium spirits – Allied Domecq, Bacardi, Brown Forman, Diageo, and Pernod Ricard.

For each firm Table 8.3 shows the top brands, the number of markets covered by each, and the concentration of sales of those brands in terms of number of markets. For that purpose, it uses the number of equivalent firms (1/H) calculated as the inverse of the Herfindahl index (H).[43] It also illustrates the number of line extensions for each of the leading brands. Finally, the table provides information on the type of beverage and the total number of other brands owned by the multinational in that beverage category.

By the beginning of the twenty-first century, the most successful brands owned by the world's leading multinationals were sold in many geographical markets. However, as illustrated by the column containing the index (1/H) with the concentration of markets, most of the sales of these brands were, in fact, in a small number of markets. For example, Jack Daniels, owned by Brown Forman, was sold in 142 markets but the sales were essentially generated in 3 markets, the United States being the most important one. Even Johnnie Walker Red, considered to be a good illustration of a global brand, had its sales concentrated in about 27 markets, despite being sold in 169. Table 8.3 also illustrates the importance of line extensions for the firms' most successful brands. The high number of mergers and acquisitions led firms to own several brands in the same beverage type.

Trading Brands

Whereas in the past, brands were usually bought as part of the purchase of the firms that owned them, more recently a trade in brands independently of firms has increased. Some brands also achieved partial independence when their owners formed alliances – often, remarkably, with direct competitors for the production and/or distribution of these brands in specific markets.[44]

In the beer business, the independence of brands was achieved mainly through alliances both in distribution and production. For example, Guinness, while part of Diageo, was distributed either through wholly owned channels, or through alliances with direct competitors such as Interbrew

---

[43] The number of equivalent markets (1/H) is the inverse of the Herfindahl Index (H), frequently used in industrial economies to measure the concentration of industries. In this case this index is adapted to measure the concentration of sales in terms of markets of destination by each firm.

[44] See Chapter 5.

Table 8.3. *Portfolios of top alcoholic beverages brands for some leading multinationals in spirits in 2002*

Multinational	Top Brands	Number of Markets for Each Top Brand	Concentration of Markets (1/H)	Number of Range/ Line Extensions for Top Brands	Type of Beverage	Number of Brands by Type of Beverage
Allied Domecq	Ballantines	49	5.21	4	Scotch whisky	44
	Presidente	52	1.10	1	Brandy	30
	Canadian Club	50	1.92	2	Canadian whiskey	57
	Kahua	52	2.03	1	Liqueur	75
	Sauza	52	1.87	5	Tequila	17
Bacardi-Martini	Martini Range	96	9.29	19	Vermouth	9
	Bacardi Breezer	51	4.01	36	Brand line extension	14
	Bacardi Carta Blanca	124	5.71	36	Rum	18
	Bacardi Silver	4	1.21	36	Brand line extension	14
	Dewar's White Label	117	3.96	4	Scotch whisky	6
Brown Forman	Jack Daniel's	142	3.09	9	U.S. whiskey	10
	Fetzer	24	1.55	0	Still wine	7
	Canadian Mist	16	1.04	2	Canadian whiskey	2
	Southern Comfort	95	2.55	4	Liqueur	5
	Finlandia Blue	140	14.63	5	Vodka	4
	Jack Daniel's Country Cocktails	1	1	9	Brand line extension	5
Diageo	Smirnoff Ice	35	3.50	12	Brand line extension	27
	Smirnoff Red	153	5.10	12	Vodka	31
	Johnnie Walker Red	169	26.60	10	Scotch whisky	92
	Baileys	147	3.99	11	Liqueur	92
	Guinness	145	9.35	19	Beer	19
	J & B Rare	145	10.80	19	Scotch whisky	29
Pernod Ricard	Ricard	19	1.30	0	Anis/pastis	6
	Seagram Coolers	58	1.00	0	Other ready to drink	13
	Chivas Regal	4	1.18	2	Scotch whisky	6
	Larios Gin	58	1.11	0	Gin/Genever	11
	Pastis 51	58	1.59	1	Aniseed	23
	Suze	58	6.85	1	Bitters / spirit aperitifs	39

Sources: Based on data from *Canadean* and *Impact International.*

(later Inbev) in France, Carlton-United Breweries in Australia, and Lion Nathan in New Zealand.[45]

The depth and length of these alliances may, however, vary. On the one hand, they are dependent on the type of activity being shared – production, distribution, marketing, or a combination. When they involve the marketing of the brand, independence is facilitated. The alliance formed in 1990 between Scottish & Newcastle and Foster's Brewing through which the latter licensed to the former the rights to produce and distribute Foster beer in Europe for an indefinite period of time, is an illustration. The economic difficulties of Elder's/Foster's in the late 1980s were behind the creation of this long-term agreement that gave the sales of such an important market in terms of alcohol consumption to another company. These long-term alliances often result in the acquisition of one company by another. An example is the alliance formed in 1956 between Heublein and Grand Metropolitan for the production and distribution of Smirnoff in Ireland and the United Kingdom. The success Grand Metropolitan achieved with this brand in Europe led to its acquisition of Heublein in 1987.[46]

Smirnoff is in fact a good illustration of a brand with a very long and independent life characterized by multiple alliances and ownerships. First launched in Russia in 1864, it became very successful in the 1870s when it was chosen by the court of the Russian royal family. With the Revolution of 1917, the firm ceased operations and the Smirnoff family emigrated. Some years later, a son of the founder set up a distillery in Poland and started producing Smirnoff using the original family recipe and selling to eastern European countries and Scandinavia. In 1933, his company formed a contract with Rudolf Kunnett, a former supplier of the Russian firm Smirnoff, who had emigrated to the United States. This contract granted Kunnett the exclusive rights and license to manufacture and sell all Smirnoff alcoholic beverages in the United States, its territories, Canada, and Mexico. In the same year, Ste Pierre Smirnoff Fils of New York was incorporated. In 1939, the licensing rights were sold to Heublein, a U.S. alcoholic beverages firm that made the brand very successful. In 1951, Heublein bought the rights to Smirnoff outside the United States.

In 1987, Smirnoff changed hands again. Heublein was in financial difficulty and was acquired by the British multinational Grand Metropolitan, which had the rights to distribute the brand in Europe. The ownership of the brand Smirnoff was in fact the main reason for this acquisition. In 1988, the brand was valued in Grand Metropolitan's balance sheet at £588 million (US$1,047 million).[47] The global success of the brand led the newly formed

[45] Diageo, Annual Reports and Accounts (2003).
[46] Interview with Sir George Bull, former Chairman of Grand Metropolitan and Diageo, London, 19 December 2003; Heublein, Annual Report and Accounts (1986), Grand Metropolitan, Annual Reports and Accounts (1988).
[47] Grand Metropolitan, Annual Report and Accounts (1988).

Diageo to keep Smirnoff in its portfolio and manage it as one of its global priority brands, that is, the brands receiving the most investment in terms of resources (management and capital) and which derive their economic profit from several countries.

In the 1990s, the increasing concentration of the industry involved a tighter control by the antitrust authorities in different countries, which, in concert with the mergers and acquisitions underway, indirectly encouraged further the trade in independent brands. Strategies for the rationalization of portfolios also played a major role in creating independent lives for brands. Some brands became targets for acquisition by multinationals. Others, even when successful within particular markets, were disposed to smaller firms, because they did not fit with firms' strategies for the creation of global brands.

The merger between Guinness and Grand Metropolitan that formed Diageo in 1997 raised important antitrust concerns. The European Office of Fair Trading ruled that the newly merged firm had to sell some of its most successful brands because the combined company had too high a share in some product categories and in some markets. For example, in scotch whisky they ruled that J&B Rare and Dewar's jointly had too large a share of the market in the United States and in some European countries. This led to the sale of Dewar's to Bacardi in 1998. Diageo kept J&B Rare as it had a broader international presence and was number one in Spain, where scotch whisky was growing strongly.

Another example is the sale of Bombay Sapphire by Diageo to Bacardi, which resembled the sale of a piece of intellectual property as it involved only transfer of stocks, the recipe, and the trademark. There were no physical production facilities involved – while the brand was owned by Grand Metropolitan, it was distilled by a third party, G. and J. Greenall in Lancashire. After its acquisition, Bacardi maintained the essential components of the brand: the very distinctive bottle (made of blue glass), the recipe, and the ingredients. However, major changes were introduced in the speed of distribution. Investments in advertising and prices also rose in step with the premium image of the brand.[48] Sales of Bombay grew from 0.5 million bottles in 1998 to 1.4 million bottles in 2004.[49]

Interbrew's acquisition of Whitbread and Bass in 2000 and 2001 was another case contested by the European Monopolies and Restrictive Practices Commission. After the failure of several appeals by Interbrew, the firm had to sell the brand Carling, Britain's largest-selling beer, to Coors in the beginning of 2002 for £1.2 billion (US$1.7 billion).[50]

The sale of Seagram to Vivendi in 2001 caused more brands to take on an independent life. Vivendi was principally concerned with Seagram's media

[48] Interview with Chris Searle, Global Marketing Manager for Bombay Sapphire – Bacardi, London, 22 January 2004.
[49] *Impact International* – Database.
[50] "Coors Agrees to Buy Carling," *Financial Times* (27 December 2001).

companies. Consequently, it sold the alcoholic beverage business of Seagram to Diageo and Pernod Ricard. The breakup of Seagram's brands became an important moment in the trade of independent brands. Owing to the scale of the sale of Seagram and the size of the acquiring companies, this transaction raised antitrust concerns in several countries. Consequently, Diageo was not allowed to buy Chivas Regal as it would have a too high share of the market of scotch whisky. The transaction also raised issues with third parties with whom Seagram had long-term agreements and alliances. One, for instance, concerned the transfer of ownership of Captain Morgan to Diageo. This was contested by Destileria Serralves from Jamaica, the exclusive producer of the brand since its launch. Destileria Serralves claimed it had first rights of refusal in the case of changes in the ownership of the brand. They did not, however, want to exercise their right to purchase, but rather wanted the brand to go to Allied Domecq, with whom Serralves had an alliance. This dispute was settled with the acquisition of Captain Morgan by Diageo and the sale of Malibu to Allied Domecq for £560 million (US$796 million) at the beginning of 2002.[51]

The increasing independence of brands in recent years has led to the emergence of new phenomena in brand lives. Some brands have been divided. For example, the Croft brand was sold by Diageo in 2001 to two firms: the port business to the Portuguese port wine group Taylor (later renamed Quinta Vineyards Bottlers) and the sherry business to the Spanish sherry firm Gonzalez Byass. This splitting up of the ownership and management of the brand is quite an innovation. Previously such divisions had only occurred when brands were sold in different geographical markets where having different brand strategies could not be so easily detected. The existence of different brand management strategies for distinct markets, in fact, evolved in a similar way as trade in alcoholic beverages, where distribution agreements gave autonomy to local distributors.

Rationalization of Portfolios

From the early 1990s, rationalizing their portfolios of brands became part of most companies' growth and survival strategies. In 1993, Allied Lyons sold several brands that had come to its domain through the acquisition of Harveys in 1966. These brands included Tio Mateo sherry, Eminence and Catador brandies, which were sold to Estevez Group in Spain for 500 million pesetas (US$3.9 million).[52] In 1999, after its creation, Diageo sold several brands, including Cinzano to Campari of Italy for an undisclosed amount,

[51] "Diageo Talks With FTC Likely to Focus on Malibu" and "Seagram Bidders Hit by Rum Hangover," *Financial Times* (24 October 2001); "Malibu Auction Attracts Drinks Companies," *Financial Times* (18 February 2002).

[52] Allied Lyons, *Annual Report and Accounts* (1994).

1. Amstel, international advert, 1970s

2. Artois "Le Bon Bock" advert, 1930s

3. Bacardi "Uncle Sam Goes to Cuba" advert, 1919–1933

4. Bass Pale Ale label, designed in 1855

5. Brahma "No Curve" advert, 2005

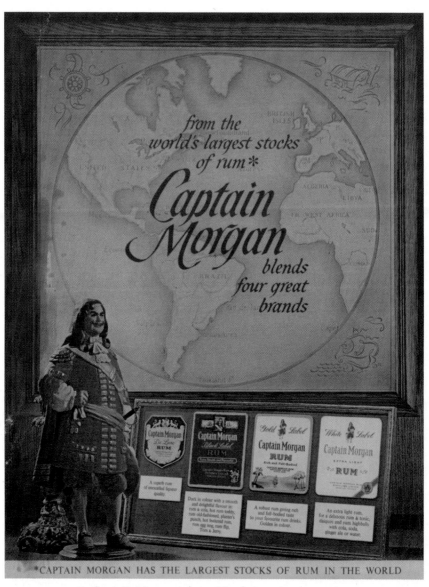

6. Captain Morgan advert, North America, late 1950s

7. Carlsberg Pilsner advert, 1952

8. Foster's, Paul Hogan campaign, Continental Europe, UK, and USA, 1981

9. "GLOBAL" illustration from Diageo annual report 2003

10. Guinness "After Work" advert, United Kingdom 1961

11. Heineken "Most Served at the Bar" advert, 1960s

12. Hennessy cognac international advert, 1959

13. J&B Scotch Whisky, "Pours More Pleasure" advert, USA, 1971

14. Johnnie Walker "Time Marches On" advert, USA, 1948

15. Martini "Sleek and Stylish" advert, 1950s © 2007 Artists Rights Society (ARS), New York/SIAE, Rome

16. Moët & Chandon "Giant Strides" advert, USA, 1903

17. Pernod "C'est la Vie!" advert, 1981

18. Ricard "Bientot la Caravane," advert 1956

19. The original Sandeman "Don" poster, 1928

20. Smirnoff "A New Cocktail Epoch" recipe booklet, 1930s

21. Suntory Whiskey Red advert, fund-raising for Tokyo Olympics, Japan 1964

22. Tuborg "The Thirsty Man" advert, 1900

Asbach of Germany and Metaxa of Greece to Bols, the Dutch group, for US$200 million. Vecchia Romagna, the leading Italian brandy, was sold to Montenegro, a Bologna-based private company. In the same year, the firm also sold eight Canadian whiskeys to Canandaigua (later renamed Constellation Brands) and four bourbons and other U.S. drinks to a consortium of three companies, the two sales raising £218 million (US$353 million).[53]

Pernod Ricard only became a global firm with the acquisition of part of Seagram brands in 2001, marking this achievement by saying, "local roots–global reach."[54] It disposed of many brands that were not considered a strategic priority. In some cases, the sales involved no future connection of the brand with Pernod Ricard. One example is the sale of Four Roses (bourbon) to Kirin. In other cases, Pernod Ricard created alliances for the distribution of the brands disposed, becoming their distributor in major international markets. The alliance formed with the Portuguese leader in wines, Sogrape, where Pernod Ricard kept the exclusive rights for the distribution of Sandeman port worldwide, is an example.

There were yet other small brands that were sold by Pernod Ricard in groups and through auction. Some of these small brands were sold almost as pieces of intellectual property. René Briand and Piave Grappa were two trademarks owned by Seagram although the company neither produced nor distributed them. The producer and distributor of these products, which had no prior ownership in the brand, then acquired them.

Despite rationalizing their portfolios, the multinationals still had competing brands. In some cases this was an indication of a certain fragmentation of markets, as many firms were able to sell competing brands in particular markets. In other cases, where heavy competition and relatively high concentration prevailed, competing brands within a portfolio indicated that the firms were pursuing sophisticated segmentation and marketing strategies that targeted their apparently competing brands to different niches. For instance, after the absorption of Seagram's brands, Diageo had four different whisky brands in South Korea: Johnnie Walker, J&B Rare, Dimple, and Windsor. The four brands were marketed according to Diageo's global segmentation study, which mapped brands' appeal to consumers according to functional benefits and consumer preferences.[55]

At early stages in the development of markets, as preferences tend to be quite similar, segmentation strategies tend to focus on the functional benefits

[53] "Cinzano Sale Completes Diageo Disposals," *Financial Times* (30 September 1999); "Diageo Close to $200 Deal With Bols," *Financial Times* (27 September 1999); "Diageo in $186m Sale of Whiskies," *Financial Times* (23 February 1999); "Diageo Sells More Spirit Brands in $171m Deal," *Financial Times* (25 February 1999).

[54] Interview with Julie Massies, Business Development Manager, Pernod Ricard, Paris, 11 June 2003.

[55] "Brand Building Opportunities for Diageo in the Alcoholic Beverages market in Korea," *Taylor Nelson Sofres* (May 2002).

and characteristics of consumers. As consumption grows, tastes become more refined and differentiated and new competitors enter the markets, segmentation based on emotional benefits and motivations becomes more significant. For example, when a market first develops in the scotch whisky category, the main motivation for consumers to drink is status. As new brands enter the scotch whisky category, consumers start to want to look different. New status categories emerge. Brand management then has to appeal to different interests in order to differentiate brands from those of competitors. In South Korea, for instance, Diageo's Johnnie Walker Black Label is directed toward ideas of sophistication, Windsor to a concept of boldness, J&B Rare to young consumers in Western bars, and Dimple to slightly older consumers and professionals who go to hostess bars.[56]

From Adaptation to Standardization

Over time, the way multinationals managed their portfolios of brands has also varied widely. At early stages in the life of firms, they have tended to use different strategies, adapted to each geographical market. Later, they used standard marketing strategies targeting the global marketplace. However, the timing for such changes varied. After Jack Daniel's whiskey was acquired by Brown Forman, the company used a standardized marketing strategy, building the pivot of its brand on its distillery and tradition. This led to a remarkably stable imagery for the brand over time and across countries that is evident in its advertisements. Even though Brown Forman works with different agencies in different countries, its commercials are similar in terms of the message they aim to convey.

Other global brands such as Ballantines and Johnnie Walker started to be advertised globally at only the end of the twentieth century. Until the mid-1980s, Johnnie Walker's imagery was very different across distinct markets, reflecting distinct power groups within the company, on the one hand, and the character of the local managers and distributors, on the other. For example, before the creation of Diageo, Johnnie Walker Red Label projected a very status-enhancing and quite passionate image in Latin America. In contrast, in the United States it had a very serious and "Wall Street"-like image. In European countries such as Greece, the brand was viewed as a cool drink, seen as a tasteful reward at the end of the day.[57]

Glenfiddich, too, adapted its imagery to local markets' tastes. When the brand was relaunched in England and Continental Europe in the late 1950s, it targeted different types of customers in distinct markets. In England, it first targeted consumers who had already tried it when they were in Scotland.

[56] Ibid; Interview with Richard Watling, Scotch whisky Global Director Marketing, Diageo, London, 5 February 2004.
[57] "Global Johnnie Walker Review Update," *Consumer Scope* (June 2003).

Thus, it was perceived as a very Scottish drink, appealing to values of authenticity and tradition. In Continental Europe, in countries such as France and Italy, where whiskies were seen as deluxe beverages, the image of Glenfiddich was one of luxury in the jet set. Over time, some common trends emerged in those markets where it was most successful, driven by consumers' preferences. By 1969, feeling the strain that comes when a brand is perceived in different ways in different markets, the company began to create a global image for the brand. The imagery was redefined to appeal to younger generations.

Yet another example is the vodka brand Smirnoff. When first sold in the United States before World War II, it was advertised as a product with no taste or smell, difficult to detect on the breath.[58] In the early 1950s, the advertisements of Smirnoff still emphasized these features. However, a new feature of excitement was added by the slogan "it leaves you breathless." Not only did the slogan hint that the drink was so fantastic you lost your breath, it also taunted whisky lovers for the strong smell of their drink. The fact that the beverage was mixable with others was also emphasized. Smirnoff began running a famous series of surrealistic advertisements, shot in Egypt, the Mojave desert, and other unusual locations. The ads focused on the vodka and emphasized the fact that the spirit was "driest of the dry."

In the 1960s, realizing that they needed to create an image for the brand beyond its functionality ("tasteless, odourless and you can mix it with your favourite drink"), Heublein hired famous personalities such as Woody Allen, Marcel Marceau, Joan Fontaine, and Zsa Zsa Gabor to build an image connoting lifestyle and sociability. They also started using women in their ads despite the fact that this was considered inappropriate by the Distilled Spirits Institute.

In the 1980s, as other vodkas such as Absolut entered the market presenting themselves in very imaginative ways, Smirnoff became more conservative, emphasizing in its advertisements its long history and status as the drink of the Russian royalty. While in the early 1990s, Smirnoff's advertisements had different proposition statements depending on the market, from the late 1990s the firm developed an aggressive campaign with a global proposition: "pure thrill." The aim was to create a compelling idea that could travel across time and borders and yet be perceived as promoting an intelligent, unexpected, and audacious brand.[59]

In extreme cases, conditions of consumption of a beverage may prevent globalization. Ricard, one of the most popular anis/pastis worldwide, generated 87 percent of its sales in its domestic market in 1997, despite the

[58] "White Whiskey" advertisements 1940s, Heublein Archive, Diageo.
[59] Graham Hankinson and Philippa Cowking, *The Reality of Global Brands* (Maidenhead: McGraw-Hill, 1996): 12–17.

brand being sold in multiple markets. The other two markets with some significance were Spain and Belgium, corresponding respectively to 9 and 2 percent of total sales.[60] In Spain, Ricard was drunk essentially by Algerian-born French who emigrated to Spain. Indeed, among most Spanish consumers, cocktail-type drinks are traditionally not very common. The drink also suffers from association with French tourists spending their summer holidays in Spain. In France, however, the brand is strongly associated with Provence and holidays. There the brand is designed to project optimism, "the sun in a bottle." The same structural difficulty prevents any penetration of Ricard in the United States. Like the Spanish, Americans do not mix water with alcohol. They drink their whisky or bourbon on the rocks, a drinking habit that is hardly favorable to Ricard. Consumer worries about the safety of what they eat and drink (and the related reluctance to mix unbranded beverages with branded ones) has certainly contributed to the persistence of this habit.

Using standardized and global marketing strategies has several advantages, such as minimizing problems associated with the presence of gray markets, where suppliers go to other countries to buy the beverages rather than using the domestic distributors. This evolution from adapted marketing strategies to global marketing strategies was also accompanied by important changes in the way firms distribute their beverages. By switching from independent distributors to wholly owned channels and alliances, firms were able to increase their control of the marketing strategies of their brands. Even in distribution agreements, the trend has been for the owners of the brands to have more power over the way the brand is managed. This is what happened to the brand José Cuervo, owned by a family firm and distributed since 1960 by leading alcoholic beverages firms (first Heublein, subsequently Grand Metropolitan, and finally, Diageo). Over time, the family has increased its control over how these multinationals manage their brands, by participating in the marketing decisions.[61]

Brands in Firms' Everyday Lives

The importance of global brands led firms to start including the market value of these brands in their financial statements. This was another factor facilitating the purchase and sale of brands independently from the firms that owned them. Grand Metropolitan was the first firm in this industry to include the value of its North American drinks brands. The enhanced strength of the company's balance sheet made it easier to finance the takeover of the food manufacturer and retailer Pillsbury in 1988. Later in the same decade,

[60] Canadean Ltd., "Pernod Ricard" (Hants: 1999).
[61] Interview with Chris Nadin, former Marketing Manager at Grand Metropolitan, London, 10 December 2003.

after the acquisition of Arthur Bell and Distillers Company, Guinness also included the market value of its new spirits brands in its balance sheet.

The strategic significance of brands led to important changes in the organizational structure of firms. In the early 1960s, firms either managed brands almost as if they were separate businesses, or organized them geographically, giving each subsidiary complete autonomy for the management of its brands. Over time, brand management changed substantially, becoming centralized. In the 1980s, companies started prioritizing brands. Grand Metropolitan started managing Smirnoff, J&B Rare, and Baileys Irish Cream as global brands. Other brands, such as Malibu, were considered regional or local, even though they later became global. This strategy was refined after the creation of Diageo in 1997, when brands were classified according to three categories: global priority brands, local priority brands, and category brands. Global priority brands were those considered to have the greatest current and future earnings potential. They were marketed consistently around the world and included leading spirits brands such as Smirnoff, Johnnie Walker, Baileys Irish Cream, and Guinness beer. Each global brand was managed by a different team of managers, with their own strategy for the brands.

Local priority brands were those in which a great deal of the economic profit was generated in one or two countries.[62] Investment decisions and management of these brands took place on a market-by-market basis. Unlike the global priority brands, they did not always have a common marketing strategy around the world. They included brands such as Bell's Extra Special whisky in the United Kingdom. This category also included brands not owned by Diageo such as Budweiser and Carlsberg, which were considered local priority brands in the Irish market. Apart from meeting the preferences of Irish consumers (considered to be very sophisticated), this also helped the local subsidiary of Diageo to achieve critical mass.[63] Category brands were those that were neither global nor local, being sold in particular markets. For example, Black & White was sold in France and Venezuela, and Gilbey's Black Velvet gin in the United Kingdom. Any brands that did not fit in these three categories were sold off.

This strategy of prioritizing brands according to their relevance in the overall portfolio of the firm was also used by brewers. Scottish & Newcastle has two categories of brands: European brands and local leading brands. Foster's and Kronenbourg were classified as European brands, which meant that they used common imagery in different European markets, even though there were still differences in terms of decisions to support advertising at the market level. Local leading brands included McEwans, consumed in

[62] Economic profit is defined as the profit after tax and investment in the balance sheet (eg. maturing stock).
[63] Interview with John Potter, Guinness Global Brand Manager, London, 21 January 2004.

Scotland, Courage in England, and Beamish Irish Stout in Ireland (where it is an alternative to Guinness), and Sagres in Portugal.[64]

In Search of an Independent and "Eternal" Life

Brands are not static but dynamic phenomena, adapting constantly to changing environments. They may outlive the entrepreneurs that created them and even become independent from firms where they were developed, ultimately being traded independently of any other assets, almost as pieces of intellectual property. They may also achieve eternal lives through the creation of line extensions and through other innovations and investments in existing brands involving other variables of the marketing mix such as original packaging or advertising. It is worth noting that unlike other kinds of intellectual property – copyrights (90 years) and patents (14 years) – there is no automatic legal limit to the length of time a firm has monopoly rights over a brand.

Independence gives the advantage to firms better able to manage a brand than the original firm that created it. This was the fate of many of the world's top brands in alcoholic beverages. Most traveled from smaller to larger firms or between leading multinational firms that had those capabilities. Yet, in other cases where brands were successful but did not have the potential to become global, they traveled from larger firms to smaller firms better able to keep them alive, or even between smaller firms. An example is Sandeman, which in recent years was owned by Seagram. The sale of Seagram to Vivendi in 2000 left Sandeman port and sherry to be acquired finally by Sogrape, Portugal's largest wines and spirits firm, and yet a small multinational firm when compared with the leading firms in the industry.[65]

The corporate governance of firms and whether they are of large or small size has had a great influence in the lives of brands, helping to explain their origin, growth, independence, and "eternity." At early stages in the lives of brands, "sticky" marketing knowledge proved to be crucial for creating and building brands, their imagery and reputation. The dynastic nature of family firms provided the stickiness in the knowledge required for their development. The managers that run those businesses were not technically specialized but had very pragmatic and path-dependent marketing knowledge transmitted through practice and experience. Even family-owned firms felt the pressure to bring "smooth" knowledge into their businesses. However, by keeping the control of the shares, families were still able to exert control over their top managers, retaining veto rights over

---

[64] Interview with Tony Froggatt, CEO of Scottish & Newcastle, Edinburgh, 11 July 2004.
[65] Teresa da Silva Lopes, "Competing with Multinationals: Strategies of the Portuguese Alcohol Industry," *Business History Review*, Vol. 79, No. 3 (2005): 559–85.

strategies that were too focused on the short term. In addition, their long-term horizons meant that they gave brands time to grow and survive, even if that implied accepting losses at the early stages in their development. Family firms are also good at rejuvenating brands and creating eternal lives for them. The knowledge required to generate successful line extensions and create innovative marketing strategies is essentially "sticky," path-dependent, and pragmatic.

In contrast, firms with shares spread over a vast number of shareholders tend not to be as good at creating and growing brands in the initial stages of their lives. Their marketing knowledge, mainly of a "smooth" nature, tends to be obtained through hiring professional managers to run the businesses and manage brands. The high levels of personnel turnover and a reward system that usually encourages top managers to achieve short-term results do not provide the opportunity for firms to create and build brands for long periods of time.

However, when firms reach maturity and need to become global, the increasing importance of "smooth" knowledge means that they are better managed by professionals. Even brands that were first-movers require investments in marketing to ensure that consumers do not perceive rival brands as acceptable substitutes.[66] In the beginning of the twenty-first century, the world's leading multinationals tended to have professional managers running their businesses and managing their brands. These hired professionals had management degrees and marketing knowledge of a broad nature that could be applied to the management of diverse kinds of brands.[67] The shift to generalist brand managers facilitated in turn the acquisition of brands independently from firms.

Conclusion

The initial success of brands tends to be associated with entrepreneurial initiatives, either by their creators, family members, descendants of the creators, or by third parties such as the distributors of those brands. At early stages in their lives, brands tend to be owned by family firms, which provide ideal environments to nurture those brands. Families tend to look at the long-term implications for their decisions and accumulate "sticky" marketing knowledge, which is pragmatic and path dependent, allowing consistency in the way brands are managed over time. Once brands achieve a certain level of success indicative of their potential to become global, then it is important that

---

[66] T. Watkins, *The Economics of the Brand* (Whitstable: McGraw-Hill, 1986): 3.

[67] Alfred D. Chandler Jr., *The Visible Hand* (Cambridge, Mass: Harvard University Press, 1977); Sherley P. Keeble, *The Ability to Manage: A Study of British Management, 1890–1990* (Manchester: Manchester University Press, 1992).

they be managed by firms with high levels of "smooth" marketing knowledge. This kind of knowledge can be applied to the management of different brands, even when firms have no previous experience in the management of those specific brands. "Sticky" marketing knowledge is no longer sufficient to develop successful local brands into successful global brands. This helps explain how brands may become independent from the firms that created them.

"Sticky" knowledge is nonetheless sufficient to explain the "eternity" of brands. Rejuvenation of brands can be successful if firms have accumulated high levels of "sticky" marketing knowledge about those brands, for example, knowing what exactly is the appeal behind the brands, and what the right market segments (either demographic or geographic) to target are. This argument, in fact, modifies existing theses, such as that of Alfred Chandler, that principally focus on capital-intensive manufacturing industries in the United States, and claimed the supremacy of the managerial enterprise over the family firm.[68] By looking at an image-based industry and multiple countries with different national systems of governance, this study demonstrates the sectoral and geographic limits of that thesis.

The generalizations provided in this chapter might also be applied to the analysis of the life of brands in other industries, in particular in consumer goods. The trend in such industries is for marketing knowledge to become increasingly "smooth" and for brands to behave as pieces of intellectual property that can be freely bought and sold. There are, however, some differences between brands from distinct industries, or businesses within the same industry. For instance, wine brands are less independent than beer and spirits brands. Emphasizing the region of origin of the brand rather than the name of the firm made wine brands dependent on the specificity of the locations. Consequently, it became more difficult to achieve a scale that made them global and independent.

If the trend of brands to become pieces of intellectual property is confirmed, the twenty-first century will be characterized by freely floating brands. Such a scenario will very likely induce several trends in the dynamic evolution of industries. There will be pressure on family owned and controlled firms – if they want to grow and survive – to hire professional managers to run their businesses. The increase in global competition will lead to further rationalization of portfolios of brands with the disposal by leading firms of brands with less relevance in their portfolios. For the surviving brands in companies' portfolios, the trend will be to widen their scope by rejuvenating them through line extensions.

Given these trends and the characteristics of the industry, the marketing-based multinational of the future will switch from a relatively pragmatic view of management of brands to a more broadly based view in which the impact

[68] Alfred D. Chandler Jr., *Scale and Scope* (Cambridge, Mass: Harvard University Press, 1990).

of the entrepreneur/manager is fully recognized. These trends provide the rationale for claiming that studies on the life of brands provide an alternative way to analyze the dynamic evolution of industries, taking into account the complexity and changes in the environment in which brands operate, the different experiences of individual brands over time, and the relationships of competition and co-operation that they create.

9

Conclusion

Growth and Survival

This book has examined the evolution of the world's largest multinationals in alcoholic beverages from 1960 until the beginning of the twenty-first century. In identifying the importance of multinationality in the growth and survival of firms, the work ultimately became a study of brands, marketing knowledge, and distribution. During the period discussed, the alcoholic beverages industry underwent several major changes. In particular, there was a profound concentration, with multiple mergers and acquisitions among leading multinational firms. As a result, many leading firms disappeared while others became even bigger. Simultaneously, there was rapid internationalization as firms became increasingly global in their strategies. There was also significant diversification as firms invested not only into related but also into unrelated businesses. Nonetheless, by the beginning of the twenty-first century, multinationals had begun to refocus on their core alcoholic beverages businesses.

Despite the similarities in the patterns of growth and survival followed by firms in this industry, there were some significant differences in terms of when these changes took place, depending on whether the firms were involved principally in beer, spirits, or wines. Concentration and internationalization were more pronounced in beer and spirits firms. In addition, beer and spirits firms were able to grow larger earlier than wine firms and encountered more adverse conditions related to the globalization of the industry in the 1980s, having to create new, firm-specific capabilities to grow and survive. In the wines business, industry rather than firm-specific factors still determined growth and survival at the beginning of the twenty-first century. These businesses were less global owing to their asset-specific nature that depended on grapes from specific geographic regions. There are also some spirits, such as scotch whisky, that were asset-specific. So, while in the late 1960s and early 1970s, the merger waves had targeted brewers and producers of processed wines such as port, champagne, and sherry, by the 1980s, spirits had become the acquisition target for firms wanting to create global brands. Only at the end of the twentieth century did similar consolidation start to occur in the wines business, as technological changes in wine production and ageing finally made global brands and distribution strategies viable.

Levels of Institutional Analysis

This study has combined three levels of institutional analysis – the country, the industry, and the firm. These levels are not mutually exclusive. They overlap and complement each other, with each level providing important determinants to explain the multinational growth and survival of firms. The country- and industry-specific determinants are predominantly exogenous, affecting all the firms in a country or in the industry equally. The firm-specific determinants are endogenous and differentiate one firm from another, promoting and limiting success. Country-specific determinants include the national systems of corporate governance in which firms are based. Industry-specific determinants include the level of competition, consumption, and regulation in the industry. Firm-specific determinants include brand ownership, marketing knowledge, distribution networks, ownership structures, and management control systems. While all these levels are considered, the analysis of the firm-specific determinants of growth and survival remains a central theme. The patterns of evolution of seventy multinational firms including their individual histories were analyzed in detail, and an original database was created to record their activity. The database provides significant information about the size and the general performance of these firms, offers details of their internationalization and diversification strategies, and indicates their leading brands. Such wide-ranging historical data allowed the analysis not only of the evolution of individual firms, but also of a whole industry.

Building Capabilities

The heritage of the companies that became the world's leading multinationals influenced their development in multiple ways. In the past, it had been possible for firms to grow and survive without constantly rebuilding their firm-specific advantages so long as the country- and industry-specific determinants were not adverse. This was a period when national systems of corporate governance protected firms from being taken over, consumption patterns of alcoholic beverages were primarily culture specific, and competition and the institutional environment in which firms operated were principally domestic. As a whole, the industry was fragmented and firms could therefore survive without having significant international activity or firm-specific advantages in relation to foreign firms. Prior to the 1960s, most of the leading firms from European countries were already highly internationalized, mainly through exports, and some through foreign direct investment.

This was obviously more common with producers of beverages such as beer, or spirits such as gin, where production did not depend on any kind of natural resources specific to one particular region.

Once these country- and industry-specific factors turned generally adverse beginning in the 1960s, however, firms could grow and survive only by constantly creating or rebuilding firm-specific advantages. This did not necessarily imply that the local environment was hostile, but rather that globalization demanded that firms learn how to deal with multiple environments even if conditions were benign at the level of particular markets. During this period, there was a convergence of strategies among the world's leading firms, and multinationality became a necessary condition for growth and survival. Mergers and acquisitions of other alcoholic beverages firms spread to all continents of the world, becoming a preferred mode of international expansion. Apart from the obvious advantages they provided – such as higher speed for market entry, risk reduction, and efficiency gains in a period of high competition – these mergers and acquisitions also gave firms the ownership of successful brands and international distribution networks that had the potential to become global.

The main factors behind the growth by merger and acquisition of the world's largest firms in alcoholic beverages were brands and marketing knowledge. These factors not only determine the nature and scope of those mergers and acquisitions, but also help explain the successive merger waves that transformed the industry since the 1960s and resulted in the progressive evolution of the boundaries of the world's leading multinationals. I employ the notion of "sticky" and "smooth" marketing knowledge. These concepts suggest the need to understand not only the role of knowledge and information in determining the changing boundaries of firms, but also the type of knowledge and information used and the way it is acquired, transferred, and accumulated by firms.

Before the 1960s, when consumption was fragmented and the level of competition and the institutional environment was local or regional, firms only entered markets that were culturally, politically, and geographically close. They acquired brands to serve these local markets and also to supply their home markets. The levels of sticky and smooth marketing knowledge were relatively low. Firms preferred to distribute their brands through modes that minimized risk and uncertainty, even if that meant having no control over the logistics or marketing of their brands. Beverages were therefore mainly distributed by agents and local distributors. Once levels of marketing knowledge grew, firms started to enter markets that were more culturally, politically, and geographically distant, and acquired and developed brands that had the potential to be sold globally.

In the 1970s and 1980s when competition increased and became global and distribution started to consolidate, new imperfections in intermediate product markets emerged. Since firms had acquired marketing knowledge associated with their international experience and success in the management and distribution of brands, they started using governance structures that involved a higher control over the management of their brands. They also tried to obtain certain economies of scale and scope in the logistics of distribution while retaining control over their marketing operations and minimizing externality costs in distribution. During this period, there was also a general trend toward vertical integration that was subsequently reversed in the 1990s when alliances became very common.

Overall, from the 1960s those firms that had not acquired high levels of sticky marketing knowledge were less likely to survive independently. As the industry matured, external processes for acquiring marketing knowledge such as mergers and acquisitions became more common. There were several processes used to guarantee the absorption of marketing knowledge through these mergers and acquisitions. One was to keep family members of the acquired firms on the board of directors of the acquiring firm.

Alliances in Distribution

In addition to being a fundamental factor in promoting collaboration between firms in an increasingly competitive environment, alliances worked as mechanisms to secure independent growth and survival. Originating in the 1930s between firms from Anglo-Saxon countries, these alliances in the 1970s and 1980s had spread to firms from Continental Europe and Japan. By the beginning of the twenty-first century, they were being formed between large multinationals as well as between firms of smaller size. It is the frequency of alliances between direct competitors in a strategic activity such as distribution that makes this study of alliances in this industry so important (as alliances in other industries normally target production). Alliances proved to be a more efficient way to organize distribution than hierarchy, because they provided the means for firms to reduce risk and uncertainty while simultaneously obtaining economies of scale and scope.

Diversification

This background of firm-specific determinants also explains the different diversification strategies followed by multinationals as they moved into related and unrelated businesses. Related diversification included not only investments in products similar to those already owned, but also investments in new geographical markets, in complementary activities (through vertical integration), and in businesses that, despite not sharing the same physical resources, made use of the same kind of knowledge. As late as the 1960s, most alcoholic beverages firms had little or no diversification. In those cases where they diversified, they relied essentially on linkages related to physical assets. Over time, they diversified into both alcoholic and nonalcoholic beverages businesses, relying on other types of linkages. Firms also started to take advantage of the efficiencies provided by knowledge linkages.

By the beginning of the twenty-first century, this situation had reversed, and the high number of low-diversified firms reflected the importance that product as well as knowledge linkages had for the efficient operation and long-term survival of these multinationals. Diversification into nonalcoholic beverages businesses reflected more than genuine efficiency gains in physical and knowledge linkages. It was, rather, a response to the diversification fads of the time and to multimarket competition. Most firms had high levels of internationalization, mainly in alcoholic beverages, even in those cases where they diversified into other businesses also.

Diversification strategies within the alcoholic beverages industry evolved in distinct cycles, depending on the original businesses of the firms. Again, the flows of knowledge acquired in the marketing and management of brands played a very important role in this process. While beer firms expanded into wines and spirits, spirits firms only invested in wines, and wines firms invested in spirits, but modestly. The sequences of diversification followed by these firms were also distinct. The last beverage type to become the target of investment by multinationals was wine. This demonstrates that, ultimately, marketing knowledge in this industry primarily resides in the management of beer. This is why beer firms diversified into wines and spirits, but neither spirits nor wine firms diversified into beer.

Corporate Governance

The country of origin proved to be an important but not determining factor in the development of leading multinational firms. Until the 1980s, the world's largest firms were all from the United States, the United Kingdom, and Canada. In these countries, capital markets were more developed, and national systems of corporate governance favored mergers and acquisitions. Once the national systems of corporate governance in Continental Europe and Japan showed some trends toward convergence during the 1980s toward those of the Anglo-Saxon countries, the number of large alcoholic beverages firms originally from those countries approached that of firms from Anglo-Saxon countries.

In this industry, contrary to Chandlerian claims about the predominance of managerial governance structures, family ownership has always been a significant determinant in explaining growth and survival of the large multinationals. While dispersed shareholdings and professional management may have permitted the investment in the capital-intensive manufacturing processes documented by Chandler, success in beverages depended on capabilities in marketing and branding, capabilities which may have been developed more effectively by continued family involvement in the business. This is related to the characteristics of an industry in which heritage is linked to brand image, products tend to have long life-cycles, and investments in technological innovation are not very significant. From the 1980s, when there was a convergence of strategies in the industry (even though these did not always result in the most efficient decision or reflect genuine economies), those publicly quoted, multinational firms that did not follow these convergent strategies were often acquired by others that did. The firms that were able to keep their independence were primarily those that were family owned.

Despite the importance of family ownership in explaining growth and survival over time, control of decision making did not necessarily remain in the hands of families. The evidence provided shows that by the beginning of the twenty-first century, even those multinationals in alcoholic beverages that were owned by families tended to be managed by professional managers. Because investments in technological innovation are not as relevant for these firms, it is easier to keep ownership concentrated while still satisfying the financial commitments required for continual growth. However, organizational complexity and growing portfolios of brands often in different product categories required hiring professional managers.

The predominant governance structures evolved from being entrepreneurial based in the beginning of the 1960s, with direct ownership and personal management control systems, to being marketing based, characterized by direct ownership and managerial control systems at the beginning of the twenty-first century. This evolution is again related to the increasingly important role of marketing knowledge and the way firms acquired that knowledge. Before the 1960s, acquisition of marketing knowledge was more pragmatic and path dependent, and was obtained internally through investments in brand innovation. As the industry started to mature, external processes became more common, and marketing knowledge was obtained through mergers and acquisitions of other firms, and through the hiring of professional managers with marketing degrees (although this practice still remained more common in the United States than elsewhere).

The Role of Global Brands

Power of Brands: Imagery and Performance

Global brands that are leaders in the industry developed far beyond their original connection to a particular product. The dimensions that brands add to products or services may, however, vary substantially. In some cases such as in alcoholic beverages, bottled water, and fragrances, brands rely mainly on associated images. In others, such as automotive and computer brands, their "personality" draws more on the performance achieved by the product. Even though there are cases of pure imagery and pure performance brands, most of the times they tend to build their personality around both these attributes.

Brands, in particular those in alcoholic beverages that work through association, usually take a long time to build, and require continual investment by the firms that own them. Multinationals are constantly appealing to new generations of customers who like to try new and different things. Firms often try to create this appeal by developing line extensions. While line extensions have been very successful, their sales may never become very significant in terms of the overall profitability of the firm. Nonetheless, they play a very important role in helping to revamp the brand, keeping it alive and looking "young."

Multiple Brand Ownerships

This capacity for brands to have independent and eternal lives helps us understand the increasing number of brands that outlive the firms that created and developed them. Brand capacity to outlive firms and to be better managed by some firms than others at particular moments in their lives raises questions concerning corporate governance and the way firms acquire marketing knowledge. The concept of marketing knowledge used here included a sticky and a smooth part. The sticky part is more pragmatic and path dependent, accumulated within the firm over time. The smooth part has a broader application and is obtained through hiring professional managers or consultants with specialist training and general marketing skills. Firms managed and owned by families with high levels of sticky marketing knowledge tended to be better at creating successful brands. Firms managed by professionals tended to accumulate more smooth marketing knowledge and for that reason, were better at acquiring and managing independent brands created elsewhere.

Apart from being able to have independent lives, successful brands also have the capacity to live "eternally" by being constantly rejuvenated. In this case, however, the kind of marketing knowledge requires a particular sticky kind, with the emphasis on the adaptation of brands to a specific market segment of a new geographical region leading to the creation of brand or line extensions. Successful brands are considered to be global when they are sold in each of the major regions of the world (even if most of their sales are concentrated in a small number of markets), and pursue an integrated strategy toward this activity. Many of these successful global brands outlive the entrepreneurs and the firms that create them, having multiple ownerships during their lives. The different ownerships of brands over time means that each owner has a particular role in building or developing the brand locally or globally. While brands are becoming established, they tend to be better managed by the entrepreneurs who created them. When they reach a certain level of growth and success they are often better managed by other entrepreneurs or firms with smooth marketing knowledge, larger brand portfolios, and global scope of their operations. Sometimes these changes in ownership are only apparent, achieved through long-term license agreements or through some other forms of alliances to target particular geographic regions or distinct product types. In recent years, many brands have changed ownership as a result of the concentration movements and the need to comply with antitrust regulations.

Staying "Forever Young"

Brands that become truly global and survive multiple ownerships help illustrate the important role they may play in shaping modern consumer society and economic growth. This is especially true when we are contemplating the waves of mergers and acquisitions that we read about in the newspapers. The power of established brands, the difficulty of building new ones, and the capacity for brands to add new dimensions to products, differentiating them from rivals designed to satisfy the same needs, suggest that brands will change ownership whenever other firms more capable of managing them exist. These capabilities are associated with the levels of marketing knowledge within the firms, a function less of the size of these particular firms than of the capacity of management to ensure that the brand can stay "forever young."

Beyond Alcoholic Beverages

While growth and survival are probably the most common topics of research in international business history owing to the prominent role of the firm in explaining modern capitalism, this book analyzes them in a distinct context – the global alcoholic beverages industry from the 1960s until the beginning of the twenty-first century. The innovations in communications and transportation during this period led to rapid and distinct rounds of globalization waves (in the sense that they involved more and larger-size firms), and internationalization strategies that tended to focus on firms' core businesses.

The innovations in communications and transportation also meant that the types of networks formed by firms around the world were distinct from those established in the nineteenth and early twentieth century. While in the first globalization wave, cross-border networks involved family members moving into foreign markets and also cross directorships, the alliances formed at the end of the twentieth and early twenty-first centuries tended to take place between direct competitors with complementary capabilities such as knowledge about their businesses (production vs. distribution) or knowledge about the target geographical markets. These latter alliances often involved several brands and products and various geographical markets.

During the period from 1960 until early twenty-first century, family firms still predominated even though internationalization no longer meant placing family members in foreign markets as professional managers were hired instead. Even though marketing-based industries do not tend to be dominant in the economies of major countries (although they still may be representative in foreign trade), they are global in their scope, and their firms rank among the world's largest multinationals. The role of different entrepreneurs in the life of brands and the ownership structures used in the international distribution of alcoholic beverages have proved to be central in explaining the growth and survival of firms.

From the 1960s, brands were the main determinant for mergers and acquisitions in alcoholic beverages. While the characteristics of alcoholic beverages in general make the role of global brands explicit, it is evident that their importance has not been limited to this or other consumer goods industries. In other industries such as consumer electronics where technological innovation is usually considered to be the prime driver, brands also play a significant role. Hence, this book shows the enormous potential of brands to explain the evolution of firms' strategies and to understand the history of those strategies. The study has shown how their position changed over time, as numerous local brands gave way to fewer global brands supported by massive marketing expenditures.

Inevitably, given the scope of the topic and its hitherto relatively unexplored nature, the structures and the sequences of change described in this book provide no more than a starting point for the analysis of the problems of any specific situation. It remains to be seen whether these findings about the impact of the industry- and firm-specific determinants on the patterns of growth and survival of firms can also be applied to the study of the growth and survival of smaller firms that nonetheless operate at a global level. Such a study would help broaden our understanding of the evolution of other non–science-based industries that, like alcoholic beverages, are characterized by a high level of competition, concentration, and globalization, and have globally branded products with long life cycles.

In addition, the study of the life of brands in alcoholic beverages might be applied in the analysis of the life of brands in consumer goods industries such as beverages like mineral water, instant coffee or colas, branded foods, or branded cosmetics. Given these trends and the characteristics of the industry, the marketing-based multinationals of the future in almost every industry will doubtless switch from a relatively pragmatic view of management of brands (based solely on knowledge acquired within the firm) to a more broadly based strategic view in which the impact of the entrepreneur/manager is fully recognized. It is based on these trends that this book claims that studies on the life of brands provide an important alternative in analyzing the dynamic evolution of industries.

Finally, the argument of this book points beyond the compilation and explanation of the past experiences of alcoholic beverages firms to the discussion of a broader research agenda for international business history. This book debates whether or not current day globalization is different from the first globalization wave that took place from the 1880s until 1929. It also challenges the all-inclusive nature of the Chandler synthesis, the complexity of capitalist development, and the different forms it takes. In particular, it notes the contribution of family enterprises to innovation and the entrepreneurial capabilities of firms. The book offers new insights on how certain country, industry, and firm determinants can help explain multinational growth and survival in marketing-based industries.

While not aiming to provide a recipe for leadership, growth, and survival of multinational firms, this book nonetheless establishes that the past matters, by providing the empirical evidence on how firms grew and survived, what firm-specific capabilities were determinant in that process, and how these capabilities and, in particular, global brands developed over a long period of time. This book is intended to restore a better balance between marketing studies and histories that focus exclusively on technology. Ultimately, a more balanced perspective will contribute, I believe, to an improved understanding of the emergence of the global economy of the twenty-first century.

Appendix 1

Value-Added Chain in Alcoholic Beverages

This Appendix provides the general characteristics of each beverage – beer, spirits, and wines – and of the value-added chain. By linking the strategically relevant stages that make up the production and marketing sequence from the raw materials to the final consumer, the value-added chain helps explain the changing boundaries of firms in alcoholic beverages, including their mergers and acquisitions and alliances.[1]

Characteristics of the Beverages

Beer is made from fermented malt, water, and yeast, and is flavored with hops. It can, however, be fabricated from a variety of raw materials such as millet, maize, sorghum, barley, wheat, and rice. These raw materials can be grown in most fertile regions, making it relatively easy to produce similar beer in different locations. Thus, although Bass Brewery once claimed that the water from Burton-on-Trent gave it a distinctive character, and Coors Brewery still makes such claims for Rocky Mountain water, the location of the breweries today has more to do with the location of consumers than with the location of raw materials. Nonetheless, in some countries – Germany in particular – beer remains remarkably "local."

Spirits are made from concentrating ethyl alcohol by distilling an already fermented product. The term *spirit* includes many types of beverages such as whisky, rum, brandy, gin, vodka, and aquavit. The most evident difference is in color. While whisky, rum, and brandy vary in shade from straw-colored to the deepest brown, gin and vodka normally are colorless. However, color is mostly produced by adding coloring to the clear distillate. The real difference between these drinks lies in the raw materials used. For example, while rum is made from sugarcane, whisky is obtained from the distillation of an aqueous extract of an infusion of malted barley and other cereals that have been fermented.[2] Given the relative indifference of both beer and

---

[1] For a definition of *value-added chain*, see John H. Dunning, *Multinational Enterprises and the Global Economy* (Wokingham, Berkshire: Addison Wesley, 1993): 189; Michael E. Porter, *Competitive Advantage* (New York: Free Press, 1985): 33.

[2] A. H. Rose (ed.), *Alcoholic Beverages*, Vol. 1 (London: Academic Press, 1977).

spirits to the place of production, these two types of alcoholic beverages have proved highly amenable to internationalization and the development of global brands.

Wine is usually made from the fermented juice of grapes. It also can be produced from other commodities. In Asia, it is made from rice, and in Africa, from palm tree sap. There are many different types of grape wines, varying according to the specific characteristics of the blend of grape varietal used. These can produce quite distinct flavors, colors, and chemical compositions. Processing methods also make major differences in the end product. In most wine making, the carbon dioxide generated during fermentation is allowed to escape. In some cases, however, this is prevented and sparkling wines – most famously, champagne – result. Similarly, in most cases, fermentation proceeds until most of the sugar in the grapes has turned into alcohol. In some cases, however, spirit is added to preserve some of the sugar. This process results in fortified wines such as port or sherry.[3]

For each type of alcoholic beverage, the quality of the beverage can vary widely depending on a variety of factors, including the raw materials and the age of the beverage. All three types of alcoholic beverages – wines, spirits, and beer – require some time to age, but wines generally require more time and are more delicate.[4]

The marketing strategies followed by wine firms naturally vary based on these differences.[5] For example, prices charged for wines are generally categorized as premium or standard. Standard or de novo wines are predominantly mass-produced and distinct from premium bottled wines in multiple ways. They tend to emphasize the blend, not the place of origin. In premium wines in contrast, appellation of origin and the characteristics of the *terroir* (the land where the grapes are grown) and the vintage (the year the grapes are harvested) are very important. Whereas traditionally wines from the old world are, to a significant degree, branded by the region (*terroir*), de novo wines are now branded by individual firms. The notion of *terroir* insists that particular wine-producing regions have their own distinct characteristics, arising from the soil and the climate. Old wine-producing regions have long used laws and treaties to protect these regions and the names – cognac, champagne, chianti, madeira, port, and so on – associated with them. The de novo wine brands, in contrast, do not associate themselves with *terroir*. These can in principle be made anywhere suitable grapes are grown. Paradoxically, whereas regionally located wines tend to be highly variable (as local conditions vary from year to year), the de novo wines, which may be

[3] Rabobank, "The World Wine Business" (1996).
[4] Tony Spawton, "Development in the Global Alcoholic Drinks Industry and Its Implications for the Future Marketing of Wine," *European Journal of Marketing*, Vol. 24, No. 4 (1990): 47–54.
[5] Datamonitor, "Strategic Review of European Drinks" (1997).

produced in different places each year, tend to be more consistent as the industrial processes used to produce them can iron out variation. As global wines, they address global tastes and thus tend to be fruitier, easier to drink, and cheaper.

Terroir wines are subject to problems of free riding by low-quality producers, who can damage the status of the region as a whole. De novo wines, by contrast, have more control over the perception of their brand. Like beer and spirits, they can be made in different geographical areas, allowing firms to take advantage of scale and scope economies. New branded wines tend to be produced in new world countries such as the United States, Chile, Argentina, Australia, and New Zealand. The brands emphasize the grape variety above the region or the date, giving the consumer an alternative (and easier) way of sorting through the wide variety of brands from the old world wines, where *terroir* and date are highly important, but highly variable. Private brands are thus a very important part of the strategy used in the marketing of new world wines.

These constraints of *terroir* wines inevitably lead to relatively small, inelastic quantities in comparison to standard table wines. As a result, the wines tend to be expensive and sold in specialty shops for niche customers. In contrast, because standard wines are easily branded, they tend to offer competitive prices and to be sold in supermarkets and liquor stores.

Description of the Value-added Chain

In Figure A1.1 beer, spirits, and wine businesses are combined into one single schematic representation of the value-added chain, despite their differences. The main stages of economic activity are grouped in four categories according to their basic function – procurement, production, marketing and sales, and complementary services. Marketing and sales make the linkage to the final consumer.

Procurement includes those activities through which the firm obtains raw materials for the production of alcoholic beverages. When not integrated vertically, alcoholic beverages firms procure raw materials from farmers, cooperatives, or brokers that may serve as intermediaries, selling larger volumes. In beer, apart from water, other important raw materials are malt, grain, or cereal, and hops, which acts as a preservative. In spirits, depending on the type of beverage, raw materials can range from fruits, grains, sugarcane, or cereals. In wine, there is usually only one raw material, grapes.[6]

---

[6] For a detailed definition of the various types of alcoholic beverages, see e.g. Christina Marfels, *Concentration, Competition and Competitiveness in the Beverages Industries of the European Community* (Luxembourg: Commission of the European Communities, 1992); Diane M. Sawinski and Wendy H. Mason, *Encyclopaedia of Global Industries* (London: Gale Research, 1996).

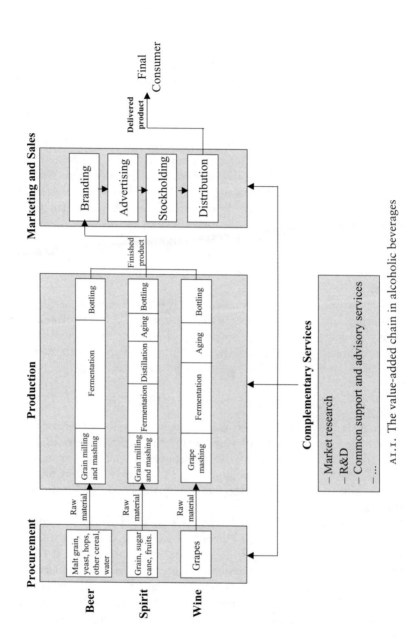

AI.I. The value-added chain in alcoholic beverages

194

Production processes vary according to beverage. In beer, the raw materials first go through a process of mashing and subsequently suffer a process of fermentation. In spirits, after the milling and mashing of the cereals or fruits and their fermentation, the beverages are subject to a distillation process. For some spirits, like whisky, the quality of the beverage improves with aging. Again, the aging process varies depending on the beverage and the quality and characteristics desired, but it may take many years. In beer, the aging process is brief, corresponding to only a few weeks. In wine, after the crushing of the grapes the juice is fermented in barrels or stainless steel containers.[7] The aging process for some types of beer and wine spans the line between production and marketing and sales, as good wine and beer actually continue to improve after bottling.

The bottling and packaging of alcoholic beverages has changed substantially in recent years as it has become an important way to indicate the quality and assert the origin of the product. Hence, the scope of the bottling function has extended to the marketing stage. Decisions about packaging, such as the type and style of bottle used, are now part of the marketing activity.

Marketing and sales include branding, stockholding, advertising and promotion, and distribution. Branding works as a link between the producer and the consumer and between the producer and distributor-wholesaler or retailer. It involves studying the marketing strategy most adequate to different cultural environments, taking into consideration specific regulations such as those on bottle labeling or alcohol advertising. For instance, in some states in the United States, the lack of other forms of advertising makes labels the main means by which firms communicate with consumers.[8]

Advertising and promotion includes any paid form of nonpersonal communication by an identified sponsor to promote a product or a company. It may involve the employment of several specific channels or media, including direct mail, newspapers, magazines, trade journals, radio, television, cinema, and outdoor posters. Advertising provides an important key to gaining distribution by creating consumer demand, which limits the retailer's choice of brands to stock. Like bottling and branding, this activity also suffered great changes in the last forty years of the twentieth century with the globalization of economies and the developments in transports and communications.[9]

---

[7] For example, port wine is considered by law to need at least three years of ageing before it achieves its full capacities. However, most table wines are considered to be in good condition to be drunk after a couple of months of fermentation.

[8] Victor J. Tremblay and Carol Horton Tremblay, *The US Brewing Industry – Data and Economic Analysis* (Cambridge, Mass: MIT Press, 2005); François Guichard, "O Vinho do Porto e mais Alguns: Gestão da Imagem," *Douro: Estudos e Documentos*, Vol. 1, No. 3 (1997): 151–52.

[9] Alfred D. Chandler Jr., *Scale and Scope* (Cambridge, Mass: Harvard University Press, 1990): 150–51; idem, *The Visible Hand* (Cambridge, Mass: Harvard University Press, 1977); Asa Briggs, *Wine for Sale* (London: Bastford, 1985): 46.

Stockholding and distribution involve the physical handling and delivery of the finished product to final customers. There have been profound changes in the world's political and economic environment since the 1960s, as well as in the modern supply-chain logistics. Consequently, it is worth spending more time on this stage of the supply chain. These changes have led to increased concentration in distribution at the wholesale and retail levels and the shortening of channels between producer and consumer.[10]

There are several differences associated with the distribution of beer, spirits, and wine. Since beer is perishable, when conservation systems had not been developed, it could only be distributed in very restricted geographical regions. The development of pasteurized keg beers and refrigeration systems for containers and trucks led to more consistent, longer-life, mass produced beers, and also altered the costs of transportation.[11]

Finally, to return to Figure A1.1, complementary services include the intermediate services that support procurement, production, and marketing and sales, and, for that reason, tend to occur parallel to the three main stages in the value-added chain. Such services include market research; research and development; administrative, financial, and advisory services; and transport services, among other activities. These activities may be performed either by alcoholic beverages firms or by third parties.

Value-added Chain Over Time

The strategic importance of each of the different activities in the value-added chain changed over time, affecting the level of horizontal and vertical integration in firms. Traditionally, production was considered the most strategic activity. Competition was low, distribution was fragmented and regional, and in beverages like beer, production technology was the central means for obtaining economies of scale and scope.

As technologies in brewing, distilling, and wine making became widespread and standardized and competition intensified and became global, marketing and sales gained increased importance. New forms of distribution

---

[10] N. A. H. Stacey and A. Wilson, *The Changing Pattern of Distribution* (Oxford: Pergamon, 1965).

[11] The main developments were more effective control of malting, brewing, fermentation, and conditioning, with the use of closed vessels, computer-aided control, among other technologies; experience with continuous brewing techniques in mashing and fermentation, which were then modified to produce accelerated batch and high-gravity systems; improved packaging, particularly in bottling and canning, with much faster process throughputs; and more effective distribution by road. For a more detailed analysis of this topic, see Terry Gourvish and Richard G. Wilson, *The British Brewing Industry, 1830–1980* (Cambridge: Cambridge University Press, 1994): chapter 13. In the 1990s there has been considerable innovation, notably improvements in the automated cleaning of brewing vessels and the emergence of new beers.

emerged as a response to the development of buyers' (or retailers') own brands, and the concentration of retailing first in the United States, subsequently in Europe, and finally in other parts of the world such as Asia, also created important threats to firms' brands.[12]

Although this shift of competitive importance from production to marketing can be considered to have begun in the 1960s, it is possible to argue that real structural and attitudinal shifts did not happen until the late 1980s. In the United Kingdom, for example, the 1989 Monopolies and Restrictive Practices Commission report led to the creation of a significant new sector of the industry, the nonbrewing pub chain.[13] This affected the level of vertical integration by firms as they aimed not only at reducing transaction costs but also extracting rents.[14]

In wines, the situation was quite distinct. By the beginning of the twenty-first century, only a few wine firms overlapped the three basic stages of the value-added chain. Most linkages between the three major stages were contracts between wineries and growers, and between wineries and foreign importers. Understandably, the relative bargaining strength of these economic entities was highly unequal. Large wineries were often in a monopsonistic position vis-à-vis competitive small-scale growers who had limited or no alternative sales outlets[15].

---

[12] Nicholas Alexander, *International Retailing* (Oxford: Blackwell, 1997); Bridget Williams, "Multiple Retailing and Brand Image," in Geoffrey Jones and Nicholas J. Morgan (eds.), *Adding Value: Brands and Marketing in Food and Drink* (London: Routledge, 1994): 292, 306–7; W. G. McClelland, *Studies in Retailing* (Oxford: Blackwell, 1963): 122.

[13] Tony Millns, "The British Brewing Industry, 1945–1995," in Richard G. Wilson and Terry Gourvish (eds.), *The Dynamics of the International Brewing Industry Since 1800* (London: Routledge, 1993).

[14] Paul Duguid, "In Vino Veritas," in Martin Kenney and Richard Florida (eds.), *Locating Global Advantage: Industry Dynamics in a Globalizing Economy* (Palo Alto, Calif: Stanford University Press, 2003).

[15] John Cavanagh, Frederick Clairmonte, and Robin Room, *The World Alcohol Industry With Special Reference to Australia, New Zealand and the Pacific Islands* (Sydney: Transnational Corporations Research Project – University of Sydney, 1985): 55.

Appendix 2

Brands Owned by the Leading Multinationals in 2005

This Appendix provides a list of the leading multinationals in 2005, their country of origin, their main brands at that time, and the country of origin of those brands. It also shows the dates when those brands were added to the portfolio of the multinationals. These are either the dates when the brands were launched by the firms that still own them, the dates when they were acquired together with the firms that owned them, or when they were acquired independently from the firms that originally owned them.

Table A2.1. *Brands owned by the leading multinationals in 2005*

Multinational	Country of Origin	Brand (origin)	Date of Addition to the Portfolio
Anheuser-Busch	US	Budweiser (US)	1876
		Busch Light (US)	1955
		Michelob (US)	1981
		Bud Light (US)	1982
		Bud Dry (US)	1988
		Bud Ice (US)	1994
Asahi Breweries	JPN	Asahi Super Dry (JPN)	1987
		Super Malts (JPN)	2000
		Asahi Honnama (JPN)	2001
Bacardi		Bacardi Carta Blanca (CUB/US)	1862
		Bacardi Breezer (CUB/US)	1990
		Martini (FRA)	1993
		Bombay Sapphire (UK)	1998
		Dewar's Scotch Whisky (UK)	1998
Brown Forman	US	Jack Daniel's (US)	1956
		Canadian Mist (CAN)	1971
		Southern Comfort (US)	1979
		Early Times (US)	1923
Carlsberg	DEN	Carlsberg (DEN)	1847
		Tuborg (DEN)	1970
		Karhu (FIN)	1997
		Tetley (UK)	1997
		Pripps (SWE)	2000
		Ringnes (NOR)	2000
		Holsten (GER)	2004
Constellation Brands	US	Almaden (US)	1994
		Inglenook (US)	1994
		Hardys (US)	2003
		Robert Mondavi (US)	2004
Diageo	UK	Guinness (IRE)	1759
		Baileys Original (IRE)	1974
		Smirnoff (RUS)	1986
		Johnnie Walker (UK)	1986
		J&B Rare (UK)	1986
		Gordon's (UK)	1986
		Captain Morgan (PR)	2000
		Cuervo (MEX)	2000
		Tanqueray (UK)	2000

(continued)

Table A2.1 *(Continued)*

Multinational	Country of Origin	Brand (origin)	Date of Addition to the Portfolio
E. & J. Gallo	US	E. & J. Gallo (US)	1933
		Carlo Rossi (US)	n/a
		Peter Vella (US)	n/a
		Thunderbird (US)	1957
Fortune Brands/American Brands	US	Jim Beam (US)	1966
		De Kuyper (NL)	1987
		Sauza (MEX)	2005
		Canadian Club (CAN)	2005
		Courvoisier (FRA)	2005
Foster's Group	AUS	Foster's (AUS)	1888
		Carlton (AUS)	1890
		Victoria Bitter (AUS)	1907
Heineken	NL	Heineken (NL)	1864
		Amstel (NL)	1968
		Warka (POL)	1988
		Moretti (IT)	1996
		Cruz Campo (SPN)	1999
Inbev	BEL/BRA	Stella Artois (BEL)	1880
		Brahma (BRA)	1888
		Antarctica (BRA)	1889
		Skol (BRA)	1967
		Jupiler (FR)	1976
		Labbatt (CAN)	1995
		Beck's (GER)	2001
Kirin Brewery	JPN	Kirin Lager (JPN)	1888
		Ichiban Shibori (JPN)	1990
		Tanrei Nama (JPN)	1998
LVMH	FRA	Moët & Chandon (FR)	1743
		Hennessy (FR)	1765
		Mercier (FR)	1970
		Veuve Cliquot (FR)	1987
Modelo	MEX	Corona (MEX)	1925
		Victoria (MEX)	1935
		Modelo Especial (MEX)	1966
Molson-Coors	US	Molson (CAN)	1786
		Original Coors (US)	1874
		Coors Light (US)	1978
		Keystone Light (US)	1989
		Bavaria (BRA)	2000
		Carling (US)	2001
		Kaiser Pilsen (BRA)	2002

Table A2.1 *(Continued)*

Multinational	Country of Origin	Brand (origin)	Date of Addition to the Portfolio
Pernod Ricard	FRA	Ricard (FRA)	1932
		Jacob's Creek (AUS)	1975
		Chivas Regal (CAN)	2000
		Martell (FRA)	2001
		Ballantines (UK)	2005
		Beefeater (UK)	2005
		Kahlua (MEX)	2005
		Malibu (UK)	2005
Rémy Cointreau	FRA	Rémi Martin (FRA)	1724
		Cointreau (FRA)	1849
		Piper Heidsieck (FRA)	1988
		Bols (NL)	2000
		Metaxa (GRE)	2001
SABMiller	SA	Pilzner Urquell (CZR)	1999
		Miller Genuine Draft (US)	2002
		Miller Lite / Lite Ice (US)	2002
		Peroni Nastro Azzuro (IT)	2003
		Aguila (COL)	2005
San Miguel	PHIL	San Miguel (PHIL)	1890
		Pale Pilsen (PHIL)	n/a
		Red Horse (PHIL)	n/a
		Gold Eagle (PHIL)	n/a
Scottish & Newcastle	UK	John Smiths (UK)	1995
		Kronenbourg (FR)	2000
		Baltika (RUS)	2002
		Sagres (POR)	2003
Sapporo	JPN	Sapporo (JAP)	1876
		Sapporo Happoh Shu (JAP)	1995
Suntory	JAP	Yamazaki (JAP)	1923
		Kakubin (JAP)	1937
		Ibiki (JAP)	1989
Tsingtao	CHI	Tsingtao (CHI)	1903

Sources: Compiled from companies' annual reports, monographs, and newspapers.

Appendix 3

Annual Sales for Each Firm in Alcoholic Beverages

Table A3.1. *Annual sales by firm in alcoholic beverages from 1960 to 2005*

Firm	1960	1961	1962	1963	1964	1965	1966	1967	1968	1969	1970
Adolph Coors	n/a	n/a	n/a	n/a	n/a	n/a	n/a	n/a	n/a	n/a	n/a
Allied Domecq	–	1,275	1,369	1,412	1,812	1,948	2,045	2,217	2,531	2,991	3,128
Ambev	–	–	–	–	–	–	–	–	–	–	–
Anheuser Busch	1,186	1,185	1,256	1,303	1,403	1,547	1,721	1,986	2,345	2,412	2,696
Arthur Bells	54	75	75	170	167	205	221	216	213	240	178
Artois	n/a	n/a	n/a	n/a	n/a	n/a	n/a	n/a	n/a	n/a	n/a
Asahi Breweries	291	411	387	410	499	472	457	1,136	918	517	533
Bacardi	n/a	n/a	n/a	n/a	n/a	n/a	n/a	n/a	n/a	n/a	n/a
Bass	431	536	863	1,062	1,250	1,333	1,504	1,766	2,434	2,723	2,794
Brauerei Beck	n/a	179	202	228	240	247	285	311	481	505	372
Brown Forman	392	390	419	455	462	506	553	587	644	720	744
Carlsberg	n/a	n/a	n/a	n/a	n/a	n/a	n/a	n/a	n/a	911	1,021
Companhia Antarctica Paulista	n/a	n/a	n/a	n/a	n/a	n/a	n/a	n/a	n/a	n/a	n/a
Companhia Cervejaria Brahma	n/a	n/a	n/a	n/a	n/a	n/a	n/a	n/a	n/a	n/a	n/a
Constellation Brands / Canandaigua	n/a	n/a	n/a	n/a	n/a	n/a	n/a	n/a	n/a	n/a	n/a
Courage	292	614	717	729	799	817	824	708	796	888	940

Diageo	–	–	–	–	–	–	–	–	–	–	–
Distillers Company	2,512	2,818	2,879	3,048	3,156	3,547	3,539	3,571	3,090	3,302	3,046
E. & J. Gallo	n/a	n/a	n/a	n/a	n/a	n/a	n/a	n/a	n/a	n/a	n/a
Fortune Brands / American Brands	5,068	5,186	5,298	5,278	5,237	5,253	5,124	5,345	6,825	9,624	9,092
Foster's Group / Foster's Brewing / Elders IXL	n/a	n/a	n/a	1,007	1,185	1,099	2,161	2,252	2,106	2,307	2,149
G. Heileman Brewing	72	72	116	90	104	111	115	151	213	289	372
Grand Metropolitan	–	–	39	193	190	242	274	268	293	372	1,979
Guinness	737	783	870	909	997	1,097	1,214	1,291	1,184	1,406	1,482
Heineken	117	132	133	140	162	174	205	236	276	517	545
Heublein	395	413	445	463	507	607	1,178	1,298	1,381	1,884	1,992
Hiram Walker	1,742	1,698	1,685	1,684	1,722	1,803	1,883	1,957	2,116	2,317	2,328
Holsten	n/a	n/a	n/a	n/a	n/a	n/a	n/a	n/a	n/a	n/a	n/a
International Distillers & Vintners	–	–	–	308	354	431	461	500	697	864	863
Inbev	–	–	–	–	–	–	–	–	–	–	–
Interbrew	–	–	–	–	–	–	–	–	–	–	–
Jim Beam	305	315	327	328	327	339	–	–	–	–	–
Kirin	806	1,002	1,214	1,388	1,667	1,650	1,892	2,101	2,417	2,806	3,569
John Labbatt	250	251	261	287	319	338	277	327	428	819	998
Liggett & Myers	2,085	1,973	1,920	1,906	1,875	1,754	2,073	2,261	2,220	2,382	2,368
Lion Nathan	–	–	–	–	–	–	–	–	–	–	–
Miller Brewing (part of Phillip Morris)	n/a	n/a	n/a	n/a	n/a	n/a	n/a	619	663	710	675
Modelo	n/a	n/a	n/a	n/a	n/a	n/a	n/a	n/a	n/a	n/a	n/a
Moët & Chandon	41	44	51	58	64	68	80	93	91	99	–

(continued)

Table A3.1 (Continued)

Firm	1960	1961	1962	1963	1964	1965	1966	1967	1968	1969	1970
Moët Hennessy	–	–	–	–	–	–	–	–	–	–	340
Moët Hennessy LV	–	–	–	–	–	–	–	–	–	–	–
Molson	n/a	n/a	n/a	n/a	536	715	722	812	919	993	1,018
Molson–Coors	–	–	–	–	–	–	–	–	–	–	–
National Distillers	2,228	2,860	2,977	2,908	3,024	3,040	3,225	3,210	3,444	3,912	3,516
Pabst Brewing	576	671	697	769	849	930	1,012	1,147	1,278	1,235	1,233
Pernod	1	1	1	1	1	2	2	3	3	3	3
Pernod Ricard	–	–	–	–	–	–	–	–	–	–	–
Rémy Cointreau	–	–	–	–	–	–	–	–	–	–	–
San Miguel	n/a	n/a	n/a	n/a	n/a	n/a	n/a	n/a	n/a	n/a	n/a
Sapporo	509	710	787	826	897	899	830	1,070	1,093	1,257	1,081
Schenley	1,467	1,552	1,421	1,517	1,511	1,687	1,716	1,854	1,978	2,325	2,275
Schlitz Brewing	637	594	708	811	890	807	987	1,088	1,285	1,514	1,572
Scottish & Newcastle	n/a	n/a	n/a	n/a	n/a	n/a	n/a	986	936	1,013	1,094
Seagram	2,950	3,037	3,151	3,278	3,346	3,685	3,964	4,168	4,515	4,855	4,886
SABMiller / South African Breweries	133	146	148	182	204	216	228	252	588	561	713
Stroh	n/a	n/a	n/a	n/a	n/a	n/a	n/a	n/a	n/a	n/a	n/a
Suntory	n/a	n/a	n/a	315	351	409	540	779	920	1,105	1,280
Truman	138	149	166	174	196	205	221	232	208	221	231
Tsingtao	n/a	n/a	n/a	n/a	n/a	n/a	n/a	n/a	n/a	n/a	n/a
Watney Mann	n/a	n/a	n/a	n/a	n/a	1,184	1,265	1,176	1,114	1,244	1,290
Whitbread	321	415	708	749	n/a	1,034	1,037	1,130	1,396	1,504	1,650

Firm	1971	1972	1973	1974	1975	1976	1977	1978	1979	1980
Adolph Coors	932	990	937	923	938	1,073	995	934	957	1,014
Allied Domecq	3,459	3,165	2,990	2,748	2,942	2,874	3,238	4,645	5,837	5,837
Ambev	–	–	–	–	–	–	–	–	–	–
Anheuser Busch	2,942	2,924	2,748	2,796	2,968	2,604	3,084	3,380	3,587	3,762
Arthur Bells	228	246	272	279	326	380	128	438	552	538
Artois	n/a	n/a	n/a	n/a	n/a	n/a	n/a	n/a	n/a	n/a
Asahi Breweries	498	573	636	451	n/a	n/a	n/a	n/a	1,067	933
Bacardi	n/a	n/a	n/a	n/a	n/a	n/a	n/a	n/a	n/a	n/a
Bass	3,068	3,296	2,956	2,451	2,620	2,616	2,658	2,934	3,125	3,351
Brauerei Beck	411	559	510	405	384	385	367	321	284	289
Brown Forman	727	818	743	609	614	662	665	683	724	772
Carlsberg	1,177	1,301	1,323	1,208	1,363	1,497	1,440	1,530	1,502	1,269
Companhia Antarctica Paulista	n/a	n/a	n/a	n/a	n/a	n/a	n/a	n/a	n/a	n/a
Companhia Cervejeira Brahma	n/a	n/a	n/a	n/a	n/a	n/a	n/a	n/a	n/a	n/a
Constellation Brands/ Canandaigua	n/a	n/a	n/a	n/a	n/a	n/a	n/a	n/a	55	58
Courage	1,085	1,280	1,864	1,030	1,190	1,199	1,217	1,290	1,319	1,433
Diageo	–	–	–	–	–	–	–	–	–	–
Distillers Company	3,299	3,315	2,729	2,507	2,463	2,283	2,479	2,512	2,572	2,680
E. & J. Gallo	n/a	n/a	n/a	n/a	n/a	n/a	n/a	n/a	n/a	n/a
Fortune Brands / American Brands	9,223	8,985	7,664	7,065	7,318	7,457	7,747	7,742	7,554	7,765

(continued)

Table A3.1 (Continued)

Firm	1971	1972	1973	1974	1975	1976	1977	1978	1979	1980
Foster's Group / Foster's Brewing / Elders IXL	1,730	2,108	3,331	3,144	1,848	1,960	2,248	2,397	2,600	2,860
G. Heileman Brewing	348	420	436	n/a	n/a	n/a	n/a	n/a	n/a	824
Grand Metropolitan	2,630	5,665	5,227	4,348	4,794	4,833	4,804	5,306	5,941	6,854
Guinness	1,697	1,781	1,407	1,258	1,353	1,345	1,458	1,843	1,881	2,079
Heineken	666	997	1,190	1,140	1,292	1,433	1,660	1,813	1,851	1,855
Heublein	2,055	2,822	2,391	2,454	2,552	2,861	2,603	2,423	2,286	2,194
Hiram Walker	2,306	2,436	2,077	1,801	1,533	1,604	1,381	1,330	1,241	2,466
Hoisten	n/a	n/a	n/a	n/a	n/a	n/a	n/a	n/a	n/a	n/a
International Distillers & Vintners	940	1,310	879	819	–	–	–	–	–	–
Inhev	–	–	–	–	–	–	–	–	–	–
Interbrew	–	–	–	–	–	–	–	–	–	–
Jim Beam	–	–	–	–	–	–	–	–	–	–
Kirin	3,966	4,857	4,079	1,529	1,659	1,791	2,093	2,559	4,897	4,813
John Labbatt	1,089	1,104	996	970	1,054	1,270	1,216	1,100	1,048	1,137
Liggett & Myers	2,456	2,202	1,762	1,507	1,467	1,540	1,583	1,384	1,364	–
Lion Nathan	–	–	–	–	–	–	–	–	–	–
Miller Brewing (part of Phillip Morris)	666	633	683	799	1,188	1,776	3,079	1,986	2,890	2,903
Modelo	n/a	n/a	n/a	n/a	n/a	n/a	n/a	n/a	n/a	n/a
Moët & Chandon	–	–	–	–	–	–	–	–	–	–

Moët Hennessy	385	482	571	411	476	494	523	635	702	790
Moët Hennessy LV	–	–	–	–	–	–	–	–	–	–
Molson	1,016	1,138	1,292	1,247	1,313	1,487	1,403	1,248	1,320	1,358
Molson–Coors	–	–	–	–	–	–	–	–	–	–
National Distillers	3,527	3,447	3,084	2,780	2,286	2,719	2,663	2,778	2,733	1,770
Pabst Brewing	1,359	1,343	1,170	1,106	1,200	1,360	1,218	1,100	1,014	974
Pernod	4	4	5	n/a	–	–	–	–	–	–
Pernod Ricard	–	–	–	–	603	800	807	872	1,584	986
Rémy Cointreau	–	–	–	–	–	–	–	–	–	–
San Miguel	n/a	n/a	n/a	n/a	n/a	n/a	n/a	n/a	n/a	n/a
Sapporo	1,281	1,472	1,484	1,086	1,166	1,068	1,303	1,559	1,482	1,393
Schenley	2,078	n/a	n/a	n/a	n/a	n/a	n/a	n/a	n/a	n/a
Schlitz Brewing	1,703	1,831	1,740	n/a	n/a	n/a	n/a	n/a	n/a	n/a
Scottish & Newcastle	1,185	1,277	1,172	925	986	1,006	1,013	1,117	1,168	1,024
Seagram	4,955	4,771	4,198	3,660	3,503	3,730	3,676	3,400	3,299	3,294
SABMiller / South African Breweries	659	689	986	1,826	2,169	2,484	2,557	2,456	2,091	2,526
Stroh	n/a	n/a	n/a	n/a	n/a	n/a	n/a	n/a	n/a	n/a
Suntory	1,458	1,850	2,140	1,985	2,141	2,542	3,035	3,910	3,605	3,469
Truman	248	–	–	–	–	–	–	–	–	–
Tsingtao	n/a	n/a	n/a	n/a	n/a	n/a	n/a	n/a	n/a	n/a
Watney Mann	1,387	–	–	–	–	–	–	–	–	–
Whitbread	1,674	1,643	1,494	1,319	1,356	1,434	1,518	1,644	1,806	1,959

(continued)

Table A3.1 (Continued)

Firm	1981	1982	1983	1984	1985	1986	1987	1988	1989	1990
Adolph Coors	1,085	1,107	1,384	1,447	1,646	1,489	1,373	1,451	1,310	1,309
Allied Domecq	5,317	5,065	4,995	4,842	5,234	5,479	6,005	7,187	7,041	7,410
Ambev	-	-	-	-	-	-	-	-	-	-
Anheuser Busch	4,488	5,534	7,523	8,303	8,993	8,691	7,730	9,257	9,815	10,242
Arthur Bells	548	519	466	436	-	n/a	814	801	-	-
Artois	n/a	n/a	n/a	230	229	n/a	-	-	-	-
Asahi Breweries	1,050	980	1,127	1,207	1,273	1,743	2,425	4,056	4,532	4,452
Bacardi	n/a	n/a	n/a	n/a	283	265	295	318	380	421
Bass	4,016	3,930	3,757	3,826	3,975	4,497	5,337	6,336	6,303	6,987
Brauerei Beck	n/a	n/a	859	969	1,089	1,000	924	862	917	928
Brown Forman	897	1,041	1,103	1,464	1,552	1,459	1,429	1,297	1,235	1,150
Carlsberg	1,223	1,255	1,457	1,441	1,498	1,822	1,983	2,052	1,946	2,158
Companhia Antarctica Paulista	n/a	n/a	1,136	10	1,141	1,126	973	n/a	n/a	n/a
Companhia Cervejeira Brahma	n/a	n/a	n/a	639	1,246	1,534	1,341	n/a	627	381
Constellation Brands / Canandaigua	70	85	98	115	172	196	174	158	157	159
Courage	1,502	1,722	-	-	-	-	-	-	-	-
Diageo	-	-	-	-	-	-	-	-	-	-
Distillers Company	2,441	2,289	2,130	1,926	2,100	-	-	-	-	-
E. & J. Gallo	n/a	n/a	n/a	n/a	n/a	n/a	n/a	n/a	n/a	926
Fortune Brands / American Brands	7,628	7,865	8,843	8,934	7,972	8,211	9,304	10,546	10,584	11,444

	3,352	3,434	4,156	6,276	6,276	5,796	7,516	11,439	13,319	10,475
Foster's Group / Foster's Brewing / Elders IXL	3,352	3,434	4,156	6,276	6,276	5,796	7,516	11,439	13,319	10,475
G. Heileman Brewing	n/a	n/a	n/a	n/a	n/a	n/a	n/a	n/a	n/a	n/a
Grand Metropolitan	7,551	8,129	8,445	8,621	9,216	8,780	9,478	10,230	14,520	14,713
Guinness	2,123	2,030	1,649	1,569	1,958	5,396	4,681	4,710	4,804	5,499
Heineken	1,689	1,908	2,015	2,442	2,476	3,088	3,341	3,518	3,455	3,915
Heublein	2,392	2,584	n/a	n/a	n/a	n/a	–	–	–	–
Hiram Walker	2,823	3,292	3,441	n/a	n/a	–	–	–	–	–
Holsten	n/a	n/a	n/a	n/a	n/a	n/a	n/a	n/a	n/a	n/a
International Distillers & Vintners	–	–	–	–	–	–	–	–	–	–
Inbev	–	–	–	–	–	–	–	–	–	–
Interbrew	–	–	–	–	–	–	–	–	1,265	1,485
Jim Beam	–	–	–	–	–	–	–	–	–	–
Kirin	5,210	5,056	5,615	6,193	6,522	8,208	8,900	8,774	8,695	8,636
John Labbatt	1,262	2,035	2,251	2,416	2,283	2,918	2,915	3,577	3,915	3,539
Liggett & Myers	–	–	–	–	–	–	–	–	–	–
Lion Nathan	–	–	–	–	–	–	–	n/a	n/a	n/a
Miller Brewing (part of Phillip Morris)	3,310	3,541	3,643	3,740	3,744	3,402	3,087	3,030	3,190	3,117
Modelo	n/a	n/a	n/a	n/a	n/a	n/a	n/a	2,638	2,607	2,129
Moët & Chandon	–	–	–	–	–	–	–	–	–	–
Moët Hennessy	897	844	872	1,000	1,099	1,601	2,240	–	–	–
Moët Hennessy LV	–	–	–	–	–	–	–	2,633	2,937	3,212
Molson	1,573	1,754	1,785	1,783	1,761	1,639	1,725	1,887	2,097	1,928
Molson–Coors	–	–	–	–	–	–	–	–	–	–

(continued)

Table A3.1 (Continued)

Firm	1981	1982	1983	1984	1985	1986	1987	1988	1989	1990
National Distillers	1,820	1,786	2,429	2,041	2,076	1,958	–	–	–	–
Pabst Brewing	947	917	997	–	–	–	–	–	–	–
Pernod	–	–	–	–	–	–	–	–	–	–
Pernod Ricard	1,382	1,340	1,238	1,216	1,218	1,924	1,810	1,870	2,138	2,727
Rémy Cointreau	–	–	–	–	–	–	–	–	–	–
San Miguel	n/a	n/a	n/a	n/a	n/a	n/a	n/a	n/a	n/a	n/a
Sapporo	1,748	1,688	1,901	2,107	2,239	3,019	3,381	3,761	3,328	3,127
Schenley	n/a	n/a	n/a	n/a	n/a	n/a	–	–	–	–
Schlitz Brewing	n/a	n/a	–	–	–	–	–	–	–	–
Scottish & Newcastle	1,378	1,311	1,213	1,176	1,166	1,284	1,375	1,547	1,606	1,942
Seagram	3,235	3,417	1,826	3,381	3,624	3,363	3,400	3,639	4,826	4,923
SABMiller / South African Breweries	3,158	3,404	4,858	4,169	3,089	2,848	3,536	3,643	3,856	4,517
Stroh	545	603	1,643	n/a	n/a	n/a	n/a	n/a	n/a	n/a
Suntory	3,818	3,899	4,470	4,095	4,201	5,035	5,482	4,697	5,375	4,851
Truman	–	–	–	–	–	–	–	–	–	–
Tsingtao	n/a	n/a	n/a	n/a	n/a	n/a	n/a	n/a	n/a	n/a
Watney Mann	–	–	–	–	–	–	–	–	–	–
Whitbread	1,834	1,778	1,893	2,014	2,381	2,544	2,548	2,865	3,529	3,897

Firm	1991	1992	1993	1994	1995	1996	1997	1998	1999	2000
Adolph Coors	1,365	1,370	1,477	1,508	1,381	1,454	1,636	1,918	2,118	2,414
Allied Domecq	8,074	8,226	7,528	7,827	7,871	6,994	6,541	6,603	6,286	3,842
Ambev	–	–	–	–	–	–	–	–	–	2,706
Arthuser Busch	9,483	9,627	10,321	10,548	9,804	10,537	11,523	10,538	11,263	12,499
Arthur Bells	–	–	–	–	–	–	–	–	–	–
Artois	–	–	–	–	–	–	–	–	–	–
Asahi Breweries	4,068	4,409	5,329	6,380	9,446	9,302	9,747	6,456	11,612	12,983
Bacardi	405							2,221	2,367	2,800
Bass	6,895	6,610	6,181	6,140	5,800	6,252	7,204	7,831	n/a	–
Brauerei Beck	1,051	n/a	711	793	931	874	795	832	802	811
Brown Forman	1,216	1,303	1,522	1,447	1,366	1,497	1,638	1,772	1,913	2,146
Carlsberg	2,017	2,167	2,227	2,397	2,489	2,586	2,635	4,050	4,246	4,272
Companhia Antarctica Paulista	284	314	667	392	1,253	1,142	n/a	n/a	n/a	–
Companhia Cervejeira Brahma	824	730	3,278	2,562	1,659	1,812	2,125	2,310	1,555	–
Constellation Brands / Canandaigua	157	214	284	567	740	824	1,019	1,122	1,418	2,162
Courage	–	–	–	–	–	–	–	–	–	–
Diageo	–	–	–	–	–	–	19,090	18,438	18,071	17,053
Distillers Company	–	–	–	–	–	–	–	–	–	–
E. & J. Gallo	981	874	1,018	883	898	1,002	1,167	1,388	1,435	1,650
Fortune Brands / American Brands	11,767	11,944	11,694	4,846	4,025	3,938	4,350	4,887	5,283	5,845

(continued)

Table A3.1 (Continued)

Firm	1991	1992	1993	1994	1995	1996	1997	1998	1999	2000
Foster's Group / Foster's Brewing / Elders IXL	7,387	6,657	4,089	3,339	n/a	1,657	1,853	2,869	1,946	1,835
G. Heileman Brewing	n/a	n/a	n/a	181	150	–	–	–	–	–
Grand Metropolitan	13,761	12,145	11,276	10,730	10,343	11,566	–	–	–	–
Guinness	6,150	6,696	6,475	6,468	6,033	6,161	–	–	–	–
Heineken	4,071	4,350	4,406	4,825	5,160	6,036	6,218	6,449	7,211	7,469
Heublein	–	–	–	–	–	–	–	–	–	–
Hiram Walker	–	–	–	–	–	–	–	–	–	–
Holsten	n/a	n/a	n/a	n/a	819	854	819	835	911	1,010
International Distillers & Vintners	–	–	–	–	–	–	–	–	–	–
Inbev	–	–	–	–	–	–	–	–	–	–
Interbrew	1,619	1,706	1,543	1,311	2,255	2,605	2,677	2,244	3,272	5,212
Jim Beam	–	–	–	–	–	–	–	–	–	–
Kirin	8,712	9,432	7,910	8,127	7,734	6,770	6,420	6,327	7,542	9,959
John Labbatt	3,706	2,776	1,532	1,532	–	–	–	–	–	–
Liggett & Myers	–	–	–	–	–	–	–	–	–	–
Lion Nathan	n/a	n/a	n/a	n/a	n/a	491	495	421	435	456
Miller Brewing (part of Phillip Morris)	3,618	3,477	3,846	3,872	3,515	3,612	3,773	3,799	4,111	4,375
Modelo	2,284	2,255	2,565	3,660	2,312	2,681	3,199	3,024	3,402	3,911
Moët & Chandon	–	–	–	–	–	–	–	–	–	–

Moët Hennessy	–	–	–	–	–	–	–	–	–	–
Moët Hennessy LV	10,670	8,623	7,138	7,390	5,082	4,872	4,539	3,894	3,578	3,484
Molson	1,181	909	627	549	497	492	538	746	738	1,970
Molson–Coors	–	–	–	–	–	–	–	–	–	–
National Distillers	–	–	–	–	–	–	–	–	–	–
Pabst Brewing	–	–	–	–	–	–	–	–	–	–
Pernod	–	–	–	–	–	–	–	–	–	–
Pernod Ricard	4,037	23,759	3,229	2,931	2,744	2,607	2,570	2,461	2,395	2,406
Rémy Cointreau	674	651	1,188	1,102	1,110	1,099	1,035	954	1,106	1,037
San Miguel	1,771	n/a	n/a	n/a	n/a	n/a	n/a	n/a	n/a	n/a
Sapporo	5,234	4,763	4,283	4,891	5,108	5,753	5,854	5,010	3,985	3,686
Schenley	–	–	–	–	–	–	–	–	–	–
Schlitz Brewing	–	–	–	–	–	–	–	–	–	–
Scottish & Newcastle	5,419	5,100	5,201	4,985	3,903	2,605	2,482	2,222	2,282	2,168
Seagram	15,686	11,658	8,769	11,279	8,137	5,226	5,441	5,649	5,549	5,465
SABMiller / South African Breweries	4,806	5,636	5,425	5,635	6,330	6,280	6,128	6,171	5,335	5,208
Stroh	–	–	n/a	n/a	n/a	n/a	n/a	n/a	n/a	n/a
Suntory	7,879	6,934	5,760	5,863	5,682	6,351	6,465	6,139	5,238	5,298
Truman	–	–	–	–	–	–	–	–	–	–
Tsingtao	3,760	2,131	1,479	1,255	n/a	n/a	n/a	n/a	n/a	n/a
Watney Mann	–	–	–	–	–	–	–	–	–	–
Whitbread	6,619	6,652	6,292	6,176	5,636	5,547	5,926	4,635	3,650	3,536

(continued)

Table A3.1 (Continued)

Firm	2001	2002	2003	2004	2005
Adolph Coors	2,494	3,856	3,664	3,618	—
Allied Domecq	4,138	4,980	4,961	4,967	—
Ambev	n/a	n/a	n/a	—	—
Anheuser Busch	13,256	13,853	12,958	12,547	12,069
Arthur Bells	—	—	—	—	—
Artois	—	—	—	—	—
Asahi Breweries	12,109	11,200	11,064	11,215	10,414
Bacardi	2,772	2,961	2,840	2,521	2,632
Bass	—	—	—	—	—
Brauerei Beck	—	—	—	—	—
Brown Forman	2,253	2,270	2,176	2,165	2,191
Carlsberg	4,246	4,597	4,815	5,047	5,092
Companhia Antarctica Paulista	—	—	—	—	—
Companhia Cervejeira Brahma	—	—	—	—	—
Constellation Brands / Canandaigua	2,285	2,662	2,502	2,985	3,281
Courage	—	—	—	—	—
Diageo	17,894	16,681	13,880	13,677	14,506
Distillers Company	—	—	—	—	—
E. & J. Gallo	1,202	1,146	1,030	1,308	1,366
Fortune Brands / American Brands	5,708	5,798	5,692	5,163	5,668
Foster's Group / Foster's Brewing / Elders IXL	2,166	2,536	2,755	2,415	2,436
G. Heileman Brewing	—	—	—	—	—
Grand Metropolitan	—	—	—	—	—
Guinness	—	—	—	—	—
Heineken	7,016	8,151	9,568	10,438	10,778
Heublein	—	—	—	—	—
Hiram Walker	—	—	—	—	—
Holsten	747	801	777	544	—
International Distillers & Vintners	—	—	—	—	—
Inbev	—	—	—	8,938	11,637

Interbrew	n/a	n/a	n/a	—	—
Jim Beam	—	—	—	—	—
Kirin	9,298	9,262	9,211	9,505	8,992
John Labbatt	—	—	—	—	—
Liggett & Myers	—	—	—	—	—
Lion Nathan	661	785	943	1,025	993
Miller Brewing (part of Phillip Morris)	n/a	2,715	—	—	—
Modelo	4,416	4,143	3,585	3,454	3,650
Moët & Chandon	—	—	—	—	—
Moët Hennessy	—	—	—	—	—
Moët Hennessy LV	11,235	12,198	12,366	13,169	13,887
Molson	1,231	1,368	1,644	1,631	—
Molson–Coors	—	—	—	3,618	4,420
National Distillers	—	—	—	—	—
Pabst Brewing	—	—	—	—	—
Pernod	—	—	—	—	—
Pernod Ricard	4,185	4,647	3,693	3,702	3,668
Rémy Cointreau	735	980	1,034	927	797
San Miguel	2,416	2,590	2,442	2,633	3,579
Sapporo	4,708	4,167	3,789	4,033	4,100
Schenley	—	—	—	—	—
Schlitz Brewing	—	—	—	—	—
Scottish & Newcastle	6,435	6,426	7,457	4,946	5,233
Seagram	—	—	—	—	—
SABMiller / South African Breweries	4,296	4,456	7,481	9,549	10,355
Stroh	—	—	—	—	—
Suntory	6,326	5,926	5,475	5,147	n/a
Truman	—	—	—	—	—
Tsingtao	4,846	6,321	n/a	n/a	n/a
Watney Mann	—	—	—	—	—
Whitbread	—	—	—	—	—

Note: Amounts stated in millions of constant U.S. dollars (2000 = 100).

Appendix 4

Selection of the Sample

The sample of firms selected for this study relied on several benchmark dates: 1960, 1970, 1980, 1990, 2000, and 2005. The use of multiple benchmark dates avoids possible bias that could occur if only one of the dates had been selected. For example, if only 2005 had been considered, firms that were important in the 1960s or after but which had not remained in the ranking of the world's largest firms until the beginning of the twenty-first century would have been eliminated from this study, either because they had not survived or because they had not kept a pace of growth that allowed them to remain in the official rankings of the largest industrials such as *Fortune 500*. In the same way, if 1960 had been chosen as the only benchmark date, firms that had emerged as the largest at the end of the period of analysis would not have been included.[1]

Several possible economic criteria could have been used in the selection of the firms to be included in this study. Value added, assets, market capitalization, and sales are just some examples of alternative measures. Although these measures might be equivalent in the long run, they offer valid but distinct perspectives on the performance of firms, each one with its own advantages and drawbacks.[2]

Value added would have been the ideal measure for the performance of firms. It would have illustrated, for example, that wine firms generate less value added than spirits and beer firms because of their less powerful brands and higher production and inventory holding costs (such as labor and

---

[1] This last kind of distortion occurs in Raymond Vernon's study on U.S. foreign direct investment between 1900 and 1967, in which he looked at only the largest firms at the end of the period and traced them back. Raymond Vernon, "International Investment and International Trade in the Product Cycle," *Quarterly Journal of Economics*, Vol. 80 (1966): 190–207; idem, *Sovereignty at Bay: the Multinational Spread of United States Enterprises* (New York: Basic Books, 1971). For a critique and alternative approach, see Geoffrey Jones and Frances Bostock, "US Multinationals in British Manufacturing Before 1962," *Business History Review*, Vol. 70 (1996): 211–12.

[2] Leslie Hannah and John Kay, *Concentration in Modern Industry* (London: Macmillan, 1976): 42–43; John Kay, *Foundations of Corporate Success* (Oxford: Oxford University Press, 1993): chapter 13.

investments in aging the wine). However, owing to the lack of availability of information, value added could not be used as a selection criterion.

Assets are another possible measure that was not selected for two main reasons. First, it is highly sensitive to inflation. Second, because firms do not always use the same criteria in accounting for assets, it is difficult to reconstruct the balance sheets in such a way as to have comparable information between firms.

Market capitalization is also frequently considered an appropriate indicator for measuring the size of firms, as it reflects the expectations on their present and future profitability irrespective of their origin. Again, this was also not used in this study because firms often only became publicly quoted in the last decades of the twentieth century (and for that reason it was not possible to obtain information about each firm covering the period starting in the beginning of the 1960s).[3] As a result of the problems presented by these alternative measures, turnover (sales), the most widely used indicator of performance, was the measure selected to assess the performance and in particular the evolution in the size of firms in this industry.[4]

---

[3] For example Anheuser Busch, a family owned and controlled firm, became publicly quoted in 1990.

[4] For a discussion of alternative measures of performance see e.g. John H. Dunning and Robert Pearce, *The World's Largest Industrial Enterprises* (Guildford: Gower, 1981).

Appendix 5

Biographies of the World's Largest Multinationals in Alcoholic Beverages

This Appendix contains brief biographies of the world's largest multinationals in alcoholic beverages at the beginning of the twenty-first century. In complex cases the historical evolution is illustrated by a graph.

Allied Domecq (See Figure A5.1) Allied Breweries was founded in 1961 through the merger of three major U.K. brewers – Ind. Coope, Tetley Walker, and Ansells Brewery – to produce and distribute three brands of beer (Double Diamond, Skol, and Long Life) as well as wines and spirits, thus becoming Britain's second largest brewer. In 1968, it acquired Showerings, a wine and cider company, owner of Babycham, which had also acquired Harveys of Bristol in 1966. Since then, Allied Breweries grew rapidly, essentially through international mergers and acquisitions. Two major examples are the acquisition of Hiram Walker from Canada in 1986, and in 1994, Pedro Domecq, the leading Spanish spirits and sherry firm that also had a prominent position in South America. Over time, Allied Domecq divested its nonalcoholic beverages and beer business. By the beginning of the twenty-first century, this multinational was pursuing a strategy of concentration in the spirits and branded wines businesses. It owned a number of top spirits brands such as Ballantines, Beefeater, Courvoisier, Hiram Walker, Kahlua, Sauza, and Malibu. In 2005, Allied Domecq was acquired by Pernod Ricard. Fortune Brands bought some of Allied Domecq's brands from Pernod Ricard.

Anheuser-Busch is the owner of the world's top-selling beer brand Budweiser. Founded in 1852, this firm owes its early growth to sales in the United States. In the late 1990s, this family firm started investing in foreign markets, especially in Asia and South America. In Asia it formed a licensing agreement with Kirin in 1993 to distribute Budweiser in Japan. It also invested in China, Argentina, and Brazil, as well as in the United Kingdom. In 1998, it made a major investment in South America with the acquisition of 50 percent of Mexico's Grupo Modelo, producer of the beer brand Corona.

Asahi Breweries is a Japanese firm, founded in 1889, whose present success is attributable to its flagship brand, Asahi Super Dry, developed in 1987.

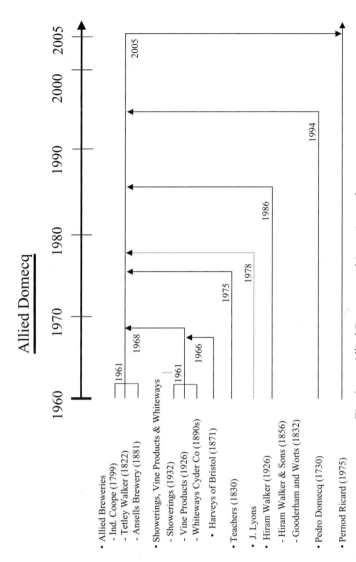

Fig. A5.1. Allied Domecq and its main predecessors

219

Since then, the firm's rate of growth has increased, leading Asahi Breweries in 2001 to surpass Kirin's market share in Japan. Despite being relatively diversified, Asahi Breweries' recent investments have targeted all fields in alcoholic beverages. It has brewing and distribution agreements with several Western alcoholic beverages firms such as Bass Brewers, Miller Brewing, and Molson, and also with wines and spirits firms.

Bacardi was founded in 1862 in Cuba. It developed essentially from sales to the U.S. market after the repeal of Prohibition, and from sales of a single product, Bacardi Rum. As a result of the 1959 revolution in Cuba, the family was forced into exile in the United States. In 1993, in an effort to diversify, the company bought a majority stake in Martini Rossi. During the following years, the firm made investments in creating line and brand extensions out of its restricted portfolio of brands. In 1998, it made further investments in widening its portfolio, acquiring Dewar's Scotch Whisky and Bombay Sapphire gin from Diageo. It is now one of the world's leading spirits firms, with a more restricted portfolio of successful and global brands.

Brown Forman is a family firm founded in 1870. At the beginning of the twenty-first century, it was a leading U.S. producer of spirits and wines, having as its major brand the famous bourbon Jack Daniel's. It is one of the few U.S. firms that during Prohibition, was allowed to produce spirits that were consumed for medical purposes. Beginning in the 1960s, the firm started merging and acquiring other spirits and wines firms in order to expand its portfolio of brands sold in the U.S. market and also to expand geographically. Some of the firms it acquired were Korbel (champagne and brandy) in 1965, Canadian Mist in 1971, and Southern Comfort in 1979. In the 1990s, it made strategic acquisitions in wines, including two producers of premium-quality California wines – Jekel Vineyards and Fetzer Vineyards – in, respectively, 1991 and 1992. It also acquired a producer of Chilean wines, Carmel vineyards, in 1993. The company began its transformation into a global player in 1994, when its domestic and international spirits companies and its wine group were merged into Brown Forman Beverages Worldwide. In 2000, it formed a global alliance with Altia Group Ltd., owner of Finlandia vodka, to market and distribute the brand internationally. In 2004 Brown Forman acquired Altia's share in the alliance, becoming the sole marketer of the brand worldwide.

Carlsberg is a Danish brewery founded in 1847. By the beginning of the twenty-first century, Carlsberg was owned by a foundation (created by its founder). It is a leading international producer of beer, especially with the brands Carlsberg and Tuborg. Tuborg, Carlsberg's major competitor in Denmark, was acquired in 1970. It produced beer in more than 100 countries through either wholly owned investments or through alliances (in particular licensing agreements). Its portfolio of regional brands includes Pripps (Sweden), Holsten (Germany), Tetley's (UK), Koff (Finland), Okocim (Poland), and Feldscholösschen (Switzerland).

Constellation Brands, formerly Canandaigua, is a family firm founded in 1945 in the United States to produce and sell wines. The firm expanded by buying a number of wineries in the 1960s and 1970s. It went public in 1973. By the beginning of the twenty-first century, it was a leading producer and marketer of wines from Australia and New Zealand, and a major producer and independent drinks wholesaler in the United Kingdom. Through its subsidiaries, this firm also sells imported beer brands such as Corona and Tsingtao in the U.S. market. It also produces and imports spirits such as Black Velvet Canadian whiskey and Barton's Blue Wave.

Diageo was formed in 1997 as a result of the merger between Guinness and Grand Metropolitan, which made it the world's largest multinational in alcoholic beverages (See Figure A5.2). The complex history of mergers and acquisitions of Guinness and Diageo explains why it owns many of the top spirits brands such as Smirnoff, Johnnie Walker Red , J&B Rare, Gordon's, and Baileys Irish Cream. Among its predecessors are leading firms that were some of the world's largest industrials, for example, Distillers Company, Liggett & Myers, Heublein, and Schenley. In 2001, Diageo formed an alliance with Pernod Ricard to buy Seagram's brands. This alliance enabled the firm to enlarge its portfolio even further. Since then, it has acquired branded wines such as the U.S. Chalone Wine Group and Bushmills Irish whiskey in 2005.

E. & J. Gallo is the world's largest producer of wines. Since its foundation in 1933, this Californian family firm essentially invested in branded standard wines. It mainly sells in the United States, where it has a very effective national distribution network.

Fortune Brands was founded in 1864 as a small tobacco company named American Tobacco Company. In 1966, this firm entered the alcoholic beverages business, acquiring Jim Beam Distillery (the same year it changed its name to American Brands). Since then, it has diversified into other unrelated businesses. In 1990, however, it started to focus on alcoholic beverages, acquiring Whyte & Mackay distillers and seven liquor brands from Seagram. In 1994, the firm sold its tobacco business, and changed its name to Fortune Brands. In 1999, it formed Maxxium Worldwide, a non-U.S. wines and spirits sales and distribution joint venture with Rémy Cointreau and Highland Distillers. In addition to the companies' own brands, this joint venture also distributes Absolut vodka, owned by the Swedish monopoly Vin & Sprit. In 2005, it bought some of Allied Domecq's brands (Courvoisier cognac,

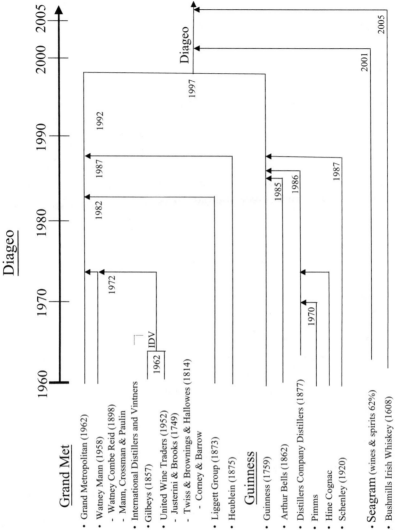

Fig. A5.2. Diageo and its main predecessors

Canadian Club, Maker's Mark, and Sauza) after its acquisition by Pernod Ricard.

Foster's is a leading Australian brewer that in recent years also made significant investments into the wines business. Having operated since 1888, this firm had a complex early start, involving several mergers and acquisitions that led to the creation of Foster brewery. In 1907, the Foster Company joined an amalgamation of six Melbourne breweries to form Carlton and United Breweries. In 1983, the conglomerate Elders IXL acquired Carlton and United Breweries, establishing Elders IXL as one of Australia's largest companies. Since then, this Australian firm expanded not only in the domestic market but also internationally, acquiring for example the British brewer Courage in 1986, and the brewing interests of Grand Metropolitan in 1991 (both businesses sold to Scottish & Newcastle in 1995). In 1990, Elders IXL was renamed Foster's Brewing Group. It entered into the wines business by acquiring the Australian wine firms Mildara Blass and Rothbury Wines in, respectively, 1995 and 1996. Despite selling its brands in many countries, over 70 percent of Foster's Brewing sales are generated in the Australian market.

Heineken, a Dutch family firm, is a very internationalized brewer, owning the famous brands Heineken and Amstel, which are sold in more than 170 countries. Founded in 1864, this firm internationalized very early. The United States has been historically an important market, not only because of the level of sales it generated, but also due to the role it played in the creation of Heineken's brand image. The U.S.-owned distributor Van Munching contributed greatly to this success. Amstel, Heineken's second beer brand, was traditionally the major competitor in the Dutch market. It was acquired in 1968. Since then, Heineken has continued expanding internationally, making several important acquisitions and alliances of brewers, owners of successful brands such as Cruz Campo in Spain, Warka in Poland, and Moretti in Italy.

Inbev is the result of the combination of two leading multinationals – Ambev from Brazil and Interbrew from Belgium (See Figure A5.3). Ambev – Companhia de Bebidas das Américas – was formed in 2000 as a result of the merger between the two leading Brazilian brewers, Companhia Antarctica Paulista and Companhia Cervejeira Brahma, both firms dating back to the nineteenth century and producing leading Brazilian beer brands like Brahma and Antarctica. Since 2000, it started internationalizing mainly in South America, through exports and also foreign direct investment. In 2001, Ambev bought controlling interest in two Uruguayan brewers, Salus and Cerveceria y Malteria Pay, and acquired Ceveceria Internacional in Paraguay. In 2002, it acquired a 36 percent voting stake in Quilmes, Argentina's top brewer. Ambev also has several licensing agreements to produce foreign beers in Brazil.

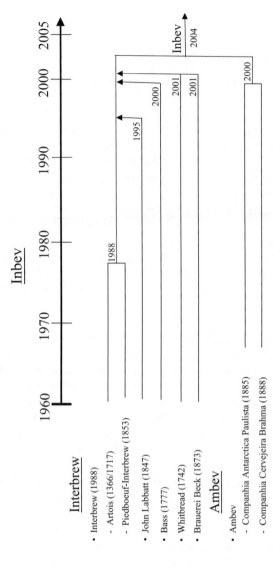

Fig. A5.3. Inbev and its main predecessors

Interbrew was formed in Belgium in 1988 as a result of the merger of the two long-established leading family firms, Piedboeuf-Interbrew and Artois. Its major acquisitions include the Canadian brewer, John Labbatt in 1995, and in 2000 the two leading British brewers, Whitbread and Bass. Owing to the concentration that these two acquisitions created in the United Kingdom brewing industry, the U.K. Competition Commission forced the firm to sell its beer brand Carling, which was acquired by Coors in 2002.

Kirin is a Japanese brewer founded in 1907. Part of the Mitsubishi Keiretsu, Kirin has been the leading brewer in terms of market share in the Japanese market since the 1950s, only being challenged by Asahi Breweries in 2001. In 1972, Kirin entered the spirits business through its joint venture with Seagram. In the 1990s, it acquired wines businesses. To compensate for the stagnation of sales in the Japanese market, Kirin concluded several distribution agreements, including one with Anheuser-Busch. It also acquired foreign brewers, including the Australian firm Lion Nathan in 1998 and the Philippines food and drink giant San Miguel.

Moët-Hennessy Louis Vuitton was formed in 1987 as a result of the merger between the champagne and cognac group, Moët Hennessy and the luggage and luxury products firm Louis Vuitton, thus becoming the world's leading champagne and cognac producer (See Figure A5.4). To manage this new group, the families that owned the merging firms hired a professional manager, Bernard Arnault, who, soon after taking control of the management, also became the firm's major shareholder. Since then, the firm has made several mergers and acquisitions, but these were mainly in the fashion and luxury products businesses. In 1987, however, it made a landmark arrangement with Guinness, through which the two multinationals distributed jointly their complementary brands worldwide.

Molson Coors is a leading multinational, the result of the 2004 merger between Coors from the United States and Molson from Canada. Coors was a leading family-owned brewer, founded in 1873. Although it was active essentially in the U.S. market, it also exported to more than thirty countries and formed alliances with direct competitors. The agreements with Molson Breweries and Foster's Brewing in 1997 to manage the distribution of its brands in Canada are examples. In 2002, Coors also bought the British brand Carling from Interbrew (later part of Inbev). Molson was a Canadian firm whose ownership changed substantially after 1960. Founded in 1876, this firm merged with the Canadian subsidiary of the Australian conglomerate Elders IXL in 1988. In 1993, the Canadian family who originally owned Molson bought back control of the shares, and since 1998 has become the only large Canadian-owned brewer. In this process, Molson internationalized, in

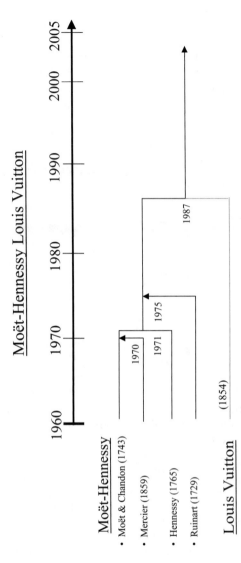

Fig. A5.4. Moët-Hennessy Louis Vuitton and its main predecessors

particular to South America. The merger led to the creation of a leading family-owned multinational brewer.

Pabst is a successor company of Best Brewing Company of Milwaukee, founded in 1844 by Jacob Best. In 1889 the firm changed its name to Pabst Brewing Company, and by the beginning of the twentieth century, was a leading U.S. beer brand. In 1985, after a period of decline, the firm was acquired by S&P. In an attempt to counter its loss of market share, Pabst closed plants and transferred production to Miller and Stroh. In 1999, S&P acquired several breweries, including Stroh Brewing Company. However, this acquisition did not significantly improve the profitability of the firm. In 2001, Pabst abandoned all its production facilities, becoming a "virtual" brewer, contracting with other brewers such as Miller and Lion Brewery to brew the beers while retaining ownership of its brands, Pabst Blue Ribbon, Lone Star, Old Milwaukee, Old Style, Schlitz, and Colt D45.

Pernod Ricard was formed in 1975 as a result of the merger between two family firms, Pernod and Ricard (See Figure A5.5). World leader in anis pastis, this firm also owns other wines and top spirits brands such as Wild Turkey bourbon. Since its formation, it has made several important international mergers and acquisitions, including Austin Nichols (Wild Turkey) acquired from Liggett & Myers in 1980. In 2001, in a joint agreement with Diageo it purchased Seagram's brands, adding to its portfolio top spirits such as Chivas Regal and Glenlivet. These brands improved Pernod Ricard's presence in North America. In 2005, it acquired Allied Domecq, becoming the second largest spirits and wines firm in the world. These acquisitions added Beefeater gin, Ballantines whisky, Kahlua, Malibu rum, Stolichnaya vodka, and Tia Maria to Pernod Ricard's portfolio. The acquisition of Allied Domecq also gave Pernod Ricard a major foothold in the British market.

Rémy Cointreau was formed in 1991 as a result of a merger between two long-established French family firms, Rémy Martin and Cointreau. In 1999, it formed Maxxium, a joint venture with Brown Forman (United States), Highland Distillers (United Kingdom), and Vin & Sprit (Sweden) to jointly distribute its beverages worldwide. In 2000, Rémy Cointreau acquired the Dutch spirits group, Bols, and also expanded its distribution capacity in Central and Eastern Europe.

SABMiller. South African Breweries (SAB) was incorporated in 1895, selling beer to workers in the new mining town of Johannesburg. In 1956, it acquired its two major competitors in the South African market, becoming almost a monopoly there and clearly the dominant beverages company in the country. After 1956, the firm made no major acquisitions either in the domestic

Pernod Ricard

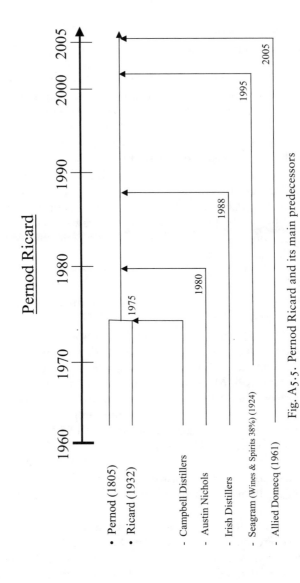

Fig. A5.5. Pernod Ricard and its main predecessors

market or abroad, in part because of restrictions imposed by the South African government. With the abolition of apartheid in 1994, SAB started investing in foreign markets. Ventures were launched in Tanzania, Zambia, Mozambique, and Angola. In May 2002, SAB acquired Miller Brewing from the tobacco group Philip Morris and changed its name to SABMiller. With this acquisition, South African Breweries became a major multinational brewer. Miller was a U.S. brewer founded in 1855 and acquired by Philip Morris in 1970. It merged with or acquired other U.S. brewers such as Stroh (which also owned G. Heileman Brewing), Schlitz, and Pabst. By the 1990s, it held the second largest market share in the United States. In May 2002, South African Breweries acquired a 64 percent equity stake in the Company, the remainder continuing to be held by Philip Morris. After the 2002 acquisition SABMiller has a wide portfolio of beer brands including Castle, Pilsner Urquell, and Miller.

San Miguel, which was founded in 1890 as a brewer, developed into the largest beverage and food firm in the Philippines. By the beginning of the twenty-first century, it controlled the beer market in the Philippines. In 2001, it allied with the Japanese brewer Kirin, giving the latter 15 percent of San Miguel's shares.

Sapporo is Japan's oldest brewer, having been founded in 1876. In the beginning of the twenty-first century, it was the number three brewer in the Japanese market after Asahi Breweries and Kirin. Selling essentially in Japan, it has other alcoholic beverages businesses besides beer, with the importation of wines being particularly important.

Scottish & Newcastle, currently the leading British brewer, was formed in 1960 as a result of the amalgamation of several brewers, its oldest predecessor having been founded in Edinburgh in 1749. In 1995, it acquired Courage, which was founded in London in 1787, an addition that made the company the largest U.K. brewer. Since 2000 it started internationalizing, making important foreign investments, such as Kronenbourg in France and Central de Cervejas in Portugal, and by forming strategic alliances, such as Baltic Beverages Holding in Russia with Carlsberg.

Seagram, a Canadian family firm that produced spirits, was founded in 1924, and relied on sales of Canadian whiskey to the U.S. (See Figure A5.6) market. Over the years, this firm became one of the leading multinationals in alcoholic beverages, owner of successful global brands like Chivas Regal, 7 Crown, Crown Royal, Captain Morgan, and Seagram's. In the 1990s, Seagram began emphasizing its investments in entertainment at the expense of its alcoholic beverages. In 2001, Seagram was sold by the family to Vivendi, the French media and water group, which subsequently sold the alcoholic

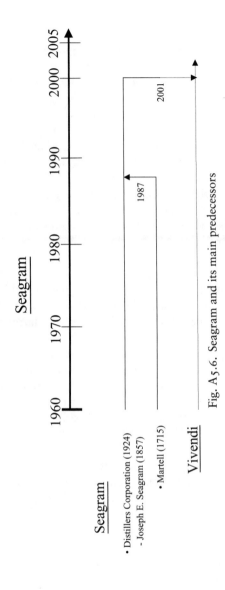

Fig. A5.6. Seagram and its main predecessors

beverages brands to Diageo and Pernod Ricard. These two firms kept the most important brands and sold the rest.

Suntory is a family firm formed in Japan in 1899 that grew out of its production of red wine and Japanese whiskey. Selling essentially in the Japanese market, Suntory also produces beer, but that is not a very significant part of its activity. The firm has multiple alliances with leading Western multinationals, which have played a very important role in the growth of the firm within the Japanese spirits and wines business.

Tsingtao is China's largest brewer. Founded in 1903 by German settlers, it was later occupied by the Japanese, and was finally retaken by the Chinese government. In 2005, the Chinese government remained the major shareholder, and Anheuser-Busch was the largest nongovernment shareholder.

Appendix 6

Types of Governance Structures in Distribution, 1900–2005

There were multiple governance structures used by firms to distribute alcoholic beverages from the beginning of the twentieth century until the present day. At different times some were more important than others. Using four periods – 1900–1960; 1961–1970; 1971–1990; 1991–2000, 2001–2005 – Table A6.1 summarizes which were the largest alcoholic beverages firms in the world, the predominant geographical scope of their operations and the main governance structures used for distributing alcoholic beverages. When a particular type of governance structure is very common in a specific period, it is represented by (++), when it is common but not a predominant governance structure, it is symbolized by a (+), and when it is not used it is classified with a (o). The bottom row in the table highlights the main types of governance structures used by the world's largest firms in each of the five periods.

The period 1900–1960 is included in this analysis to help explain the rapid pace of change that occurred in international distribution from the 1960s. The benchmark dates used (1960, 1970, 1990, 2000) correspond to periods of change. In each of these periods there were important technological innovations and changes in the strategic role of brands in the growth of firms globally.[1]

Figure A6.1 positions the alternatives means of distribution of alcoholic beverages from 1900 to 2005 along two axes. The vertical axis takes into consideration the level of control of the markets and of the information by the firm. The horizontal axis measures the level of resources invested in each type of alliance. This figure takes into consideration situations where products are distributed from producers to wholesalers and from producers to retailers.

According to the literature on distribution channels, it is possible to identify eight principal types of channels used in the distribution of alcoholic beverages during the period 1900–2005: networks of merchant houses, agents, distributors, direct sale, employees working in the market of destination; wholly owned channels; channel-alliances; and e-commerce.

---

[1] For further discussion of this periodization see Chapters 2 and 3.

Table A6.1. *Evolution of governance structures in the distribution of alcoholic beverages*

	Period				
	Before 1960	1961–1970	1971–1990	1991–2000	2001–2005
Largest firms	Seagram / Distillers / National Distillers / Guinness	Seagram / Distillers / National Distillers / Allied	Grand Metropolitan / Anheuser-Busch / Kirin / Allied	Diageo (Grand Metropolitan / Guinness) / Anheuser-Busch / Kirin / Seagram	Diageo (Grand Metropolitan / Guinness) / Anheuser-Busch / Kirin / Pernod Ricard
Geographical scope	Domestic (regional)	Domestic (national)/ International	International/ Multinational	Multinational/ Global	Multinational/ Global
Governance Structures in Distribution					
Market alliances	+	o	o	o	o
With distributors					
Local Agents	++	+	o	o	o
Local Distributors	o	++	+	+	+
Networks of merchant houses	+	+	+	+	o
With Competitors					
Leader in domestic market	+	++	++	++	++
Multinational	o	o	++	++	++
Direct sale to retailers	o	+	+	+	+
Hierarchy					
Employee working abroad	+	+	+	++	++
E-commerce	–	–	–	++	++
Wholly owned channels	+	+	++	+	+
Main forms used by firms	Local Agents	Local Distributors / Competitors: leaders in domestic market	Wholly owned channels / Competitors: leaders in domestic market	Wholly owned channels / Competitors: leaders in domestic market / Competitors: multinationals	Competitors: multinationals Wholly owned channels / Competitors: leaders in domestic market

Note: the author; ++: Very usual; +: usual; o: not usual; -: not applicable.

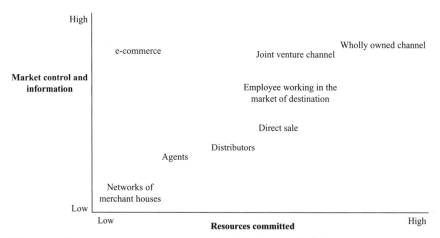

Fig. A6.1. Governance structures in the distribution of alcoholic beverages, 1900–2005.[2]

The "networks of merchant houses" were private organizations that essentially operated in distant markets in Asia, Africa, or Latin America. Begun mostly in the eighteenth and nineteenth centuries, they played a fundamental role in fostering trade between European and the developing countries. Although their core business was to provide intermediation services, they also owned assets in several countries. They could specialize in the trade of one product to different regions or distribute several products to one specific region. Alcoholic beverages were only one of the possible types of products they could handle in their portfolios. Depending on the product, the market, the level of demand for the product, and the firm supplying the product, merchant houses could either carry products on their own account and handle all the activities related to the export of the product (administration, logistics and marketing), or work under commission, being responsible for only some of those activities.

"Agents" were very important intermediaries in the distribution of alcoholic beverages until World War II. Their activities covered very limited regions and they worked under commission or consignment, receiving a percentage proportional to their sales. They assumed a very limited risk as they never owned the products they carried, nor had responsibility for those products in case of deterioration or theft. Each firm tended to use several agents per country, the span of activity and the level of sales of each being very small. Frequently, agents used subagents, who covered specific locations within an already limited region. There existed essentially three types of agents. The exclusive agents who represented only one firm in a given market; the

[2] Axes are based on Stephen Young, James Hamill, Colin Wheeler and J. Richard Davies, *International Market Entry and Development* (Exeter: Harvester Wheatsheaf, 1989): 87.

semi-exclusive agents who represented only one firm for a particular type of alcoholic beverage (e.g., beer, whisky, gin, or port), but who could trade other goods or different types of alcoholic beverages; and the nonexclusive agents, the least common type of agents, who could simultaneously represent various competing firms producing the same type of alcoholic beverage.

According to Bucklin's study of the U.S. market, "distributors" (wholesalers) developed after World War II and took the place of agents.[3] The majority of these distributors were small family businesses whose activity was based on the personal contacts of the founders with their customers. In other markets, distributors generally encompassed a much broader range of functions than those usually allocated in the United States. They were usually responsible for many of the marketing functions for those markets. Distributors were distinct from agents, as they operated in wider geographical regions (often the whole country or even several countries geographically close), and took responsibility for the products they handled. Very often they were also responsible for bottling the beverages.[4] By the beginning of the twenty-first century, they were still a very important channel of distribution for smaller firms that lacked the size to trade on their own with large supermarkets and hypermarkets. They were particularly important for those firms that wanted to target market niches or markets where the retailing industry was less developed.

Another type of distribution channel is the "direct sale." Basically, there are three different groups of "direct sale" retail institutions for alcoholic beverages. One group refers to the "off-premises" licensed take-home outlets and includes supermarket chains, cooperatives, independent grocery stores, outlets that exclusively sell alcoholic beverages, Duty Free Stores (whose genesis dates to 1949 and which decreased in importance after 1997 as a result of the European economic integration), and military sales outlets. Another major set of take-home outlets are public sector and private establishments with exclusive control over the sale of alcoholic beverages in markets such as Canada and Scandinavian countries. In these markets, alcohol can only be sold through these outlets.[5] The other group includes "on-premises" outlets such as restaurants, pubs, cafés, and hotels.

---

[3] Louis P. Bucklin, *Competition and Evolution in the Distributive Trades* (Englewood Cliffs, NJ: Prentice Hall, 1972): 206.

[4] There were other types of distributors that were specific to the kind of alcoholic beverage. One example is export bottlers, who were very important in the distribution of beer until World War II, but basically their role was similar to that of the distributors. See, e.g., S. R. Dennison and Oliver MacDonagh, *Guinness 1886–1939: From Incorporation to the Second Word War* (Dublin: Cork University Press, 1998): chapters 5 and 13; Terry Gourvish and Richard G. Wilson, *The British Brewing Industry, 1830–1980* (Cambridge: Cambridge University Press, 1994).

[5] Frederick Clairmonte and John Cavanagh, *Merchants of Drink: Transnational Control of World Beverages* (Penang: Third World Network, 1988): 175–90.

The large supermarkets and hypermarkets carrying wide assortments of goods are particularly important today in the retailing of consumer goods. The trend towards concentration of distribution had started in the United States in the 1930s, spreading to the rest of North America in the 1940s and to Western Europe in the 1950s.[6] However, it was the process of globalization of the world economy and the changes in consumer lifestyles from the 1960s that dramatically transformed the retailing of consumer goods. The advent of large retailers has done more than erode manufacturers' traditional hold on consumer markets. Channels of distribution were no longer passive physical conduits of goods but had an active role as generators of value addition, especially in logistics and marketing.[7]

The second group of "direct sale" retail institutions refers to "on premise" sales. Although the general pattern was for firms to sell to restaurants, hotels, and cafés through distributors or agents, there were some cases where orders were processed directly by the firms. A third group, widely seen in some Asian countries, comprises vending machines, and the purchase is made without any relation to a vendor or retailer. In addition, firms often had their own retail chains.

Another seldom-used distribution channel is "employees working in the market of destination." These employees who lived abroad established contacts in those markets, distributed the products, and simultaneously provided reliable feedback to the firms. They were especially important while firms were penetrating new markets or when those markets were considered to be strategic, but where demand did not justify having a wholly owned distribution channel (a subsidiary). In these situations, there was no autonomous subsidiary (either wholly owned by the firm or in alliance with a partner) but merely an employee (or employees) living abroad. Although the risk involved and the resources committed were higher than when using agents or distributors, they were not particularly significant and the level of flexibility of the firm to pull out of the market if necessary remained high.

The "wholly owned channels," often used in previous centuries more by entrepreneurial based firms than by large firms from different sectors of alcoholic beverages only developed to become an important part in the strategy of firms from the 1970s and 1980s. The wholly owned distribution subsidiaries, which were legally autonomous corporations, played a similar role

[6] Erderner Kaynak (ed.), *Trans-National Retailing* (New York: W. de Gruyter, 1988); Luca Pellegrini and Srinivas K. Reddy (eds.), *Retail and Marketing Channels* (London: Routledge, 1989).

[7] Susan Segal-Horn and John McGee, "Strategies to Cope with Retailer Buyer Power," in Pellegrini and Reddy, *Retail and Marketing*: 27. In developing countries there was a time lag of around twenty years before the "direct sales" channels developed. By the beginning of the twenty-first century, while large supermarkets and hypermarkets accounted for an important part of the trade of consumer goods in the Western World, in developing countries small retailers still distributed a substantial proportion of these consumer goods.

to the "employee working in the market of destination," the main difference being the volume of sales they were able to handle, their increased capacity to respond to customers' orders, their greater control of decision taking, the higher risk and the lower flexibility to pull out of the market if necessary.

"Joint venture channels" involve the creation of distribution channels where control and costs are spread over the marketing and distribution of products. These joint venture alliances can take several forms and involve distinct partners, such as a large multinational with a local producer of alcoholic beverages, a large multinational with another multinational, a large multinational with a local distributor, and two small competing firms. The size of the partners involved and the scope of the alliances tend to vary over time.

Finally, developments in information systems including the Internet at the end of the twentieth century, led to the emergence of a new type of distribution channel that involved a relatively low commitment of resources while simultaneously providing a high level of market control and information. Through this type of distribution channel, firms (even those of small size) could have direct contact with wholesalers, retailers, or final customers in any part of the world, and respond to large or small purchasing orders without incurring high risks and intermediation costs. These developments clearly marked the end of relationships with some wholesalers and retailers and the beginning of new arrangements where these intermediaries still played an important role, since many of the e-commerce companies were essentially brokers.

Appendix 7

Schematic Representation: Alliances as Dynamic Processes for Acquiring Marketing Knowledge

This appendix provides a schematic representation of the main types of alliances used by a standard leading alcoholic beverages firm, P_1, over time. It offers a visual illustration of the process through which firms acquire and transfer marketing knowledge using four main types of alliances: with local agents, with local distributors, with different kinds of competitors – leading alcoholic beverages firms in their domestic markets, and other leading multinationals in the industry.

Each of the four columns represents a different country.[1] Country 1 is the origin of P_1. The second, third, and fourth columns change with the type of alliance. There are n countries, each one dominated by an alcoholic beverages firm. Countries 1 and n develop large multinationals and countries 2 and i only develop large firms, leaders in their domestic markets.

The analysis in Figure A7.1 is static, and does not reflect that at a particular moment in time firms from different countries might form distinct types of alliances. Production and distribution operations are symbolized by squares, marketing knowledge by a circle, and knowledge about brands by a triangle. Ownership of production and distribution by P_1 is indicated by shading; otherwise, these activities appear unshaded or with stripes. When ownership is shared in an alliance, the square appears half-shaded.

Flows of marketing knowledge, which include the routines and procedures within the firm about marketing methods and the management of brands and distribution channels, are represented by single arrows.[2] They connect the

---

[1] Figure A7.1 employs the conventions introduced and refined by Buckley and Casson's work on the theory of the multinational firm. Peter J. Buckley and Mark Casson, "A Theory of Co-operation in International Business," in F. J. Contractor and P. Lorange (eds.), *Co-operative Strategies in International Business* (Lexington, Mass: Lexington Books, 1988); idem, "Analysing Foreign Market Entry Strategies: Extending the Internalisation Approach," *Journal of International Business Studies*, Vol. 29, No. 3 (1998): 539–61; Mark Casson, *The Organisation of International Business* (Aldershot: Elgar, 1995); idem, *Information and Organisation: A New Perspective on the Theory of the Firm* (Oxford: Clarendon, 1996).

[2] For a more comprehensive definition of marketing knowledge, see Chapter 1.

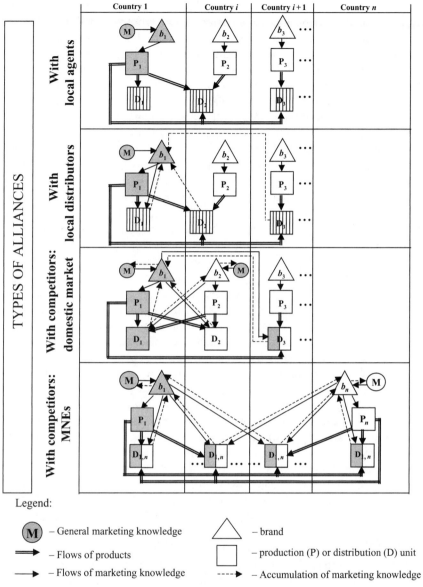

Legend:

(M) – General marketing knowledge △ – brand

⟹ – Flows of products ☐ – production (P) or distribution (D) unit

→ – Flows of marketing knowledge ⤍ – Accumulation of marketing knowledge

Fig. A7.1. Types of alliances in the distribution of alcoholic beverages.

unit in the firm that accumulates general marketing knowledge (M) with the unit that centralizes the specific or sticky marketing knowledge about the brands (*b*), and production operations (P) as well as distribution units (R) (wholly or partially owned).

Flows of products are represented by double arrows and connect production with retail distribution, which can either be wholly owned (represented by a shaded square), partially owned through an alliance (represented by a half-shaded square) or owned by a third party (represented by a square with stripes). The direction of the double arrows represents the flow of products. The direction of the single arrows represents the direction of the flows of acquisition and transfer of knowledge.

The construction of Figure A7.1 relied on eight sets of assumptions on the role of brands in the evolution of multinationals. First, the long-term goal of the largest firms in alcoholic beverages is survival, and the choice of the most efficient distribution channel for their brands helps prevent firms from becoming a target for takeovers. Second, P_I is constantly changing the modes through which it distributes its beverages, responding to the transformations in the environment, and, when entering a market for the first time, seeks to minimize risk. It is only later that P_I chooses the mode of distribution that provides a higher level of control, marketing knowledge, and economies of scale and scope. Third, while P_n ranks among the largest firms worldwide, the diagram only analyzes the alternative modes for P_I's distribution strategy. Fourth, P_I acquires marketing knowledge through its exposure to overseas markets. Fifth, there is no information asymmetry and opportunism in the formation of alliances. Sixth, the distribution activity includes distribution subsidiaries (which have their own sales force) and also retail outlets such as pubs/inns and specialty shops. Seventh, brands $1, 2, n - 1$, and n are assumed to be complementary. Eighth, P_I only uses one channel of distribution in each country.

The first diagram in Figure A7.1 represents an alliance between P1 and local agents in different markets who also distribute other brands. It illustrates the lack of transfer or accumulation of marketing knowledge, as well as P_I's lack of control of the marketing of its brand b_I.

The second diagram describes an alliance between P_I and a local distributor, and shows that it is possible for P_I to accumulate sticky marketing knowledge. There is, however, still no control over the marketing of b_I or the transfer of knowledge about the marketing of the brand to the distributor.

The third diagram shows a situation in which the firm is vertically integrated in the domestic market and has an alliance with a local competitor abroad, a leader in its own market. It illustrates the transfer and accumulation of sticky marketing knowledge, with some control by P_I of the operations and the decision making of the marketing of the brand.

Finally, the last diagram represents a situation in which P_I (a large multinational) forms an alliance with another large multinational. The situation includes multiple markets and sales through jointly owned and managed distribution channels. In this situation, control is shared. Acquisition and transfer of marketing knowledge and also the possibility of obtaining economies of scale and scope are illustrated by the large number of complementary brands – 1, 2, $n - 1$, and n. Overall, Figure A7.1 shows the benefits of alliances with direct competitors, where firms minimize risk and control and yet are able to acquire marketing knowledge.

Appendix 8

Diversification Strategies

Table A8.1. *Percentage of sales in alcoholic beverages to total sales, 1960–2005*

Origin / Year	Distillers Company UK	IDV UK	Grand Metropolitan UK	Diageo UK	Guinness UK	Allied UK	Hiram Walker CAN	Seagram CAN	Pernod Ricard FRA	Heineken NL	LVMH FRA	Anheuser-Busch US
1960	80	100	0	–	n/a	n/a	n/a	100	–	n/a	–	n/a
1961	82	100	0	–	91	n/a	n/a	100	–	n/a	–	n/a
1962	88	100	0	–	94	n/a	n/a	100	–	n/a	–	n/a
1963	86	100	0	–	96	n/a	n/a	100	–	n/a	–	n/a
1964	83	100	0	–	98	n/a	n/a	100	–	97	–	n/a
1965	81	100	0	–	92	n/a	n/a	100	–	96	–	n/a
1966	n/a	100	0	–	92	n/a	n/a	100	–	94	–	n/a
1967	n/a	100	0	–	89	n/a	n/a	100	–	95	–	n/a
1968	91	100	0	–	87	n/a	n/a	100	–	96	–	n/a
1969	91	100	0	–	84	n/a	n/a	100	–	78	–	n/a
1970	90	100	0	–	84	n/a	n/a	100	–	80	–	n/a
1971	89	100	5	–	85	n/a	n/a	98	–	84	–	n/a
1972	89	100	33	–	85	n/a	n/a	98	–	86	–	n/a
1973	88	100	34	–	81	n/a	n/a	98	–	84	–	n/a
1974	88	100	29	–	81	n/a	n/a	97	–	86	–	n/a
1975	86	–	32	–	79	n/a	n/a	94	75	86	–	n/a
1976	86	–	n/a	–	77	n/a	n/a	92	n/a	87	–	n/a

Year											
1977	n/a	—	89	n/a	92	58	n/a	74	—	n/a	—	86
1978	n/a	—	88	n/a	93	60	58	61	—	n/a	—	84
1979	n/a	—	87	n/a	93	62	64	62	—	49	—	84
1980	n/a	—	88	n/a	88	57	66	64	—	50	—	84
1981	n/a	—	89	n/a	100	50	70	69	—	57	—	84
1982	98	—	90	n/a	100	43	69	73	—	35	—	83
1983	81	—	n/a	n/a	100	41	67	84	—	43	—	83
1984	83	—	88	n/a	100	—	64	85	—	31	—	67
1985	77	—	87	61	100	—	64	69	—	30	—	60
1986	77	—	87	64	100	—	66	73	—	33	—	—
1987	77	56	87	64	85	—	67	79	—	38	—	—
1988	77	54	87	60	78	—	72	95	—	43	—	—
1989	78	52	87	65	79	—	71	98	—	30	—	—
1990	76	52	87	64	78	—	75	98	—	24	—	—
1991	76	53	86	62	77	—	77	99	—	28	—	—
1992	76	50	n/a	55	76	—	60	100	—	36	—	—
1993	n/a	47	87	53	76	—	59	100	—	42	—	—
1994	n/a	42	n/a	49	72	—	56	100	—	43	—	—
1995	n/a	38	86	48	74	—	63	100	—	41	—	—
1996	n/a	37	n/a	50	48	—	62	—	—	40	—	—
1997	82	26	n/a	67	39	—	57	—	61	—	—	—
1998	82	27	n/a	68	39	—	56	—	62	—	—	—
1999	83	26	87	70	—	—	51	—	61	—	—	—
2000	82	20	85	69	—	—	88	—	60	—	—	—
2001	82	20	100	42	—	—	89	—	59	—	—	—
2002	82	18	100	70	—	—	91	—	77	—	—	—
2003	82	18	100	97	—	—	92	—	95	—	—	—
2004	81	18	100	97	—	—	93	—	100	—	—	—
2005	80	19	100	98	—	—	—	—	100	—	—	—

Sources: Companies' annual inputs.

Table A8.2. *Percentage of sales generated outside the continent of origin of the firm, 1960–2005*

Year	Distillers Company	IDV	Grand Metropolitan	Diageo	Guinness	Allied	Hiram Walker	Seagram	Pernod Ricard	Heineken	LVMH	Anheuser-Busch
Origin	UK	UK	UK	UK	UK	UK	CAN	CAN	FRA	NL	FRA	US
1960	n/a	n/a	n/a	–	n/a	n/a	n/a	n/a	–	n/a	–	n/a
1961	n/a	n/a	n/a	–	n/a	n/a	n/a	n/a	–	n/a	–	n/a
1962	n/a	n/a	n/a	–	n/a	n/a	n/a	n/a	–	n/a	–	n/a
1963	n/a	n/a	n/a	–	n/a	n/a	n/a	n/a	–	n/a	–	n/a
1964	n/a	n/a	n/a	–	n/a	n/a	n/a	n/a	–	n/a	–	n/a
1965	n/a	n/a	n/a	–	91	n/a	n/a	n/a	–	n/a	–	n/a
1966	n/a	29	n/a	–	n/a	n/a	n/a	n/a	–	n/a	–	n/a
1967	36	30	0	–	16	n/a	n/a	n/a	–	n/a	–	n/a
1968	44	30	4	–	19	n/a	n/a	n/a	–	n/a	–	n/a
1969	48	30	1	–	28	n/a	n/a	n/a	–	n/a	–	n/a
1970	47	30	1	–	31	n/a	n/a	n/a	–	n/a	–	n/a
1971	46	30	3	–	21	n/a	n/a	n/a	–	n/a	–	n/a
1972	46	20	4	–	19	n/a	n/a	n/a	–	n/a	–	n/a
1973	46	25	6	–	17	n/a	n/a	n/a	–	n/a	–	n/a
1974	44	28	5	–	20	n/a	n/a	n/a	0	n/a	–	n/a
1975	42	–	n/a	–	26	n/a	n/a	n/a	n/a	n/a	–	n/a
1976	39	–	n/a	–	n/a	n/a	n/a	n/a	n/a	n/a	–	n/a
1977	37	–	n/a	–	21	n/a	n/a	n/a	n/a	n/a	–	n/a
1978	40	–	n/a	–	20	4	n/a	23	n/a	n/a	–	n/a
1979	38	–	6	–	22	11	n/a	26	n/a	n/a	–	n/a
1980	39	–	11	–	18	11	n/a	30	n/a	n/a	–	n/a

Year												
1981	40	–	23	–	24	11	15	32	n/a	n/a	–	n/a
1982	44	–	27	–	21	12	14	31	n/a	n/a	–	n/a
1983	45	–	31	–	20	14	12	32	n/a	n/a	–	n/a
1984	45	–	36	–	20	17	12	29	n/a	n/a	–	n/a
1985	52	–	38	–	19	18	11	32	n/a	n/a	–	n/a
1986	–	–	34	–	27	16	–	36	n/a	n/a	–	n/a
1987	–	–	34	–	30	18	–	43	n/a	n/a	52	n/a
1988	–	–	32	–	41	26	–	51	n/a	n/a	56	n/a
1989	–	–	45	–	40	25	–	47	n/a	27	60	n/a
1990	–	–	54	–	39	27	–	47	n/a	24	56	n/a
1991	–	–	56	–	38	24	–	52	n/a	25	51	n/a
1992	–	–	60	–	41	23	–	52	n/a	25	60	n/a
1993	–	–	65	–	44	24	–	55	n/a	27	63	n/a
1994	–	–	69	–	45	26	–	55	20	30	62	5
1995	–	–	67	–	43	28	–	54	19	30	62	6
1996	–	–	69	–	44	24	–	44	19	29	61	6
1997	–	–	–	66	–	19	–	41	19	31	70	7
1998	–	–	–	65	–	21	–	43	19	29	63	6
1999	–	–	–	65	–	23	–	49	19	10	63	6
2000	–	–	–	65	–	43	–	51	19	10	66	6
2001	–	–	–	68	–	74	–	–	26	32	64	7
2002	–	–	–	68	–	72	–	–	44	32	63	7
2003	–	–	–	69	–	72	–	–	43	34	62	8
2004	–	–	–	68	–	72	–	–	44	33	62	12
2005	–	–	–	–	–	–	–	–	60	24	65	17

Source: Companies' annual reports.

Table A8.3. *Diversification by the largest multinational in alcoholic beverages in* 2000

Multinational	Country of Origin	Total Sales	Level of Diversification	Alcoholic Beverages (%)	Other Businesses (%)	Other Businesses' Scope of Operation
Allied Domecq	UK	3,842	Low diversification	Wines and spirits (88%)	Quick-service restaurants (12%)	Global market
Ambev	BRA	2,706	Medium diversification	Beer (79%)	Soft drinks (21%)	Domestic market
Anheuser-Busch	US	12,499	No diversification	Beer (100%)		Domestic market
Asahi Breweries	JAP	12,983	Low diversification	Wines, spirits, and beer (81%)	Soft drinks and food (16%) Others (3%)	Domestic market
Bacardi	CB/BER	2,800	No diversification	Spirits and wines (100%)		
Brown Forman	US	2,146	Medium diversification	Wines and spirits (72%)	Luggage and chinaware (28%)	Domestic market
Carlsberg	DEN	4,272	Low diversification	Beer (99%)	Other businesses (1%)	Domestic market
Adolph Coors	US	2,414	No diversification	Beer (100%)		
Constellation Brands / Canandaigua	US	2,162	No diversification	Wines and spirits (73%) Beer (distribution 27%)		
Diageo	UK	17,053	High diversification	Wines, spirits, and beer (60%)	Quick-service restaurants (8%) Packaged foods (32%)	Global market

Company	Country		Revenue	Products		Market
E. & J. Gallo	US	No	1,650	Wines (100%)		Domestic market
Fortune Brands / American Brands	US	High	5,845	Wines and spirits (21%)	Home products (38%), Office products (25%), Golf products (16%)	Domestic market
Foster Brewing	AUS	High	1,835	Beer (48%), Wines and spirits (20%), Other (5%)	Leisure and hospitality (27%), Other (5%)	Domestic market
Heineken	NL	Low	7,469	Beer (80%), Wines and spirits (5%)	Soft drinks (11%), Other (4%)	Domestic market
Interbrew	BEL	Low	5,212	Beer (98%)	Other (2%)	Domestic market
Kirin	JAP	Medium	14,669	Beer (71%)	Soft drinks (20%), Other (9%)	Domestic market
LVMH	FRA	High	10,670	Wines and spirits (20%)	Fashion and leather goods (28%), Perfumes and cosmetics (18%), Selective retailing (28%), Watches and jewelry (5%), Other (1%)	Global market
Philip Morris (Miller)	US	Unrelated	4,806*	Beer (5%)	Tobacco (61%), Food (33%), Financial services (1%)	Domestic market

(continued)

247

Table A8.3 *(Continued)*

Multinational	Country of Origin	Total Sales	Level of Diversification	Alcoholic Beverages (%)	Other Businesses (%)	Other Businesses' Scope of Operation
Molson	CAN	1,181	None	Beer and related (100%)		
Pernod Ricard	FRA	4,037	High	Wines and spirits (69%)	Processed fruits (31%)	Domestic market
Rémy Cointreau	FRA	674	None	Wines and spirits (100%)		
Scottish & Newcastle	UK	5,419	Low	Beer (58%) Retail (pub, restaurant) (31%)	Leisure (11%)	Domestic market
Seagram	CAN	15,686	High	Wines and spirits (39%)	Music (54%) Entertainment, recreation (7%)	Global market
South African Breweries	SA	4,806	Medium	Beer (72%)	Other beverages (22%) Hotels and gaming (6%)	Domestic market
Suntory	JAP	7,879	High	Wines and spirits (24%) Beer (17%)	Food (44%) Other (15%)	Domestic market

Note: Amounts in millions of current U.S. dollars.
*Total Sales for Miller only, the brewing business of Philip Morris.
Source: Various annual reports and newspapers.

Appendix 9

Patterns of Diversification within Alcoholic Beverages

Table A9.1. *Patterns of diversification within the alcoholic beverages industry*

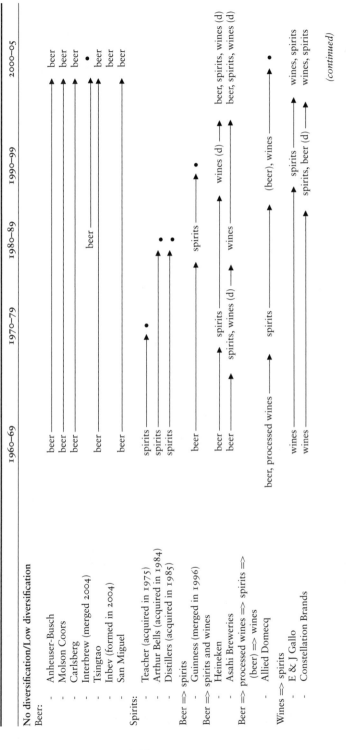

	1960–69	1970–79	1980–89	1990–99	2000–05
No diversification/Low diversification					
Beer:					
- Anheuser-Busch	beer			→	beer
- Molson Coors	beer			→	beer
- Carlsberg	beer			→	beer
- Interbrew (merged 2004)	beer		beer	→	• beer
- Tsingtao	beer			→	beer
- Inbev (formed in 2004)	beer			→	beer
- San Miguel	beer			→	beer
Spirits:					
- Teacher (acquired in 1975)	spirits	→ •			
- Arthur Bells (acquired in 1984)	spirits		→ •		
- Distillers (acquired in 1985)	spirits		→ •		
Beer ⇒ spirits					
- Guinness (merged in 1996)	beer		→ spirits	•	
Beer ⇒ spirits and wines					
- Heineken	beer	→ spirits		→ wines (d)	→ beer, spirits, wines (d)
- Asahi Breweries	beer	→ spirits, wines (d)		→	→ beer, spirits, wines (d)
Beer ⇒ processed wines ⇒ spirits ⇒ (beer) ⇒ wines					
- Allied Domecq	beer, processed wines	→ spirits	→ wines	→ (beer), wines	•
Wines ⇒ spirits					
- E & J Gallo	wines			→ spirits	→ wines, spirits
- Constellation Brands	wines			→ spirits, beer (d)	→ wines, spirits

(*continued*)

249

Table A9.1 (Continued)

	1960–69	1970–79	1980–89	1990–99	2000–05
Spirits ⇒ wines					
- Rémy Cointreau	spirits —————————→		wines —————→		spirits, wines
- Bacardi	spirits ——————————————————→			wines ——→	spirits, wines
- Highland Distillers	spirits ——————————————————→			wines (d) ——→	spirits, wines (d)
Medium diversification					
Beer:					
- Ambev (formed in 2000, merged 2004)					Beer
Beer ⇒ spirits and wines					
- Kirin Breweries	beer —————————→	spirits, wines (d) ——→	wines —→		beer, spirits, wines
- Sapporo	beer —————————→	wines and spirits ——→			beer, spirits, wines
- SABMiller	beer ————————————————————→			spirits, wines ——→	beer, spirits, wines
Spirits ⇒ processed wines ⇒ wines					
- Brown Forman	spirits, processed wines (d) ———————————→			wines ——————→	spirits, wines
High diversification					
Spirits and wines:					
- Pernod Ricard (formed in 1975)		processed wines, spirits ——————————————————→			wines, spirits
- Moët-Hennessy (formed in 1971)		processed wines, spirits ——————————————————→			wines, spirits
Spirits ⇒ wines					
- Seagram	spirits, wines —————————————————————————————————————→				spirits, wines
- Fortune Brands	spirits ——————————————————————————→			wines ——→	spirits, wines
Beer ⇒ processed wines, wines and spirits ⇒ (beer)					
- Grand Metropolitan (merged in 1996)	beer ——————————→	spirits, wines ——→	(beer)	•	
Beer ⇒ wines					
- Foster's	beer ——————————————————————————→			wines ——→	beer, wines
Beer, wines and spirits:					
- Diageo (formed in 1997)				beer, spirits, wines ——→	beer, spirits, wines
- Suntory	spirits, wines, beer ——→				spirits, wines, beer

Notes: ● – firm merged or acquired; (d) – distribution; (beer) – divestment from the beer business

250

Appendix 10

Schematic Representation: Brands and Marketing Knowledge in Mergers and Acquisitions

Figure A10.1 provides a schematic representation of the process of growth of the largest multinationals of alcoholic beverages at the beginning of the twenty-first century. It illustrates how brands influenced that evolution by constantly changing the boundaries of firms in a series of different stages. It is based on the assumption that a standard multinational of alcoholic beverages P_I evolves in several stages corresponding largely to "waves" of international mergers and acquisitions. Penrose's concepts on the growth of the firm, and Johanson and Vahlne's stages model of the internationalization of the firm are used to help explain the internationalization process, despite not directly addressing entry into foreign markets through globalization of brands.[1] The figure shows that the world's largest alcoholic beverages firms first grew through geographical expansion using their existing successful brands, and through international mergers, acquisitions, and alliances. It highlights the increasing importance of marketing knowledge in the development of firms. Figure A10.1 does not, however, suggest that the industry evolved over time into a monopoly, but rather that P_I grew from being the leader in its domestic market to being a globalized multinational firm.

The schematic representation focuses in particular on three types of growth strategies of firms – exports, mergers and acquisitions, and alliances. As in other industries in developed economies, these were the predominant forms of international expansion of alcoholic beverages firms since the 1960s.[2] However, since the evolution in the patterns of ownership in mergers is very similar to that of acquisitions, they are not included in the schematic representation.

---

[1] Edith Penrose, *The Theory of the Growth of the Firm* (Oxford: Blackwell, 1959); J. Johanson and J. E. Vahlne, "The Internationalisation Process of the Firm: A Model of Knowledge Development and Increasing Market Commitment," *Journal of International Business Studies*, Vol. 8 (1977): 23–32.

[2] John M. Stopford and Louis T. Wells, *Managing the Multinational Enterprise* (London: Longman, 1972); Brent D. Wilson, "The Propensity of Multinational Firms to Expand Through Acquisitions," *Journal of International Business Studies*, Vol. 11, No. 2 (1980): 59–65.

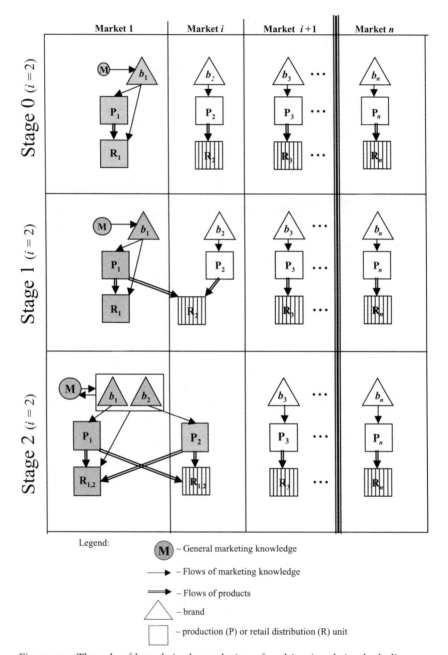

Fig. A10.1. The role of brands in the evolution of multinationals in alcoholic beverages

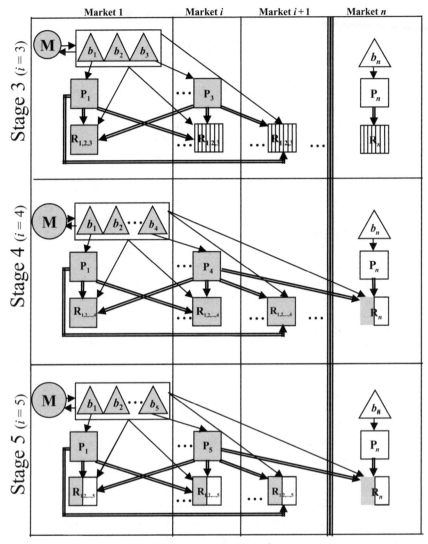

Fig. A10.1 (*Continued*)

Each of the four columns represents a different country.[3] The two middle columns change with the evolution of firm P_1 (in stages). There are n

[3] Figure A10.1 employs the conventions introduced and refined by Buckley and Casson's work on the theory of the multinational firm. Peter J. Buckley and Mark Casson, "A Theory of Co-operation in International Business," in F. J. Contractor and P. Lorange (eds.), *Co-operative Strategies in International Business* (Lexington, Mass: Lexington Books, 1988); idem, "Analysing Foreign Market Entry Strategies: Extending the Internalisation Approach," *Journal of International Business Studies*, Vol. 29, No. 3 (1998): 539–61; Mark Casson,

countries, each one dominated by an alcoholic beverages firm. Markets from 1 to $i + 1$ are culturally and politically similar and geographically proximate, with i corresponding to different markets ranging from 2 to $n - 1$, and referring to the number of relevant markets at a particular stage in the development of the firm. Country 1 in the first column is the origin of P_1. Country n is culturally and geographically distant from the other markets.

The symbols used for production and distribution operations, flows of products and flows of marketing knowledge, as well as the assumptions on the role of brands in the evolution of markets, are the same as used in Appendix 7.

The construction of Figure A10.1 relies on eight sets of assumptions, based on the evidence provided by the evolution of the world's largest multinationals analyzed in previous sections. First, their long-term goals are survival and maximization of shareholders' wealth, or at least the maintenance of a level of market capitalization that prevents them from becoming targets for takeovers, within a context of modern global capital markets. Despite some short-term moves to outmaneuver competitors, it is assumed that these long-term goals can be achieved through one main strategy – the merger and acquisition of firms that own successful brands with global potential. This is why firms follow several stages in their evolution, first selling in markets culturally, politically, and geographically proximate, then acquiring production firms and distribution channels in those markets, and only subsequently entering markets with a high cultural and geographic distance (especially by forming alliances).

Second, P_1 produces brand 1 (b_1), which from the late 1950s until the beginning of the twenty-first century, develops into one of the world's largest multinationals in the industry. It grows in evolutionary stages (correlated with the waves of mergers and acquisitions) by merging and acquiring other large firms in distinct markets, and constantly changing its boundaries. In its international strategy, P_1 first acquires firms in those markets to which it was already exporting and which are culturally, politically, and geographically closer, and only later enters more distant markets. Third, all the firms from P_1 to P_n rank among the largest firms worldwide, but only P_1's growth and survival is analyzed. Firms P_2 to P_n are close followers of P_1.

Fourth, P_1 has firm-specific advantages over its competitors,[4] and ranks among the world's largest firms. These firm-specific advantages, which are

---

The Organisation of International Business (Aldershot: Elgar, 1995); idem, *Information and Organisation: A New Perspective on the Theory of the Firm* (Oxford: Clarendon, 1996).

[4] John H. Dunning, "Reappraising the Eclectic Paradigm in an Age of Alliance Capitalism," *Journal of International Business Studies*, Vol. 26, No. 3 (1995): 461–91. The definition of firm-specific advantages is based on John Dunning's concept of "ownership advantage," in John H. Dunning, "Trade, Location of Economic Activity and the MNE: A Search for an Eclectic Approach," in B. Ohlin, P. O. Hesselborn, and P. M. Wijkman (eds.), *The International Allocation of Economic Activity* (London: Macmillan, 1977); Stephen Hymer, "On Multinational Corporations and Foreign Direct Investment," selected by John H. Dunning

endogenous and differentiate the firm from its competitors promoting its success, include its marketing knowledge, in particular its superior capacity to manage brands, and also its ownership structure, entrepreneurial capabilities of its managers, organizational structure, first-mover advantages, economies of scale and scope, technology, and distribution networks. These are advantages that form the basis for the international growth and survival of firms in alcoholic beverages. Fifth, with each acquisition P_I acquires additional marketing knowledge. Sixth, all the firms acquired own successful brands; brands can only be acquired with the firms that produce them; search for brands is rational and there are no costs associated with information asymmetry and opportunism in their acquisition. In the real world, the process of growth involves both decisions to grow a handful of local and regional brands into global brands, and also to eliminate the majority of other brands considered lacking in growth potential. However, as the aim of the schematic representation is to explain how successful brands contribute to the evolution of multinationals in alcoholic beverages, these issues are not discussed here.[5] It is assumed that all brands are successful and remain so during the period of analysis. The schematic representation also does not discuss whether and how the definition of a "successful brand" changes over time and does not concern itself with the decision to divest brands. Seventh, only one single level of distribution is considered. This links production to final demand and includes distribution subsidiaries (which have their own sales force).

From stages 0 to 3, the environment is assumed to be benign (no wars or major crisis) and the relevant level of competition to be local. In stages 4 and 5, competition becomes global. Stages 0 and 1 do not correspond to the period analyzed in this book, but help the understanding of the evolution of P_I in the subsequent stages. These preliminary stages correspond to the evolution of multinationals of alcoholic beverages and their predecessors before the 1960s. Stages 2 to 5 rely on the empirical evidence presented in previous sections, and relate to the period from 1960 until 2005.

Stages 0 and 1 illustrate that before the 1960s, when the world alcoholic beverages industry was still fragmented, the largest alcoholic beverages firms had a restricted regional scope, relying on organic growth to expand geographically and using the existing brands. At this stage, very few firms got involved in international mergers and acquisitions. Stage 0 shows the starting point for P_I, a standard leading firm, from market 1. At this stage, it is assumed there is one leading firm in each market and no trade takes place between markets since P_I's levels of general and sticky marketing knowledge

from "The International Operations of National Firms: A Study of Foreign Direct Investment" (PhD dissertation, MIT, 1960), in C. N. Pitelis and R. Sugden (eds.), *The Nature of the Transnational Firm* (London: Routledge, 1991): 23–43; Richard Nelson, "Why Do Firms Differ and How Does It Matter," *Strategic Management Journal*, Vol. 14 (1991): 61–74.
[5] For a discussion of this topic, see Chapter 7, "Acquiring brands."

(which is specific to the firm) are very low, and the firm owns only one single successful brand (b_1).

In stage 1, P_1 creates firm-specific advantages and decides to start selling/exporting to market 2 using an independent distributor. In this process it also develops additional firm-specific advantages over the local competitor P_2, in particular by obtaining additional marketing knowledge, which facilitates the acquisition of P_2 in the subsequent stage.

In stage 2, with the acquisition of P_2, P_1 is able to obtain economies of scale and scope in distribution, and also to import brand b_2 into its home market. In this process P_1 acquires additional general market knowledge. In stage 3 (which corresponds to the period from the 1960s to the 1980s), P_1 acquires P_3, a close competitor (owner of b_3), which also has an established international activity. The purpose of this acquisition of a firm that owns an already successful brand (b_3) is to transform it into a global brand.

In stages 4 and 5 (which correspond to the period from the 1980s), entry in markets culturally, politically, and geographically distant becomes possible because P_1 has acquired extensive marketing knowledge that provides the ability to explore the potential of other brands. In stage 4 (corresponding to the merger wave between 1985–1988), P_1 continues to acquire firms that own successful brands and distribute those brands through wholly owned distribution channels in markets culturally, politically, and geographically proximate. However, it also enters markets culturally, politically, and geographically distant by using wholly owned distribution channels, and also by forming alliances with local partners or other large competitors. In stage 5 (which corresponds essentially to the 1990s), P_1 disintegrates vertically, and alternatively forms alliances in distribution with another multinational P_6, covering with that alliance multiple markets worldwide.

This model provides a more formal explanation of the growth process of large multinational firms in alcoholic beverages since the 1960s. It shows the impact of brands and marketing knowledge on the pattern and pace of growth of firms, and how their interaction constantly changed the boundaries of firms. Over time, successful brands became increasingly a major determinant for mergers, acquisitions, and alliances with distributors or competitors. They also had an indirect role in accelerating the process of multinational growth and long-term survival of firms, as their acquisition allowed firms to acquire knowledge more rapidly.

Appendix 11

Evolution of Sales of the World's Leading Brands by Beverage Type

Table AII.1. *Leading brands in wines, champagnes, and low-alcohol refreshers*

Type of Wine / Brand Name	Date Brand Launched / Foundation	Country of Origin of the Brand	Owner	Country of Owner	Total Sales, 1990	Total Sales, 1997	Total Sales, 2002
Table Wine							
Gallo / E. & J. Wine	1933	US	E. & J. Gallo	US	19.4	23.2	24.6
Franzia	1981	US	The Wine Group	US	6.40	17.90	20.96
Carlo Rossi	1964	US	E. & J. Gallo	US	13.0	12.09	10.65
Tavernello	1966	IT	Caviro Societa Cooperative Arl	IT	5.2	9.3	10.7
Almaden	1852	US	Constellation Brands	US	7.8	7.62	9.75
Champagne							
Moët & Chandon	1743	FRA	LVMH	FRA	2.00	2.19	2.12
Veuve Cliquot	1772	FRA	LVMH	FRA	0.79	0.94	1.18
Vranken Laffitte	1848/1976	FRA	Vranken Pommery Monopole	FRA	0.22	0.47	0.58
Mumm	1827	FRA	Seagram	FRA	0.83	0.64	0.56
Lanson	1760	FRA	Lanson	FRA	0.61	0.45	0.55

(continued)

Table A11.1 (*Continued*)

Type of Wine / Brand Name	Date Brand Launched / Foundation	Country of Origin of the Brand	Owner	Country of Owner	Total Sales, 1990	Total Sales, 1997	Total Sales, 2002
Ready to Drink							
Smirnoff Ice	2002	US	Diageo	UK	–	–	43.9
Bacardi Breezer	1990	US/BER	Bacardi-Martini	US/BER	4.43	4.93	16.19
Skyy Blue	2002	US	Campari	ITA	–	–	6.88
Bacardi Silver	2002	US	Bacardi	US/BER	–	–	5.68
Jim Beam and Cola	1986	US	Jim Beam Brands	US	0.75	2.29	4.41

Note: Amounts stated in millions of 9-L cases. n/a – not available.

Sources for Tables A11.1 and A11.2: Impact International (various publications); Seagram Collection (Wilmington Delaware, Hagley Museum and Library, USA); Moët & Chandon Archive (Epernay, France); Charles Craig, *The Scotch Whisky Industry Record* (Dumbarton: Index Publishing Limited, 1994); Janice Jorgensen (ed.), *Encyclopaedia of Consumer Brands* (London: St James Press, 1994); Bartles & Jaymes, Consumer Relations (June 2002).

Table A11.2. *Leading brands in premium spirits*

Type of Premium Spirit / Brand Name	Date Brand Launched / Foundation	Country of Origin of the Brand	Owner	Country of Owner	Total Sales, 1990	Total Sales, 1997	Total Sales, 2002
Other Whisky (Excluding Scotch)							
Jack Daniels	1866	US	Brown Forman	US	4.29	5.19	6.6
Jim Beam	1795	US	American/Fortune Brands	US	4.63	4.92	4.64
Crown Royal	1934	CAN	Diageo	UK	1.97	2.74	3.63
Seagram's 7 Crown	1857	CAN	Diageo	UK	4.03	2.84	2.57
Suntory Kakubin	1989	JPN	Suntory	JP	2.80	2.89	2.41
Scotch Whisky							
Johnnie Walker Red Label	1820	UK	Diageo	UK	5.75	7.29	6.90
J & B Rare	1749	UK	Diageo	UK	5.41	5.95	5.52
Ballantines Finest	1872	UK	Allied Domecq	UK	4.78	4.59	4.90
Grants Family Reserve	1899	UK	William Grant	UK	2.21	3.75	3.67
Dewar's White Label	1846	UK	Bacardi	CB/BER	3.14	2.87	3.48
Vodka Premium Brands							
Smirnoff	1864	RUS	Diageo	UK	13.58	13.52	17.0
Absolut	1879	SWE	Vin & Spirit	SWE	3.09	4.37	7.50
Bols	1995/1575	NL	Remy Cointreau	FRA	–	0.64	1.76
Stolichnaya	1953	RUS	Soyuzplodimport (SPI)	RUS	1.36	1.29	2.40
Finlandia	1970	FIN	Brown Forman	US	0.92	1.65	1.70

(continued)

Table AII.2 (*Continued*)

Type of Premium Spirit / Brand Name	Date Brand Launched / Foundation	Country of Origin of the Brand	Owner	Country of Owner	Total Sales, 1990	Total Sales, 1997	Total Sales, 2002
Gin/Genever Premium Brands							
Gordons Gin	1769	UK	Diageo	UK	6.26	5.22	4.83
Seagram Gin	1857	US/CAN	Pernod Ricard	FRA	4.06	3.28	2.99
Beefeater	1820	UK	Allied Domecq	UK	1.99	2.11	2.27
Larios	1863	SPN	Pernod Ricard	FRA	3.36	2.25	2.02
Tanqueray	1830	UK	Diageo	UK	1.44	1.39	1.48
Rum							
Tanduay 5 year Gold	1876	PHIL	Tanduay Distillery	PHIL	n/a	11.20	19.7
Bacardi Carta Blanca	1862	CB	Bacardi	CB/BER	16.22	13.24	13.05
Captain Morgan Spiced Rum	1983	JAM	Diageo	US/CAN	0.72	1.85	3.67
Brugal Gold	1888	SPN	Brugal & Co	SPN	1.85	1.79	2.70
Bacardi Oro	1862	CB	Bacardi	CB/BER	2.93	2.25	2.41
Cognac and Other Brandy							
Dreher	1910	BRA	Campari	IT	2.56	3.80	2.70
Presidente	1958	SPN	Allied Domecq	UK	5.36	4.47	2.42
Hennessy	1765	FRA	LVMH	FRA	1.89	1.48	2.01
Wilthener Goldkrone	n/a	GER	Hardenberg Wilthen	GER	1.00	2.00	2.03
E. & J.	n/a	US	E. & J. Gallo	US	2.55	1.82	1.94
Liqueurs							
Baileys Irish Cream	1974	IRE	Diageo	UK	3.36	4.13	5.84

De Kuyper	De Kuyper	NL	1920	NL	2.31	2.39	2.68
Kahlua	Allied Domecq	MEX	1937	UK	2.59	2.29	2.23
Malibu	Diageo	UK	1980	UK	1.30	1.60	2.26
Southern Comfort	Brown Forman	US	1880	US	2.47	2.25	2.14
Other Flavored Spirits (Excluding Liqueurs)							
Ricard	Pernod Ricard	FRA	1932	FRA	7.08	6.03	6.53
Jagermeister	Mast-Jagermeister AG	GER	1935	GER	1.67	2.52	3.19
Campari	Campari	ITA	1860	ITA	2.32	2.57	2.61
Pastis 51	Pernod Ricard	FRA	1954	FRA	2.55	1.98	2.01
Fernet Branca	Fratelli Branca	ITA	1845	ITA	1.43	1.37	1.37
Tequila							
Cuervo Gold	Cuervo	MEX	1980	MEX	1.38	1.64	4.08
Sauza Gold	Allied Domecq	UK	1873	MEX	0.26	0.64	0.73
Cuervo Anejo Super	Cuervo	MEX	1790	MEX	0.06	0.21	0.63
Sauza 100 Anos	Allied Domecq	UK	2000	MEX	–	–	0.53
Sauza Blanco	Allied Domecq	UK	1873	MEX	1.07	1.19	0.34

Note: Amounts stated in millions of 9-L cases.

Table A11.3. *Leading brands in beer*

Brand Name	Date Brand Launched / Foundation	Country of Origin of the Brand	Owner	Country of Owner	Total Sales, 1990	Total Sales, 1997	Total Sales, 2002
Budweiser	1876	US	Anheuser-Busch	US	60.5	54.7	50.1
Bud (range)	1982	US	Anheuser-Busch	US	14.0	30.5	45.6
Skol	1964	BRA	Ambev	BRA	6	15	32.3
Corona	1925	MEX	Grupo Modelo / Anheuser-Busch	US	10.6	19.4	26.7
Heineken	1864	NL	Heineken	NL	15.5	18.8	22.9
Coors Light	1993	US	Coors	US	14.4	17.8	21.6
Asahi Super Dry	1987	JPN	Asahi Breweries	JPN	14.3	21.7	21.1
Miller Lite	1975	US	Miller	US	23.4	19.8	18.8
Brahma Chopp	1888	BRA	Ambev	BRA	18.4	23.0	18.0
Busch (range)	1955	US	Anheuser-Busch	US	11	16.1	16.5
Castle Lager	1895	SA	SABMiller	SA	6.4	15.0	13.8
Polar (range)	1941	VEN	Cerveceria Polar	VEN	10.2	13.9	11.8
Amstel	1870	NL	Heineken	NL	n/a	9.7	10.8
Carlsberg	1847	DEN	Carlsberg	DEN	9.5	9.5	10.7
San Miguel	1890	PHIL	San Miguel Corp.	PHL	13.1	11.7	10.4
Beijing Beer	1941	CHN	Beijing Yanjing	CHN	n/a	7.0	10.3
Guinness Stout	1759	IRE	Guinness	IRE/UK	8	8.8	10.2
Kaiser	1982	BRA	Molson	CAN	6.8	11.7	9.2
Baltika	1990	RUS	Baltic Beverages Holding	RUS	n/a	2.9	9.1
Stella Artois	1880	BEL	Interbrew	BEL	n/a	4.9	8.85

Note: Amounts stated in millions of hectoliters.
Sources: For 1990, *Impact International*; for 1997 and 2002, *Plato Logic Limited.*

Bibliography

Primary Sources

Annual Reports

When available, annual reports were obtained from the firms in question. Where annual reports were not readily available from the firms, alternatives sources were used. The annual reports deposited at Companies House and Guildhall Library proved especially valuable for the British firms, and the annual reports deposited in the Baker Library at Harvard Business School were particularly useful, especially for firms where direct access had not been possible. The annual reports analyzed, when available, included the period from 1960 to 2000 and the firms researched were as follows:

Adoph Coors
Allied Domecq from 1995 / Allied Lyons from 1982 / Allied Breweries from 1963/ Ind. Coope
    Tetley Ansell Limited
Ambev
Anheuser-Busch
Arthur Bells
Asahi Breweries
Bacardi
Bass
Bavaria
Braueri Beck from 1979 / Haake Beck-Brauerei
Brown Forman
Carlsberg from 1987 / United Breweries
Carlton United Breweries
Companhia Cervejeira Brahma
Companhia Antarctica Paulista
Constellation Brands from 2001 / Canandaigua
Courage
Diageo
Distillers Company
Doosan
E. & J. Gallo
Fortune Brands from 1997 / American Brands from 1969 / American Tobacco Company
Foster's Group from 2001 / Foster Brewing from 1991 / Elders IXL from 1982 / Elder Smith
    Gold
G. Heileman Brewing
Gilbeys

Grand Metropolitan
Guinness
Heineken
Heublein
Hiram Walker
Holsten
Inbev from 2004 / Interbrew
International Distillers & Vintners
Jim Beam
John Labbatt
Kirin
Liggett & Myers
Miller Brewing and also Phillip Morris (since it acquired Miller in 1970)
Modelo
Moët & Chandon
Moët Hennessy
Lion Nathan
Louis Vuitton Moët-Hennessy
Molson
Molson-Coors
National Distillers
Orkla
Pabst Brewing
Pernod
Pernod Ricard
Rémy Cointreau
San Miguel
Sapporo
Schenley
Schlitz Brewing
Scottish & Newcastle
Seagram from 1975 / Distillers Corporation–Seagram Ltd.
SABMiller from 2002 / South African Breweries
Stroh
Suntory
Teachers
Truman
Tsingtao
Tuborg
Watney Mann
Whitbread

Archives

Research was conducted in the confidential corporate archives of the following companies:
Allied Domecq (statistics department)
Carlsberg (only the nonconfidential material)
Diageo
Distillers Company
Heublein (Diageo)
Hiram Walker (information department)
Moët & Chandon

Seagram Collection, Record Group 2; Series VI: Sales and Distribution (Hagley Museum and Library).
Suntory (information department)

Interviews

Allied Domecq (Portugal): David Orr, Finance and Tax Director of Cockburn (Oporto, 2 Nov. 1998).
Allied Domecq (United Kingdom): Michael Jackaman, former Chairman of Allied Domecq and also former Chairman of the Wines, Spirits and Soft Drinks Division of Allied Domecq (Somerset, 8 December 1998; Somerset, 19 June 2000).
Allied Domecq (United Kingdom): Phil Taylor, Insight and Analytics Director (Bristol, 19 January 1999).
Bacardi (Bermuda): José Louis Martin, President of Bacardi-Martini Spain (Barcelona, 22 July 1999).
Bacardi (Bermuda): Salvador Guedes, Partner in the alliance Bacardi Martini and Sogrape and President and CEO of Sogrape (Oporto, 26 November 1998).
Bacardi (Bermuda): Xavier Serra, General Manager Bacardi-Martini Spain (Barcelona, 22 July 1999).
Brown Forman (United States): Ian Kennedy, former brand manager of Jack Daniels in the United Kingdom, through the agency contract Brown Forman had with International Distillers and Vintners (London, 4 February 2004).
California Wine Institute (United States): Interview with John de Lucca, President of the California Wine Institute (San Francisco, 20 March 2001).
Carlsberg (Denmark): Andrew Arnold, Director of Corporate Communications (1 May 2002).
Carlsberg (Denmark): Bajrne Maurer, Corporate Communications (Copenhagen, 18 May 2001).
Cobra (India): Karan F. Bilmaria, Chairman and CEO of Cobra Brewing (Reading, 1 March 2002).
Diageo (United Kingdom): Andy Fennell, President of Global Marketing for Smirnoff and Captain Morgan (Connecticut, 13 January 2004).
Diageo (United Kingdom): Chris Searle, Brand Manager that launched Piat D'Or (London, 22 January 2004).
Diageo (United Kingdom): Chris Searle, Global Marketing Manager for Bombay Sapphire – Bacardi (London, 22 January 2004).
Diageo (United Kingdom): Jack Keenan, former CEO of Diageo and former Deputy Chief Executive of Guinness/UDV (Cambridge, 14 May 2003; London, 3 June 2003; Oxford, 5 August 2003).
Diageo (United Kingdom): John Potter, Guinness Brand Manager (London, 21 January 2004).
Diageo (United Kingdom): Peter Dee, Global Marketing Director for Johnnie Walker, Diageo (London, 14 January 2005).
Diageo (United Kingdom): Peter O'Connor, Brand Manager of Baileys Irish Cream (London, 22 January 2004).
Diageo (United Kingdom): Richard Watling, Scotch Whisky Global Marketing Director for Diageo (London, 5 February 2004; London, 8 March 2004).
Diageo (United Kingdom): Steve Wilson, former Brand Innovation Manager at International Distillers and Vintners (London, 17 February 2004).
Diageo (United Kingdom): Steve Wilson, Global Brand Innovation Manager, Diageo (London, 17 February 2004).

Grand Metropolitan (United Kingdom): Chris Nadin, former Marketing Manager at Grand Metropolitan (London, 10 December 2003).

Grand Metropolitan (United Kingdom): Sir George Bull, former CEO of Grand Metropolitan and Diageo (London, 19 November 2003).

Grand Metropolitan (United Kingdom): Tim Ambler, former consultant from Grand Metropolitan (London, 12 July 2000).

Heineken (The Netherlands): Jan Beijerinck, former Worldwide Client Service Director (Utrecht, 10 March 2000; 26 November 2001).

Inbev (Interbrew): Charles Adrianssen, Member of the Board of Directors of Interbrew and family member (London, 11 June 2004).

Inbev (Interbrew): Philippe Spoelberch, Member of the Board of Directors of Interbrew and family member (Brussels, 5 July 2004).

International Distillers and Vintners (United Kingdom): James Espey, former Chairman of IDV-UK (Wimbledon, 23 February 2000).

LouisVuitton Moët-Hennessy (France): Colin Campbell, Director of Moët Hennessy (Paris, 22 November 1999).

Pedro Domecq (Spain): José Isasi-Isasmendi y Adaro, former President of Pedro Domecq and also family member (Madrid, 18 July 2000).

Pernod Ricard (France): Julie Massies, Business Development Manager, Pernod Ricard (Paris, 11 June 2003).

Pernod Ricard (France): Thierry Jacquillat, former CEO of Pernod Ricard and family member (London, 22 October 2003; London, 20 January 2004).

Sandeman (United Kingdom): John Jones, former Director of Sandeman London (London, 18 April 2000).

Scottish & Newcastle (United Kingdom): Interview with Tony Frogatt, CEO of Scottish & Newcastle (Edinburgh, 11 July 2004).

Seagram (Canada/United States): George Sandeman, Managing Director of Seagram Iberia and Chairman of the House of Sandeman (Oporto, 19 January 2000).

Seagram (Canada/United States): James Espey, former Chairman of Seagram Distillers (Wimbledon, 3 December 1999).

Seagram (Canada/United States): Tony Frogatt, President of Seagram Europe and former president of Cinzano and IDV Europe (London, 10 February 1999).

Suntory (Japan): Kozo Chiji, Manager of Corporate Planning Department (Tokyo, 16 September 1999).

Suntory (Japan): Kunimasa Himeno, Manager International Division of Suntory (Tokyo, 16 September 1999).

Suntory (Japan): Yoshi Kunimoto, Executive Vice President of Suntory-Allied (Tokyo, 16 September 1999).

United Distillers/Guinness Plc (United Kingdom): James Espey, former Managing Director (Wimbledon, 4 September 2000).

William Grant (United Kingdom): David Grant, family member of William Grant and Marketing Director (London, 7 January 2004).

Magazines and Newspapers

Drinks International Bulletin
Evening Standard
Financial Times
Fortune
Hoover.com
Impact International

International Wine and Spirit Record
New York Times
PR Newswire
Revista dos Vinhos
Spiritscan
St Louis Pot-Dispatch
Taylor Nelson Sofres
The Christchurch Press
The Economist
The Graphic
The Independent
The Times 1000
The Wall Street Journal
Trade Mark Journal
World Reporter

Reports from Consultants

ABN AMRO, "Spirits Consolidation: The Next Moves" (March 1998).
ABN AMRO, "The Sting is in the Tail" (1999).
Barclays de Zoete Wedd Report, "LVMH" (1988).
BNP Paribas, "Global Wine Industry" (2003).
Canadean Ltd., "Global Drink Trends" (Basingstoke, 1999).
Canadean Ltd., "The Spirits & Wine: Global Spirits Trends, 1999" (1999).
Commission of the European Communities, "A Study of the Evolution of Concentration in the Dutch Beverage Industry" (1976).
Conseil Interprofessionnel des Vins du Languedoc et Syndicat des Vins de Pays d'Oc, "Réflexion sur la Valeur Ajoutée des Vins de Pays d'Oc et des A.O.C. du Languedoc" (Languedoc, 2001).
Datamonitor, "Strategic Review of European Drinks" (1997).
Goldman, Sachs & Co., "James B. Beam Distilling Co" (1961).
Hoovers Directory of World Business (Austin, Tex: Reference Press, 2002).
Impact International, "The US Wine Market: Impact Databank Review and Forecast" (1998).
Impact International, "The US Wine Market: Impact Databank Review and Forecast" (1999).
International Wine and Spirit Record, "Mergers and Acquisitions: 1992 Number Four" (December 1992).
James Capel & Co. Ltd., "United Distillers Group" (Nov. 1988).
M. Shanken Communications, "Impact World Directory" (New York, 1996).
Rabobank, "The World Wine Business" (1996).

Secondary Sources

Aaker, David A. and Erich Joachimsthaler, "The Lure of Global Branding," *Harvard Business Review* (Nov–Dec, 1999): 137–44.
Aaker, David A. and Kevin Lane Keller, "Consumer Evaluations of Brand Extensions," *Journal of Marketing*, Vol. 54 (1990): 27–41.
Aaker, David A., "Brand Extensions: The Good, the Bad and the Ugly," *Sloan Management Review*, Vol. 32, No. 4 (1990): 47–56.
Aaker, David A., *Building Strong Brands* (New York: Free Press, 1996).
Adler, Paul S., "Market, Hierarchy, and Trust: The Knowledge Economy and the Future of Capitalism," *Organization Science*, Vol. 12, No. 2 (2001): 215–34.

Alexander, Nicholas, *International Retailing* (Oxford: Blackwell, 1997).

Amatori, Franco and Geoffrey Jones (eds.), *Business History Around the World* (New York: Cambridge University Press, 2003).

Anderson, Erin and Anne T. Coughlan, "International Market Entry and Expansion via Independent or Integrated Channels of Distribution," *Journal of Marketing*, Vol. 51 (1987): 71–82.

Anderson, James C. and James A. Narus, "A Model of Distributor Firm and Manufacturer Firm Working Partnerships," *Journal of Marketing*, Vol. 54 (January, 1990): 42–58.

Ansoff, H. I., "Strategies for Diversification," *Harvard Business Review*, Vol. 35, No. 5 (1957): 113–24.

Ansoff, H. I., "A Model for Diversification," *Management Science*, Vol. 4 (1958): 392–414.

Arrow, Kenneth J., "Classification Notes on the Production and Transmission of Technical Knowledge," *American Economic Review*, No. 52 (1969): 29–35.

Balasubramanyam, V. N. and M. A. Salisu, "Brands and the Alcoholic Drinks Industry," in Geoffrey Jones and Nicholas J. Morgan (eds.), *Adding Value: Brands and Marketing in Food and Drink* (London: Routledge, 1994).

Balasubramanyam, V. N., "Entrepreneurship and the Growth of the Firm: The Case of the British Food and Drink Industries in the 1980s," in Jonathan Brown and Mary Rose (eds.), *Entrepreneurship, Networks and Modern Business* (Manchester: Manchester University Press, 1993).

Bamberg, James, "OLI and OIL: BP in the US in Theory and Practice, 1968–98," in Geoffrey Jones and Lina Gálvez-Munöz (eds.), *Foreign Multinationals in the United States* (London: Routledge, 2002).

Bamberg, James, *British Petroleum and Global Oil, 1950–1975: The Challenge of Nationalism* (Cambridge: Cambridge University Press, 2000).

Barwise, P. and T. Robertson, "Brand Portfolios," *European Management Journal*, Vol. 10, No. 3 (1992): 277–85.

Bebchuk, Lucian Arye and Mark J. Roe, "A Theory of Path Dependence in Corporate Ownership and Governance," *Stanford Law Review*, Vol. 52, No. 1 (1999): 127–70.

Berle, Adolf A. and Gardiner C. Means, *The Modern Corporation and Private Property* (New York: Harcourt, Brace & World, 1932) (New revised edition, New Brunswick, NJ: Transaction Publishers, 1991).

Bielenberg, Andy, "The Irish Brewing Industry and the Rise of Guinness 1790–1914," in Richard G. Wilson and Terry R. Gourvish (eds.), *The Dynamics of the International Brewing Since 1800* (London: Routledge, 1998).

Bilkey, W. J. and E. Nes, "Country-of-Origin Effects on Products Evaluations," *Journal of International Business Studies*, Vol. 13, No. 1 (1982): 89–99.

Bishop, M. and John Kay (eds.), *European Mergers and Merger Policy* (Oxford: Oxford University Press, 1993).

Bonin, Hubert, Christophe Bouneau, Ludovic Cailluet, Alexandre Fernandez and Silvia Marzagalli (eds.), *Transnational Companies, Nineteenth and Twentieth Centuries* (Paris: PLAGE, 2002).

Bonin, Hubert, *Les Groupes Financiers Français* (Paris: Presses Universitaires de France, 1995).

Boyce, Gordon, *Information, Mediation and Institutional Development* (Manchester: Manchester University Press, 1995).

Briggs, Asa, *Wine for Sale: Victoria Wine and the Liquor Trade, 1860–1984* (London: B. T. Bastford, 1985).

Bronfman, Edgar M., *Good Spirits: The Making of a Businessman* (New York: G. P. Putnam's Sons, 1998).

Bronfman, Samuel, "...From Little Acorns...," in Distillers Corporation-Seagrams Ltd., *Annual Report and Accounts* (1970).

Brown, John Seely and Paul Duguid, "Knowledge and Organization: A Social-Practice Perspective," *Organization Science*, Vol. 12, No. 2 (2001): 198–213.

Brown, John Seely and Paul Duguid, *The Social Life of Information* (Boston, Mass: Harvard Business School Press, 2000).

Brown, Jonathan and Mary B. Rose (eds.), *Entrepreneurship, Networks and Modern Business* (Manchester: Manchester University Press, 1993).

Buckley, Peter J. and Mark Casson, "A Theory of Co-Operation in International Business," in F. J. Contractor and P. Lorange (eds.), *Co-operative Strategies in International Business* (Lexington, Mass: Lexington Books, 1988).

Buckley, Peter J. and Mark Casson, "Analysing Foreign Market Entry Strategies: Extending the Internalisation Approach," *Journal of International Business Studies*, Vol. 29 No. 3 (1998): 539–62.

Buckley, Peter J. and Mark Casson, *The Future of the Multinational Enterprise* (London: Macmillan, 1976).

Bucklin, Louis P., *Competition and Evolution in the Distributive Trades* (Englewood Cliffs, NJ: Prentice Hall 1972).

Business History Review, Vol. 71, No. 2 (1997).

Butel, Paul and Alain Huetz de Lemps, *Hennessy: Histoire de la Société et de la Famille, 1765–1990* (Cognac: Hennessy, 1999).

Campbell, John L., and Leon N. Lindberg, "The Evolution of Governance Regimes," in John L. Campbell, J. Rogers Hollingsworth, and Leon N. Lindberg (eds.), *Governance of the American Economy* (Cambridge: Cambridge University Press, 1991).

Cantwell, John A., "Historical Shifts in Corporate Technological Diversification," in J. A. Cantwell, A. Gambardella and O. Granstrand (eds.), *The Economics and Management of Technological Diversification* (London: Routledge, 2004).

Carleton, Jim, *Apple: The Insider Story of Intrigue, Egomania and Business Blunders* (New York: Times Business Books, 1997).

Carroll, Glenn R. and Michael T. Hannan, *The Demography of Corporations and Industries* (Princeton: Princeton University Press, 2000).

Cassis, Youssef, *Big Business: The European Experience in the Twentieth Century* (Oxford: Oxford University Press, 1997).

Casson, Mark (ed.), *The Railway Revolution*, 8 volumes (London: Routledge, 1998).

Casson, Mark and Howard Cox, "International Business Networks: Theory and History," *Business and Economic History*, Vol. 22, No. 1 (1993): 42–53.

Casson, Mark and Mary Rose (eds.), "Institutions and the Evolution of Modern Business," Special Issue: *Business History*, Vol. 39, No. 4 (1997).

Casson, Mark, "Brands: Economic Ideology and Consumer Society," in Geoffrey Jones and Nicholas J. Morgan (eds.), *Adding Value: Brands and Marketing in Food and Drink* (London: Routledge, 1994).

Casson, Mark, "Contractual Arrangements for Technology Transfer: New Evidence From Business History," *Business History*, Vol. 28, No. 4 (1986): 5–35.

Casson, Mark, "General Theories of the Multinational Enterprise: Their Relevance to Business History," in Peter Hertner and Geoffrey Jones (eds.), *Multinationals: Theory and History* (Aldershot: Gower, 1986).

Casson, Mark, "Institutional Economics and Business History: A Way Forward?" *The University of Reading: Discussion Papers in Economics and Management*, No. 362 (1997/98).

Casson, Mark, "Internalization Theory and Beyond," in Peter J. Buckley (ed.), *Recent Research on the Multinational Enterprise* (Aldershot: Elgar, 1991).

Casson, Mark, "The Economic Analysis of Multinational Trading Companies," in Geoffrey Jones (ed.), *The Multinational Traders* (London: Routledge, 1998).

Casson, Mark, "The Economics of the Family Firm: An Analysis of the Dynastic Motive," *The University of Reading: Discussion Papers in Economics and Management*, No. 391 (1998).

Casson, Mark, "The Nature of the Firm Reconsidered: Information Synthesis and Entrepreneurial Organisation," *Management International Review*, Vol. 36, No. 1 (1996): 55–94.

Casson, Mark, "The Organization and Evolution of the Multinational Enterprise: An Information Cost Approach," Special Issue: *Management International Review*, Vol. 39 (1999): 77–121.

Casson, Mark, *Alternatives to the Multinational Enterprise* (London: Macmillan, 1979).

Casson, Mark, *Economics of International Business: A New Research Agenda* (Cheltenham: Elgar, 2000).

Casson, Mark, *Enterprise and Competitiveness: A Systems View of International Business* (Oxford: Clarendon, 1990).

Casson, Mark, *Enterprise and Leadership: Studies on Firms, Markets and Networks* (Cheltenham: Elgar, 2000).

Casson, Mark, *Information and Organization: A New Perspective on the Theory of the Firm* (Oxford: Clarendon, 1997).

Casson, Mark, *The Entrepreneur: An Economic Theory* (Oxford: Martin Robertson, 1982).

Casson, Mark, *The Firm and the Market* (Oxford: Basil Blackwell, 1987).

Casson, Mark, *The Organization of International Business* (Aldershot: Elgar, 1995).

Casson, Mark, *The Railway Revolution*, 8 volumes (London: Routledge, 1998).

Cavanagh, John and Frederick F. Clairmonte, *Alcoholic Beverages: Dimensions of Corporate Power* (London: Croom & Helm, 1985).

Cavanagh, John, Frederick Clairmonte, and Robi Room, *The World Alcohol Industry With Special Reference to Australia, New Zealand and the Pacific Islands* (Sydney: Transnational Corporations Research Project – University of Sydney, 1985).

Caves, Richard E., "International Corporations: The Industrial Economics of Foreign Direct Investment," *Economica*, Vol. 38 (1971): 1–27.

Caves, Richard E., Michael E. Porter, M. A. Spence, and J. T. Scott, *Competition in the Open Economy: A Model Applied to Canada* (Cambridge, Mass: Harvard University Press, 1980).

Caves, Richard E., *Multinational Enterprise and Economic Analysis* (Cambridge: Cambridge University Press, 1982).

Cavusgil, S. Tamer, "Perspectives: Knowledge Development in International Marketing," *Journal of International Marketing*, Vol. 6, No. 2 (1998): 103–12.

Chandler Jr., Alfred D., "Comparative Business History," in D. C. Coleman and Peter Mathias, *Enterprise and History: Essays in Honour of Charles Wilson* (Cambridge: Cambridge University Press, 1984).

Chandler Jr., Alfred D., "Managerial Enterprise and Competitive Capabilities," *Business History*, Vol. 34, No. 1 (1992): 11–41.

Chandler Jr., Alfred D., "Organizational Capabilities and the Economic History of the Industrial Enterprise," *Journal of Economic Perspectives*, Vol. 6, No. 3 (1992): 79–100.

Chandler Jr., Alfred D., "The Emergence of Managerial Capitalism," *Business History Review*, Vol. 58 (1984): 473–503.

Chandler Jr., Alfred D., "The Enduring Logic of Industrial 'Success," *Harvard Business Review* (March-April, 1990): 130–40.

Chandler Jr., Alfred D., "The Growth of the Transnational Industrial Firm in the United States and the United Kingdom: A Comparative Analysis," *Economic History Review*, Vol. 33, No. 3 (1980): 296–410.

Chandler Jr., Alfred D., Franco Amatori and Takashi Hikino (eds.), *Big Business and the Wealth of Nations* (Cambridge: Cambridge University Press, 1997).

Chandler Jr., Alfred D., *Scale and Scope: The Dynamics of Industrial Capitalism* (Cambridge, Mass: Harvard University Press, 1990).

Chandler Jr., Alfred D., *Strategy and Structure* (Cambridge, Mass: The MIT Press, 1962).

Chandler Jr., Alfred D., *The Visible Hand* (Cambridge, Mass: Harvard University Press, 1977).

Channon, Derek F., *The Strategy and Structure of British Enterprise* (London: Macmillan, 1973).

Cheffins, Brian R., "History and the Global Corporate Governance Revolution: The UK Perspective," *Business History*, Vol. 43, No. 4 (2001): 87–118.

Chernatony, L. de and G. McWilliam, "The Varying Nature of Brands as Assets," *International Journal of Advertising*, Vol. 8 (1989): 339–49.

Chernatony, Leslie de (ed.), *Brand Management* (Aldershot: Ashgate, 1998).

Chernatony, Leslie de and Francesca Dall'Olmo Riley, "Brand Consultants' Perspectives and the Concept of the Brand," *Marketing and Research Today*, Vol. 25, No. 1 (1997): 45–52.

Chernatony, Leslie de and Francesca Dall'Olmo Riley, "Defining a Brand: Beyond the Literature with Experts' Interpretations," *Journal of Marketing Management*, Vol. 14, No. 5 (1998): 417–43.

Chernatony, Leslie de and Francesca Dall'Olmo Riley, "Modelling the Components of the Brand," *European Journal of Marketing*, Vol. 32, No. 11/12 (1998): 1077–90.

Chernatony, Leslie de, and Malcom McDonald, *Creating Powerful Brands in Consumer, Service And Industrial Markets* (Oxford: Butterworth-Heinemann, 1998).

Christiansen, Clayton, *The Innovator's Dilemma* (Cambridge, Mass: Harvard University Press, 1996).

Church, Roy and Christine Clark, "The Origins of Competitive Advantage in the Marketing of Branded Packaged Consumer Goods: Colman's and Reckitt's in Early Victorian Britain," *Journal of Industrial History*, Vol. 3 No. 2 (2000): 98–199.

Church, Roy, "Advertising Consumer Goods in Nineteenth-Century Britain: Reinterpretations," *Economic History Review*, Vol. 53, No. 4 (2000): 621–45.

Church, Roy, "Family Firm and Managerial Capitalism: The Case of the International Motor Industry" *Business History*, Vol. 28, No. 2 (1986): 165–80.

Church, Roy, "The Family Firm in Industrial Capitalism: International Perspectives on Hypothesis and History," *Business History*, Vol. 35, No. 4 (1993): 17–43.

Church, Roy, "The Limitation of the Personal Capitalism Paradigm," in Roy Church, Albert Fishlow, Neil Fligstein, Thomas Hughes, Jürgen Kocka, Hidemasa Morikawa, and Frederic M. Scherer (eds.), "Scale and Scope: A Review Colloquium," *Business History Review*, Vol. 64, No. 3 (1990): 690–735.

Clairmonte, Frederick F. and John Cavanagh, *Merchants of Drink: Transnational Control of World Beverages* (Penang: Third World Network, 1988).

Clayton, Christiansen, *The Innovator's Dilemma* (Cambridge, Mass: Harvard University Press, 1996).

Coase, Ronald H., "The Nature of the Firm: Influence," in Oliver E. Williamson and Sydney G. Winter (eds.), *The Nature of the Firm: Origins, Evolution and Development* (Oxford: Oxford University Press, 1993).

Coase, Ronald H., "The Nature of the Firm," *Economica*, NS. 4 (1937): 386–405.

Coelho, Alfredo and António de Sousa, "Stratégies de Développement des Groupes Multinationaux des Vins et Spiritueux," *Économies et Sociétés*, Vol. 10–11, No. 24 (2000): 257–70.

Coleman, D. C., "Failings and Achievements: Some British Businesses, 1910–80," *Business History*, Vol. 29, No. 4 (1987): 1–17.

Colli, Andrea and Mary B. Rose, "The Culture and Evolution of Family Firms in Britain and Italy," *Scandinavian Economic History Review*, Vol. 47, No. 1 (1999): 24–47.

Colli, Andrea, *The History of the Family Firm* (Cambridge: Cambridge University Press, 2003).

Collis, David John, "The Value Added Structure and Competition Within Industries" (Harvard University, Ph.D. dissertation, 1986).

Competition Commission, "Interbrew SA and Bass plc: A Report on the Acquisition by Interbrew SA of the Brewing Interests of Bass plc" (January 2001).

Corley, T. A. B., "Firms and Markets: Towards a Theory of Business History," *Business and Economic History*, Vol. 22, No. 1 (1993): 54–66.

Craig, H. Charles, *The Scotch Whisky Industry Record* (Dumbarton: Index Publishing Limited, 1994).

Craig, Tim, "Achieving Innovation Through Bureaucracy: Lessons From the Japanese Brewing Industry," *California Management Review*, Vol. 38, No. 1 (1995): 8–36.

Craig, Tim, "The Japanese Beer Wars: Initiating and Responding to Hyper-Competition in New Product Development," *Organization Science*, Vol. 7, No. 3 (1996): 302–321.

Crestin-Billet, Frédérique, *La Naissance d'une Grande Maison de Champagne* (Épernay: Calmann-Lévy, 1996).

Cullen, L. M., *The Brandy Trade Under the Ancien Régime* (Cambridge: Cambridge University Press, 1998).

Dennison, S. R. and Oliver MacDonagh, *Guinness 1886–1939: From Incorporation to the Second Word War* (Dublin: Cork University Press, 1998).

Desbois-Thibault, Claire, *L'Extraordinaire Aventure du Champagne: Moët & Chandon: Une Affaire de Famille, 1792–1914* (Paris: PUF, 2003).

Dierickx, Ingemar and Karen Cool, "Asset Stock Accumulation and the Sustainability of Competitive Advantage," *Management Science*, Vol. 35, No. 12 (1989): 1504–11.

Ditrichsen, J., "The Development of Diversified and Conglomerate Firms in the US, 1920–1970," *Business History Review*, Vol. 46, No. 2 (1972): 202–219.

Dosi, G., David Teece and S. Winter, "Toward a Theory of Corporate Coherence: Preliminary Remarks," in G. Dosi, R. Gianetti and P. A. Toninelli (eds.), *Technology and Enterprise in an Historical Perspective* (Oxford: Clarendon Press, 1992).

Downar, William L., *Dictionary of the History of the American Brewing and Distilling Industries* (London: Greenwood Press, 1980).

Doyle, Peter, "Building Successful Brands: The Strategic Options," *Journal of Marketing Management*, Vol. 5, No. 11 (1989): 77–95.

Doz, Yves, José Santos and Peter Williamson, *From Global to Metanational – How Companies Win in the Knowledge Economy* (Boston, Mass: Harvard Business School Press, 2002).

Duguid, Paul (ed.) "Networks in the Trade of Alcohol," Special Issue: *Business History Review*, Vol. 79, No. 3 (2005).

Duguid, Paul and Teresa da Silva Lopes, "Divide and Rule: Regulation and Response in the Port Wine Trade 1812–1840," in Terry Gourvish (ed.), *European Yearbook of Business History* (Aldershot: Ashgate, 2000).

Duguid, Paul and Teresa da Silva Lopes, "Institutions and Organisations of Port Wine Trade, 1814–1834," *Scandinavian Economic History Review*, Vol. 47, No. 1 (1999): 84–102.

Duguid, Paul, "Developing the Brand: The Case of Alcohol, 1800–1880," *Enterprise and Society*, Vol. 4, No. 3 (2003): 405–441.

Duguid, Paul, "In Vino Veritas," in Martin Kenney and Richard Florida (eds.), *Locating Global Advantage: Industry Dynamics in a Globalizing Economy* (Palo Alto, Calif: Stanford University Press, 2003).

Duguid, Paul, "Lavradores, Exportadores, Intermediários e Capitalistas: Componentes da Região do Vinho do Porto," *Douro: Estudos e Documentos*, Vol. 1, No. 2 (1996): 201–224.

Duguid, Paul, "The Changing of the Guard: British Firms in the Port Trade, 1774–1840," in Gaspar Martins Pereira (ed.), *A História do Vinho do Porto e do Vale do Douro*, Vol. IV (Porto: GEHVID/Afrontamento, 2002).

Dunning, John H. and Howard Archer, "The Eclectic Paradigm and the Growth of UK Multinational Enterprise 1870–1983," *Business and Economic History*, Vol. 16 (1987): 19–49.

Dunning, John H. and Robert Pearce, *The World's Largest Industrial Enterprises* (Guildford: Gower, 1981).

Dunning, John H., "Globalization and the Theory of the MNE Activity," in N. Hood and S. Young (eds.), *The Globalization of Multinational Enterprise Activity* (London: Macmillan, 1999).

Dunning, John H., "Globalization, Technological Change and the Spatial Organization of Economic activity," in Alfred D. Chandler Jr., Peter Hasgtröm, and Orjan Sölvell (eds.), *The Dynamic Firm* (Oxford: Oxford University Press, 1998).

Dunning, John H., "Location and the Multinational Enterprise: A Neglected Factor," *Journal of International Business Studies*, Vol. 29, No. 1 (1998): 45–66.

Dunning, John H., "Reappraising the Eclectic Paradigm in an Age of Alliance Capitalism," *Journal of International Business Studies*, Vol. 26, No. 3 (1995): 461–91.

Dunning, John H., "The Eclectic Paradigm as an Envelope for Economic and Business Theories of the MNE Activity," *The University of Reading: Discussion Papers in International Investment and Management*, No. 263 (1998/99).

Dunning, John H., "The Eclectic Paradigm of International Production: A Restatement and Some Possible Extensions," *Journal of International Business Studies*, Vol. 19, No. 1 (1988): 1–31.

Dunning, John H., "The Globalization of Firms and the Competitiveness of Countries," in John H. Dunning, Bruce Kogut, and Magnus Blomström (eds.), *Globalization of Firms and the Competitiveness of Nations* (Lund: Institute of Economic Research, 1990).

Dunning, John H., "Towards an Eclectic Theory of International Production: Some Empirical Tests," *Journal of International Business Studies*; Vol. 11, No. 1 (1980): 9–31.

Dunning, John H., "Trade, Location of Economic Activity and the MNE: A Search for an Eclectic Approach," in B. Ohlin, P. O. Hesselborn, and P. M. Wijkman (eds.), *The International Allocation of Economic Activity* (London: Macmillan, 1977).

Dunning, John H., *Alliance Capitalism and Global Business* (London: Routledge, 1997).

Dunning, John H., *American Investment in British Manufacturing Industry* (London: George Allen and Unwin, 1958). (New revised edition, London: Routledge, 1998)

Dunning, John H., *Explaining International Production* (London: Unwin Hyman, 1988).

Dunning, John H., *International Production and the Multinational Enterprise*, (London: Allen & Unwin, 1981).

Dunning, John H., *Multinational Enterprises and the Global Economy* (Wokingham, Berkshire: Addison Wesley, 1993).

Erickson, G., R. Jacobson, and J. Johansson, "Competition for Market Share in the Presence of Strategic Invisible Assets," *International Journal of Research in Marketing*, Vol. 9, No. 1 (1992): 23–37.

Eriksson, Kent, Anders Majkgard, and D. Deo Sharma, "Path Dependence and Knowledge Development in the Internationalisation Process," *Management International Review*, Vol. 40, No. 4 (2000): 307–28.

Espey, James, "A Multinational Approach to New Product Development," *European Journal of Marketing*, Vol. 19, No. 2 (1985): 5–18.

Espey, James, "The Development of a Worldwide Strategy for International Distillers and Vintners Limited," (Kensington University Ph.D., 1981).

European Commission, *European Economy*, No. 69 (Brussels: EU, 1999).

Eveno, Patrick, "La Construction d'un Groupe International: LVMH," in Jacques Marseille (ed.), *Le Luxe en France du Siècle des 'Lumières' à nos Jours* (Paris: ADHE, 1999).

Fama, Eugene F., "Efficient Capital Markets II," *Journal of Finance*, Vol. 46, No. 5 (1991): 1575–617.

Farok J. and Peter Lorange (eds.), *Cooperative Strategies in International Business* (Toronto: Lexington Books, 1988).

Federal Trade Commission: Bureau of Economics, *The Brewing Industry* (USA, Dec. 1978).

Feldwick, P., "Defining a Brand," in D. Cowley (ed.), *Understanding Brands* (London: Kogan Page, 1991).

Fielden, Christopher, *A Drink Dynasty: The Suntory Story* (Throwbride: Wine Source, 1996).

Fieldhouse, D. K., *Merchant Capital and Economic Decolonization* (Oxford: Clarendon Press, 1994).

Foster, Peter, *Family Spirits: The Bacardi Saga* (Toronto: MacFarlane Walter & Ross, 1990).

Foster, Richard N. and Sarah Kaplan, *Creative Destruction* (New York: Doubleday, 2001).

Fridenson, Patrick, "France: The Relatively Slow Development of Big Business in the Twentieth Century," in Alfred D. Chandler Jr., Franco Amatori, and Takashi Hikino (eds.), *Big Business and the Wealth of Nations* (Cambridge: Cambridge University Press, 1997).

Fruin, W. Mark, *The Japanese Enterprise System* (Oxford: Clarendon, 1992).

Galambos, Louis, "Business History and the Theory of the Growth of the Firm," *Explorations in Entrepreneurial History*, Vol. 4, No. 1 (1966): 3–14.

Galambos, Louis, "Identity and the Boundaries of Business History – An Essay on Consensus and Creativity," in Franco Amatori and Geoffrey Jones (eds.), *Business History Around the World* (New York: Cambridge University Press, 2003).

Gales, Ben P. A. and Keetie E. Sluyterman, "Outward Bound. The Rise of Dutch Multinationals," in Geoffrey Jones and Harm G. Schröter (eds.), *The Rise of Multinationals in Continental Europe* (Aldershot: Elgar, 1993).

Gates, William, *The Road Ahead* (New York: Viking, 1996).

Gerlach, Michael L., *Alliance Capitalism: The Social Organization of Japanese Business* (Berkeley: University of California Press, 1992).

Giddens, Anthony, *The Constitution of Society: Outline of the Theory of Structuration* (Cambridge: Cambridge University Press, 1984).

Glamann, Kristof, *Jacobsen of Carlsberg – Brewer and Philanthropist* (Copenhagen: Gyldendal, 1991).

Glamann, Kristof, *Voresool – Og Hele Verdens* (Copenhagen: Carlsberg, 1997).

Gomes-Casseres, Benjamin, "Joint Venture Cycles: The Evolution of Ownership Strategies of US MNEs, 1945–75," in F. J. Contractor and P. Lorange (eds.), *Cooperative Strategies in International Business* (Lexington, Mass: Lexington Books, 1988).

Gort, M., *Diversification and Integration in American Industry* (Princeton, NJ: Princeton University Press, 1962).

Gourvish, Terry and Richard G. Wilson, *The British Brewing Industry, 1830–1980* (Cambridge: Cambridge University Press, 1994).

Gourvish, Terry, "British Business and the Transition to a Corporate Economy: Entrepreneurship and Management Structures," *Business History*, Vol. 29, No. 4 (1987): 18–45.

Gourvish, Terry, "Business History: in Defence of the Empirical Approach?," *Accounting Business and Financial History*, Vol. 5, No. 1 (1995): 3–16.

Gourvish, Terry, "Concentration, Diversity and the Firm Strategy in European Brewing, 1945–90," in Richard Wilson and Terry Gourvish (eds.), *The Dynamics of the International Brewing Industry Since 1800* (London: Routledge, 1998).

Gourvish, Terry, "Economics of Brewing, Theory and Practice: Concentration and Technological Change in the USA, UK and West Germany Since 1945," *Business and Economic History*, Vol. 23, No. 1 (1994): 253–61.

Granovetter, Mark S., "Economic Action and Social Structure: The Problem of Embeddedness," *American Journal of Sociology*, Vol. 91, No. 3 (1985): 481–510.

Grove, Andrew, *Only the Paranoid Survive* (New York: Doubleday, 1996).

Guichard, François and Philippe Roudié, *Vins, Vignerons et Coopérateurs de Bordeaux et de Porto* (Paris: CNRS, 1985).

Guichard, François, "O Vinho do Porto e Mais Alguns: Gestão da Imagem," *Douro: Estudos e Documentos*, Vol. 1, No. 3 (1997): 145–57.

Guichard, François, *Rótulos e Cartazes no Vinho do Porto* (Lisboa: INAPA, 2001).

Hamilton, C., *Absolut: Biography of a Bottle* (London: Texere, 2000).

Hankinson, Graham and Philippa Cowking, *The Reality of Global Brands* (Maidenhead: McGraw-Hill, 1996).

Hannah, Leslie, "La Evolución de las Grandes Empresas en el Siglo XX: Un Análisis Comparativo," *Revista de Historia Industrial*, Vol. 10 (1996): 93–125.

Hannah, Leslie, "Scale and Scope: Towards a European Visible Hand?," *Business History*, Vol. 33, No. 2 (1991): 297–309.

Hannah, Leslie, and John Kay, *Concentration in Modern Industry* (London: Macmillan, 1976).

Hannah, Leslie, *The Rise of the Corporate Economy* (London: Methuen, 1976).

Hannan, Michael T. and John Freeman, "The Population Ecology of Organisations," *American Journal of Sociology*, Vol. 82 (1977): 929–64.

Hannan, Michael T. and John Freeman, *Organizational Ecology* (Cambridge, Mass: Harvard University Press, 1989).

Harper Trade Journals, *The Harpers Handbook to the Wine Trade* (London: Harper Trade Journals, 1997).

Hart, Peter E. and Robert D. Pearce, "Growth Patterns of the World's Largest Firms 1962–1982," *The University of Reading: Discussion Papers in International Investment and Business Studies*, No. 83 (1984).

Hart, Peter E., "Corporate Governance in Britain and Germany," *National Institute of Economic and Social Research: Discussion Paper*, No. 31 (1992).

Hart, Susannah and John Murphy, *Brands: The New Wealth Creators* (London: Macmillan, 1998).

Harvey, Charles and Geoffrey Jones (eds.), "Organisational Capability and Competitive advantage," Special Issue: *Business History*, Vol. 34, No. 1 (1992).

Hawkins, K. H. and C. L. Pass, *The Brewing Industry* (London: Heinemann, 1979).

Hennart, Jean-François, "Internationalisation in Practice: Early Foreign Direct Investment in Malaysian Tin Mining," *Journal of International Business Studies*, 17 (1986): 131–43.

Henry, Thomas, *Harveys of Bristol* (London: Good Books, 1986).

Hertner, Peter and Geoffrey Jones (eds.), *Multinationals: Theory and History* (Hants: Gower, 1986).

Hewat, Tim, *The Elders Explosion – One Hundred and Fifty Years of Progress From Elder to Elliot* (Sydney: Bay Books, 1988).

Hirsh, S., "An International Trade and Investment Theory of the Firm," *Oxford Economic Papers*, Vol. 28 (1976): 258–70.

Hodgson, Geoffrey M., *How Economics Forgot History* (London: Routledge, 2001).

Hollingsworth, J. Rogers and Robert Boyer, "The Co-Ordination of Economic Actors as Social Systems of Production," in J. R. Hollingsworth and R. Boyer (eds.), *Contemporary Capitalism: The Embeddedness of Institutions* (Cambridge: Cambridge University Press, 1997).

Hoover's Directory of World Business (Austin, Tex: Reference Press, 2002).

Horst, Thomas, "Firm and Industry Determinants of the Decision to Invest Abroad: An Empirical Study," *Review of Economics and Statistics*, Vol. 54 (1972): 258–66.

Horst, Thomas, *At Home Abroad: A study of the Domestic and Foreign Operations of the American Food-Processing Industry* (Cambridge, Mass: Ballinger, 1974).

Hoskisson, Robert E. and Michael A. Hitt, "Antecedents and Performance Outcomes of Diversification: A Review and Critique of Theoretical Perspectives," *Journal of Management*, Vol. 16, No. 2 (1990): 461–509.

Hurst, Wendy, Ed Gregory, and Thomas Gussman, *Alcoholic Beverages Taxation and Control Policies* (Ottawa: Brewers Association of Canada, 1997).

Hymer, Stephen H., "The Large Multinational Corporation: An Analysis of Some Motives for the International Integration of Business," *Revue Economique*, Vol. 19, No. 6 (1968): 949–73.

Hymer, Stephen, "On Multinational Corporations and Foreign Direct Investment," selected by John H. Dunning from "The International Operations of National Firms: A Study of Foreign Direct Investment" (MIT Ph.D., 1960), in Christos N. Pitelis and Roger Sugden (eds.), *The Nature of the Transnational Firm* (London: Routledge, 1991).

Inkpen, Andrew C. and Paul W. Beamish, "Knowledge, Bargaining Power, and the Instability of International Ventures," *Academy of Management Review*, Vol. 22, No. 1 (1997): 177–202.

Innis, Harold, *The Bias of Communication* (Toronto: University of Toronto Press, 1991).

International Journal of the Economics of Business, Vol. 8, No. 2 (2001).

International Monetary Fund, *International Financial Statistics Yearbook* (Washington, D.C.: IMF, 1988).

International Monetary Fund, *International Financial Statistics Yearbook* (Washington, D. C.: IMF, 1990).

International Monetary Fund, *International Financial Statistics Yearbook* (Washington, D. C.: IMF, 2002).

International Monetary Fund, *International Financial Statistics Yearbook* (Washington, D. C.: IMF, 2005).

Iterson, Ad van and RenéOlie, "European Business Systems: the Dutch Case," in Richard Whitley (ed.), *European Business Systems: Firms and Markets in Their National Contexts* (London: Sage, 1992).

Jackson, Michael, *The World Guide for Beer* (London: Quarto, 1977).

Jacobs, M. G. P. A. and W. H. G. Mass, *Heineken History* (Amsterdam: De Bussy Ellerman Harms bv., 1992).

Jayachadran, Satish, Javier Gimeno and P. Rajan Varadarajan, "The Theory of Multimarket Competition: A Synthesis and Implication for Marketing Strategy," *Journal of Marketing*, Vol. 63 (1999): 49–66.

Jeanneau, Jacques, "La société Cointreau, D'Angers au Marché Mondial," in Alain Huetz de Lemps and Phillipe Roudié (eds.), *Eaux-de-Vie et Spiritueux* (Paris: Centre National de la Recherche Scientifique, 1985).

Jeffreys, James B. and Derek Knee, *Retailing in Europe: Present Structure and Future Trends* (London: Macmillan, 1962).

Jenkinson, Tim and Colin Mayer, "The Assessment: Corporate Governance and Corporate Control," *Oxford Review of Economic Policy*, Vol. 8, No. 3 (1992): 1–10.

Jensen, Michael and William H. Meckling, "Theory of the Firm: Managerial Behavior, Agency Costs and Ownership Structure," *Journal of Financial Economics*, Vol. 3 (1976): 305–60.

Johansen, Hans Chr., "Marketing and Competition in Danish Brewing," in Geoffrey Jones and Nicholas J. Morgan (eds.), *Adding Value: Brands and Marketing in Food and Drink* (London: Routledge, 1994).

Johanson, J. and J. E. Vahlne, "The Internationalisation Process of the Firm: A Model of Knowledge Development and Increasing Market Commitment," *Journal of International Business Studies*, Vol. 8 (1977): 23–32.

John, Richard R., "Elaborations, Revisions, Dissents: Alfred D. Chandler, Jr's, The Visible Hand After Twenty Years," *Business History Review*, 71 (1997): 151–200.

Jones, Geoffrey (ed.), "The Making of the Global Enterprise," Special Issue: *Business History*, Vol. 36, No. 1 (1994).

Jones, Geoffrey (ed.), *Coalitions and Collaboration in International Business* (Aldershot: Elgar, 1993).

Jones, Geoffrey and Frances Bostock, "US Multinationals in British Manufacturing Before 1962," *Business History Review*, Vol. 70 (1996): 207–56.

Jones, Geoffrey and Harm G. Schröter (eds.), *The Rise of Multinationals in Continental Europe* (Aldershot: Elgar, 1993).

Jones, Geoffrey and Keetie E. Sluyterman, "British and Dutch Business History," in Franco Amatori and Geoffrey Jones (eds.), *Business History Around the World* (Cambridge: Cambridge University Press, 2002, forthcoming).

Jones, Geoffrey and Mary B. Rose (eds.), "Family Capitalism," Special Issue: *Business History*, Vol. 35, No. 4 (1993).

Jones, Geoffrey and Nicholas J. Morgan (eds.), *Adding Value: Brands and Marketing in Food and Drink* (London: Routledge, 1994).

Jones, Geoffrey, "Business History: Theory and Concepts," *The University of Reading: Discussion Papers in Economics*, No. 295 (1994).

Jones, Geoffrey, "Company History and Business History in the 1990s," in Wilfried Feldenkirchen and Terry Gourvish (eds.), *European Yearbook of Business History*, 2 (Aldershot: Ashgate, 1999).

Jones, Geoffrey, "Corporate Governance and British Industry," *Entreprises et Histoire*, No. 21 (1999): 29–43.

Jones, Geoffrey, "Unique Firms in a Global Economy: Does the History of Business Matter to its Future?," Inaugural Lecture (Rotterdam: Centrum voor Bedrijfsgeschiedenis: Erasmus Universiteit Rotterdam, 10 December 1999).

Jones, Geoffrey *British Multinational Banking, 1830–1990* (Oxford: Clarendon Press, 1993).

Jones, Geoffrey *Merchants to Multinationals* (Oxford: Oxford University Press, 2000).

Jones, Geoffrey, *Multinationals and Global Capitalism – From the Nineteenth to the Twenty First Century* (Oxford: Oxford University Press, 2005)

Jones, Geoffrey, *Renewing Unilever – Transformation and Tradition* (Oxford: Oxford University Press, 2005).

Jones, Geoffrey, *The Evolution of International Business* (London: Routledge, 1996).

Jones, Peter, Colin Clarke-Hill, David Hillier, and Peter Shears, "A Case of Bargain Booze," *British Food Journal*, Vol. 103, No. 7 (2001): 453–59.

Jones, S. R. H., "Transaction Costs and the Theory of the Firm: The Scope and Limitations of the New Institutional Approach," *Business History*, Vol. 39, No. 4 (1997): 9–25.

Jorgensen, Janice (ed.), *Encyclopaedia of Consumer Brands*, Vol. 1 (London: St James Press, 1994).

Kaminsky, Peter, *The World of Bacardi-Martini* (Barcelona: Bacardi, 1996).

Kapferer, Jean-Noël, *Strategic Brand Management* (London: Kogan Page, 1992).

Kay, John, *Foundations of Corporate Success* (Oxford: Oxford University Press, 1993).

Kay, Neil M., *Pattern in Corporate Evolution* (Oxford: Oxford University Press, 1997).

Kaynak, Erderner (ed.), *Trans-National Retailing* (New York: W. de Gruyter, 1988).

Keeble, Sherley P., *The Ability to Manage: A Study of British Management, 1890–1990* (Manchester: Manchester University Press, 1992).

Keller, Kevin Lane, "The Brand Report Card," *Harvard Business Review* (Jan–Feb. 2000): 147–57.

Keller, Kevin Lane, *Strategic Brand Management* (London: Prentice Hall, 1998).

Kerr, K. Austin, *Organized for Prohibition: A New History of the Anti-Saloon League* (New Haven: Yale University Press, 1985).

Kim, C. K. and J. Y. Chung, "Brand Popularity, Country Image and Market Share: an Empirical Study," *Journal of International Business Studies*, Vol. 28, No. 2 (1997): 361–86.

King, Steven, *Developing New Brands* (Bath: Wiley, 1973).

Kipping, Matthias and Ove Bjarnar, *The Americanisation of European Business: The Marshall Plan and the Transfer of US Management Models* (London: Routledge, 1998).

Klein, Benjamin, Robert Crawford, and Armen Alchian, "Vertical Integration, Appropriable Rents and the Competitive Contracting Process," *Journal of Law and Economics*, Vol. 21, No. 2 (1978): 297–326.

Klein, Maury, "Coming Full Circle: The Study of Big Business Since 1950," *Enterprise and Society*, Vol. 2, No. 3 (2001): 425–60.

Klepper, Steven and Kenneth L. Simons, "Innovation and Industry Shakeouts," *Business and Economic History*, Vol. 25, No. 1 (1996): 81–9.

Kochan, Nicholas (ed.), *The World's Greatest Brands* (Basingstoke: Macmillan, 1996).

Koehn, Nancy F., *Brand New: How Entrepreneurs Earned Consumers' Trust from Wedgwood to Dell* (Boston, Mass: Harvard Business School Press, 2001).

Kogut, Bruce, "A Study of the Life Cycle of Joint Ventures," in F. J. Contractor and P. Lorange (eds.), *Cooperative Strategies in International Business* (Lexington, Mass: Lexington Books, 1988).

Kogut, Bruce, and Udo Zander, "Knowledge of the Firm and the Evolutionary Theory of the Multinational Corporation," *Journal of International Business Studies*, Vol. 24 (1993): 625–645.

Kumar, Nirmalya, "The Power of Trust in Manufacturer-Retailer Relationships," in Harvard Business Review (ed.), *Managing the Value Chain* (Boston, Mass: Harvard Business School Press, 2000).

Laborde, Pierre, "*La Société Izarra de Bayonne*," in Alain Huetz de Lemps and Phillipe Roudié (eds.), *Eaux-de-Vie et Spiritueux* (Paris: Centre National de la Recherche Scientifique, 1985).

Lamoreaux, Naomi R., Daniel M. G. Raff and Peter Temin, "New Economic Approaches to the Study of Business History," *Business and Economic History*, Vol. 26, No. 1 (1997): 57–79.

Lamoreaux, Naomi R., *Insider Lending: Banks, Personal Connections and Economic Development in Industrial New England* (Cambridge: Cambridge University Press, 1994).

Langlois, Richard and Paul Robertson, *Firms, Markets and Economic Change* (London: Routledge, 1995).

Lazonick, William and William Mass (eds.), *Organizational Capability and Competitive Advantage* (Aldershot: Elgar, 1995).

Lazonick, William, "Controlling the Market for Corporate Control," *Industrial and Corporate Change*, Vol. 1 No. 3 (1992): 445–88.

Lazonick, William, "The Japanese Economy and Corporate Reform: What Path to Sustainable Prosperity?" *Industrial and Corporate Change*, Vol. 8, No. 4 (1999): 607–34.

Lazonick, William, "Understanding Innovative Enterprise – Toward the Integration of Economic Theory and Business History," in Franco Amatori and Geoffrey Jones (eds.), *Business History Around the World* (Cambridge: Cambridge University Press, 2003).

Lazonick, William, *Business Organization and the Myth of the Market Economy*, (Cambridge, Mass: Harvard University Press, 1991).

Lemps, Alain Huetz de, R. Pijassou, Phillipe Roudié, and G. Bernard (eds.), *Eaux-de-vie et Spiritueux* (Paris: Centre Nacional de Recherche Scientifique, 1985).

Levine, R. "Financial Development and Economic Growth: Views and Agenda" *Journal of Economic Literature*, No. 35 (1997): 688–726.

Levitt, Theodore, "The Globalisation of Markets," *Harvard Business Review* (May-June, 1983): 92–102.

Lopes, Teresa da Silva, "A Evolução das Estruturas Internacionais de Comercialização de Vinho do Porto no Século XX," *Revista de História Económica e Social*, Série 2, No. 1 (2001): 91–132.

Lopes, Teresa da Silva, "Brands and the Evolution of Multinationals in Alcoholic Beverages," *Business History*, Vol. 44, No. 3 (2002): 1–30.

Lopes, Teresa da Silva, "Brands, Mergers and Acquisitions in the Alcoholic Beverages Industry," in Hubert Bonin (ed.), *Transnational Companies, Nineteenth and Twentieth Centuries* (Paris: PLAGE, 2001).

Lopes, Teresa da Silva, "Competing with Multinationals: Strategies of the Portuguese Alcohol Industry," *Business History Review*, Vol. 79, No. 3 (2005): 559–85.

Lopes, Teresa da Silva, "Growth and Survival in the Global Alcoholic Beverages Industry, 1960–2001," paper presented at the Annual Conference of the European Business History Association (Oslo, 31 August–1 September 2001).

Lopes, Teresa da Silva, "The Impact of Multinational Investment on Alcohol Consumption Since the 1960s," *Business and Economic History*, Vol. 28, No. 2 (1999): 109–22.

Lopes, Teresa da Silva, "Transaction Costs in the Internationalisation of Port Wine," paper presented at the International Conference on Business History and Theory (Glasgow, 2–4 July 1999).

Lopes, Teresa da Silva, *Internacionalização e Concentração no Vinho do Porto, 1945–1995* (Porto: GEHVID/ICEP, 1998).

Lucas, William F., "Nothing Better in the Market: Brown Forman's Century of Quality 1870–1970," *The Newcomen Society in North America* (New York: Newcomen Society, 1970).

Maddison, A., *L'Économie Mondiale 1820–1992* (Paris: OCDE, 1995).

Maeda, Kazutoshi, "The Evolution of Retailing Industries in Japan," in Akio Okochi and Koichi Shimokawa (eds.), *Development of Mass Marketing, The International Conference on Business History*, Vol. 7 (1981): 265–89.

Marchildon, Gregory P., "Promotion, Finance and Mergers in Canadian Manufacturing Industry, 1885–1918" (London School of Economics Ph.D., 1990).

Marfels, Christina, *Concentration, Competition and Competitiveness in the Beverages Industries of the European Community* (Luxembourg: Commission of the European Communities, 1992).

Marris, Robin (ed.), *The Corporate Society* (London: Macmillan, 1974).

Marris, Robin, *The Economic Theory of Managerial Capitalism* (London: Macmillan, 1964).

Marrus, Michael R., *Samuel Bronfman: The Life and Times of Seagram's Mr. Sam* (London: Brandey University Press, 1991).

Mathias, Peter, *The Brewing Industry in England, 1700–1830* (Cambridge: Cambridge University Press, 1959).

Mayer, Colin, "Firm Control," Inaugural Lecture delivered to the University of Oxford (18 February 1999).

Mayer, Michael and Richard Whittington, "National Institutions and Corporate Change: Strategy, Structure and 'Systemness' in France, Germany and the United Kingdom, 1950–1993," *Industrial and Corporate Change*, Vol. 8, No. 3 (1999): 519–51.

McClelland, W. G., *Studies in Retailing* (Oxford: Blackwell, 1963).

McCraw, Thomas K., *The Essential Alfred Chandler: Essays Towards a Historical Theory of Big Business* (Boston, Mass: Harvard Business School Press, 1988).

McGahan, A. M., "The Emergence of the National Brewing Oligopoly: Competition in the American Market, 1933–1958," *Business History Review*, Vol. 65 (1991): 229–284.

McGowan, Richard, *Government Regulation of the Alcohol Industry* (Westport, Connecticut, 1997).

McKenna, Christopher, "The World's Newest Profession: Management Consulting in the Twentieth Century" (Johns Hopkins University Ph.D., 2000).

Merrett, David (ed.), *Business Institutions and Behaviour in Australia* (London: Frank Cass, 2000).

Merrett, David and Greg Whitwell, "The Empire Strikes Back: Marketing Australian Beer and Wine in the United Kingdom," in Geoffrey Jones and Nicholas J. Morgan (eds.), *Adding Value: Brands and Marketing in Food and Drink* (London: Routledge, 1994).

Merrett, David, "Corporate Governance, Incentives and the Internationalisation of Australian Business," paper presented at the Business History Conference (Hagley, 19–21 April 2002).

Michel, G. and Tim Ambler, "Establishing Brand Essence Across Borders," *The Journal of Brand Management*, Vol. 6, No. 5 (1999): 333–45.

Millns, Tony, "The British Brewing Industry, 1945–1995," in Richard Wilson and Terry Gourvish (eds.), *The Dynamics of the International Brewing Industry Since 1800* (London: Routledge, 1998).

Moldoveanu, M. C., N. Nohria, and H. Stevenson, "The Path-Dependent Evolution of Organizations," *Harvard Business School Working Papers* (July 1995).

Monopolies Commission, *Elders IXL and Allied Lyons PLC. A Report on the Proposed Merger* (London, September 1986).

Monopolies Commission, *Unilever Ltd. and Allied Breweries Ltd. A Report on the Proposed Merger*, PP (1968–69, LX, HC297) (9 June 1969).

Montgomery, C. A., "Corporate Diversification," *Journal of Economic Perspective*, 8 (1994): 163–78.

Montgomery, C. A., "The Measurement of Firm Diversification: Some More Empirical Evidence," *Academy of Management Journal*, Vol. 25 (1982): 299–307.

Moreland, P. W., "Alternative Disciplinary Mechanisms in Different Corporate Systems," *Journal of Economic Behaviour and Organization*, Vol. 26, No. 1 (1995): 17–34.

Morikawa, Hidemasa, *A History of Top Management in Japan: Managerial Enterprises and Family Enterprises* (Oxford: Oxford University Press, 2001).

Moss, Michael S. and John H. Hume, *The Making of Scotch Whisky* (Edinburgh: James & James, 1981).

Murphy, John M., "Assessing the Value of Brands," in J. Murphy (ed.), *Branding a Key Marketing Tool* (London: Macmillan, 1992).

Napier, C., "Brand Accounting in the United Kingdom," in Geoffrey Jones and Nicholas J. Morgan (eds.), *Adding Value: Brands and Marketing in Food and Drink* (London: Routledge, 1994).

Nayyar, Praveen R., "On the Measurement of Corporate Diversification Strategy: Evidence From Large US Service Firms," *Strategic Management Journal*, Vol. 13 (1992): 219–35.

Nelson, Richard R. and Sidney G. Winter, *An Evolutionary Theory of Economic Change* (Cambridge, Mass: Harvard University Press, 1982).

Nelson, Richard R., "Why Do Firms Differ, and How It Matter?" *Strategic Management Journal*, Vol. 14 (1991): 61–74.

Neuman, Manfred, *Competition Policy: History, Theory and Practice* (Cheltenham: Elgar, 2001).

Newkirk, Brian, and Rob Atkinson, "Buying Wine Online – Rethinking the 21st Amendment for the 21st Century," *Policy Report* (January 2003).

North, Douglass C., *Institutions, Institutional Change and Economic Performance* (Cambridge: Cambridge University Press, 1990).

Odlyzko, Andrew, "The Internet and Other Networks: Utilizations Rates and Their Implications," *Information Economics Policy*, Vol. 12, No. 4 (2000): 341–365.

Office of Management and Budget, *Standard Industrial Classification Manual* (Washington: US Government Printing Office, 1972).

Österberg, Esa (ed.), Proceedings of the International Seminar on Alcohol Retail Monopolies: Exchange of Information and Experience (Saariselkä, September 21–23, 1999).

O'Sullivan, Mary, "Change and Continuity in the French System of Corporate Governance," in *Corporate Governance, Innovation and Economic Performance in the EU* (project funded by the European Commission, 2001).

O'Sullivan, Mary, *Contests for Corporate Control* (Oxford: Oxford University Press, 2000).

Owen, Colin C., *The Greatest Brewery in the World: A History of Bass, Ratcliff & Gretton* (Chesterfield: Derbyshire Record Society, 1992).

Owen, Geoffrey, "Corporate Governance in Britain: Is Incremental Reform Enough?" *Corporate Governance, Innovation and Economic Performance in the EU* (part of a project funded by the European Commission, 2001).

Pajunen, Kalle, "Hinnankorotuksia ja Saatavuudemajoituksia: Valtion Alkoholipolitiikan Vaikutukset Alkoholijuomien Hintoihin, Kulutukseen, Tuontiin ja Kotimaiseen Tuotantoon 1930-ja 1960-luvuilla" (University of Jyväskylä, Finland, Bachelor of Arts Dissertation, 1998).

Pearce, Robert D., "Concentration, Diversification and Penetration: Some Dimensions of Industry Structure and Interaction," *The University of Reading: Discussion Papers in Industrial Economics*, No. 13 (1989).

Pearce, Robert D., "The Internationalisation of Sales by Leading Enterprises: Some Firm, Industry and Country Determinants, *The University of Reading: Discussion Papers in International Investment and Business Studies*, No. 101 (1987).

Pearce, Robert D., *The Growth and Evolution of Multinational Enterprise: Patterns of Geographical and Industrial Diversification* (Aldershot: Elgar, 1993).

Pellegrini, Luca and Srinivas K. Reddy (eds.), *Retail and Marketing Channels* (London: Routledge, 1989).

Penrose, Edith, *The Growth of Firms, Middle East Oil and Other Essays* (London: Frank Cass, 1971).

Penrose, Edith, *The Large International Firm in Developing Countries: The International Petroleum Industry* (London: Allen & Unwin, 1968).

Penrose, Edith, *The Theory of the Growth of the Firm* (Oxford: Blackwell, 1959). (New, revised edition, Oxford: Oxford University Press, 1995)

Peterden, Torben and Steen Thomsen, "European Patterns of Corporate Ownership: a Twelve-Country Study," *Journal of International Business Studies*, Vol. 28, No. 4 (1997): 759–778.

Plavchan, Ronald Jan, *A History of Anheuser-Busch, 1852–1933* (New York: ARNO Press, 1976).

Polanyi, Micheal, *The Tacit Dimension* (London: Routledge, 1966).

Pollard, Sidney, *The International Economy Since 1945* (London: Routledge, 1997).

Porta, R. La, F. Lopez-de-Silanes, A. Schleifer, and R. Vishny, "Legal Determinants of External Finance," *Journal of Finance*, No. 52 (1997): 1131–50.

Porter, Glenn and Harold C. Livesay, *Merchants and Manufacturers* (Baltimore: Johns Hopkins Press, 1971).

Porter, Michael E., *Competitive Advantage: Creating and Sustaining Superior Performance* (New York: Free Press, 1985).

Quelch, J. and E. Hoff, "Customising Global Marketing," *Harvard Business Review* (May–June 1986): 59–68.

Raadschelders, Jos C. N., "Evolution, Institutional Analysis and Path Dependency: an Administrative-History Perspective on Fashionable Approaches and Concepts," *International Review of Administrative Sciences*, Vol. 64 (1998): 565–82.

Ramanujam, Vasudevan and P. Varadarajan, "Research on Corporate Diversification: a Synthesis," *Strategic Management Journal*, Vol. 10 (1989): 523–51.

Räsänen, Keijo and Richard Whipp, "National Business Recipes: A Sector Perspective," in Richard Whitley (ed.), *European Business Systems: Firms and Markets in their National Contexts* (London: Sage, 1992).

Reader, William J. and Judy Slinn, "Grand Metropolitan" (unpublished manuscript, 1992).

Reddy, S. K., S. L. Holak and S. Bhat, "To Extend or not to Extend: Success Determinants of Line Extensions," *Journal of Marketing Research*, Vol. 31 (1994): 243–62.

Refait, Michel, *Moët & Chandon: De Claude Moët à Bernard Arnault* (Saints Geosmes: Dominique Guéniot, 1998).

Richardson, George B., "The Organization of Industry," *Economic Journal*, Vol. 82 (1972): 883–96.

Roberts, Alan, "The Very Idea of Theory in Business History," *The University of Reading: Discussion Papers in Accounting and Finance*, No. 54 (1998).

Rose, A. H. (ed.), *Alcoholic Beverages*, Vol. 1 (London: Academic Press, 1977).

Rose, Mary B., "Family Firm Community and Business Culture: A Comparative Perspective on the British and American Cotton Industries," in Andrew Godley and Oliver Westall (eds.), *Business and Culture* (Manchester: Manchester University Press, 1996).

Rosen, B., J. Boddewyn, and E. Louis, "US Brands Abroad: an Empirical Study of Global Branding," *International Marketing Review*, Vol. 6, No. 1 (1989): 7–19.

Roudié, Philippe, "Une Vénérable Entreprise Bordelaise de Liqueurs Marie Brizard et Roger," in Alain Huetz de Lemps and Philippe Roudié (eds.), *Eaux-de-Vie et Spiritueux* (Paris: Centre National de la Recherche Scientifique, 1985).

Rugman, Alan and Alan Verbeke, "Towards a Theory of Regional Multinationals: A Transactions Cost Economics Approach," *Management International Review*, Vol. 44, No. 4 (2004): 3–15.

Rumelt, Richard P., *Strategy, Structure and Economic Performance* (Cambridge, Mass: Harvard University Press, 1974).

Sako, Mari, *Prices, Quality and Trust – Inter-Firm Relationships in Britain and Japan* (Cambridge: Cambridge University Press, 1992).

Sawinski, Diane M. and Wendy H. Mason, *Encyclopaedia of Global Industries* (London: Gale Research, 1996).

Scarbrough, Harry, "Path(ological) Dependency? Core Competencies From an Organizational Perspective," *British Journal of Management*, Vol. 9 (1998): 219–32.

Schamlensee, R., "Product Differentiation Advantages of Pioneering Brands," *American Economic Review*, Vol. 72, No. 3 (1982): 349–65.

Schleifer, A., and R. W. Vishny, "Large Shareholders and Corporate Control," *Journal of Political Economy*, Vol. 94 (1986): 461–88.

Schmitz, Christopher, "The World's Largest Industrial Companies of 1912," *Business History*, Vol. 37, No. 4 (1995): 85–96.

Schoemaker, Paul J. H. and Raphael Amit, "Investment in Strategic Assets: Industry and Firm specific perspectives," *Advances in Strategic Management*, Vol. 10 (1994): 3–33.

Schramm-Nielsen, Jette, Peter Laurence, and Karl Henrik Sivesind, *Management in Scandinavia – Culture, Context and Change* (Cheltenham: Elgar, 2004).

Schröter, Harm G., "Small European Nations: Cooperative Capitalism in the Twentieth Century," in Alfred D. Chandler Jr., Franco Amatori, and Takashi Hikino (eds.), *Big Business and the Wealth of Nations* (Cambridge: Cambridge University Press, 1997).

Schumpeter, Joseph A., *Capitalism, Socialism and Democracy* (London: Unwin University Books, 1943).

Schumpeter, Joseph A., *History of Economic Analysis*, (New York: Oxford University Press, 1954).

Scott, John and Catherine Griff, *Directors of Industry: The British Corporate Network 1904–76* (Cambridge: Polity Press, 1984).

Severn, Alan K., "Investor Evaluation of Foreign and Domestic Risk," *Journal of Finance*, No. 29 (1974): 545–50.

Simon, Herbert A., *Models of Man* (New York: Wiley, 1957).

Sluyterman, K. E. and H. H. Vleesenbeek, *Three Centuries of De Kuyper 1695–1995* (Shiedam: Prepress Center Assen, 1995).

Smith, Adam, *An Enquiry Into the Nature and Causes of the Wealth of Nations* (New York: Modern Library, 1776/1937).

Smith, D. E., and H. S. Soolgaard, "The Dynamics of Shifts in European Alcoholic Drinks Consumption," *Journal of International Consumer Marketing*, Vol. 12, No. 3 (2000): 85–109.

Spahni, Pierre, *The International Wine Trade* (Cambridge: Woodhead, 1995).

Spawton, Tony, "Development in the Global Alcoholic Drinks Industry and Its Implications for the Future Marketing of Wine," *European Journal of Marketing*, Vol. 24, No. 4 (1990): 47–54.

Spinelli, Laurence, *Dry Diplomacy: The United States, Great Britain and Prohibition* (Wilmington, Del: S.R. Books, 1989).

Stack, Martin, "Local and Regional Breweries in America's Brewing Industry, 1865 to 1920', *Business History Review*, Vol. 74 No. 3 (2000): 535–63.

Stockman, Frans N., Rolf Ziegler and John Scott, *Networks of Corporate Power: A Comparative Analysis of Ten Countries* (Cambridge: Polity Press, 1985).

Stopford, John M. and John H. Dunning, *Multinationals: Company Performance and Global Trends* (London: Macmillan, 1983).

Stopford, John M. and Louis T. Wells Jr., *Managing the Multinational Enterprise* (London: Longman, 1972).

Taylor, Graham D. and Peter A. Baskerville, *A Concise History of Business in Canada* (Toronto: Oxford University Press, 1994).

Tedlow, Richard S. and Geoffrey Jones (eds.), *The Rise & Fall of Mass Marketing* (London: Routledge, 1993).

Tedlow, Richard, "The Fourth Phase of Marketing: Marketing History and the Business World Today," in Richard Tedlow and Geoffrey Jones (eds.), *The Rise and Fall of Mass Marketing* (London: Routledge, 1993).

Tedlow, Richard, *New and Improved: The Story of Mass Marketing in America* (Oxford: Heinemann, 1990).

Teece, David, "Economies of Scale and Scope of the Enterprise," *Journal of Economic Behaviour and Organisation*, Vol. 1, No. 3 (1980): 223–47.

Teece, David, "Towards an Economic Theory of the Multiproduct Firm," *Journal of Economic Behaviour and Organization* 3 (1982): 39–63.

Teiser, Ruth, "Recollections of a Career With the Gallo Winery and the Development of the California Wine Industry, 1942–1989," manuscript of an interview to Charles Crawford (University of California, Berkeley: The Wine Spectator California Winemen Oral Series, 1989).

The Lanham Trade-Mark Act (1947).

Thomsen, Steen and Torben Pedersen, "Industry and Ownership Structure," *International Review of Law and Economics*, Vol. 18 (1999): 385–402.

Thomsen, Steen, "Foreign Ownership and Survival," paper presented at the Second Aarhus Workshop in International Business History (Aarhus, 25–26 May 2001).

Tolliday, Steven, "Rethinking the Japanese Industrial Policy Debate: Controversies Over Transwar Continuities," paper presented at the Business History Conference (Miami, 20–22 April 2001).

Tolliday, Steven, *The Economic Development of Modern Japan, 1868–1945: From Meiji Restoration to the Second World War*, 2 volumes (Cheltenham: Elgar, 2001).

Toms, Steve and John Wilson, "The Evolution of British Business? A New Paradigm," a paper presented at the Annual Conference of the British Business History Association (Portsmouth, 29–30 June 2001).

Tremblay, Victor J., and Carol Horton Tremblay, *The U.S. Brewing Industry – Data and Economic Analysis* (Cambridge, Mass: MIT Press, 2005).

Troesker, Werner, "Exclusive Dealing and the Whiskey Trust, 1890–1895," *Journal of Economic History*, Vol. 58, No. 3 (1998): 755–78.

Troester, M., "Absolut Vodka," in Janice Jorgensen (ed.), *Encyclopaedia of Consumer Brands* (London: St James Press, 1994).

United Nations, *Demographic Yearbook* (New York: UN, 1998).

United Nations, *Demographic Yearbook* (New York: UN, 2005).

United Nations, *World Investment Report: Cross-border Mergers and Acquisitions and Development* (New York: UN, 2000).

Unwin, Tim, *The Wine and the Vine* (London: Routledge, 1991).

Urban, G. S., Gaskin T. Carter and Z. Mucha, "Market Share Reward of Pioneering Brands," *Management Science*, Vol. 32 (1984): 645–59.

Useem, Michael, *Executive Defence: Shareholder Power and Corporate Reorganization* (Cambridge, Mass: Harvard University Press, 1993).

Vachani, Sushil, "Distinguishing Between Related and Unrelated International Geographic Diversification: A Comprehensive Measure of Global Diversification," *Journal of International Business Studies*, Vol. 22, No. 2 (1991): 307–22.

Vernon, Raymond, "International Investment and International Trade in the Product Cycle," *Quarterly Journal of Economics*, 80 (1966): 190–207.

Vernon, Raymond, *Sovereignty at Bay: The Multinational Spread of United States Enterprises* (New York: Basic Books, 1971).

Ville, Simon and David Merrett, "The Development of Large Scale Enterprise in Australia, 1910–64," in David Merrett (ed.), *Business Institutions and Behaviour in Australia* (London: Frank Cass, 2000).

Ward, S., L. Light and J. Goldstine, "What High-Tech Managers Need to Know About Brands," *Harvard Business Review* (July–August 1999): 85–95.

Watkins, Trevor, *The Economics of the Brand: A Marketing Analysis* (Whitstable: McGraw-Hill, 1986).

Waugh, Alec, *Merchants of Wine: Being a Century Account of the Fortunes of the House of Gilbey* (London: Cassell, 1957).

Weir, Ronald B., "Alcohol Controls and Scotch Whisky Exports 1870–1939," *British Journal of Addiction*, No. 83 (1988): 1289–97.

Weir, Ronald B., "D.C.L.: Acquisitions, 1940–1986" (*mimeo*, 1999).

Weir, Ronald B., "D.C.L.: Acquisitions and Major Shareholdings, 1877–1940" (*mimeo*, 1990).

Weir, Ronald B., "Managing Decline: Brands and Marketing in Two Mergers 'The Big Amalgamation' 1925 and Guinness DCL 1986," in Geoffrey Jones and Nicholas J. Morgan (eds.), *Adding Value: Brands and Marketing in Food and Drink* (London: Routledge, 1994).

Weir, Ronald B., "The Export Marketing of Scotch Whisky 1870–1939," in Erik Aerts, Louis M. Cullen, and Richard Wilson (eds.), *Proceedings from the Tenth Economic History Congress* (Leuvein, August, 1990).

Weir, Ronald B., *The History of Distillers Company 1877–1939* (Oxford: Oxford University Press, 1995).

Wernerfelt, Birger, "A Resource-Based View of the Firm," *Strategic Management Journal*, No. 5 (1984): 171–80.

Whitley, Richard (ed.), *European Business Systems: Firms and Markets in their National Contexts* (London: Sage, 1992).

Whitley, Richard, "Business Systems, Industrial Sectors and Strategic Choices," in Richard Whitley (ed.), *European Business Systems: Firms and Markets in Their National Contexts* (London: Sage, 1992).

Whitley, Richard, "Dominant Forms of Economic Organization in Market Economies," *Organization Studies*, Vol. 15, No. 2 (1994): 153–82.

Whitley, Richard, "Eastern Asian Enterprise Structures and the Comparative Analysis of Forms of Business Organization," *Organization Studies*, Vol. 11, No. 1 (1990): 47–54.

Whitley, Richard, *Business Systems in East Asia: Firms Markets and Societies* (London: Sage, 1992).

Whitley, Richard, *Divergent Capitalism: The Social Structuring and Change of Business Systems* (Oxford: Oxford University Press, 1999).

Whittington, Richard and Michael Mayer, *The European Corporation: Strategy, Structure and Social Science* (Oxford: Oxford University Press, 2000).

Wilkins, Mira and Frank E. Hill, *American Business Abroad: Ford on Six Continents* (Detroit: Wayne State University, 1964).

Wilkins, Mira, "Business History as a Discipline," *Business and Economic History*, Vol. 17 (1988): 1–7.

Wilkins, Mira, "The Neglected Intangible Asset: The Influence of the Trademark on the Rise of the Modern Corporation," *Business History*, Vol. 34, No. 1 (1992): 66–99.

Wilkins, Mira, "When and Why Brands in Food and Drink?," in Richard S. Tedlow and Geoffrey Jones (eds.), *The Rise and Fall of Mass Marketing* (London: Routledge, 1993).

Wilkins, Mira, *The Emergence of Multinational Enterprise: American Business Abroad From the Colonial Era to 1914* (Cambridge, Mass: Harvard University Press, 1970).

Wilkins, Mira, *The History of Foreign Investment in the United States to 1914* (Cambridge, Mass: Harvard University Press, 1989).

Wilkins, Mira, *The History of Foreign Investment in the United States 1914–1945* (Cambridge, Mass: Harvard University Press, 2004).

Wilkins, Mira, *The Maturing of Multinational Enterprise: American Business Abroad From 1914 to 1970* (Cambridge, Mass: Harvard University Press, 1974).

Williams, Bridget, "Multiple Retailing and Brand Image," in Geoffrey Jones and Nicholas J. Morgan (eds.), *Adding Value: Brands and Marketing in Food and Drink* (London: Routledge, 1994).

Williamson, Oliver E. and Sidney G. Winter (eds.), *The Nature of the Firm: Origins, Evolution and Development* (Oxford: Oxford University Press, 1991).

Williamson, Oliver E., "The Modern Corporation: Origins, Evolution, Attributes," *Journal of Economic Literature*, 19 (1981): 1537–68.

Williamson, Oliver E., "Transaction-Cost Economics: The Governance of Contractual Relations," *Journal of Law and Economics*, Vol. 22 (1979): 3–61.

Williamson, Oliver E., *Markets and Hierarchies – Analysis and Antitrust Implications* (New York: Free Press, 1975).

Williamson, Oliver E., *The Economic Institutions of Capitalism* (New York: Free Press, 1985).

Wilson, Brent D., "The Propensity of Multinational Firms to Expand Through Acquisitions," *Journal of International Business Studies*, Vol. 11, No. 2 (1980): 59–65.

Wilson, Charles H., *The History of Unilever*, 2 volumes (London: Cassel, 1954) and 1 volume (London: Praeger, 1968).

Wilson, Richard G. and Terry Gourvish (eds.), *The Dynamics of the International Brewing Industry Since 1800* (London: Routledge, 1998).

Winter, Sydney G., "Knowledge and Competence as Strategic Assets," in David Teece (ed.), *The Competitive Challenge: Strategies for Industrial Renewal* (Cambridge, Mass: Ballinger, 1987).

Winter, Sydney G., "On Coase, Competence and Corporation," in Oliver E. Williamson and Sidney G. Winter (eds.), *The Nature of the Firm: Origins, Evolution and Development* (Oxford: Oxford University Press, 1991).

World Drink Trends (Henley-on-Thames: NTC Publications, 1998).

World Drink Trends (Henley-on-Thames: NTC Publications, 2005).

Wrigley, Leonard, "Divisional Autonomy and Diversification" (Harvard Business School Ph.D., 1970).

Yeoung, Bernard, "The Future of Multinational Enterprise: 25 Years Later," Special Issue: *Journal of International Business Studies*, Vol. 34, No. 2 (2003).

Young, Stephen, James Hamill, Colin Wheeler, and J. Richard Davies, *International Market Entry and Development* (Exeter: Harvester Wheatsheaf, 1989).

Zanden, Jan L. van, *The Economic History of the Netherlands 1914–1995* (London: Routledge, 1998).

Zeitlin, Jonathan and Gary Herrigel, *Americanization and Its Limits: Reworking US Technology and Management in Post-War Europe and Japan* (Oxford: Oxford University Press, 2000).

Index

287